CBSE Term II 2022

Mathematics
Class IX

- Complete Theory in Sync with Syllabus
- Case Based Questions
- Short/Long Answer Questions
- 3 Practice Papers with Explanations

Author
Vishal Kumar Mehta

arihant

ARIHANT PRAKASHAN (School Division Series)

ARIHANT PRAKASHAN (School Division Series)

ॐ **Administrative & Production Offices**

Regd. Office
'Ramchhaya' 4577/15, Agarwal Road, Darya Ganj, New Delhi -110002
Tele: 011- 47630600, 43518550

ॐ **Head Office**
Kalindi, TP Nagar, Meerut (UP) - 250002, Tel: 0121-7156203, 7156204

ॐ **Sales & Support Offices**
Agra, Ahmedabad, Bengaluru, Bareilly, Chennai, Delhi, Guwahati,
Hyderabad, Jaipur, Jhansi, Kolkata, Lucknow, Nagpur & Pune.

ॐ **ISBN :** 978-93-25796-50-8

PO No : TXT-XX-XXXXXXX-X-XX

Published by Arihant Publications (India) Ltd.

For further information about the books published by Arihant, log on to www.arihantbooks.com or e-mail at info@arihantbooks.com

Follow us on   

Contents

Watch Free Learning Videos

Subscribe **arihant** You**Tube** Channel

- ☑ Video Solutions of CBSE Sample Papers
- ☑ Chapterwise Important MCQs
- ☑ CBSE Updates

Syllabus

CBSE Term II Class IX

No.	Unit Name	Marks
I	Algebra (cont.)	12
II	Geometry (cont.)	15
III	Mensuration (cont.)	09
IV	Statistics & Probability (cont.)	04
	Total	**40**
	Internal Assessment: Term II	**10**
	Grand Total	**50**

UNIT ALGEBRA

1. Polynomials

Definition of a polynomial in one variable, with examples and counter examples. Coefficients of a polynomial, terms of a polynomial and zero polynomial. Degree of a polynomial. Constant, linear, quadratic and cubic polynomials. Monomials, binomials, trinomials. Factors and multiples. Zeros of a polynomial. Factorization of $ax^2 + bx + c$, $a \neq 0$ where a, b and c are real numbers, and of cubic polynomials using the Factor Theorem.

Recall of algebraic expressions and identities. Verification of identities

$$(x + y + z)^2 = x^2 + y^2 + z^2 + 2xy + 2yz + 2zx$$
$$(x \pm y)^3 = x^3 \pm y^3 \pm 3xy\,(x \pm y)$$
$$x^3 \pm y^3 = (x \pm y)\,(x^2 \mp xy + y^2$$

and their use in factorization of polynomials.

UNIT GEOMETRY

2. Quadrilaterals

1. (Prove) The diagonal divides a parallelogram into two congruent triangles.
2. (Motivate) In a parallelogram opposite sides are equal, and conversely.
3. (Motivate) In a parallelogram opposite angles are equal, and conversely.

4. (Motivate) A quadrilateral is a parallelogram if a pair of its opposite sides is parallel and equal.
5. (Motivate) In a parallelogram, the diagonals bisect each other and conversely.
6. (Motivate) In a triangle, the line segment joining the mid-points of any two sides is parallel to the third side and in half of it and (motivate) its converse.

3. CIRCLES

Through examples, arrive at definition of circle and related concepts-radius, circumference, diameter, chord, arc, secant, sector, segment, subtended angle.

1. (Prove) Equal chords of a circle subtend equal angles at the centre and (motivate) its converse.
2. (Motivate) The perpendicular from the centre of a circle to a chord bisects the chord and conversely, the line drawn through the centre of a circle to bisect a chord is perpendicular to the chord.
3. (Motivate) Equal chords of a circle (or of congruent circles) are equidistant from the centre (or their respective centres) and conversely.
4. (Motivate) The angle subtended by an arc at the centre is double the angle subtended by it at any point on the remaining part of the circle.
5. (Motivate) Angles in the same segment of a circle are equal.
6. (Motivate) The sum of either of the pair of the opposite angles of a cyclic quadrilateral is 180° and its converse.

4. CONSTRUCTIONS

1. Construction of bisectors of line segments and angles of measure 60°, 90°, 45° etc., equilateral triangles.
2. Construction of a triangle given its base, sum/difference of the other two sides and one base angle.

UNIT MENSURATION

5. SURFACE AREAS AND VOLUMES

Surface areas and volumes of cubes, cuboids, spheres (including hemispheres) and right circular cylinders/cones.

UNIT STATISTICS & PROBABILITY

6. PROBABILITY

History, Repeated experiments and observed frequency approach to probability. Focus is on empirical probability. (A large amount of time to be devoted to group and to individual activities to motivate the concept; the experiments to be drawn from real - life situations, and from examples used in the chapter on statistics).

CBSE Circular

Exam Scheme Term I & II

केन्द्रीय माध्यमिक शिक्षा बोर्ड
(शिक्षा मंत्रालय, भारत सरकार के अधीन एक स्वायत संगठन)

CENTRAL BOARD OF SECONDARY EDUCATION
(An Autonomous Organisation under the Ministry of Education, Govt. of India)

CBSE/DIR (ACAD)/2021

Date: July 05, 2021
Circular No: Acad-51/2021

All the Heads of Schools affiliated to CBSE

Subject: Special Scheme of Assessment for Board Examination Classes X and XII for the Session 2021-22

COVID 19 pandemic caused almost all CBSE schools to function in a virtual mode for most part of the academic session of 2020-21. Due to the extreme risk associated with the conduct of Board examinations during the second wave in April 2021, CBSE had to cancel both its class X and XII Board examinations of the year 2021 and results are to be declared on the basis of a credible, reliable, flexible and valid alternative assessment policy. This, in turn, also necessitated deliberations over alternative ways to look at the learning objectives as well as the conduct of the Board Examinations for the academic session 2021-22 in case the situation remains unfeasible.

CBSE has also held stake holder consultations with Government schools as well as private independent schools from across the country especially schools from the remote rural areas and a majority of them have requested for the rationalization of the syllabus, similar to last year in view of reduced time permitted for organizing online classes. The Board has also considered the concerns regarding differential availability of electronic gadgets, connectivity and effectiveness of online teaching and other socio-economic issues specially with respect to students from economically weaker section and those residing in far flung areas of the country. In a survey conducted by CBSE, it was revealed that the rationalized syllabus notified for the session 2020-21 was effective for schools in covering the syllabus and helped learners in achieving learning objectives in a less stressful manner.

In the above backdrop and in line with the Board's continued focus on assessing stipulated learning outcomes by making the examinations competencies and core concepts based, student-centric, transparent, technology-driven, and having advance provision of alternatives for different future scenarios, the following schemes are introduced for the Academic Session for Class X and Class XII 2021-22.

केन्द्रीय माध्यमिक शिक्षा बोर्ड

(शिक्षा मंत्रालय, भारत सरकार के अधीन एक स्वायत संगठन)

CENTRAL BOARD OF SECONDARY EDUCATION

(An Autonomous Organisation under the Ministry of Education, Govt. of India)

Special Scheme for 2021-22

A. Academic session to be divided into 2 Terms with approximately 50% syllabus in each term:

The syllabus for the Academic session 2021-22 will be divided into 2 terms by following a systematic approach by looking into the interconnectivity of concepts and topics by the Subject Experts and the Board will conduct examinations at the end of each term on the basis of the bifurcated syllabus. This is done to increase the probability of having a Board conducted classes X and XII examinations at the end of the academic session.

B. The syllabus for the Board examination 2021-22 will be rationalized similar to that of the last academic session to be notified in July 2021. For academic transactions, however, schools will follow the curriculum and syllabus released by the Board vide Circular no. F.1001/CBSE-Acad/Curriculum/2021 dated 31 March 2021. Schools will also use alternative academic calendar and inputs from the NCERT on transacting the curriculum.

C. Efforts will be made to make Internal Assessment/ Practical/ Project work more credible and valid as per the guidelines and Moderation Policy to be announced by the Board to ensure fair distribution of marks.

Details of Curriculum Transaction

- Schools will continue teaching in distance mode till the authorities permit in-person mode of teaching in schools.

- **Classes IX-X: Internal Assessment** (throughout the year-irrespective of Term I and II) would include the *3 periodic tests, student enrichment, portfolio and practical work/ speaking listening activities/ project.*

- **Classes XI-XII: Internal Assessment** (throughout the year-irrespective of Term I and II) would include end of topic or unit tests/ exploratory activities/ practicals/ projects.

- Schools would create a student profile for all assessment undertaken over the year and retain the evidences in digital format.

- CBSE will facilitate schools to upload marks of Internal Assessment on the CBSE IT platform.

- Guidelines for Internal Assessment for all subjects will also be released along with the rationalized term wise divided syllabus for the session 2021-22.The Board would also provide additional resources like sample assessments, question banks, teacher training etc. for more reliable and valid internal assessments.

केन्द्रीय माध्यमिक शिक्षा बोर्ड

(शिक्षा मंत्रालय, भारत सरकार के अधीन एक स्वायत्त संगठन)

CENTRAL BOARD OF SECONDARY EDUCATION

(An Autonomous Organisation under the Ministry of Education, Govt. of India)

<u>Term I Examinations:</u>

- At the end of the first term, the Board will organize **Term I Examination** in a flexible schedule to be conducted between November-December 2021 with a window period of 4-8 weeks for schools situated in different parts of country and abroad. Dates for conduct of examinations will be notified subsequently.

- The Question Paper will have Multiple Choice Questions (MCQ) including case-based MCQs and MCQs on assertion-reasoning type. Duration of test will be **90 minutes** and it will cover only the rationalized syllabus of **Term I only** (i.e. approx. 50% of the entire syllabus).

- Question Papers will be sent by the CBSE to schools along with marking scheme.

- The exams will be conducted under the supervision of the External Center Superintendents and Observers appointed by CBSE.

- The responses of students will be captured on OMR sheets which, after scanning may be directly uploaded at CBSE portal or alternatively may be evaluated and marks obtained will be uploaded by the school on the very same day. The final direction in this regard will be conveyed to schools by the Examination Unit of the Board.

- Marks of the **Term I** Examination will contribute to the final overall score of students.

<u>Term II Examination/ Year-end Examination:</u>

- At the end of the second term, the Board would organize **Term II or Year-end Examination** based on the rationalized syllabus of Term II only (i.e. approximately 50% of the entire syllabus).

- This examination would be held around **March-April 2022** at the examination centres fixed by the Board.

- The paper will be of **2 hours duration** and have questions of different formats (case-based/ situation based, open ended- short answer/ long answer type).

- In case the situation is not conducive for normal descriptive examination **a 90 minute MCQ based exam** will be conducted at the end of the Term II also.

- Marks of the Term II Examination would contribute to the final overall score.

केन्द्रीय माध्यमिक शिक्षा बोर्ड

(शिक्षा मंत्रालय, भारत सरकार के अधीन एक स्वायत संगठन)

CENTRAL BOARD OF SECONDARY EDUCATION

(An Autonomous Organisation under the Ministry of Education, Govt. of India)

<u>Assessment / Examination as per different situations</u>

A. In case the situation of the pandemic improves and students are able to come to schools or centres for taking the exams.

Board would conduct Term I and Term II examinations at schools/centres and the theory marks will be distributed equally between the two exams.

B. In case the situation of the pandemic forces complete closure of schools during November-December 2021, but Term II exams are held at schools or centres.

Term I MCQ based examination would be done by students online/offline from home - in this case, the weightage of this exam for the final score would be reduced, and weightage of Term II exams will be increased for declaration of final result.

C. In case the situation of the pandemic forces complete closure of schools during March-April 2022, but Term I exams are held at schools or centres.

Results would be based on the performance of students on Term I MCQ based examination and internal assessments. The weightage of marks of Term I examination conducted by the Board will be increased to provide year end results of candidates.

D. In case the situation of the pandemic forces complete closure of schools and Board conducted Term I and II exams are taken by the candidates from home in the session 2021-22.

Results would be computed on the basis of the Internal Assessment/Practical/Project Work and Theory marks of Term-I and II exams taken by the candidate from home in Class X / XII subject to the moderation or other measures to ensure validity and reliability of the assessment.

In all the above cases, data analysis of marks of students will be undertaken to ensure the integrity of internal assessments and home based exams.

Dr. Joseph Emmanuel
Director (Academics)

CHAPTER 01

Polynomials

In this Chapter...

- Polynomials in One Variable
- Zeroes of a Polynomial
- Factorisation of a Quadratic Polynomial
- Factorisation of a Cubic Polynomial
- Algegraic Identities

A combination of constants and variables, connected by the four fundamental arithmetical operations $+$, $-$, $\times$ and $\div$, is called an **algebraic expression**.

e.g. $6x^2 - 5y^2 + 2xy$ is an algebraic expression, where x and y are variables and 6, -5, 2 are constants. An algebraic expression in which the variables involved, only non-negative integral power, is called a **polynomial.**

Polynomial in One Variable

A polynomial in one variable x of degree n is an algebraic expression of the form

$$p(x) = a_n x^n + a_{n-1} x^{n-1} + a_{n-2} x^{n-2} + \cdots + a_2 x^2 + a_1 x + a_0$$

where, $a_0, a_1, a_2, \ldots, a_n$ are constants and $a_n \neq 0$.

e.g. $p(x) = 3x^3 + 2x^2 - 7x + 5$ is a polynomial in the variable x (one variable).

Term and Coefficient of a Polynomial

The part of a polynomial separated by '$+$' or '$-$' sign is called a **term** of the polynomial. Each term of a polynomial has a **coefficient**, which is the constant associated with that term.

e.g. In polynomial $x^2 - 4x + 7$, the expressions x^2, $4x$ and 7 are called terms of the polynomial and here coefficient of x^2 is 1, coefficient of x is -4.

Degree of a Polynomial

Highest power of the variable in a polynomial is known as the **degree** of that polynomial.

Degree of a Polynomial in One Variable

For a polynomial in one variable, the highest power of the variable is called the degree of a polynomial.

e.g. $2x^4 - 6x^3 + 4x + 1$ is a polynomial in x of degree 4.

[since, the highest power of x is 4]

Degree of a Polynomial in Two or More Variables

In a polynomial in more than one variable, the sum of the powers of the variables in each term is taken up and the highest sum so obtained is called the degree of a polynomial.

e.g. $7x^3 - 5x^2 y^2 + 3xy + 6y + 8$ is a polynomial in x and y of degree 4.

[since, the highest sum of powers of x and y is $2 + 2$, i.e. 4]

Classifications of Polynomials

On the Basis of Number of Terms

On the basis of number of terms, the polynomials can be classified as:

(i) **Monomial** A polynomial containing one non-zero term, is called a **monomial** ('mono' means 'one').

e.g. $5x$, 7, $3x^3$, $-7x^2$ and u^4 are all monomials.

(ii) **Binomial** A polynomial containing two non-zero terms, is called a binomial ('bi' means 'two').

e.g. $y^{30} + 1$ and $z^{23} - z^2$ are binomials.

(iii) **Trinomial** A polynomial containing three non-zero terms, is called a trinomial ('tri' means 'three').

e.g. $(8 + 3x + x^2), (7 + 5xy + 6xy^2)$ and $(\sqrt{2} + x - x^2)$ are trinomials.

On the Basis of Degree of Variables

On the basis of degree of variables, the polynomials can be classified as:

(i) **Constant Polynomial** A polynomial of degree zero, is called constant polynomial.

e.g. $3, -7$ and $7/4$ are constant polynomials.

(ii) **Linear Polynomial** A polynomial of degree 1, is called a linear polynomial.

e.g. $2x + 5$ is a linear polynomial in x.

So, standard form of a linear polynomial in x will be $ax + b$, where a, b are constants and $a \neq 0$.

(iii) **Quadratic Polynomial** A polynomial of degree 2, is called a quadratic polynomial.

e.g. $3x^2 + 7x + 9$ is a quadratic polynomial in x.

So, a quadratic polynomial in x is of the form $ax^2 + bx + c$, where a, b, c are constants and $a \neq 0$.

(iv) **Cubic Polynomial** A polynomial of degree 3, is called a cubic polynomial.

e.g. $7x^3 - 5x^2 + 3x - 9$ is a cubic polynomial in x.

So, a cubic polynomial in x is of the form $ax^3 + bx^2 + cx + d$, where a, b, c, d are constants and $a \neq 0$.

(v) **Biquadratic Polynomial** A polynomial of degree 4, is called a biquadratic polynomial.

e.g. $5x^4 - 7x^3 + 8x^2 - 12x - 10$ is a biquadratic polynomial in x.

A biquadratic polynomial in x is of the form $ax^4 + bx^3 + cx^2 + dx + e$, where a, b, c, d, e are constants and $a \neq 0$.

(vi) **n Degree Polynomial** A polynomial of degree n in x is an expression of the form

$$p(x) = a_n x^n + a_{n-1} x^{n-1} + a_{n-2} x^{n-2}$$
$$+ \cdots + a_2 x^2 + a_1 x + a_0$$

where, $a_n, a_{n-1}, \ldots, a_2, a_1, a_0$ are constants and $a_n \neq 0$.

Here, $a_n x^n, a_{n-1} x^{n-1}, a_{n-2} x^{n-2}, \ldots, a_2 x^2, a_1 x, a_0$ are known as the terms of the polynomial $p(x)$ and $a_n, a_{n-1}, a_{n-2}, \ldots, a_2, a_1, a_0$ are known as their coefficients.

(vii) **Zero Polynomial** If $a_0 = a_1 = a_2 = \ldots = a_n = 0$ (all constants are zero), then we get the zero polynomial, which is denoted by 0.

Zeroes of a Polynomial

Value of a Polynomial

The value of a polynomial obtained on putting a particular value of the variable is called the value of a polynomial. The value of a polynomial $p(x)$ at $x = a$ (say) is denoted by $p(a)$.

e.g. Let $\quad p(x) = 5x^3 - 2x^2 + 3x - 2$

At $x = 1, \quad p(1) = 5(1)^3 - 2(1)^2 + 3(1) - 2$
$$= 5 - 2 + 3 - 2 = 8 - 4 = 4$$

So, 4 is the value of given polynomial $p(x)$ at $x = 1$.

Zero of a Polynomial

Zero of a polynomial $p(x)$ is a number α, such that $p(\alpha) = 0$. Zero of a polynomial is also called the **root** of polynomial equation $p(x) = 0$.

e.g. Let $p(x) = 5x + 7$

At $x = \dfrac{-7}{5}, p\left(\dfrac{-7}{5}\right) = 5\left(\dfrac{-7}{5}\right) + 7 = -7 + 7 = 0$

Hence, $x = -\dfrac{7}{5}$ is a zero (or root) of $p(x)$.

Method to Check Whether the Given Value is a Zero of a Polynomial or Not

If a polynomial in one variable (say x) is given to us and a value of variable $x = c$ (say) is also given, then to check that given value of x is a zero of given polynomial or not, we use the following steps

   Step I Firstly, consider the given polynomial say $p(x)$.

   Step II Put $x = c$ in given polynomial $p(x)$ and find the value of $p(c)$.

Step III If $p(c) = 0$, then $x = c$ will be a zero of given polynomial and if $p(c) \neq 0$, then $x = c$ will not be a zero of given polynomial.

Factorisation of a Quadratic Polynomial

By Splitting the Middle Term

Let factors of the quadratic polynomial $ax^2 + bx + c$ be $(px + q)$ and $(rx + s)$.

Then, $ax^2 + bx + c = (px + q)(rx + s)$
$$= prx^2 + (ps + qr)x + qs$$

On comparing the coefficients of x^2, x and constant terms from both sides, we get

$$a = pr, b = ps + qr \text{ and } c = qs$$

Here, b is the sum of two numbers ps and qr, whose product is $(ps)(qr) = (pr)(qs) = ac$.

Thus, to factorise $ax^2 + bx + c$, write b as the sum of two numbers, whose product is ac.

By Using Factor Theorem

Write the given polynomial $p(x) = ax^2 + bx + c$ in the form

$$p(x) = a\left(x^2 + \frac{b}{a}x + \frac{c}{a}\right) = a\, g(x) \qquad \text{...(i)}$$

where, $\quad g(x) = x^2 + \frac{b}{a}x + \frac{c}{a}$

i.e. firstly make the coefficient of x^2 equal to one if it is not one.

Find all the possible factors of constant term $\left(\dfrac{c}{a}\right)$ of $g(x)$.

Using trial method, find the factors at which $g(x) = 0$ say, $x = \alpha$ and $x = \beta$. Further, write $g(x)$ as the product of factors, then $g(x) = (x - \alpha)(x - \beta)$ and put this value of $g(x)$ in Eq. (i) to get required factors of $p(x)$.

Factorisation of a Cubic Polynomial

To factorise a cubic polynomial, we use the following steps:

Step I Write the given cubic polynomial
$p(x) = ax^3 + bx^2 + cx + d$ in the form

$$p(x) = a\left(x^3 + \frac{b}{a}x^2 + \frac{c}{a}x + \frac{d}{a}\right) = ag(x) \qquad \text{...(i)}$$

where, $g(x) = x^3 + \dfrac{b}{a}x^2 + \dfrac{c}{a}x + \dfrac{d}{a}$

i.e. first make the coefficient of x^3 equal to one if it is not one and then find the constant term.

Step II Find all the possible factors of constant term $\left(\dfrac{d}{a}\right)$ of $g(x)$.

Step III Check at which factor of constant term, $p(x)$ is zero by using trial method and get one factor of $p(x)$, (i.e. $x - \alpha$).

Step IV Write $p(x)$ as the product of this factor and a quadratic polynomial,

i.e. $\quad p(x) = (x - \alpha)(a_1 x^2 + b_1 x + c_1)$

Step V Apply splitting the middle term method or factor theorem in quadratic polynomial to get another two factors. Thus, we get all the three factors of given cubic polynomial.

Algebraic Identities

An identity is an equality, which is true for all values of its variables in the equality, i.e. an identity is a universal truth. Some useful algebraic identities are given below:

(i) $(x + y)^2 = x^2 + 2xy + y^2$

(ii) $(x - y)^2 = x^2 - 2xy + y^2$

(iii) $x^2 - y^2 = (x - y)(x + y)$

(iv) $(x + a)(x + b) = x^2 + (a + b)x + ab$

(v) $(x + y + z)^2 = x^2 + y^2 + z^2 + 2xy + 2yz + 2zx$

$$= \Sigma x^2 + 2\Sigma xy$$

(vi) $(x + y)^3 = x^3 + y^3 + 3xy(x + y)$

$$= x^3 + y^3 + 3x^2 y + 3xy^2$$

(vii) $(x - y)^3 = x^3 - y^3 - 3xy(x - y)$

$$= x^3 - y^3 - 3x^2 y + 3xy^2$$

(viii) $x^3 - y^3 = (x - y)(x^2 + xy + y^2) = (x - y)\left[(x - y)^2 + 3xy\right]$

(ix) $x^3 + y^3 = (x + y)(x^2 - xy + y^2) = (x + y)\left[(x + y)^2 - 3xy\right]$

(x) $x^3 + y^3 + z^3 - 3xyz$

$$= (x + y + z)(x^2 + y^2 + z^2 - xy - yz - zx)$$

$$= (x + y + z)\left[(x + y + z)^2 - 3(xy + yz + zx)\right]$$

if $(x + y + z) = 0$ then $x^3 + y^3 + z^3 = 3xyz$

(xi) $x^2 + y^2 + z^2 - xy - yz - zx$

$$= \frac{1}{2}\left[(x - y)^2 + (y - z)^2 + (z - x)^2\right]$$

Solved Examples

Example 1. Which of the following expressions are polynomials in one or more variable(s)? State reasons for your answers.

(i) $5x^{3/2} + 2y + 1$ (ii) $x^4 + 2y + 1$

(iii) $\dfrac{x^4 + x^3 + x}{x}$ (iv) $\sqrt{y^3} + y^2 + 3$

Sol. (i) Given, expression is $5x^{3/2} + 2y + 1$.

Here, expression is in two variables and all powers of variables are not non-negative integers.

Hence, it is not a polynomial.

(ii) Given, expression is $x^4 + 2y + 1$.

Here, expression is in two variables and all powers of variables are non-negative integers.

Hence, it is a two variable polynomial.

(iii) Given, expression is $\dfrac{x^4 + x^3 + x}{x}$

Which can be written as $x^3 + x^2 + 1$.

Here, expression is in one variable and all powers of a variable are non-negative integers.

Hence, it is a one variable polynomial.

(iv) Given, expression is $\sqrt{y^3} + y^2 + 3$.

Here, expression is in one variable and all powers of a variable are not non-negative integers.

Hence, it is not a polynomial.

Example 2. Identify the types of following polynomials on the basis of terms.

(i) $20y^3 + 3y + 8$

(ii) 4

(iii) $x^2 + 5x$

Sol. (i) We have, $20y^3 + 3y + 8$

Here, number of terms in given polynomial is 3.
Hence, it is a trinomial.

(ii) We have, 4

Here, number of terms in given polynomial is 1.
Hence, it is a monomial.

(iii) We have, $x^2 + 5x$

Here, number of terms in given polynomial is 2.
Hence, it is a binomial.

Example 3. If $p = 3$, find the degree of the polynomial $g(x) = (p - x)^3 + 14$.

Sol. Given, $g(x) = (p - x)^3 + 14$

On putting $p = 3$, we get

$$g(x) = (3 - x)^3 + 14$$

$$= 27 - x^3 - 27x + 9x^2 + 14$$

$$[\because (a - b)^3 = a^3 - b^3 - 3a^2b + 3ab^2]$$

$$= -x^3 + 9x^2 - 27x + 41$$

Here, the highest power of x is 3, so its degree is 3.

Example 4. Verify whether the following are zeroes of the polynomial indicated against them.

(i) $p(z) = z^2 + z - 6$ at $z = -3$.

(ii) $p(x) = 2x^3 - 9x^2 + x + 12$ at $x = \dfrac{3}{2}$.

Sol. (i) Given polynomial is $p(z) = z^2 + z - 6$ ...(i)

On putting $z = -3$ in Eq. (i), we get
$p(-3) = (-3)^2 + (-3) - 6 = 9 - 3 - 6 = 9 - 9 = 0$

So, $z = -3$ is a zero of the given polynomial.

(ii) Given polynomial is $p(x) = 2x^3 - 9x^2 + x + 12$ ...(i)

On putting $x = \dfrac{3}{2}$ in Eq. (i), we get

$$p\left(\frac{3}{2}\right) = 2\left(\frac{3}{2}\right)^3 - 9\left(\frac{3}{2}\right)^2 + \frac{3}{2} + 12$$

$$= \frac{27}{4} - \frac{81}{4} + \frac{3}{2} + 12$$

$$= \frac{27 - 81 + 6 + 24}{4} = -\frac{24}{4} = -6$$

So, $x = \dfrac{3}{2}$ is not a zero of the given polynomial.

Example 5. Find the zero of the following polynomials.

(i) $p(x) = 4 - 3x$ (ii) $p(t) = 2t - \dfrac{5}{2}$

Sol. (i) Given polynomial is $p(x) = 4 - 3x$

On putting $p(x) = 0$, we get

$$4 - 3x = 0$$
$$\Rightarrow \quad 3x = 4$$
$$\Rightarrow \quad x = \frac{4}{3}$$

Hence, $x = \dfrac{4}{3}$ is the zero of the given polynomial.

(ii) Given polynomial is $p(t) = 2t - \dfrac{5}{2}$

On putting $p(t) = 0$, we get

$$2t - \frac{5}{2} = 0$$
$$\Rightarrow \quad 2t = \frac{5}{2}$$
$$\Rightarrow \quad t = \frac{5}{4}$$

Hence, $t = \dfrac{5}{4}$ is the zero of the given polynomial.

Example 6. If $x^2 + px - 30 = (x - 5)(x + 6)$, for all x, find the value of p.

Sol. Since $(x - 5)$ and $(x + 6)$ are factors of polynomial

$p(x) = x^2 + px - 30$

$\therefore x = 5$ and $x = -6$ are zeroes of the polynomial

$\Rightarrow \qquad p(5) = 0$ and $p(-6) = 0$

$\Rightarrow \qquad 5^2 + p(5) - 30 = 0$

$\Rightarrow \qquad 25 + 5p - 30 = 0$

$\Rightarrow \qquad 5p - 5 = 0$

$\Rightarrow \qquad 5p = 5$

$\Rightarrow \qquad p = 1$

Alternative Method

We have, $x^2 + px - 30 = (x - 5)(x + 6)$

$\qquad = x^2 - 5x + 6x - 30$

$\qquad = x^2 + x - 30$

On comparing the coefficient of x, we get $p = 1$

Example 7. Find the zeroes of the polynomial $p(x) = (x - 2)^2 - (x + 2)^2$.

Sol. Given, polynomial is $p(x) = (x - 2)^2 - (x + 2)^2$

For, zeroes of polynomial, put $p(x) = 0$

$\Rightarrow \qquad (x - 2)^2 - (x + 2)^2 = 0$

$\Rightarrow \quad (x - 2 + x + 2)(x - 2 - x - 2) = 0$

$\qquad\qquad$ [using identify $a^2 - b^2 = (a + b)(a - b)$]

$\Rightarrow \qquad 2x(-4) = 0$

$\Rightarrow \qquad -8x = 0$

$\Rightarrow \qquad x = 0$

Hence, zero of given polynomial is 0.

Example 8. If $f(t) = 4t^2 - 3t + 6$, find (i) $f\left(\dfrac{2}{3}\right)$, (ii) $f(-5)$

Sol. Given, $f(t) = 4t^2 - 3t + 6$

(i) $\quad f\left(\dfrac{2}{3}\right) = 4 \times \left(\dfrac{2}{3}\right)^2 - 3 \times \dfrac{2}{3} + 6$

$\qquad = 4 \times \dfrac{4}{9} - 2 + 6$

$\qquad = \dfrac{16}{9} + 4$

$\qquad = \dfrac{16 + 36}{9} = \dfrac{52}{9}$

(ii) $\quad f(-5) = 4(-5)^2 - 3(-5) + 6$

$\qquad = 100 + 15 + 6 = 121$

Example 9. Find $p(0)$, $p(1)$ and $p(-2)$ for the following polynomials.

$\qquad p(x) = 10x - 4x^2 - 3$

Sol. Given, $p(x) = 10x - 4x^2 - 3$

So, $\quad p(0) = 10 \times 0 - 4 \times (0)^2 - 3$

$\Rightarrow \quad p(0) = 0 - 0 - 3 = -3$

$\qquad p(1) = 10 \times (1) - 4(1)^2 - 3$

$\qquad = 10 - 4 - 3 = 3$

$\qquad p(-2) = 10 \times (-2) - 4(-2)^2 - 3$

$\qquad = -20 - 16 - 3 = -39$

Hence, $p(0) = -3$, $p(1) = 3$ and $p(-2) = -39$

Example 10. If $(x + 4)$ is a factor of the polynomial $x^3 - x^2 - 14x + 24$, find its other factors.

Sol. Given $x^3 - x^2 - 14x + 24$

Since $(x + 4)$ is a factor of $x^3 - x^2 - 14x + 24$

Therefore by dividing $x^3 - x^2 - 14x + 24$ by $(x + 4)$, we get

$\qquad\qquad x^2 - 5x + 6$

By splitting middle term $= x^2 - 3x - 2x + 6$

$\qquad = x(x - 3) - 2(x - 3)$

$\qquad = (x - 3)(x - 2)$

Therefore other factors of $x^3 - x^2 - 14x + 24$ are $(x - 3)$ and $(x - 2)$.

Example 11. Factorise $x^4 - 3x^2 + 2$.

Sol. Let $\quad p(x) = x^4 - 3x^2 + 2$

Put $x^2 = y$, then the given expression becomes

$\qquad p(x) = y^2 - 3y + 2$

$\Rightarrow \quad p(x) = y^2 - 2y - y + 2$

$\qquad = y(y - 2) - 1(y - 2) = (y - 2)(y - 1)$

Put $y = x^2$, we get

$p(x) = (x^2 - 2)(x^2 - 1) = [(x)^2 - (\sqrt{2})^2][(x)^2 - (1)^2]$

$\qquad = (x - \sqrt{2})(x + \sqrt{2})(x - 1)(x + 1)$

$\qquad\qquad [\because (a^2 - b^2) = (a - b)(a + b)]$

Example 12. Factorise $x^2 + \dfrac{1}{x^2} - 2 - 3x + \dfrac{3}{x}$.

Sol. $x^2 + \dfrac{1}{x^2} - 2 - 3x + \dfrac{3}{x}$

$\qquad = \left(x^2 + \dfrac{1}{x^2} - 2\right) - 3\left(x - \dfrac{1}{x}\right)$

$\qquad = \left(x - \dfrac{1}{x}\right)^2 - 3\left(x - \dfrac{1}{x}\right) = \left(x - \dfrac{1}{x}\right)\left(x - \dfrac{1}{x} - 3\right)$

$\qquad\qquad [\because (a - b)^2 = a^2 + b^2 - 2ab]$

Example 13. Factorise $5(3x + y)^2 + 6(3x + y) - 8$.

Sol. Let $(3x + y) = p$, then the given expression becomes

$\qquad 5p^2 + 6p - 8 = 5p^2 + 10p - 4p - 8$

$\qquad\qquad$ [by splitting the middle term]

$\qquad = 5p(p + 2) - 4(p + 2)$

$\qquad = (p + 2)(5p - 4)$

On putting $p = 3x + y$ in above expression we get,

$\qquad = (3x + y + 2)(15x + 5y - 4)$

Example 14. If $\sqrt{u} + \sqrt{v} - \sqrt{w} = 0$, find the value of $(u + v - w)$.

Sol. Given,

$$\sqrt{u} + \sqrt{v} - \sqrt{w} = 0$$

$$\Rightarrow \qquad \sqrt{u} + \sqrt{v} = \sqrt{w}$$

Squaring both sides,

$$(\sqrt{u} + \sqrt{v})^2 = (\sqrt{w})^2$$

Using identity, $(x + y)^2 = x^2 + 2xy + y^2$

$$\Rightarrow \qquad u + v + 2\sqrt{u.v} = w$$

$$\Rightarrow \qquad u + v - w = -2\sqrt{u.v}$$

Example 15. Find $y^2 + \dfrac{1}{y^2}$ and $y^4 + \dfrac{1}{y^4}$, if $y - \dfrac{1}{y} = 9$.

Sol. Given, $y - \dfrac{1}{y} = 9$

Squaring both sides, we get

$$\Rightarrow \qquad y^2 + \frac{1}{y^2} - 2 \times y \times \frac{1}{y} = 81$$

$$[\because (a - b)^2 = a^2 + b^2 - 2ab]$$

$$\Rightarrow \qquad y^2 + \frac{1}{y^2} = 83$$

Again, squaring both sides, we get

$$\left(y^2 + \frac{1}{y^2}\right)^2 = (83)^2$$

$$\Rightarrow \quad y^4 + \frac{1}{y^4} + 2 \times y^2 \times \frac{1}{y^2} = 6889$$

$$[\because (a + b)^2 = a^2 + b^2 + 2ab]$$

$$\Rightarrow \qquad y^4 + \frac{1}{y^4} = 6887$$

Chapter Practice

Objective Questions

- ## Multiple Choice Questions

1. Which one of the following is a polynomial?

(a) $\dfrac{x^2}{2} - \dfrac{2}{x^2}$ (b) $\sqrt{2x} - 1$ (c) $x^2 + \dfrac{3x^{3/2}}{\sqrt{x}}$ (d) $\dfrac{x-1}{x+1}$

2. Degree of the zero polynomial is

(a) 0 (b) 1
(c) any natural number (d) not defined

3. $\sqrt{2}$ is a polynomial of degree

(a) 2 (b) 0 (c) 1 (d) $\dfrac{1}{2}$

4. Degree of the polynomial $4x^4 + 0x^3 + 0x^5 + 5x + 7$ is **[NCERT Exemplar]**

(a) 4 (b) 5 (c) 3 (d) 7

5. Zero of the zero polynomial is

(a) 0 (b) 1
(c) any real number (d) not defined

6. If $p(x) = x + 3$, then $p(x) + p(-x)$ is equal to

(a) 3 (b) $2x$ (c) 0 (d) 6

7. Zero of the polynomial $p(x) = 2x + 5$ is **[NCERT Exemplar]**

(a) $-\dfrac{2}{5}$ (b) $-\dfrac{5}{2}$ (c) $\dfrac{2}{5}$ (d) $\dfrac{5}{2}$

8. The value of the polynomial $5x - 4x^2 + 3$, when $x = -1$ is

(a) -6 (b) 6 (c) 2 (d) -2

9. If $p(x) = x^2 - 2\sqrt{2}x + 1$, then $p(2\sqrt{2})$ is equal to

(a) 0 (b) 1
(c) $4\sqrt{2}$ (d) $8\sqrt{2} + 1$

10. One of the zeroes of the polynomial $2x^2 + 7x - 4$ is **[NCERT Exemplar]**

(a) 2 (b) $\dfrac{1}{2}$
(c) $-\dfrac{1}{2}$ (d) -2

11. $(x + 1)$ is a factor of the polynomial

(a) $x^3 + x^2 - x + 1$ (b) $x^3 + x^2 + x + 1$
(c) $x^4 + x^3 + x^2 + 1$ (d) $x^4 + 3x^3 + 3x^2 + x + 1$

12. If $x + 1$ is a factor of the polynomial $2x^2 + kx$, then the value of k is

(a) -3 (b) 4
(c) 2 (d) -2

13. The factorisation of $4x^2 + 8x + 3$ is **[NCERT Exemplar]**

(a) $(x + 1)(x + 3)$ (b) $(2x + 1)(2x + 3)$
(c) $(2x + 2)(2x + 5)$ (d) $(2x - 1)(2x - 3)$

14. The value of $249^2 - 248^2$ is

(a) 1^2 (b) 477 (c) 487 (d) 497

15. One of the factors of $(25x^2 - 1) + (1 + 5x)^2$ is

(a) $5 + x$ (b) $5 - x$ (c) $5x - 1$ (d) $10x$

16. The coefficient of x in the expansion of $(x + 3)^3$ is

(a) 1 (b) 9 (c) 18 (d) 27

17. If $49x^2 - b = \left(7x + \dfrac{1}{2}\right)\left(7x - \dfrac{1}{2}\right)$, then the value of b is **[NCERT Exemplar]**

(a) 0 (b) $\dfrac{1}{\sqrt{2}}$

(c) $\dfrac{1}{4}$ (d) $\dfrac{1}{2}$

18. Which of the following is a factor of $(x + y)^3 - (x^3 + y^3)$?

(a) $x^2 + y^2 + 2xy$ (b) $x^2 + y^2 - xy$
(c) xy^2 (d) $3xy$

19. If $\dfrac{x}{y} + \dfrac{y}{x} = -1$ (where $x, y \neq 0$), then the value of $x^3 - y^3$ is **[NCERT Exemplar]**

(a) 1 (b) -1 (c) 0 (d) $\dfrac{1}{2}$

20. One of the dimensions of the cuboid whose volume is $36Kx^2y - 21Kxy^2 + 3Ky^3$, is

(a) $3Ky$ (b) $4x - y$ (c) $3x - y$ (d) All of these

• Case Based MCQs

21. An object which is thrown or projected into the air, subject to only the acceleration of gravity is called a projectile, and its path is called its trajectory. This curved path was shown by Galileo to be a parabola. Parabola is represented by a polynomial. If the polynomial to represent the distance covered is

$$P(x) = -3x^2 + 24x + 12$$

(i) What is the degree of the polynomial?

   (a) 0   (b) 1   (c) 2   (d) 3

(ii) Find the height of the projectile 5 seconds after its launch.

   (a) 57 m   (b) 32 m

   (c) 85 m   (d) 68 m

(iii) The polynomial is classified as .... on the basis of number of terms.

   (a) Linear polynomial   (b) Monomial

   (c) Binomial   (d) Trinomial

(iv) The name of polynomial on the basis of degree is

   (a) Cubic polynomial   (b) Constant polynomial

   (c) Quadratic polynomial   (d) Bi-quadratic polynomial

(v) If equation of parabola is given by $p(x) = 3x^2 - 2x - 4$, then value of $p(2)$ is

   (a) 8   (b) 4   (c) 12   (d) 6

22. D.A.V School of Delhi decided different types of tours for the students to educated them. So in class IX, $\dfrac{1}{12}$th times the square of the total number of students planned to visit historical monuments $\dfrac{7}{12}$th times the member of students planned to visit old age homes while 15 students decided to teach poor children.

(i) Using above information, express the total numbers of students as a polynomial in term of x.

   (a) $\dfrac{x^2}{12} + \dfrac{7}{12}x + 15$ (b) $\dfrac{x^2}{4} + \dfrac{7}{4}x + 10$

   (c) $\dfrac{7x^2}{12} + \dfrac{1}{12} + 10$ (d) $\dfrac{x^2}{4} + \dfrac{7}{4} + 15$

(ii) Write the coefficient of x in polynomial.

   (a) $\dfrac{9}{13}$ (b) $\dfrac{7}{12}$ (c) $\dfrac{11}{12}$ (d) $\dfrac{13}{12}$

(iii) Write the coefficient of x^2 in polynomial.

   (a) $\dfrac{1}{13}$ (b) $\dfrac{1}{10}$ (c) $\dfrac{1}{12}$ (d) 15

(iv) Value of $p(x)$ at $x = 2$

   (a) $\dfrac{33}{2}$ (b) $\dfrac{11}{2}$ (c) $\dfrac{22}{3}$ (d) $\dfrac{14}{3}$

(v) Value of $p(x)$ at $x = -1$

   (a) $\dfrac{19}{2}$ (b) $\dfrac{29}{2}$ (c) $\dfrac{9}{2}$ (d) $\dfrac{39}{2}$

23. Pulkit along with his four friends visited. The house of Sumit, who was a common friend. There they meet his father, who was having interest in mathematics. Sumit's father wanted to test the practical knowledge of all his friends, so he showed many objects like a cuboid shaped geometry box, a rectangular photo frame, a circular cardboard, square shaped files and a cube. He started asking following question on by one.

(Cuboid Geometry Box)   (Rectangular Photo Frame)

(Circular Cardboard)

(i) If the area of circular cardboard is $49\pi x^2 + 70\pi x + 25\pi$, what is the radius of this object?

   (a) $(7x + 5)$ (b) $\pi(7x + 5)$

   (c) $-5/7$ (d) $7/5$

(ii) If the volume of geometry box is $x^3 - 2x^2 - x + 2$, what are the possible dimensions of this box?

   (a) $(x + 1), (x + 1), (x + 2)$ (b) $(x + 1), (x - 1), (x + 2)$

   (c) $(x - 1), (x + 1), (x - 2)$ (d) $(x - 1), (x - 1), (x - 2)$

(iii) If the area of a file is $4x^2 + 4x + 1$ what is the perimeter of this file?

   (a) $2x + 1$ (b) $4x + 1$

   (c) $4(2x + 1)$ (d) $(8x + 2)$

(iv) If the area of rectangular photo frame is $12x^2 - 7x + 1$, what are the possible dimensions of photo frame?

   (a) $(3x - 1)(4x - 1)$ (b) $(3x + 1), (4x + 1)$

   (c) $(3x - 1)(4x + 1)$ (d) $(3x + 1), (4x - 1)$

(v) If the volume of cube is $8a^3 - b^3 - 12a^2b + 6ab^2$, what is the side of cube?

   (a) $(2a + b)$ (b) $(2a - b)$

   (c) $(2a + 3b)$ (d) $(3a - 2b)$

PART 2
Subjective Questions

• Short Answer Type Questions

1. Identify the following types of polynomials, on the basis of degree.
   (i) $3x^2 + 5$ (ii) $z^3 + 4z + 1$
   (iii) $4t$

2. Find the coefficient of x^2 in
$$(3x + x^3)\left(x + \dfrac{1}{x}\right).$$

3. Which of the following are polynomials? Justify your answer.
   (i) $x^3 + 3x^2 + 2$
   (ii) $\sqrt{x^5} + 4x + 2$
   (iii) $\dfrac{x^4 + x^3 + 3x}{x} + 2$

4. Find the zero of a polynomial $2x + 4$.

5. If $x = 3$ and $x = 0$ are zeroes of the polynomial $2x^3 - 8x^2 + ax + b$, then find the values of a and b.

6. Verify that whether -2 and 3 are zeroes of the polynomial $x^2 - x - 6$.

7. $x - 1$ is a factor of the polynomial. Yes or No?

8. Find m and n, if $(x + 2)$ and $(x + 1)$ are the factors of $x^3 + 3x^2 - 2mx + n$.

9. If $p(x) = x^3 - 4x^2 + x + 6$, then show that $p(3) = 0$ and hence factorise $p(x)$.

10. Factorise $x^3 + 2x^2 - 5x - 6$.

11. Factorise $x^2 - 5x + 6$ by using factor theorem.

12. Using factor theorem, factorise $x^3 - 6x^2 + 3x + 10$.

13. Factorise the following $x^3 - x^2 + ax + x - a - 1$.

14. Factorise $x^3 - 2x^2y + 3xy^2 - 6y^3$.

15. Factorising $2x^2 + 7x + 3$ by splitting the middle term.

16. Factorise (i) $2x^2 - \dfrac{5}{6}x + \dfrac{1}{12}$.
   (ii) $7\sqrt{2}\,x^2 - 10x - 4\sqrt{2}$.

17. Factorise $(x^2 + 4) - 2a - a^2 - 5$.

18. If $a^2 + \dfrac{9}{a^2} = 31$, what is the positive value of $a - \dfrac{3}{a}$?

19. Factorise $x^2 + \dfrac{1}{x^2} + 2 - 2x - \dfrac{2}{x}$.

20. Simplify $\sqrt{2a^2 + 2\sqrt{6}\,ab + 3b^2}$.

21. Find the product
$$\left(a - \dfrac{1}{a}\right)\left(a + \dfrac{1}{a}\right)\left(a^2 + \dfrac{1}{a^2}\right)\left(a^4 + \dfrac{1}{a^4}\right) \text{ using a}$$
suitable identity.

22. Factorise $a^{12}y^4 - a^4y^{12}$.

23. Simplify $27x^3 - (3x - y)^3$.

24. Factorise $\dfrac{x^3}{8} - 64 - 3x^2 + 24x$ by using suitable identity.

25. Evaluate $(104)^3$ by using suitable identity.

26. Factorise $a^3(b - c)^3 + b^3(c - a)^3 + c^3(a - b)^3$

27. Factorise $25x^2 + 4y^2 + 9z^2 - 20xy - 12yz + 30zx$ by using suitable identity.

28. If $x + y + z = 1$, $xy + yz + zx = -1$ and $xyz = -1$, find the value of $x^3 + y^3 + z^3$.

29. Factorise the following.
   (i) $9x^2 + 4y^2 + 16z^2 + 12xy - 16yz - 24xz$
   (ii) $16x^2 + 4y^2 + 9z^2 - 16xy - 12yz + 24xz$

30. Simplify the following expressions.
   (i) $(x + y + z)^2 + (x + y - z)^2$
   (ii) $(2x + p - c)^2 - (2x - p + c)^2$

31. Factorise the following expressions.
   (i) $25x^2 + 9y^2 + 9z^2 - 30xy - 18yz + 30xz$
   (ii) $9x^2 + 16y^2 + 4z^2 - 24xy + 16yz - 12xz$

32. If $a + b + c = 9$ and $ab + bc + ca = 40$, then the value of $a^2 + b^2 + c^2$.

• Long Answer Type Questions

33. Identify the types of following polynomials on the basis of their degree.
   (i) 5
   (ii) $2x - 3$
   (iii) $2t^3 - 3t^2 + 5t - 4$
   (iv) $3y^2 - 4y + 5$
   (v) $2x^4 - 5x^3 + 4x^2 - 3x + 2$

34. Find the coefficient of x^2 in the following polynomials.

    (i) $(x-4)(x-4)$

    (ii) $1 - x^2 - x^3 + 2x^7$

    (iii) $(2x-5)(2x^2 - 3x + 1)$

    (iv) $(x-1)(4x^2 - 5x - 7)$

35. Evaluate the following value.

    (i) If $f(x) = x - 9$, find $f(x) - f(-x)$.

    (ii) If $p(x) = 4x^5 - 3x^4 - 5x^3 + x^2 - 8$, then find $p(-1)$.

    (iii) If $q(x) = x^3 + 3x^2 + 3x + 1$, find

$$q(-2) + q(-3) + q\left(\frac{1}{2}\right).$$

36. Find the zeroes of the polynomial in each of the following.

    (i) $p(x) = x - 4$

    (ii) $g(x) = 3 - 6x$

    (iii) $q(x) = 2x - 7$

    (iv) $h(y) = 2y$

    (v) $f(x) = 4 - 8x$

37. Factorise $x^2 + 5x - 66$ by using factor theorem.

38. Factorise $3u^3 - 4u^2 - 12u + 16$.

39. Factorise $2x^3 - 5x^2 - 19x + 42$.

40. If both $x - 2$ and $x - \dfrac{1}{2}$ are factors of $px^2 + 5x + r$, then show that $p = r$.

41. Factorise $3x^2 + 7x - 6$ by splitting the middle term.

42. If $x = (2+\sqrt{5})^{1/2} + (2-\sqrt{5})^{1/2}$ and $y = (2+\sqrt{5})^{1/2} - (2-\sqrt{5})^{1/2}$, evaluate $x^2 + y^2$.

43. Simplify

$$\frac{(a^2 - b^2)^3 + (b^2 - c^2)^3 + (c^2 - a^2)^3}{(a-b)^3 + (b-c)^3 + (c-a)^3}.$$

44. Factorise the following

    (i) $3a^3 b - 243ab^3$

    (ii) $x^4 - 625$

    (iii) $a^3 + b^3 + a + b$

    (iv) $x(x-y)^3 + 3x^2 y(x-y)$

45. If $x^2 + \dfrac{1}{x^2} = 14$, find $x^3 + \dfrac{1}{x^3}$.

46. One-fourth of a herd of camels was seen in the forest. Twice the square root of the herd had gone to mountains and the remaining 15 camels were seen on the bank of a river. Find the total number of camels.

● **Case Based Questions**

47. A car moves on a highway, the path trace by the car is shown below

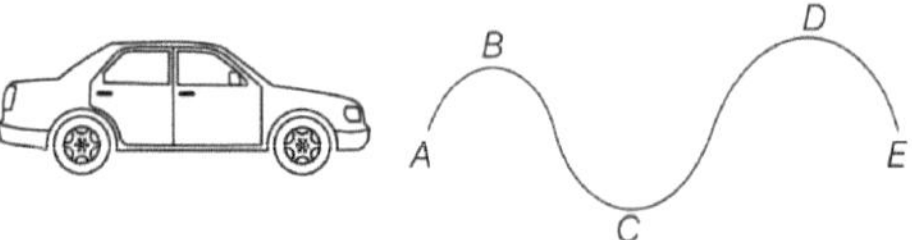

The pattern curve path traced in the shape of parabolic. In mathematician form, the given path followed the polynomial expression,
$$p(x) = a_n x^n + a_n x^{n-1} \ \cdots\cdots$$

For a polynomial $p(x)$ of degree ≥ 1, $p(a) = 0$, where a is a real number, then $(x-a)$ is a factor of the polynomial $p(x)$.

    (i) If $p(x) = x^3 - 3x^2 + 4x - 12$ then what is the value of $p(3)$ and $p(-3)$?

    (ii) For what value of k, the polynomial $2x^4 + 3x^3 + 2kx^2 + 3x + 6$ exactly divisible by $(x+1)$?

    (iii) Find the value of k if $x+1$ is a factor of $4x^3 + 3x^2 - 4x + k$.

SOLUTIONS

Objective Questions

1. (c)

(a) Now, $\dfrac{x^2}{2} - \dfrac{2}{x^2} = \dfrac{x^2}{2} - 2x^{-2}$, it is not a polynomial, because exponent of x is -2 which is not a whole number.

(b) Now, $\sqrt{2x} - 1 = \sqrt{2}x^{1/2} - 1$, it is not a polynomial, because exponent of x is $-\dfrac{1}{2}$ which is not a whole number.

(c) Now, $x^2 + \dfrac{3x^2}{\sqrt{x}} = x^2 + 3x^{2-\frac{1}{2}} = x^2 + 3x^{\frac{3}{2}} = x^2 + 3x$, it is a polynomial, because exponent of x is a whole number.

(d) $\dfrac{x-1}{x+1}$, it is not a polynomial because it is a rational function.

2. (d) The degree of zero polynomial is not defined, because in zero polynomial, the coefficient of any variable is zero i.e. $0x^2$ or $0x^5$, etc.

Hence, we cannot exactly determine the degree of variable in zero polynomial.

3. (b) $\sqrt{2} = \sqrt{2}x^0$. Hence, $\sqrt{2}$ is a polynomial of degree 0, becaucse exponent of x is 0.

4. (a) Degree of $4x^4 + 0x^3 + 0x^5 + 5x + 7$ is equal to the highest power of variable x.
Here, the highest power of x is 4.
Hence, the degree of this polynomial is 4.

5. (c) Zero of the zero polynomial is any real number.
e.g. Let us consider zero polynomial be $0(x-k)$, where k is a real number For determining the zero, put $x - k = 0 \Rightarrow x = k$
Hence, zero of the zero polynomial be any real number.

6. (d) Given $p(x) = x+3$, put $x = -x$ in the given equation, we get $p(-x) = -x + 3$
Now, $p(x) + p(-x) = x + 3 + (-x) + 3 = 6$

7. (b) Given, $p(x) = 2x+5$
For zero of the polynomial, put $p(x) = 0$

$\therefore \qquad 2x + 5 = 0 \Rightarrow x = -\dfrac{5}{2}$

Hence, zero of the polynomial $p(x)$ is $\dfrac{-5}{2}$.

8. (a) Let $p(x) = 5x - 4x^2 + 3$ ...(i)

On putting $x = -1$ in Eq. (i), we get
$p(-1) = 5(-1) - 4(-1)^2 + 3$
$= -5 - 4 + 3 = -6$

9. (b) Given, $p(x) = x^2 - 2\sqrt{2}x + 1$ ...(i)

On putting $x = 2\sqrt{2}$ in Eq. (i), we get
$p(2\sqrt{2}) = (2\sqrt{2})^2 - (2\sqrt{2})(2\sqrt{2}) + 1$
$= 8 - 8 + 1 = 1$

10. (b) Let $p(x) = 2x^2 + 7x - 4$
$= 2x^2 + 8x - x - 4$ [by splitting middle term]
$= 2x(x+4) - 1(x+4)$
$= (2x-1)(x+4)$

For zeroes of $p(x)$, put $p(x) = 0$
$\therefore \qquad (2x-1)(x+4) = 0$
$\Rightarrow \qquad 2x - 1 = 0 \quad$ and $\quad x + 4 = 0$
$\Rightarrow \qquad x = \dfrac{1}{2}$ and $x = -4$

Hence, one of the zeroes of the polynomial $p(x)$ is $\dfrac{1}{2}$.

11. (b) We know that, $(x - a)$ is a factor of $p(x)$, if $p(a) = 0$.

Let $p(x) = x^3 + x^2 - x + 1$,
$\quad q(x) = x^3 + x^2 + x + 1$,
$\quad r(x) = x^4 + x^3 + x^2 + 1$
and $s(x) = x^4 + 3x^3 + 3x^2 + x + 1$

Then, $p(-1) = (-1)^3 + (-1)^2 - (-1) + 1$
$= -1 + 1 + 1 + 1 = 2$
$q(-1) = (-1)^3 + (-1)^2 + (-1) + 1$
$= -1 + 1 - 1 + 1 = 0$
$r(-1) = (-1)^4 + (-1)^3 + (-1)^2 + 1$
$= 1 - 1 + 1 + 1 = 2$
and $s(-1) = (-1)^4 + 3(-1)^3 + 3(-1)^2 + (-1) + 1$
$= 1 - 3 + 3 - 1 + 1 = 1$

Since, $q(-1) = 0$, therefore $(x + 1)$ is a factor of $x^3 + x^2 + x + 1$.

12. (c) Let $\qquad p(x) = 2x^2 + kx$
Since, $(x + 1)$ is a factor of $p(x)$, then
$$p(-1) = 0$$
$\therefore \qquad 2(-1)^2 + k(-1) = 0$
$\Rightarrow \qquad 2 - k = 0 \Rightarrow k = 2$
Hence, the value of k is 2.

13. (b) Now, $4x^2 + 8x + 3 = 4x^2 + 6x + 2x + 3$
    [by splitting middle term]
$= 2x(2x + 3) + 1(2x + 3)$
$= (2x + 3)(2x + 1)$

14. (d) Now, $249^2 - 248^2 = (249 + 248)(249 - 248)$
    [using identity, $a^2 - b^2 = (a-b)(a+b)$]
$= 497 \times 1 = 497$

15. (d) Now, $(25x^2 - 1) + (1 + 5x)^2$
$= 25x^2 - 1 + 1 + 25x^2 + 10x$
    [using identity, $(a+b)^2 = a^2 + b^2 + 2ab$]
$= 50x^2 + 10x = 10x(5x + 1)$

Hence, one of the factor of given polynomial is $10x$.

16. (d) Now, $(x + 3)^3 = x^3 + 3^3 + 3x(3)(x + 3)$

$\qquad$ [using identity, $(a + b)^3 = a^3 + b^3 + 3ab(a + b)$]

$\qquad = x^3 + 27 + 9x(x + 3)$

$\qquad = x^3 + 27 + 9x^2 + 27x$

Hence, the coefficient of x in $(x + 3)^3$ is 27.

17. (c) Given, $(49x^2 - b) = \left(7x + \dfrac{1}{2}\right)\left(7x - \dfrac{1}{2}\right)$

$\Rightarrow \quad [49x^2 - (\sqrt{b})^2] = \left[(7x)^2 - \left(\dfrac{1}{2}\right)^2\right]$

$\qquad$ [using identity, $(a + b)(a - b) = a^2 - b^2$]

$\Rightarrow \quad 49x^2 - (\sqrt{b})^2 = 49x^2 - \left(\dfrac{1}{2}\right)^2$

$\Rightarrow \quad -(\sqrt{b})^2 = -\left(\dfrac{1}{2}\right)^2$

$\Rightarrow \quad (\sqrt{b})^2 = \left(\dfrac{1}{2}\right)^2$ [multiplying both sides by -1]

$\therefore \qquad b = \dfrac{1}{4}$

18. (d) Now, $(x + y)^3 - (x^3 + y^3) = (x + y)^3 - (x + y)(x^2 - xy + y^2)$

$\qquad$ [using identity, $a^3 + b^3 = (a + b)(a^2 - ab + b^2)$]

$\qquad = (x + y)[(x + y)^2 - (x^2 - xy + y^2)]$

$\qquad = (x + y)(x^2 + y^2 + 2xy - x^2 + xy - y^2)$

$\qquad$ [using identity, $(a + b)^2 = a^2 + b^2 + 2ab$]

$\qquad = (x + y)(3xy)$

Hence, one of the factor of given polynomial is $3xy$.

19. (c) Given, $\dfrac{x}{y} + \dfrac{y}{x} = -1$

$\Rightarrow \quad \dfrac{x^2 + y^2}{xy} = -1$

$\Rightarrow \quad x^2 + y^2 = -xy$

$\Rightarrow \quad x^2 + y^2 + xy = 0 \qquad\qquad\qquad$ ...(i)

Now, $\quad x^3 - y^3 = (x - y)(x^2 + xy + y^2)$

$\qquad$ [using identity, $a^3 - b^3 = (a - b)(a^2 + ab + b^2)$]

$\qquad = (x - y) \times 0 = 0 \qquad$ [from Eq. (i)]

20. (d) Volume $= 36Kx^2y - 21Kxy^2 + 3Ky^3$

$\qquad = 3Ky[12x^2 - 7xy + y^2]$

$\qquad = 3Ky[12x^2 - 4xy - 3xy + y^2]$

$\qquad = 3Ky[4x(3x - y) - y(3x - y)]$

$\qquad = 3Ky(4x - y)(3x - y)$

Hence, according to the given options, possible expression for the length/breadth/height is $3Ky$ or $4x - y$ or $3x - y$.

21. (i) (c) The degree of polynomial in one variable is the highest power in the algebraic expression.

$\qquad$ The degree of the equation is 2.

(ii) (a) Given,

$\qquad P(x) = -3x^2 + 24x + 12$

$\qquad P(5) = -3(5)^2 + 24 \times 5 + 12$

$\qquad = -75 + 120 + 12$

$\qquad = -75 + 132 = 57 \text{ m}$

So, the total height of the projectile is 57 m.

(iii) (d) Since, the total number of terms is 3. The polynomial is classified as trinomial on the basis of number of terms.

(iv) (c) The degree of the polynomial is 2. So this polynomial is called quadratic polynomial.

(v) (b) Given, $p(x) = 3x^2 - 2x - 4$

$\qquad p(2) = 3(2)^2 - 2(2) - 4$

$\qquad = 12 - 4 - 4 = 12 - 8 = 4$

22. (i) (a) Let the total number of students be x then $\dfrac{1}{12}$ th times the square of total students $= \dfrac{x^2}{12}$

Then $\dfrac{7}{12}$ th times the number of students $= \dfrac{7x}{12}$

Then total students $= \dfrac{x^2}{12} + \dfrac{7x}{12} + 15$

Hence the polynomial will be $\dfrac{x^2}{12} + \dfrac{7x}{12} + 15$.

(ii) (b) $\dfrac{7}{12}$ is coefficient of x.

(iii) (c) $\dfrac{1}{12}$ is coefficient of x^2.

(iv) (a) $p(x) = \dfrac{x^2}{12} + \dfrac{7x}{12} + 15$

$\qquad p(2) = \dfrac{(2)^2}{12} + \dfrac{7 \times 2}{12} + 15$

$\qquad p(2) = \dfrac{4}{12} + \dfrac{7}{6} + 15 = \dfrac{2 + 7 + 90}{6}$

$\qquad p(2) = \dfrac{99}{6} = \dfrac{33}{2}$

(v) (b) $p(-1) = \dfrac{(-1)^2}{12} + \dfrac{7(-1)}{12} + 15$

$\qquad p(-1) = \dfrac{1}{12} - \dfrac{7}{12} + 15 = \dfrac{1 - 7 + 180}{12} = \dfrac{174}{12} = \dfrac{29}{2}$

23. (i) (a) Given,

Area of circular cardboard $= 49\pi x^2 + 70\pi x + 25\pi$

We know that,

Area of circle $= \pi r^2$

$\qquad = \pi(49x^2 + 70x + 25)$

$\qquad = \pi(49x^2 + 35x + 35x + 25)$

$\qquad = \pi[7x(7x + 5) + 5(7x + 5)]$

$\qquad = \pi[(7x + 5)^2]$

$\qquad = \pi(7x + 5)(7x + 5)$

Hence the radius of the circle is $(7x + 5)$.

(ii) (c) Volume $= x^3 - 2x^2 - x + 2$
$$= x^3 - x^2 - x^2 + x - 2x + 2$$
$$= x^2(x - 1) - x(x - 1) - 2(x - 1)$$
$$= (x^2 - x - 2)(x - 1)$$
$$= (x - 1)(x^2 - 2x + x - 2)$$
$$= (x - 1)(x(x - 2) + 1(x - 2))$$
$$= (x - 1)(x - 2)(x + 1)$$

(iii) (c) We have, Area of a file $= 4x^2 + 4x + 1$

We know that area $= (\text{Side})^2 = (4x^2 + 4x + 1) = (2x + 1)^2$
$$[\because (a + b)^2 = a^2 + b^2 + 2ab]$$

$\therefore$ Perimeter $= 4 \times (2x + 1) = 4(2x + 1)$

(iv) (a) Area of rectangle $= l \times b$
$$= 12x^2 - 7x + 1$$
$$= 12x^2 - 4x - 3x + 1$$
$$= 4x(3x - 1) - (3x - 1)$$
$$= (4x - 1)(3x - 1)$$

(v) (b) Volume of cube $= 8a^3 - b^3 - 12a^2b + 6ab^2$

Volume of cube $= (2a)^3 - (b)^3 - 6ab(2a - b)$
$$= (2a - b)[4a^2 + 2ab + b^2] - 6ab[2a - b]$$
$$= (2a - b)[4a^2 - 4ab + b^2]$$
$$= (2a - b)(2a - b)^2$$
$$= (2a - b)^3 \quad [\because \text{ volume of cube} = (\text{side})^3]$$

Hence, the side of cube is $(2a - b)$.

Subjective Questions

1. (i) We have, $3x^2 + 5$

Here, degree of polynomial $3x^2 + 5$ is 2. Hence, it is a quadratic polynomial.

(ii) We have, $z^3 + 4z + 1$

Here, degree of polynomial $z^3 + 4z + 1$ is 3. Hence, it is a cubic polynomial.

(iii) We have, $4t$

Here, degree of polynomial $4t$ is 1. Hence, it is a linear polynomial.

2. We have, $(3x + x^3)\left(x + \dfrac{1}{x}\right)$
$$= 3x \times x + 3x \times \frac{1}{x} + x^3 \times x + x^3 \times \frac{1}{x}$$
$$= 3x^2 + 3 + x^4 + x^2 = x^4 + 4x^2 + 3$$

So, the coefficient of x^2 is 4.

3. (i) Given expression is $x^3 + 3x^2 + 2$.

Here, we see that a variable has all positive integer powers. Hence, it is a polynomial.

(ii) Given expression is $\sqrt{x^5} + 4x + 2$ or $x^{5/2} + 4x + 2$.

Here, we see that a variable x has no all integer powers, i.e. $x^{5/2}$ is not an integer power.
Hence, it is not a polynomial.

(iii) Given expression is $\dfrac{x^4 + x^3 + 3x}{x} + 2$ or $x^3 + x^2 + 5$.

Here, we see that a variable has all positive integer powers.
Hence, it is a polynomial.

4. Given polynomial is $p(x) = 2x + 4$ ...(i)

On putting $p(x) = 0$, we get $2x + 4 = 0$
$$\Rightarrow \qquad 2x = -4$$
$$\Rightarrow \qquad x = -\frac{4}{2} = -2$$

Hence, $x = -2$ is the zero of the polynomial $2x + 4$.

5. Let $p(x) = 2x^3 - 8x^2 + ax + b$

Since, $x = 3$ is a zero of the polynomial.
$$\therefore \qquad\qquad p(3) = 0$$
$$\Rightarrow \qquad 2(3)^3 - 8(3)^2 + a \times 3 + b = 0$$
$$\Rightarrow \qquad 2 \times 27 - 8 \times 9 + 3a + b = 0$$
$$\Rightarrow \qquad 54 - 72 + 3a + b = 0$$
$$\Rightarrow \qquad -18 + 3a + b = 0$$
$$\Rightarrow \qquad 3a + b = 18 \qquad \text{...(i)}$$

Also, $x = 0$ is a zero of the polynomial.
$$\therefore \qquad\qquad p(0) = 0$$
$$\Rightarrow \qquad 2(0)^3 - 8(0)^2 + a \times 0 + b = 0$$
$$\Rightarrow \qquad 0 - 0 + 0 + b = 0$$
$$\Rightarrow \qquad\qquad b = 0 \qquad \text{... (ii)}$$

On putting $b = 0$ in Eq. (i), we get
$$3a + 0 = 18$$
$$\Rightarrow \qquad 3a = 18$$
$$\therefore \qquad a = \frac{18}{3} = 6$$

Hence, $a = 6$ and $b = 0$.

6. Let given polynomial be $p(x) = x^2 - x - 6$ ...(i)

On putting $x = -2$ in Eq. (i), we get
$$p(-2) = (-2)^2 - (-2) - 6 = 4 + 2 - 6 = 0$$

Again, on putting $x = 3$ in Eq (i), we get
$$p(3) = (3)^2 - (3) - 6 = 9 - 3 - 6 = 0$$

Here, $p(-2) = 0$ and $p(3) = 0$

So, $x = -2$ and $x = 3$ are zeroes of the given polynomial.

7. Yes, let assume $(x - 1)$ is a factor of $x^3 - x^2 - x + 1$.

So, $\qquad x = 1$ is zero of $x^3 - x^2 - x + 1$
$$\therefore \qquad (1)^3 - (1)^2 - (1) + 1 = 0$$
$$\Rightarrow \qquad 1 - 1 - 1 + 1 = 0$$
$$\Rightarrow \qquad\qquad 0 = 0$$

Hence, our assumption is true.

8. Let $f(x) = x^3 + 3x^2 - 2mx + n$

Since, $(x + 2)$ and $(x + 1)$ are the factors of $f(x)$.
$$\therefore \qquad f(-2) = 0 \text{ and } f(-1) = 0$$
$$\Rightarrow \quad (-2)^3 + 3(-2)^2 - 2m(-2) + n = 0$$
$$\text{and} \quad (-1)^3 + 3(-1)^2 - 2m(-1) + n = 0$$
$$\Rightarrow \qquad -8 + 12 + 4m + n = 0$$
$$\text{and} \qquad -1 + 3 + 2m + n = 0$$
$$\Rightarrow \qquad 4m + n = -4 \qquad \text{...(i)}$$
$$\text{and} \qquad 2m + n = -2 \qquad \text{...(ii)}$$

On multiplying Eq. (ii) by 2 and then subtracting Eq. (i) from Eq. (ii), we get

$4m + 2n - (4m + n) = -4 - (-4) \Rightarrow n = 0$

On putting $n = 0$ in Eq. (i), we get $4m + 0 = -4 \Rightarrow m = -1$

Hence, $m = -1$ and $n = 0$.

9. Given, $p(x) = x^3 - 4x^2 + x + 6$ ...(i)

Put $x = 3$ in Eq. (i), we get

$p(3) = (3)^3 - 4(3)^2 + 3 + 6 = 27 - 36 + 9 = 0$

Since, $p(3) = 0$, therefore $x - 3$ is a factor of $p(x)$.

Therefore by dividing $x^3 - 4x^2 + x + 6$ by $(x - 3)$, we get $x^2 - x - 2$

$\therefore \quad p(x) = (x - 3)(x^2 - x - 2) = (x - 3)(x^2 - 2x + x - 2)$

$$[\because -2 + 1 = -1 \text{ and } -2 \times 1 = -2]$$

$$= (x - 3)[x(x - 2) + 1(x - 2)]$$

$$= (x - 3)(x + 1)(x - 2)$$

10. Let $f(x) = x^3 + 2x^2 - 5x - 6$

$\Rightarrow f(2) = (2)^3 + 2(2)^2 - 5 \times 2 - 6 = 8 + 8 - 10 - 6 = 0$

Using synthetic division, we have $x^2 + 4x + 3$ is the other factor

$\Rightarrow (x - 2)(x^2 + 4x + 3) = (x - 2)(x^2 + 3x + x + 3)$

$$= (x - 2)[x(x + 3) + 1(x + 3)]$$

$$= (x - 2)(x + 1)(x + 3)$$

11. Let given polynomial be $f(x) = x^2 - 5x + 6$.

Here, coefficient of x^2 is 1, so we do not need to write it in the form a $g(x)$.

Now, constant term is 6 and all factors of 6 are

$\pm 1, \pm 2, \pm 3$ and ± 6.

At $x = 2$, $f(2) = 2^2 - 5 \times 2 + 6$

$$= 4 - 10 + 6 = 10 - 10 = 0$$

At $x = 3$, $f(3) = 3^2 - 5 \times 3 + 6$

$$= 9 - 15 + 6 = 15 - 15 = 0$$

Hence, $(x - 2)$ and $(x - 3)$ are the factors of given quadratic polynomial.

12. Let $p(x) = x^3 - 6x^2 + 3x + 10$

Here, constant term = 10 and coefficient of x^3 is one.

All possible factors of 10 are $\pm 1, \pm 2, \pm 5$ and ± 10.

At $x = -1$, $p(-1) = (-1)^3 - 6(-1)^2 + 3(-1) + 10$

$$= -1 - 6 - 3 + 10 = 0$$

So, $(x + 1)$ is a factor of $p(x)$.

On dividing $p(x)$ by $(x + 1)$, we get

Quotient $= x^2 - 7x + 10$

So, $p(x) = (x + 1)(x^2 - 7x + 10)$

By splitting the middle term, we get

$$p(x) = (x + 1)\{x^2 - (5 + 2)(x) + 10\}$$

$$[\because 2 + 5 = 7 \text{ and } 2 \times 5 = 10]$$

$$= (x + 1)\{x^2 - 5x - 2x + 10\}$$

$$= (x + 1)\{x(x - 5) - 2(x - 5)\}$$

$$= (x + 1)(x - 2)(x - 5)$$

13. $x^3 - x^2 + ax + x - a - 1 = x^3 - x^2 + ax - a + x - 1$

$$= x^2(x - 1) + a(x - 1) + 1(x - 1)$$

$$= (x - 1)(x^2 + a + 1)$$

14. Given, $x^3 - 2x^2y + 3xy^2 - 6y^3$

Take x^2 common from first two terms and $3y^2$ from last two terms.

$\Rightarrow \quad x^2(x - 2y) + 3y^2(x - 2y)$

Now, take $(x - 2y)$ common from the terms,

$\Rightarrow \quad (x - 2y)(x^2 + 3y^2)$

15. Given polynomial is $2x^2 + 7x + 3$.

On comparing with $ax^2 + bx + c$, we get

$$a = 2, b = 7 \text{ and } c = 3$$

Now, $\quad ac = 2 \times 3 = 6$

So, all possible pairs of factors of 6 are 1 and 6, 2 and 3.

Clearly, pair 1 and 6 gives $1 + 6 = 7 = b$

$\therefore 2x^2 + 7x + 3 = 2x^2 + (1 + 6)x + 3$

$$= 2x^2 + x + 6x + 3$$

$$= x(2x + 1) + 3(2x + 1) = (2x + 1)(x + 3)$$

16. (i) $2x^2 - \dfrac{5}{6}x + \dfrac{1}{12} = \dfrac{24x^2 - 10x + 1}{12}$

$$= \dfrac{1}{12}[24x^2 - (6 + 4)x + 1]$$

$$= \dfrac{1}{12}[24x^2 - 6x - 4x + 1]$$

$$= \dfrac{1}{12}[6x(4x - 1) - 1(4x - 1)]$$

$$= \dfrac{1}{12}(4x - 1)(6x - 1)$$

(ii) $7\sqrt{2}x^2 - 10x - 4\sqrt{2}$

$$= 7\sqrt{2}x^2 - 14x + 4x - 4\sqrt{2}$$

$$[\text{by splitting the middle term}]$$

$$= 7\sqrt{2}x(x - \sqrt{2}) + 4(x - \sqrt{2})$$

$$= (x - \sqrt{2})(7\sqrt{2}x + 4)$$

17. $(x^2 + 4) - 2a - a^2 - 5$

$$= x^2 - 2a - a^2 - 1 = x^2 - (1 + 2a + a^2)$$

$$= x^2 - (1 + a)^2 \qquad [\because (a + b)^2 = a^2 + b^2 + 2ab]$$

$$= [x - (1 + a)][x + (1 + a)] \quad [\because (a^2 - b^2) = (a - b)(a + b)]$$

$$= (x - 1 - a)(x + 1 + a)$$

18. Given, $a^2 + \dfrac{9}{a^2} = 31$

We know $\left(a - \dfrac{3}{a}\right)^2 = a^2 + \dfrac{9}{a^2} - 6$ [by $(a - b)^2 = a^2 + b^2 - 2ab$]

Putting value of $a^2 + \dfrac{9}{a^2} = 31$

$\Rightarrow \qquad \left(a - \dfrac{3}{a}\right)^2 = 31 - 6$

$\Rightarrow \qquad \left(a - \dfrac{3}{a}\right)^2 = 25$

Now taking square root

$$\Rightarrow \qquad \left(a - \frac{3}{a}\right) = \pm 5$$

Since, we have to take positive value therefore $a - \dfrac{3}{a} = 5$.

19. $x^2 + \dfrac{1}{x^2} + 2 - 2x - \dfrac{2}{x}$

$$= (x)^2 + \frac{1}{(x)^2} + 2 \times x \times \frac{1}{x} - 2\left(x + \frac{1}{x}\right)$$

$$= \left(x + \frac{1}{x}\right)^2 - 2\left(x + \frac{1}{x}\right) \qquad [\because (a+b)^2 = a^2 + b^2 + 2ab]$$

$$= \left(x + \frac{1}{x}\right)\left(x + \frac{1}{x} - 2\right)$$

$$= \left(x + \frac{1}{x}\right)\left(\sqrt{x} - \frac{1}{\sqrt{x}}\right)^2 \qquad [\because (a-b)^2 = a^2 + b^2 - 2ab]$$

$$= \left(x + \frac{1}{x}\right)\left(\sqrt{x} - \frac{1}{\sqrt{x}}\right)\left(\sqrt{x} - \frac{1}{\sqrt{x}}\right)$$

20. We have, $\sqrt{2a^2 + 2\sqrt{6}\,ab + 3b^2}$

$$2a^2 + 2\sqrt{6}\,ab + 3b^2$$

Above expression can be written as

$$(\sqrt{2}a)^2 + 2 \times \sqrt{2}a \times \sqrt{3}b + (\sqrt{3}b)^2$$

As we know,

$$(p + q)^2 = p^2 + q^2 + 2pq$$

Here, $p = \sqrt{2}a$ and $q = \sqrt{3}b$

$$(\sqrt{2}a + \sqrt{3}b)^2$$

So, $\sqrt{2a^2 + 2\sqrt{6}\,ab + 3b^2} = \sqrt{(\sqrt{2}a + \sqrt{3}b)^2}$

$$= \sqrt{2}a + \sqrt{3}b$$

21. Using $(a^2 - b^2) = (a - b)(a + b)$, we get

$$\left(a - \frac{1}{a}\right)\left(a + \frac{1}{a}\right)\left(a^2 + \frac{1}{a^2}\right)\left(a^4 + \frac{1}{a^4}\right)$$

$$= \left[\left(a^2 - \frac{1}{a^2}\right)\left(a^2 + \frac{1}{a^2}\right)\right]\left(a^4 + \frac{1}{a^4}\right)$$

$$= \left[(a^2)^2 - \frac{1}{(a^2)^2}\right]\left[a^4 + \frac{1}{a^4}\right]$$

$$= \left(a^4 - \frac{1}{a^4}\right)\left(a^4 + \frac{1}{a^4}\right)$$

$$= a^8 - \frac{1}{a^8}$$

22. $a^{12}y^4 - a^4 y^{12} = a^4 y^4 (a^8 - y^8)$

$$= a^4 y^4 [(a^4)^2 - (y^4)^2]$$

$$= a^4 y^4 [(a^4 + y^4)(a^4 - y^4)]$$

$$\qquad\qquad [\because (a^2 - b^2) = (a + b)(a - b)]$$

$$= a^4 y^4 [(a^4 + y^4)\{(a^2)^2 - (y^2)^2\}]$$

$$= a^4 y^4 [(a^4 + y^4)(a^2 + y^2)(a^2 - y^2)]$$

$$= a^4 y^4 [(a^4 + y^4)(a^2 + y^2)(a + y)(a - y)]$$

23. $27x^3 - (3x - y)^3 = (3x)^3 - (3x - y)^3$

$$= [3x - (3x - y)][(3x)^2 + (3x - y)^2$$

$$+ 3x \times (3x - y)]$$

$$[\because a^3 - b^3 = (a - b)(a^2 + b^2 + ab)]$$

$$= y\,(9x^2 + 9x^2 + y^2 - 6xy + 9x^2 - 3xy)$$

$$= 27x^2 y + y^3 - 9xy^2$$

24. We have, $\dfrac{x^3}{8} - 64 - 3x^2 + 24x$

We can rewrite the given expression as

$$\left(\frac{x}{2}\right)^3 - (4)^3 - 3x(x - 8)$$

$$= \left(\frac{x}{2}\right)^3 - (4)^3 - 3 \times \frac{x}{2} \times 4\left(\frac{x}{2} - 4\right) = \left(\frac{x}{2} - 4\right)^3$$

$$[\because a^3 - b^3 - 3ab\,(a - b) = (a - b)^3]$$

$$= \left(\frac{x}{2} - 4\right)\left(\frac{x}{2} - 4\right)\left(\frac{x}{2} - 4\right)$$

25. Given number without power is 104. Since, it is greater than 100, so it can be written as $100 + 4$.

$$\therefore \qquad (104)^3 = (100 + 4)^3$$

On comparing $(100 + 4)^3$ with $(x + y)^3$, we get

$$x = 100$$

and $\qquad\qquad\qquad y = 4$

By using the algebraic identity,

$$(x + y)^3 = x^3 + y^3 + 3xy\,(x + y), \text{ we get}$$

$$(104)^3 = (100 + 4)^3 = (100)^3 + (4)^3 + 3(100)(4)(100 + 4)$$

$$= 1000000 + 64 + 1200\,(104)$$

$$= 1000000 + 64 + 124800 = 1124864$$

26. $a^3(b - c)^3 + b^3(c - a)^3 + c^3(a - b)^3$

$$= [a(b - c)]^3 + [b(c - a)]^3 + [c(a - b)]^3$$

On putting $a(b - c) = x$, $b(c - a) = y$
and $c(a - b) = z$, we get

$$a^3(b - c)^3 + b^3(c - a)^3 + c^3(a - b)^3$$

$$= x^3 + y^3 + z^3 = 3xyz \qquad [\because x + y + z = 0]$$

$$= 3\,[a(b - c)]\,[b(c - a)]\,[c(a - b)]$$

$$= 3abc(a - b)(b - c)(c - a)$$

27. We have, $25x^2 + 4y^2 + 9z^2 - 20xy - 12yz + 30zx$

We can rewrite the given expression as

$$(5x)^2 + (2y)^2 + (3z)^2 - 2 \times 5x \times 2y$$

$$- 2 \times 2y \times 3z + 2 \times 3z \times 5x$$

$$= (5x)^2 + (-2y)^2 + (3z)^2 + 2(5x)(-2y)$$

$$+ 2(-2y)(3z) + 2(3z)(5x)$$

$$= (5x - 2y + 3z)^2$$

$$[\because a^2 + b^2 + c^2 + 2ab + 2bc + 2ca = (a + b + c)^2]$$

28. Given, $x + y + z = 1$ $\qquad\qquad$ ...(i)

$$xy + yz + zx = -1 \qquad\qquad \text{...(ii)}$$

$$xyz = -1 \qquad\qquad \text{...(iii)}$$

Now, $(x + y + z)^2 = x^2 + y^2 + z^2 + 2(xy + yz + zx)$

$\Rightarrow \qquad (1)^2 = x^2 + y^2 + z^2 + 2(-1)$

[using Eqs. (i) and (ii)]

$\Rightarrow \quad x^2 + y^2 + z^2 = 3 \qquad \qquad \text{...(iv)}$

Again, $x^3 + y^3 + z^3 - 3xyz$

$\qquad = (x + y + z)[x^2 + y^2 + z^2 - (xy + yz + zx)]$

$\Rightarrow x^3 + y^3 + z^3 - 3 \times (-1) = (1)[3 - (-1)]$

[using Eqs. (ii), (iii) and (iv)]

$\Rightarrow x^3 + y^3 + z^3 + 3 = 4 \Rightarrow x^3 + y^3 + z^3 = 1$

29. (i) $9x^2 + 4y^2 + 16z^2 + 12xy - 16yz - 24xz$

$\qquad = (3x)^2 + (2y)^2 + (-4z)^2 + 2(3x)(2y)$

$\qquad \qquad \qquad + 2(2y)(-4z) + 2(-4z)(3x)$

$\qquad = (3x + 2y - 4z)(3x + 2y - 4z)$

$\qquad \quad [\because (a + b + c)^2 = a^2 + b^2 + c^2 + 2ab + 2bc + 2ca]$

(ii) $16x^2 + 4y^2 + 9z^2 - 16xy - 12yz + 24xz$

$\qquad = (4x)^2 + (-2y)^2 + (3z)^2 + 2(4x)(-2y)$

$\qquad \qquad \qquad + 2(-2y)(3z) + 2(4x)(3z)$

$\qquad = (4x - 2y + 3z)(4x - 2y + 3z)$

30. (i) $(x + y + z)^2 + (x + y - z)^2$

$\qquad = (x^2 + y^2 + z^2 + 2xy + 2yz + 2zx)$

$\qquad \qquad \quad + (x^2 + y^2 + z^2 + 2xy - 2yz - 2zx)$

$\qquad = 2x^2 + 2y^2 + 2z^2 + 4xy$

(ii) $(2x + p - c)^2 - (2x - p + c)^2$

$\qquad = (4x^2 + p^2 + c^2 + 4xp - 2pc - 4xc)$

$\qquad \qquad \quad - (4x^2 + p^2 + c^2 - 4xp - 2pc + 4xc)$

$\qquad = 8xp - 8xc = 8x(p - c)$

31. (i) $25x^2 + 9y^2 + 9z^2 - 30xy - 18yz + 30xz$

$\qquad = (5x)^2 + (-3y)^2 + (3z)^2 + 2 \times 5x \times (-3y)$

$\qquad \qquad \quad + 2 \times (-3y) \times 3z + 2 \times 3z \times 5x$

$\qquad = (5x - 3y + 3z)^2$

(ii) $9x^2 + 16y^2 + 4z^2 - 24xy + 16yz - 12xz$

$\qquad = (-3x)^2 + (4y)^2 + (2z)^2 + 2 \times (-3x) \times (4y) + 2 \times (4y)(2z)$

$\qquad \qquad \qquad + 2 \times (2z) \times (-3x)$

$\qquad = (-3x + 4y + 2z)^2$

32. Given that, $a + b + c = 9$

On squaring both sides, we get $(a + b + c)^2 = (9)^2$

$\Rightarrow \qquad a^2 + b^2 + c^2 + 2ab + 2bc + 2ca = 81$

$\Rightarrow \qquad a^2 + b^2 + c^2 + 2(ab + bc + ca) = 81$

On putting $ab + bc + ca = 40$, we get

$\qquad a^2 + b^2 + c^2 + 2 \times 40 = 81$

$\therefore \qquad a^2 + b^2 + c^2 = 81 - 80 = 1$

33. (i) We have, 5 or $5x°$.

$\qquad$ Here, degree of polynomial 5 is 0.

$\qquad$ Hence, it is a constant polynomial.

(ii) We have, $2x - 3$

$\qquad$ Here, degree of polynomial $2x - 3$ in 1.

$\qquad$ Hence, it is a linear polynomial.

(iii) We have, $2t^3 - 3t^2 + 5t - 4$

$\qquad$ Here, degree of polynomial $2t^3 - 3t^2 + 5t - 4$ is 3.

$\qquad$ Hence, it is a cubic polynomial.

(iv) We have, $3y^2 - 4y + 5$

$\qquad$ Here, degree of polynomial $3y^2 - 4y + 5$ is 2.

$\qquad$ Hence, it is a quadratic polynomial.

(v) We have, $2x^4 - 5x^3 + 4x^2 - 3x + 2$

$\qquad$ Here, degree of polynomial $2x^4 - 5x^3 + 4x^2 - 3x + 2$ is 4.

$\qquad$ Hence, it is a biquadratic polynomial.

34. (i) We have, $(x - 4)(x - 4)$

$\qquad = x \times x - x \times 4 - 4 \times x + 4 \times 4$

$\qquad = x^2 - 4x - 4x + 16$

$\qquad = x^2 - 8x + 16$

$\qquad$ So, the coefficient of x^2 is 1.

(ii) We have, $1 - x^2 - x^3 + 2x^7$

$\qquad$ Here, coefficient of x^2 is -1.

(iii) We have, $(2x - 5)(2x^2 - 3x + 1)$

$\qquad = 2x \times 2x^2 - 2x \times 3x + 2x \times 1 - 5 \times 2x^2 + 5 \times 3x - 5 \times 1$

$\qquad = 4x^3 - 6x^2 + 2x - 10x^2 + 15x - 5$

$\qquad = 4x^3 - 16x^2 + 17x - 5$

$\qquad$ So, the coefficient of x^2 is -16.

(iv) We have, $(x - 1)(4x^2 - 5x - 7)$

$\qquad = x \times 4x^2 - x \times 5x - x \times 7 - 1 \times 4x^2 + 1 \times 5x + 1 \times 7$

$\qquad = 4x^3 - 5x^2 - 7x - 4x^2 + 5x + 7$

$\qquad = 4x^3 - 9x^2 - 2x + 7$

$\qquad$ So, the coefficient of x^2 is -9.

35. (i) We have, $f(x) = x - 9$

$\qquad$ On putting $x = -x$ in $f(x)$, we get $f(-x) = -x - 9$

$\qquad$ Now, $f(x) - f(-x) = x - 9 - (-x - 9)$

$\qquad \qquad \qquad \qquad = x - 9 + x + 9 = 2x$

(ii) We have, $p(x) = 4x^5 - 3x^4 - 5x^3 + x^2 - 8$

$\qquad$ On putting $x = -1$ in $p(x)$, we get

$\qquad \quad p(-1) = 4(-1)^5 - 3(-1)^4 - 5(-1)^3 + (-1)^2 - 8$

$\qquad \qquad \qquad = -4 - 3 + 5 + 1 - 8$

$\qquad \qquad \qquad = -15 + 6$

$\qquad \qquad \qquad = -9$

(iii) We have, $q(x) = x^3 + 3x^2 + 3x + 1$

$\qquad$ On putting $x = -2$ in $q(x)$, we get

$\qquad \quad q(-2) = (-2)^3 + 3(-2)^2 + 3(-2) + 1$

$\qquad \qquad \qquad = -8 + 12 - 6 + 1$

$\qquad \qquad \qquad = 13 - 14$

$\qquad \qquad \qquad = -1$

$\qquad$ On putting $x = -3$ in $q(x)$, we get

$\qquad \quad q(-3) = (-3)^3 + 3(-3)^2 + 3(-3) + 1$

$\qquad \qquad \qquad = -27 + 27 - 9 + 1$

$\qquad \qquad \qquad = -8$

On putting $x = \dfrac{1}{2}$ in $q(x)$, we get

$$q\left(\dfrac{1}{2}\right) = \left(\dfrac{1}{2}\right)^3 + 3\left(\dfrac{1}{2}\right)^2 + 3\left(\dfrac{1}{2}\right) + 1$$

$$= \dfrac{1}{8} + \dfrac{3}{4} + \dfrac{3}{2} + 1$$

$$= \dfrac{1 + 6 + 12 + 8}{8} = \dfrac{27}{8}$$

Now, $q(-2) + q(-3) + q\left(\dfrac{1}{2}\right) = -1 - 8 + \dfrac{27}{8}$

$$= -9 + \dfrac{27}{8}$$

$$= \dfrac{-72 + 27}{8} = \dfrac{-45}{8}$$

36. (i) Given, polynomial is

$$p(x) = x - 4$$

For zero of polynomial, put $p(x) = 0$

$\therefore \qquad x - 4 = 0$

$\Rightarrow \qquad x = 4$

Hence, zero of polynomial is 4.

(ii) Given, polynomial is

$$g(x) = 3 - 6x$$

For zero of polynomial, put $g(x) = 0$

$\therefore \qquad 3 - 6x = 0 \Rightarrow 6x = 3$

$\Rightarrow \qquad x = \dfrac{3}{6} = \dfrac{1}{2}$

Hence, zero of polynomial is $\dfrac{1}{2}$.

(iii) Given, polynomial is $q(x) = 2x - 7$

For zero of polynomial, put $q(x) = 0$

$\therefore \qquad 2x - 7 = 0$

$\Rightarrow \qquad 2x = 7 \Rightarrow x = \dfrac{7}{2}$

Hence, zero of polynomial is $\dfrac{7}{2}$.

(iv) Given polynomial is $h(y) = 2y$

For zero of polynomial, put $h(y) = 0$

$\therefore \qquad 2y = 0 \Rightarrow y = 0$

Hence, the zero of polynomial is 0.

(v) Given, polynomial is $f(x) = 4 - 8x$

For zero of polynomial, put $f(x) = 0$

$\therefore 0 = 4 - 8x \Rightarrow 8x = 4 \Rightarrow x = \dfrac{1}{2}$

Hence, the zero of polynomial is $\dfrac{1}{2}$.

37. Let given polynomial be $f(x) = x^2 + 5x - 66$.

Here, coefficient of x^2 is 1, so we do not used to write it in the form of a $g(x)$.

Now, constant term is -66 and all factors of -66 are

$$\pm 1, \pm 2, \pm 3, \pm 4, \pm 6, \pm 11, \pm 14, \pm 66$$

At $x = 6$, $f(6) = 6^2 + 5 \times 6 - 66$

$$= 36 + 30 - 66 = 66 - 66 = 0$$

At $x = -11$, $f(-11) = (-11)^2 - 5 \times 11 - 66$

$$= 121 - 55 - 66 = 121 - 121 = 0$$

Hence, $(x - 6)$ and $(x + 11)$ are the factors of given quadratic polynomial.

38. Let $p(u) = 3u^3 - 4u^2 - 12u + 16$

Here, we see that coefficient of x^3 is not one, so firstly we make the coefficient of x^3 is one.

i.e. $p(u) = 3\left(u^3 - \dfrac{4}{3}u^2 - \dfrac{12}{3}u + \dfrac{16}{3}\right)$ ...(i)

$$= 3g(u)$$

where, $g(u) = u^3 - \dfrac{4}{3}u^2 - 4u + \dfrac{16}{3}$

Here, constant term is $\dfrac{16}{3}$ and its factors are

$$\pm 1, \pm 2, \pm 4, \pm 8, \pm 16$$

At $u = 2$, $g(2) = (2)^3 - \dfrac{4}{3}(2)^2 - 4(2) + \dfrac{16}{3} = 8 - \dfrac{16}{3} - 8 + \dfrac{16}{3} = 0$

So, $(u - 2)$ is a factor of $g(u)$.

On dividing $g(u)$ by $(u - 2)$, we get.

Quotient $= \left(u^2 + \dfrac{2}{3}u - \dfrac{8}{3}\right)$

$\therefore \quad g(u) = (u - 2)\left(u^2 + \dfrac{2}{3}u - \dfrac{8}{3}\right)$

From Eq. (i),

$$p(u) = 3(u - 2)\left(u^2 + \dfrac{2}{3}u - \dfrac{8}{3}\right)$$

$$= (u - 2)(3u^2 + 2u - 8)$$

$$= (u - 2)(3u^2 + 6u - 4u - 8)$$

$$= (u - 2)[3u(u + 2) - 4(u + 2)]$$

$$= (u - 2)(u + 2)(3u - 4)$$

39. Let $p(x) = 2x^3 - 5x^2 - 19x + 42$

Here, we see that coefficient of x^3 is not one, so firstly we make the coefficient of x^3 is one.

i.e. $\quad p(x) = 2\left(x^3 - \dfrac{5}{2}x^2 - \dfrac{19}{2}x + \dfrac{42}{2}\right) = 2g(x)$ ...(i)

where, $g(x) = x^3 - \dfrac{5}{2}x^2 - \dfrac{19}{2}x + 21$

Here, constant term is 21 and its all factors are $\pm 1, \pm 3, \pm 7, \pm 21$.

At $x = 1$, $g(1) = (1)^3 - \dfrac{5}{2}(1)^2 - \dfrac{19}{2}(1) + 21$

$$= 1 - \dfrac{5}{2} - \dfrac{19}{2} + 21 = \dfrac{44 - 24}{2} = -12 + 22 = 10 \neq 0$$

So, $(x - 1)$ is not a factor of $g(x)$.

At $x = -3$, $g(-3) = (-3)^3 - \dfrac{5}{2}(-3)^2 - \dfrac{19}{2}(-3) + 21$

$$= -27 - \dfrac{5}{2} \times 9 + \dfrac{57}{2} + 21$$

$$= \dfrac{-54 - 45 + 57 + 42}{2} = \dfrac{-99 + 99}{2}$$

So, $(x + 3)$ is a factor of $g(x)$.

On dividing $g(x)$ by $(x + 3)$, we get

$$\text{Quotient} = \left(x^2 - \frac{11}{2}x + 7 \right)$$

$$\therefore \qquad g(x) = (x + 3)\left(x^2 - \frac{11}{2}x + 7 \right)$$

From Eq. (i), $p(x) = 2(x + 3)\left(\dfrac{2x^2 - 11x + 14}{2} \right)$

$$= (x + 3)(2x^2 - 11x + 14)$$
$$= (x + 3)(2x^2 - 4x - 7x + 14)$$
$$= (x + 3)[2x(x - 2) - 7(x - 2)]$$
$$= (x + 3)(x - 2)(2x - 7)$$

40. Let $f(x) = px^2 + 5x + r$

Since, $x - 2$ is a factor of $f(x)$, then $f(2) = 0$

$\therefore \quad p(2)^2 + 5(2) + r = 0$

$\Rightarrow \qquad 4p + 10 + r = 0 \qquad \qquad \text{...(i)}$

Since, $x - \dfrac{1}{2}$ is a factor of $f(x)$, then $f\left(\dfrac{1}{2}\right) = 0$

$$\therefore \qquad p\left(\frac{1}{2}\right)^2 + 5\left(\frac{1}{2}\right) + r = 0$$

$$\Rightarrow \qquad p \times \frac{1}{4} + \frac{5}{2} + r = 0$$

$$\Rightarrow \qquad p + 10 + 4r = 0 \qquad \qquad \text{...(ii)}$$

Since, $x - 2$ and $x - \dfrac{1}{2}$ are factors of $f(x) = px^2 + 5x + r$.

From Eqs. (i) and (ii), $4p + 10 + r = p + 10 + 4r \Rightarrow 3p = 3r$

$\therefore \qquad \qquad p = r$

41. Given polynomial is $3x^2 + 7x - 6$

On comparing with $ax^2 + bx - c$, we get

$$a = 3,\ b = 7 \text{ and } c = -6$$

Now, $ac = 3 \times -6 = -18$

So, all possible pairs of factors of -18 are 1 and -18, -1 and 18, 2 and -9, -2 and 9, 3 and -6, -3 and 6.

Clearly, pair -2 and 9 gives $-2 + 9 = 7 = b$

$\therefore \quad 3x^2 + 7x - 6 = 3x^2 + (-2 + 9)x - 6$

$$= 3x^2 - 2x + 9x - 6$$
$$= x(3x - 2) + 3(3x - 2)$$
$$= (x + 3)(3x - 2)$$

42. We have,

$$x = (2 + \sqrt{5})^{1/2} + (2 - \sqrt{5})^{1/2} \qquad \text{...(i)}$$
$$y = (2 + \sqrt{5})^{1/2} - (2 - \sqrt{5})^{1/2} \qquad \text{...(ii)}$$

Multiplying Eq. (i) by Eq. (ii),

$$xy = [\sqrt{(2 + \sqrt{5})^2} + \sqrt{2 - \sqrt{5}}\sqrt{2 + \sqrt{5}}$$
$$\qquad - \sqrt{2 - \sqrt{5}}\sqrt{2 + \sqrt{5}} - (\sqrt{2 - \sqrt{5}})^2]$$

$$\Rightarrow \quad xy = 2 + \sqrt{5} - 2 + \sqrt{5} = 2\sqrt{5} \qquad \text{...(iii)}$$

$$x + y = 2\sqrt{2 + \sqrt{5}} \qquad \text{...(iv)}$$

Squaring Eq. (iv) on both sides,

$$(x + y)^2 = 4(2 + \sqrt{5})$$
$$\Rightarrow \qquad x^2 + y^2 + 2xy = 8 + 4\sqrt{5}$$
$$\Rightarrow \quad x^2 + y^2 + 2 \times 2\sqrt{5} = 8 + 4\sqrt{5} \qquad \text{[using Eq. (iii)]}$$
$$\Rightarrow \qquad \qquad x^2 + y^2 = 8$$

43. Here, $(a^2 - b^2) + (b^2 - c^2) + (c^2 - a^2) = 0$

$\therefore (a^2 - b^2)^3 + (b^2 - c^2)^3 + (c^2 - a^2)^3$

$$= 3(a^2 - b^2)(b^2 - c^2)(c^2 - a^2)$$
$$= 3(a - b)(a + b)(b - c)(b + c)(c - a)(c + a)$$
$$\qquad [\because (a^2 - b^2) = (a - b)(a + b)]$$

Similarly, $(a - b) + (b - c) + (c - a) = 0$

$\therefore \quad (a - b)^3 + (b - c)^3 + (c - a)^3$

$$= 3(a - b)(b - c)(c - a)$$

Now, $\quad \dfrac{(a^2 - b^2)^3 + (b^2 - c^2)^3 + (c^2 - a^2)^3}{(a - b)^3 + (b - c)^3 + (c - a)^3}$

$$= \frac{3(a - b)(a + b)(b - c)(b + c)(c - a)(c + a)}{3(a - b)(b - c)(c - a)}$$

$$= (a + b)(b + c)(c + a)$$

44. (i) $3a^3b - 243ab^3 = 3ab(a^2 - 81b^2)$

$$= 3ab[(a)^2 - (9b)^2]$$
$$= 3ab(a - 9b)(a + 9b)$$
$$\qquad [\because (a^2 - b^2) = (a - b)(a + b)]$$

(ii) $x^4 - 625$

$$= (x^2)^2 - (25)^2 = (x^2 - 25)(x^2 + 25)$$
$$= [(x)^2 - (5)^2](x^2 + 25)$$
$$= (x + 5)(x - 5)(x^2 + 25)$$

(iii) $a^3 + b^3 + (a + b)$

$$= (a + b)(a^2 - ab + b^2) + (a + b)$$
$$= (a + b)(a^2 - ab + b^2 + 1)$$

(iv) $x(x - y)^3 + 3x^2y(x - y)$

$$= (x - y)[x(x - y)^2 + 3x^2y]$$
$$= x(x - y)(x^2 + y^2 - 2xy + 3xy)$$
$$= x(x - y)(x^2 + y^2 + xy)$$

45. $\because \quad \left(x + \dfrac{1}{x} \right)^2 = x^2 + \dfrac{1}{x^2} + 2$

$$\Rightarrow \quad \left(x + \frac{1}{x} \right)^2 = 14 + 2 = 16$$

$$\Rightarrow \qquad x + \frac{1}{x} = \pm 4$$

Case I   When $x + \dfrac{1}{x} = 4$, then

$$\left(x + \frac{1}{x} \right)^3 = x^3 + \frac{1}{x^3} + 3\left(x + \frac{1}{x} \right)$$

$$\Rightarrow \qquad (4)^3 = x^3 + \frac{1}{x^3} + 3 \times 4$$

$$\therefore \qquad x^3 + \frac{1}{x^3} = 64 - 12 = 52$$

Case II When $x + \dfrac{1}{x} = -4$, then

$$\left(x + \frac{1}{x}\right)^3 = x^3 + \frac{1}{x^3} + 3\left(x + \frac{1}{x}\right)$$

$$\Rightarrow \qquad (-4)^3 = x^3 + \frac{1}{x^3} + 3(-4)$$

$$\therefore \qquad x^3 + \frac{1}{x^3} = -64 + 12$$

$$= -52$$

46. Let the total number of Camels be x.

Then number of Camels seen in the forest $= \dfrac{x}{4}$

Number of Camels gone to mountain $= 2\sqrt{x}$

Number of Camels on the bank of river $= 15$

Total number of Camels $= \dfrac{x}{4} + 2\sqrt{x} + 15$

By hypothesis, we have

$$\Rightarrow \qquad \frac{x}{4} + 2\sqrt{x} + 15 = x$$

$$\Rightarrow \qquad 3x - 8\sqrt{x} - 60 = 0$$

$$3y^2 - 8y - 60 = 0 \qquad [\text{Let } x = y^2]$$

$$3y^2 - 18y + 10y - 60 = 0$$

$$(3y + 10)(y - 6) = 0$$

$$y = 6, \frac{-10}{3}$$

Now, $y = \dfrac{-10}{3} \Rightarrow x = \left(\dfrac{-10}{3}\right)^2 = \dfrac{100}{9}$ (Not possible)

$$\therefore \quad y = 6 \Rightarrow x = (6)^2 = 36$$

Hence, the number of Camels $= 36$

47. (i) Given,

$$p(x) = x^3 - 3x^2 + 4x - 12$$

$$p(3) = (3)^3 - 3(3)^2 + 4(3) - 12$$

$$\Rightarrow p(3) = 27 - 27 + 12 - 12$$

$$\Rightarrow p(3) = 0$$

and $p(-3) = (-3)^3 - 3(-3)^2 + 4(-3) - 12$

$$\Rightarrow \qquad p(-3) = -27 - 27 - 12 - 12$$

$$\Rightarrow \qquad p(-3) = -54 - 24$$

$$\Rightarrow \qquad p(-3) = -78$$

Hence the value of $p(3) = 0$ and $p(-3) = -78$

(ii) Let $p(x) = 2x^4 + 3x^3 + 2kx^2 + 3x + 6$

and $(x + 1)$ is divisible of $p(x)$

$$\therefore \qquad x + 1 = 0$$

$$x = -1$$

then $p(-1) = 0$

$$p(-1) = 2(-1)^4 + 3(-1)^3 + 2k(-1)^2 + 3(-1) + 6$$

$$\Rightarrow \qquad 0 = 2 + (-3) + 2k + (-3) + 6$$

$$\Rightarrow \qquad 0 = 2 - 3 + 2k - 3 + 6$$

$$\Rightarrow \qquad 2k = -2$$

$$\Rightarrow \qquad k = -1$$

(iii) Let $p(x) = 4x^3 + 3x^2 - 4x + k$

and $(x + 1)$ is a factor of $p(x)$

$$\therefore \qquad x + 1 = 0$$

$$x = -1$$

$$\Rightarrow \qquad p(-1) = 0$$

Now, $p(-1) = 4(-1)^3 + 3(-1)^2 - 4(-1) + k$

$$0 = -4 + 3 + 4 + k$$

$$k = -3$$

Chapter Test

Multiple Choice Questions

1. Which one of the following algebraic expressions is a polynomial in variable x?

(a) $3x^2 - 5x$ (b) $\sqrt{x} + \dfrac{1}{\sqrt{x}}$

(c) $x^2 + \dfrac{2}{x^2}$ (d) None of these

2. If $x = 2$ and $x = 0$ are zeroes of the polynomial $2x^3 - 5x^2 + ax + b$, turn the values of a and b.

(a) 1, 3 (b) 2, 0
(c) 3, 5 (d) 2, 4

3. If $x - 3$ is a factor of $k^2x^3 - x^2 + 3x - 1$, then the value of k is

(a) $\pm \dfrac{1}{3\sqrt{3}}$ (b) $\pm\sqrt{3}$

(c) $\pm \dfrac{1}{2\sqrt{2}}$ (d) None of these

4. Using factor theorem, If $p(x) = x^{19} + 1$, then the value of zeroes.

(a) 1 (b) –1
(c) 2 (d) 3

5. Evaluate 105×106 without multiplying directly, then the value is

(a) 15348 (b) 16368
(c) 11130 (d) None of these

Case Study

6. A maths teacher explains the concept of polynomials in 9th class. He told them about different type of polynomial, concept of degree of polynomial value of polynomial, factor theorem and them he told about algebraic identities.

(i) Which of the following are not polynomial.

(a) $\sqrt{x} + \dfrac{1}{\sqrt{x}}$ (b) $x^2 - 3x + 5$

(c) $\dfrac{x^{3/2}}{\sqrt{x}} - 1$ (d) None of these

(ii) Find the zero of the polynomial $q(u) = 3u$.

(a) 0 (b) 3
(c) 2 (d) 1

(iii) Find the zeroes of the polynomial $p(x) = 3x^2 + 7x + 2$.

(a) $1, -1/3$ (b) $-1/3, -2$
(c) $2/3, 1$ (d) $1/3, 2$

(iv) Find $p(1)$, if $p(x) = x^3 - 22x^2 + 141x - 120$.

(a) –1 (b) –12
(c) 0 (d) 9

(v) $(x + y)^2 - (x - y)^2$ is equal to

(a) xy (b) $2xy$
(c) x^2y (d) $4xy$

Short Answer Type Questions

7. Which of the following expressions are polynomials in one or more variable(s)? State reasons for your answer.

(i) $3x^2 - 5x$ (ii) $5y^2 + 8x$

8. Expand $\left(x - \dfrac{1}{2}y + \dfrac{1}{3}z \right)^2$.

Long Answer Type Questions

9. Using factor theorem, factorise $x^3 - 6x^2 + 3x + 10$.

10. Find the square root of $(x^2 + 4x + 4)(x^2 + 6x + 9)$.

Answers

1. (a) *2.* (b) *3.* (a) *4.* (b) *5.* (c) *6.* (i) (a) (ii) (a) (iii) (b) (iv) (c) (v) (d)

7. (i) One variable polynomial, (ii) two variable polynomial

8. $x^2 + \dfrac{1}{4}y^2 + \dfrac{1}{9}z^2 - xy - \dfrac{yz}{3} + \dfrac{2zx}{3}$ *9.* $(x + 1)(x - 2)(x - 5)$ *10.* $x^2 + 5x + 6$

For Detailed Solutions

Scan the code

CHAPTER 02

Quadrilaterals

In this Chapter...

- Quadrilateral and its Types
- Important Theorem Related to Parallelogram

The closed figure formed by joining four non-collinear points in an order is called a **quadrilateral**.

A closed figure having four sides, four angles and four vertices, is called a quadrilateral.

In a quadrilateral *ABCD*, given along side *AB*, *BC*, *CD* and *DA* are the four sides; *A*, *B*, *C* and *D* are the four vertices and ∠*A*, ∠*B*, ∠*C* and ∠*D* are the four angles formed at the vertices.

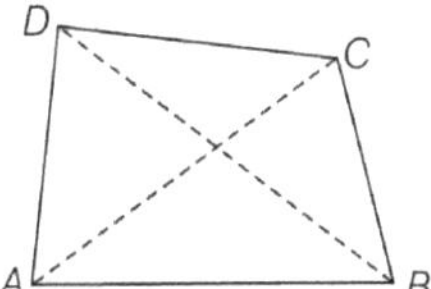

Terms Related to Quadrilateral

- **Opposite Sides** Two sides of a quadrilateral which have no common end point (vertex) i.e. do not intersect each other are called opposite sides.
  In quadrilateral *ABCD*; *AB*, *CD* and *BC*, *AD* are two pairs of opposite sides.
- **Consecutive or Adjacent Sides** Two sides of a quadrilateral which have a common end point, i.e. intersect each other, are called consecutive sides.
  In quadrilateral *ABCD*; *AB*, *BC*; *BC*, *CD*; *CD*, *DA* and *DA*, *AB* are four pairs of consecutive sides.
- **Opposite Angles** Two angles of a quadrilateral are said to be opposite angles, if they do not have a common arm.

In quadrilateral *ABCD*; ∠*A*, ∠*C* and ∠*B*, ∠*D* are two pairs of opposite angles.

- **Consecutive or Adjacent Angles** Two angles of a quadrilateral are said to be consecutive or adjacent angles, if they have a common arm.
  In quadrilateral *ABCD*; ∠*A*, ∠*B*; ∠*B*, ∠*C*; ∠*C*, ∠*D* and ∠*D*, ∠*A* are four pairs of consecutive angles.
- **Diagonals** In a quadrilateral, the line segment joining the opposite vertices is called a diagonal of the quadrilateral.
  In quadrilateral *ABCD*; *AC* and *BD* are two diagonals.

Angle Sum Property of a Quadrilateral

The sum of the four angles of a quadrilateral is 360°.

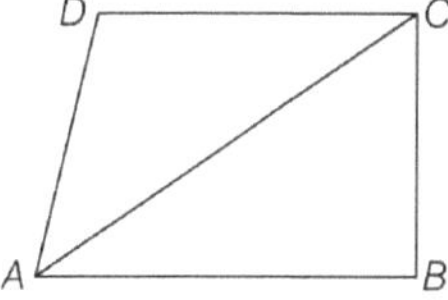

Verification Let *ABCD* be a quadrilateral and *AC* be a diagonal.

We know that, in △*ADC*,

$$\angle DAC + \angle ACD + \angle ADC = 180° \qquad ...(i)$$

[since, sum of angles of a triangle is 180°.]

Similarly, in △*ABC*,

$$\angle CAB + \angle ACB + \angle ABC = 180° \qquad ...(ii)$$

[since, sum of angles of a triangle is 180°.]

On adding Eqs. (i) and (ii), we get

$$\angle DAC + \angle ACD + \angle ADC + \angle CAB + \angle ACB + \angle ABC$$
$$= 180° + 180° = 360° \qquad \text{…(iii)}$$

Also, $\quad \angle DAC + \angle CAB = \angle BAD$

and $\quad \angle ACD + \angle ACB = \angle BCD$ $\qquad$ …(iv)

So, from Eqs. (iii) and (iv), we get

$$\angle ABC + \angle ADC + \angle BAD + \angle BCD = 360°$$
$$\Rightarrow \qquad \angle B + \angle D + \angle A + \angle C = 360°$$

Hence, the sum of the angles of a quadrilateral is 360°.

Various Types of Quadrilaterals

1. Trapezium

A quadrilateral in which one pair of opposite sides are parallel is called a trapezium.

In the figure, $ABCD$ is a trapezium, in which $AB \| CD$.

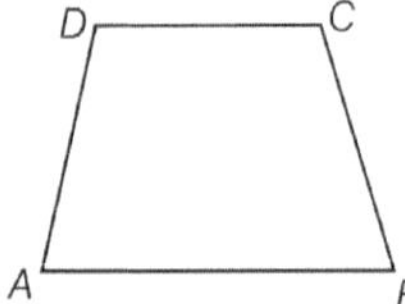

If two non-parallel sides of a trapezium are equal, then it is called an isosceles trapezium.

2. Parallelogram

A quadrilateral in which both pairs of opposite sides are parallel, is called parallelogram and it is written as $\|_{gm}$.

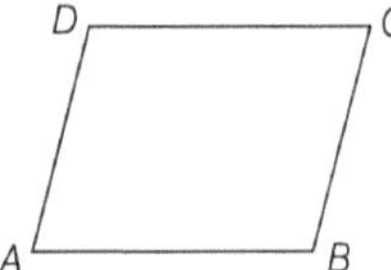

In the above figure, $ABCD$ is a parallelogram in which $AB \| DC$ and $BC \| AD$.

3. Rhombus

A parallelogram in which all sides are equal, is called a rhombus.

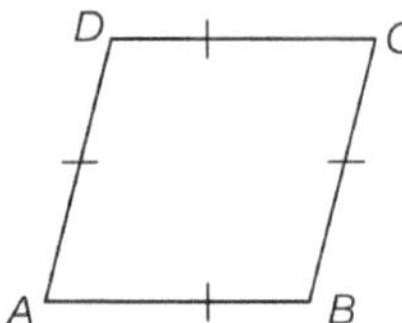

In other words, a quadrilateral in which all four sides are equal and both pairs of opposite sides are parallel, is called a rhombus.

In the above figure, $ABCD$ is a rhombus in which

$$AB = BC = CD = DA$$

and $\quad AB \| DC$ and $BC \| AD$

4. Rectangle

A parallelogram in which one of its angles is right angle, is called rectangle. In other words, a quadrilateral in which opposite sides are parallel and equal and one angle is 90°, is called a rectangle.

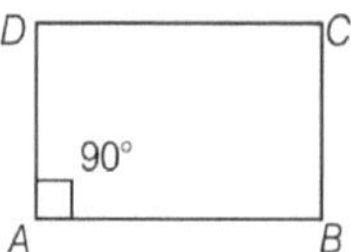

In the above figure, $ABCD$ is a rectangle in which

$$AB \| DC \text{ and } AB = DC$$

Also, $\qquad BC \| AD$ and $BC = AD$

Also, $\qquad \angle A = 90°,$

therefore, $\qquad \angle B = \angle C = \angle D = 90°$

5. Square

A rectangle whose two consecutive sides are equal, is called a square.

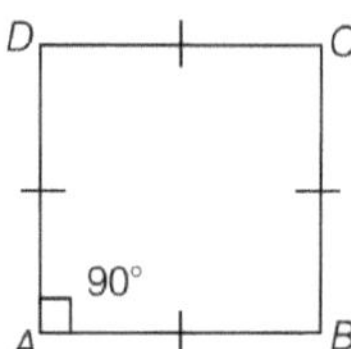

In the above figure, $ABCD$ is a square, in which

$$AB \| DC \text{ and } BC \| AD$$

and $\qquad AB = BC = CD = DA$

Also, $\qquad \angle A = \angle B = \angle C = \angle D = 90°$

6. Kite

A quadrilateral in which two pairs of adjacent sides are equal is known as kite.

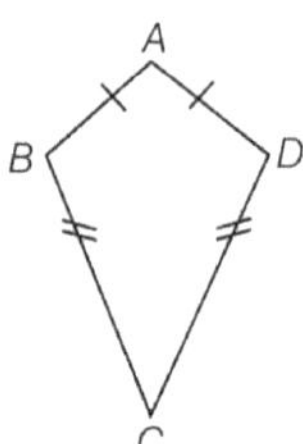

In the above figure, $ABCD$ is a kite, in which

$$AB = AD \text{ and } BC = CD$$

Important Theorem Related to Parallelogram

Theorem 1

A diagonal of a parallelogram divides it into two congruent triangles.

Given $ABCD$ is a parallelogram and AC is its one diagonal.

To prove $\triangle ABC \cong \triangle CDA$

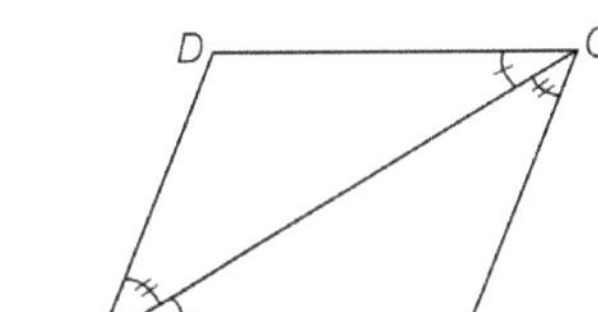

Proof Since, $ABCD$ is a parallelogram.

$\therefore \qquad AB \parallel DC$

and $\qquad BC \parallel AD$

In $\triangle ABC$ and $\triangle CDA$,

$$\angle BCA = \angle DAC$$

$[\because BC \parallel AD$ and AC is transversal,

so a pair of alternate angles are equal]

$$\angle BAC = \angle DCA$$

$[\because AB \parallel DC$ and AC is transversal,

so a pair of alternate angles are equal]

$$AC = AC \qquad \text{[common side]}$$

$\therefore \qquad \triangle ABC \cong \triangle CDA \qquad$ [by ASA congruence rule]

Similarly, we can prove that $\triangle ABD \cong \triangle CDB$

Hence, diagonal of a parallelogram divides it into two congruent triangles.

Theorem 2

In a parallelogram, opposite sides are equal.

Given $ABCD$ is a parallelogram.

To prove $AB = DC$

and $\qquad BC = AD$

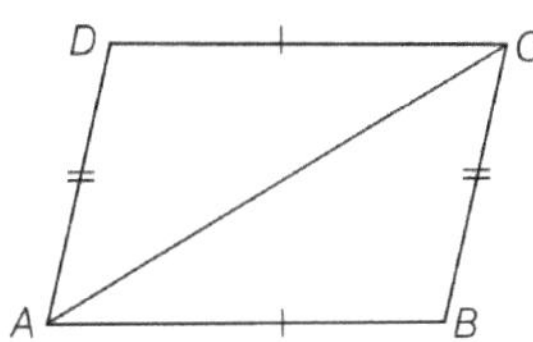

Construction Join AC.

Proof We know that, diagonal of a parallelogram divides it into two congruent triangles.

$\therefore \qquad \triangle ABC \cong \triangle CDA$

Then, $\qquad AB = DC \qquad$ [by CPCT]

Also, $\qquad \triangle ABD \cong \triangle CDB$

$\therefore \qquad BC = AD \qquad$ [by CPCT]

Hence, opposite sides of a parallelogram are equal.

Theorem 3

If each pair of opposite sides of a quadrilateral is equal, then it is a parallelogram.

Given $ABCD$ is a quadrilateral in which opposite sides are equal,

i.e. $\qquad AB = DC$ and $BC = AD$.

To prove $ABCD$ is a parallelogram,

i.e. $\qquad AB \parallel DC$ and $BC \parallel AD$.

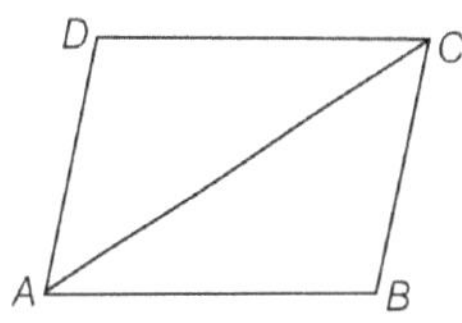

Construction Join AC.

Proof In $\triangle ABC$ and $\triangle CDA$,

$$AC = AC \qquad \text{[common side]}$$

$$AB = DC \qquad \text{[given]}$$

$$BC = AD \qquad \text{[given]}$$

$\therefore \qquad \triangle ABC \cong \triangle CDA \qquad$ [by SSS congruence rule]

Then, $\qquad \angle BAC = \angle ACD$

and $\qquad \angle BCA = \angle CAD \qquad$ [by CPCT]

But these are pairs of alternate angles.

$\therefore \qquad AB \parallel DC$ and $BC \parallel AD$.

Hence, $ABCD$ is a parallelogram.

Theorem 4

In a parallelogram, opposite angles are equal.

Given $ABCD$ is a parallelogram.

$\therefore AB \parallel DC$ and $BC \parallel AD$.

To prove $\angle A = \angle C$ and $\angle B = \angle D$.

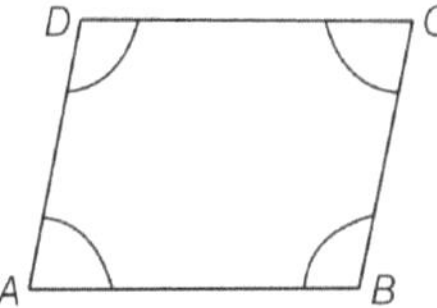

Proof Since, $AB \parallel DC$ and AD is a transversal, then $\angle A + \angle D = 180°$ $\qquad$ ...(i)

$[\because$ consecutive interior angles]

Similarly, $AD \parallel BC$ and CD is a transversal, then

$$\angle D + \angle C = 180° \qquad \text{...(ii)}$$

$[\because$ consecutive interior angles]

From Eqs. (i) and (ii), we get

$$\angle A + \angle D = \angle D + \angle C$$

$\Rightarrow \qquad \angle A = \angle C$

Similarly, we can prove that $\angle B = \angle D$.

Hence, opposite angles of a parallelogram are equal.

Theorem 5

If in a quadrilateral, each pair of opposite angles are equal, then it is a parallelogram.

Given $ABCD$ is a quadrilateral in which $\angle A = \angle C$ and $\angle B = \angle D$.

To prove $ABCD$ is a parallelogram.

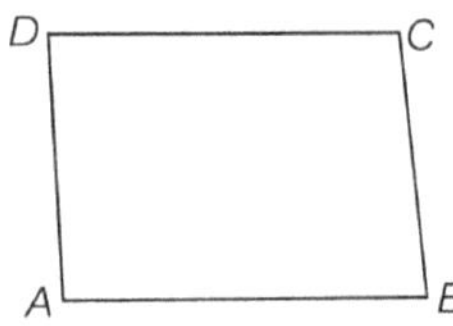

Proof   In quadrilateral $ABCD$,

$$\angle A = \angle C \qquad \text{[given] ...(i)}$$
$$\angle B = \angle D \qquad \text{[given] ...(ii)}$$

On adding Eqs. (i) and (ii), we get

$$\angle A + \angle B = \angle C + \angle D \qquad \text{...(iii)}$$

or $\qquad \angle A + \angle D = \angle B + \angle C$

$$\text{[using Eqs. (i) and (ii)] ...(iv)}$$

Now, by angle sum property of a quadrilateral, we have

$$\angle A + \angle B + \angle C + \angle D = 360° \qquad \text{...(v)}$$

On putting the value of $\angle C$ and $\angle D$ from Eq. (iii) in Eq. (v), we get

$$\angle A + \angle B + \angle A + \angle B = 360°$$
$$\Rightarrow \qquad 2(\angle A + \angle B) = 360°$$
$$\Rightarrow \qquad \angle A + \angle B = 180°$$
$$\therefore \qquad \angle A + \angle B = \angle C + \angle D = 180°$$
$$\text{[from Eq. (iii)]}$$

Since, line AB intersects AD and BC at points A and B, respectively, such that $\angle A + \angle B = 180°$

$$\text{[}\because \text{consecutive interior angles]}$$

$\therefore \qquad\qquad AD \parallel BC$

Similarly, on putting the value $\angle B + \angle C$ from Eq. (iv) in Eq. (v), we get

$$2(\angle A + \angle D) = 360°$$
$$\Rightarrow \qquad \angle A + \angle D = 180°$$
$$\therefore \qquad \angle A + \angle D = \angle B + \angle C = 180° \quad \text{[from Eq. (iv)]}$$

Since, line AD intersects AB and DC at points A and D, respectively, such that

$$\angle A + \angle D = 180° \qquad \text{[}\because \text{consecutive interior angles]}$$

$\therefore \qquad\qquad AB \parallel DC$

Hence, $ABCD$ is a parallelogram.

Theorem 6

The diagonals of a parallelogram bisect each other.

Given $ABCD$ is a parallelogram. Its diagonals AC and BD intersect each other at O.

To prove $OA = OC$ and $OB = OD$.

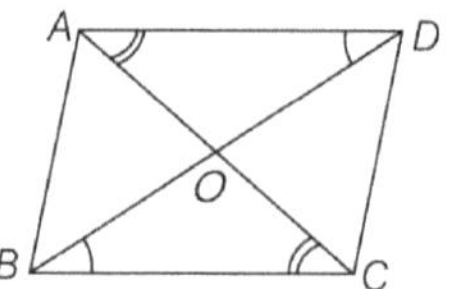

Proof   In ΔAOD and ΔCOB,

$$\angle ADO = \angle CBO$$
$$\text{[}\because BC \parallel AD \text{ and } BD \text{ is transversal,}$$
$$\text{so alternate angles are equal]}$$
$$\angle DAO = \angle BCO$$
$$\text{[}\because BC \parallel AD \text{ and } AC \text{ is transversal, so alternate}$$
$$\text{angles are equal]}$$

and $\qquad\qquad AD = BC$

$$\text{[}\because \text{opposite sides of parallelogram } ABCD \text{ are equal]}$$

$\therefore \qquad\qquad \Delta AOD \cong \Delta COB \qquad \text{[by ASA congruence rule]}$

Then, $\qquad\quad OA = OC$ and $OB = OD \qquad\quad$ [by CPCT]

Hence, the diagonals of a parallelogram bisect each other.

Theorem 7

If the diagonals of a quadrilateral bisect each other, then it is a parallelogram.

Given $ABCD$ is a quadrilateral whose diagonals AC and BD bisect each other at O.

i.e. $\qquad OA = OC$ and $OB = OD$

To prove $ABCD$ is a parallelogram.

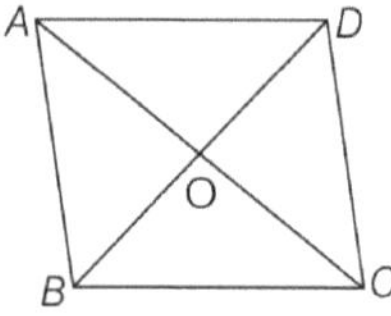

Proof   In ΔAOB and ΔCOD,

$$OA = OC \qquad\qquad\qquad\qquad \text{[given]}$$
$$OB = OD \qquad\qquad\qquad\qquad \text{[given]}$$
$$\angle AOB = \angle COD \quad \text{[}\because \text{vertically opposite angles]}$$
$$\therefore \qquad \Delta AOB \cong \Delta COD \qquad \text{[by SAS congruence rule]}$$

Then, $\qquad\quad \angle ODC = \angle OBA \qquad\qquad\qquad$ [by CPCT]

But these are alternate angles which are formed when transversal BD intersects lines AB and DC.

$\therefore \qquad\qquad AB \parallel DC$

Similarly, we can prove that $BC \parallel AD$.

Hence, $ABCD$ is a parallelogram.

Theorem 8

A quadrilateral is a parallelogram, if a pair of opposite sides is equal and parallel.

Given $ABCD$ is a quadrilateral in which $AB = DC$ and $AB \parallel DC$.

To prove $ABCD$ is a parallelogram.

Construction Join AC.

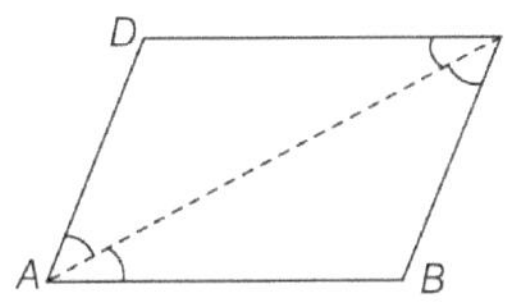

Proof In $\triangle ABC$ and $\triangle CDA$,

$$AB = DC \qquad \text{[given]}$$
$$AC = AC \qquad \text{[common side]}$$
$$\angle DCA = \angle BAC$$

[∵ $AB \| DC$ and AC is transversal, so alternate angles are equal]

$\therefore \qquad \triangle ABC \cong \triangle CDA \qquad$ [by SAS congruence rule]

Then, $\qquad \angle BCA = \angle DAC \qquad$ [by CPCT]

But these are alternate angles which are formed when lines BC and AD are intersect by transversal AC.

$\therefore \qquad AD \parallel BC$

Thus, $\qquad AB \parallel DC$

and $\qquad AD \parallel BC$

Hence, quadrilateral $ABCD$ is a parallelogram.

Theorem 9 (Converse of Mid-Point Theorem)

The line segment joining the mid-points of any two sides of a triangle is parallel to the third side and equal to half of it.

Given In a $\triangle ABC$, E and F are the mid-points of AB and AC, respectively.

To prove $EF \parallel BC$ and $EF = \dfrac{1}{2} BC$.

Construction Through vertex C, draw $CD \| BA$ and let it meets extended EF at D.

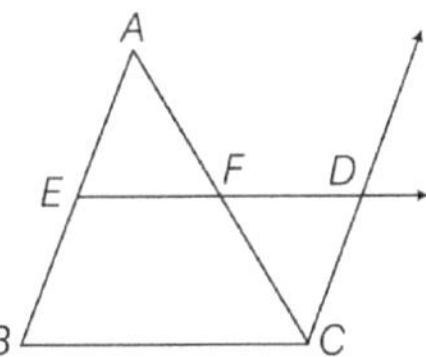

Proof Now, in $\triangle AEF$ and $\triangle CDF$,

$$\angle AFE = \angle CFD \qquad \text{[∵ vertically opposite angles]}$$
$$AF = FC \qquad \text{[∵ since, } F \text{ is mid-point of } AC]$$

and $\qquad \angle EAF = \angle FCD$

[∵ alternate angles between parallel lines BA and CD]

$\therefore \qquad \triangle AEF \cong \triangle CDF \qquad$ [by ASA congruence rule]

Then, $AE = CD$ and $EF = FD \qquad$ [by CPCT]...(i)

Also, $\quad AE = BE \qquad\qquad\qquad\qquad$ ...(ii)

[∵ since, E is the mid-point of AB]

From Eqs. (i) and (ii), we get

$$AE = BE = CD \qquad \text{...(iii)}$$

and $\qquad\qquad BE \| CD \qquad$ [by construction]

So, $BCDE$ is a parallelogram.

[∵ one pair of opposite sides is parallel and equal]

Then, $\qquad ED \| BC$ or $EF \| BC$

and $\qquad\qquad ED = BC$

Now, $\qquad\qquad BC = ED = EF + FD = 2EF$

[from Eq. (i), $EF = FD$]

$\Rightarrow \qquad\qquad EF = \dfrac{1}{2} BC$

Hence, the line segment joining the mid-points of two sides of a triangle is parallel to the third side and equal to half of it.

$\qquad\qquad\qquad\qquad\qquad\qquad\qquad$ **Hence proved.**

Theorem 10 (Converse of Mid-Point Theorem)

The line drawn through the mid-point of one side of a triangle, parallel to another side bisect the third side.

Given In a $\triangle ABC$, E is the mid-point of AB and $EF \| BC$.

To prove F is the mid-point of AC.

Construction Draw $CM \| BA$ and extend EF such that it intersects CM at D.

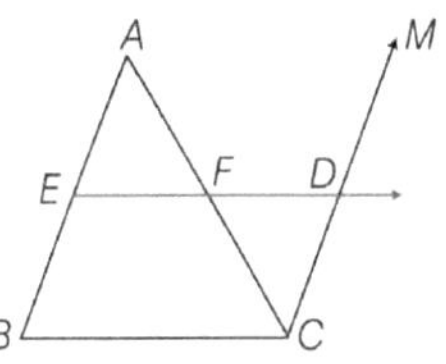

Proof In $\triangle AEF$ and $\triangle CDF$,

$$\angle FAE = \angle FCD \qquad \text{[∵ } AB \| CM \text{ and } AC \text{ is}$$

a transversal, so alternate angles are equal]

$$\angle AEF = \angle FDC \qquad \text{[∵ } AB \| CM \text{ and } ED \text{ is a}$$

transversal, so alternate angles are equal]

$$CD = AE \qquad \text{[∵ } BCDE \text{ is a parallelogram, so}$$
$$CD = BE = AE]$$

$\therefore \qquad \triangle AEF \cong \triangle CDF \qquad$ [by ASA congruence rule]

Then, $\qquad AF = CF \qquad\qquad\qquad$ [by CPCT]

Hence, F is a mid-point of AC.

Solved Examples

Example 1. Three angles of a quadrilateral are respectively equal to 110°, 60° and 80°. Find its fourth angle.

Sol. Let fourth angle be x.

$$110° + 60° + 80° + x = 360°$$

[∵ angle sum property of quadrilateral]

$$\Rightarrow \quad x = 360° - 250° = 110°$$

Example 2. If angles of a quadrilateral are x, $x + 3$, $x + 8$ and $x + 9$, then find the value of x. Also, find all the angles.

Sol. Here, $x + x + 3 + x + 8 + x + 9 = 360°$

[∵ sum of angles of quadrilateral = 360°]

$$\Rightarrow \quad 4x + 20 = 360 \Rightarrow x = \frac{360 - 20}{4} = 85$$

∴ Angles of quadrilateral are 85°, 88°, 93° and 94°

Example 3. If angles A, B, C and D of the quadrilateral $ABCD$, taken in order are in the ratio $3 : 7 : 6 : 4$, then show that $ABCD$ is a trapezium.

Sol. Let $3x$, $7x$, $6x$ and $4x$ be the angles A, B, C and D of quadrilateral $ABCD$.

$$3x + 7x + 6x + 4x = 360°$$

[∵ angle sum property of quadrilateral]

$$\Rightarrow \quad x = 18°$$

$$\therefore \quad \angle A = 54°, \angle B = 126°, \angle C = 108° \text{ and } \angle D = 72°$$

Since, line AB intersect AD and BC at points A and B such that

$$\angle A + \angle B = 180° \quad [\because \text{ consecutive interior angles}]$$

$$\therefore \quad AD \,\|\, BC$$

Hence, $ABCD$ is a trapezium.

Example 4. In the given figure, $ABCD$ is a parallelogram, what is the sum of the angles x, y and z?

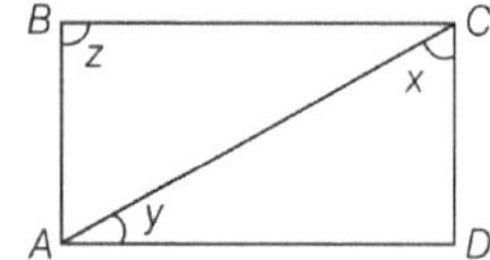

Sol. In $\triangle ADC$, $x + y + \angle ADC = 180°$

[∵ angle sum property of a triangle]

$$\Rightarrow \quad \angle ADC = 180° - (x + y) \qquad ...(i)$$

$$\because \quad \angle ABC = \angle ADC$$

[∵ opposite angles of a parallelogram]

$$\therefore \quad z = 180° - (x + y) \qquad [\text{using Eq. (i)}]$$

$$\Rightarrow \quad z + x + y = 180°$$

Example 5. In the given figure, $ABCD$ is a parallelogram. E and F are points on opposite sides AD and BC, respectively, such that $ED = \dfrac{1}{2} AD$ and $BF = \dfrac{1}{3} BC$. If $\angle ADF = 60°$, then find $\angle BFD$.

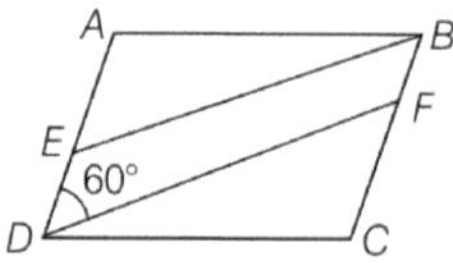

Sol. $ABCD$ is a parallelogram.

$$\therefore \qquad AD \,\|\, BC$$

$$\Rightarrow \qquad AD \,\|\, BF$$

and DF is a transversal.

$$\therefore \qquad \angle ADF + \angle BFD = 180°$$

[∵ if a transversal intersects two parallel lines, then each pair of interior angles on the same sides of the transversal is supplementary]

$$\Rightarrow \qquad \angle BFD = 180° - 60° = 120°$$

Example 6. In the given figure, it is given that $BDEF$ and $FDCE$ are parallelograms. If $BD = 8$ cm, then determine CD.

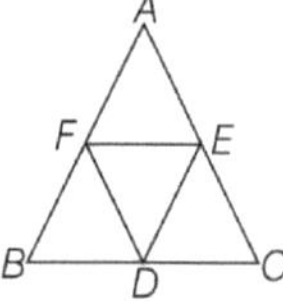

Sol. Using opposite sides of parallelograms are parallel and equal.

In parallelogram $BDEF$

$$BD \,\|\, FE \text{ and } BD = FE \qquad ...(i)$$

In parallelogram $FDCE$,

$$DC \,\|\, FE \text{ and } DC = FE \qquad ...(ii)$$

From Eqs. (i) and (ii), we get

$$BD = DC = FE = 8 \text{ cm}$$

$$\therefore \qquad CD = 8 \text{ cm}$$

Example 7. In the adjoining figure, $PQRS$ is a parallelogram in which PQ is produced to T, such that $QT = PQ$. Prove that ST bisects RQ.

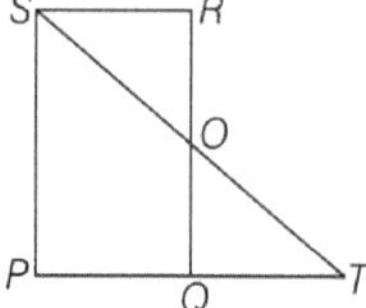

Sol. $PQRS$ is a parallelogram.

$$\therefore \qquad PQ = SR \qquad \text{...(i)}$$

Given, $\qquad PQ = QT \qquad$ ...(ii)

From Eqs. (i) and (ii),

$$PQ = SR = QT \qquad \text{...(iii)}$$

Now, In ΔSOR and ΔQOT,

$$\angle OSR = \angle OTQ \quad [\because \text{alternate interior angles}]$$
$$SR = QT \qquad [\text{from Eq. (iii)}]$$
$$\angle ORS = \angle OQT \quad [\because \text{alternate interior angles}]$$
$$\therefore \qquad \Delta SOR \cong \Delta QOT \quad [\text{by ASA congruence rule}]$$

then, $\qquad OQ = OR \qquad [\text{by CPCT}]$

Example 8. In a quadrilateral $ABCD$, $\angle B = 130°$, $\angle C = 60°$ and angle bisectors of $\angle A$ and $\angle D$ meet at P. Find $\angle APD$.

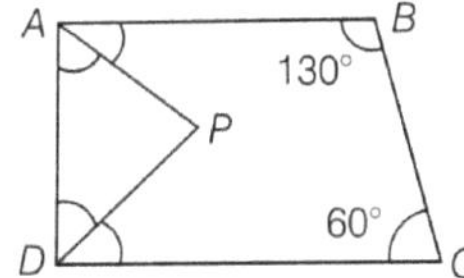

Sol. Since, sum of all angles of quadrilateral $= 360°$

$$\angle A + \angle B + \angle C + \angle D = 360°$$
$$\Rightarrow \quad \frac{1}{2}\angle A + \frac{1}{2}\angle B + \frac{1}{2}\angle C + \frac{1}{2}\angle D = \frac{1}{2} \times 360°$$

[dividing both sides by 2]

$$\Rightarrow \quad \angle PAD + 65° + 30° + \angle PDA = 180°$$

[$\because \angle B = 130°$, $\angle C = 60°$ and angle bisectors of $\angle A$ and $\angle D$ meet at P (given)]

$$\Rightarrow \qquad \angle PAD + \angle PDA = 85°$$
$$\Rightarrow \qquad 180° - \angle APD = 85°$$
$$\Rightarrow \qquad \angle APD = 95°$$

Example 9. In the given figure, $ABCD$ is a rhombus, then find the value of x.

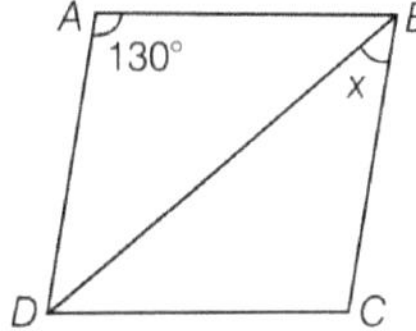

Sol. Given, $ABCD$ is a rhombus in which $\angle BAD = 130°$ and $\angle DBC = x$

$$\therefore \quad \angle ABC = 2\angle DBC = 2x$$

[$\because$ since, diagonals bisect the angles in rhombus]

Now, $\angle DAB + \angle ABC = 180° \qquad [\because \text{co-interior angles}]$

$$\Rightarrow \qquad 130° + 2x = 180°$$
$$\Rightarrow \qquad 2x = 180° - 130° = 50°$$
$$\Rightarrow \qquad x = 25° \qquad [\text{divide both sides by 2}]$$

Example 10. Given, a trapezium $ABCD$, in which $AB \parallel CD$ and $AD = BC$. If $\angle D = 70°$, then find the measure of $\angle C$.

Sol. Given, a trapezium $ABCD$, in which $AB \parallel CD$ and $AD = BC$, also $\angle D = 70°$.

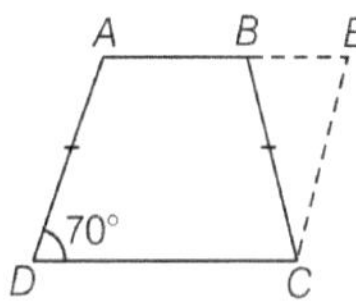

Now, we produce side AB to E and join EC such that $AD = EC$ and then $AECD$ is a parallelogram.

$$\therefore \qquad \angle D = \angle E = 70°$$

[$\because$ since, opposite angles of a parallelogram are equal]

Also, $\qquad AD = BC \qquad$ [given]

and $\qquad AD = EC \qquad$ [by construction]

$$\Rightarrow \qquad BC = EC \Rightarrow \angle E = \angle CBE = 70°$$

[$\because$ angles opposite to equal sides are equal]

Now, $\quad \angle ABC = 180° - \angle CBE = 180° - 70° = 110°$

[linear pair axioms]

Also, we have, $\angle ABC + \angle BCD = 180°$

[$\because$ interior angles on the same side of transversal BC]

$$\Rightarrow 110° + \angle BCD = 180° \Rightarrow \angle BCD = 70°$$

Example 11. In ΔABC, D, E and F are the mid-points of the sides AB, BC and AC, respectively. Then, prove that quadrilateral $DECF$ is a parallelogram.

Sol. In ΔABC, D and F are the mid-points of the sides AB and AC, respectively.

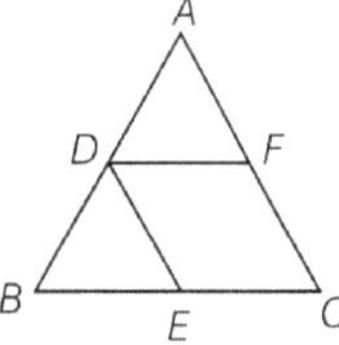

$\therefore$ By mid-point theorem,

$$DF \parallel BC \qquad \text{...(i)}$$
$$\Rightarrow \qquad DF \parallel EC$$

and $\qquad DF = \dfrac{1}{2} BC$

$$\Rightarrow \qquad DF = EC \qquad \text{...(ii)}$$

[$\because$ since, E is mid-point of BC]

From Eqs. (i) and (ii), we have

$$DF \parallel EC \quad \text{and} \quad DF = EC$$

Since, a pair of opposite sides of a quadrilateral $DECF$ are equal and parallel.

Hence, $DECF$ is a parallelogram.   **Hence proved.**

Example 12. In the adjoining figure, $ABCD$ is a parallelogram in which P is the mid-point of DC and Q is a point on AC, such that $CQ = \dfrac{1}{4}AC$. Also, PQ when produced meets BC at R. Prove that R is the mid-point of BC.

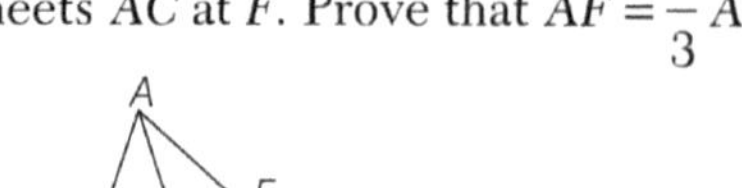

Sol. In a parallelogram $ABCD$, $AO = OC$

$\qquad$ [∵ diagonals of a parallelogram bisect each other]

$\qquad AC = AO + OC \Rightarrow AC = 2OC$

$\therefore \qquad CQ = \dfrac{1}{4}AC = \dfrac{1}{4}\times(2OC) = \dfrac{1}{2}OC$

Thus, Q is the mid-point of OC.

Now, in $\triangle CDO$, P and Q are the mid-points of CD and CO, respectively.

$\therefore PQ \parallel DO$ and, therefore $QR \parallel OB$

$\qquad\qquad$ [∵ $PQ \parallel DO \Rightarrow PQR \parallel DOB$]

Now, in $\triangle COB$, Q is the mid-point of CO and

$\qquad QR \parallel OB$. $\qquad\qquad$ [by converse of mid-point]

$\therefore R$ is the mid-point of BC. $\qquad\qquad$ **Hence proved.**

Example 13. In $\triangle ABC$, AD is the median and $DE \parallel AB$, such that E is a point on AC. Prove that BE is another median.

Sol. Given, AD is median of $\triangle ABC$ and $DE \parallel BA$.

Now, AD is median, so D is the mid-point of BC.

Also, $DE \parallel AB$

So by converse of mid point theorem, E is mid point of AC

Hence, BE is another median of $\triangle ABC$. $\qquad$ **Hence proved.**

Example 14. In the following figure, AD is a median of $\triangle ABC$ and E is the mid-point of AD. Also, BE produced meets AC at F. Prove that $AF = \dfrac{1}{3}AC$.

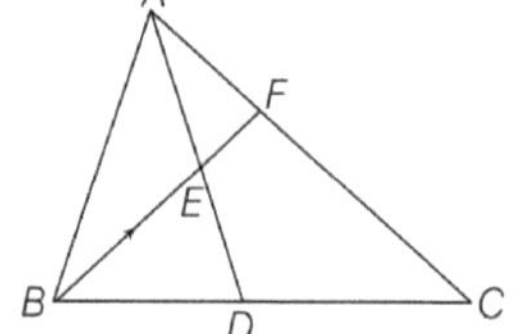

Sol. Given, In $\triangle ABC$, AD is a median and E is mid-point of AD.

To prove $\qquad AF = \dfrac{1}{3}AC$

Construction Draw $DP \parallel BF$

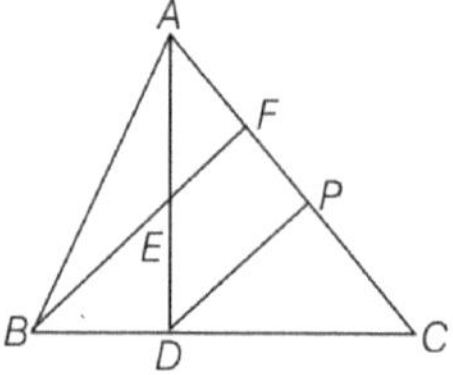

Proof In $\triangle ADP$, E is the mid-point of AD and $EF \parallel DP$.

$\qquad\qquad\qquad$ [∵ $BF \parallel DP$]

$\therefore F$ is the mid-point of AP. $\qquad\qquad$ ...(i)

$\qquad\qquad$ [by converse of mid-point theorem]

In $\triangle FBC$, D is the mid-point of BC and $DP \parallel BF$.

$\qquad\qquad$ [∵ AD is a median of $\triangle ABC$]

$\therefore P$ is the mid-point of FC. $\qquad\qquad$ ...(ii)

$\qquad\qquad$ [by converse of mid-point theorem]

Thus, $\qquad AF = FP = PC$

$\therefore \qquad AF = \left(\dfrac{1}{3}\right)AC \qquad$ [from Eqs. (i) and (ii)]

$\qquad\qquad\qquad\qquad\qquad$ **Hence proved.**

Chapter Practice

Objective Questions

• Multiple Choice Questions

1. If $ABCD$ is a trapezium, in which $AB \parallel DC$ and $\angle A = \angle B = 55°$. Then, $\angle C$ and $\angle D$ of a trapezium.
(a) $\angle C = 125°$ and $\angle D = 135°$
(b) $\angle C = 125°$ and $\angle D = 145°$
(c) $\angle C = \angle D = 125°$
(d) $\angle C = \angle D = 135°$

2. Two angles of a quadrilateral are $50°$ and $70°$ and other two angles are in the ratio $13 : 11$, then measures of the remaining two angles.
(a) $130°$ and $110°$ (b) $165°$ and $170°$
(c) $125°$ and $115°$ (d) $175°$ and $189°$

3. In quadrilateral $PQRS$, if $\angle P = 60°$ and $\angle Q : \angle R : \angle S = 2 : 3 : 7$, then the value of $\angle S$ is
(a) $155°$ (b) $175°$
(c) $165°$ (d) $170°$

4. One angle of a quadrilateral is of $108°$ and the remaining three angles are equal. Then, each of the three equal angles are   [**NCERT Exemplar**]
(a) $84°$ (b) $94°$
(c) $86°$ (d) $83°$

5. In quadrilateral $ABCD$, $\angle A + \angle D = 180°$. Then, the name can be given to this quadrilateral?
(a) Rhombus   (b) Rectangle
(c) Square   (d) Trapezium

6. In the given figure, $ABCD$ is a parallelogram with $\angle B = 110°$. Find the values of x and y.

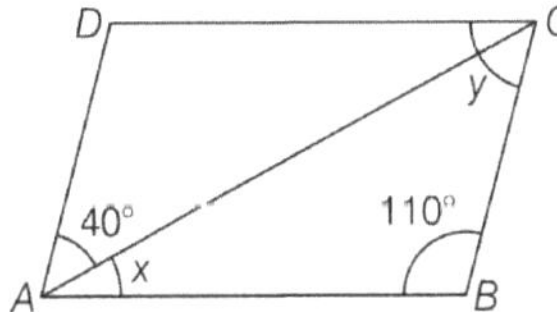

(a) $x = 60°$ and $y = 70°$ (b) $x = 30°$ and $y = 95°$
(c) $x = 30°$ and $y = 70°$ (d) $x = 40°$ and $y = 50°$

7. In the given figure, $ABCD$ is a parallelogram. If $\angle A = 65°$, then value of $\angle B + \angle D$.

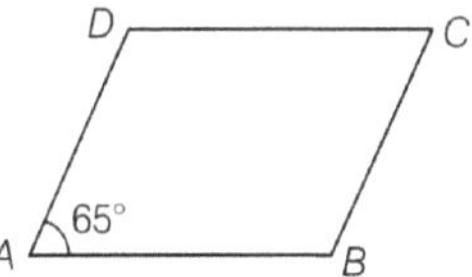

(a) $235°$
(b) $230°$
(c) $220°$
(d) $225°$

8. If $ABCD$ is a trapezium, in which $AB \parallel DC$ and $\angle A = \angle B = 45°$. Then, $\angle C$ and $\angle D$ of a trapezium is   [**NCERT Exemplar**]
(a) $135°$ (b) $145°$
(c) $155°$ (d) $165°$

9. In the given figure, $ABCD$ is a rectangle whose diagonals AC and BD intersect at O. If $\angle AOB = 32°$, then find $\angle OCD$ is

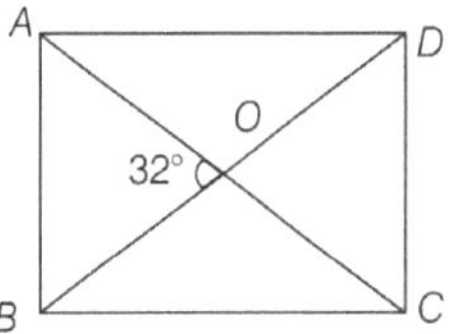

(a) $74°$ (b) $73°$
(c) $84°$ (d) None of these

10. In the given figure, $ABCD$ is a parallelogram, then the sum of the angles x, y and z is

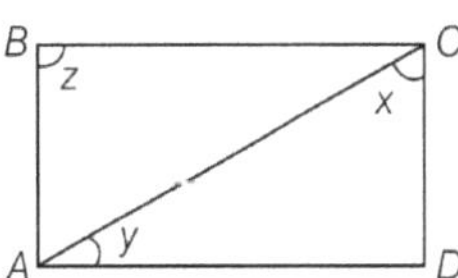

(a) $170°$ (b) $90°$
(c) $180°$ (d) $210°$

11. If $ABCD$ is a parallelogram in which $\angle ADC = 75°$ and side AB is produced to point E as shown in the figure. Then, $x + y$ is

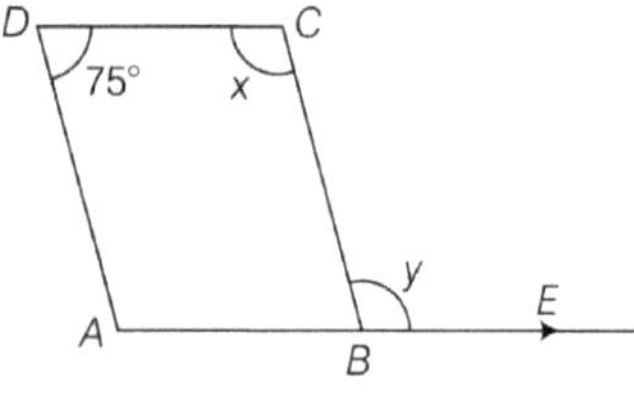

(a) 215°   (b) 210°   (c) 110°   (d) 220°

12. Diagonals of quadrilateral $ABCD$ bisect each other. If $\angle A = 35°$, then the value of $\angle B$. [NCERT Exemplar]

(a) 145°   (b) 165°   (c) 175°   (d) 135°

13. In adjoining figure, $ABCD$ and $AEFG$ are two parallelograms. If $\angle C = 55°$, then $\angle F$ is

[NCERT Exemplar]

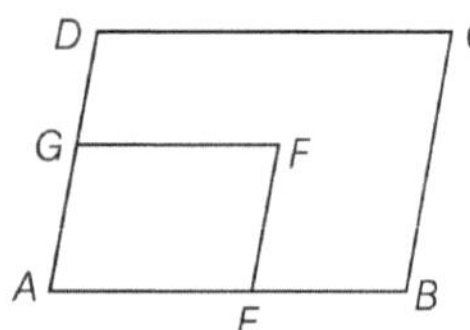

(a) 55°   (b) 95°   (c) 65°   (d) 35°

14. The perimeter of a parallelogram is 32 cm. If the longer side measures 9.5 cm, then what is the measure of the shorter side is

(a) 6.5 cm   (b) 7.5 cm   (c) 7 cm   (d) 6 cm

15. In the given figure, $ABCD$ is rhombus, $AO = 4$ cm and $DO = 3$ cm. Then, the perimeter of the rhombus is

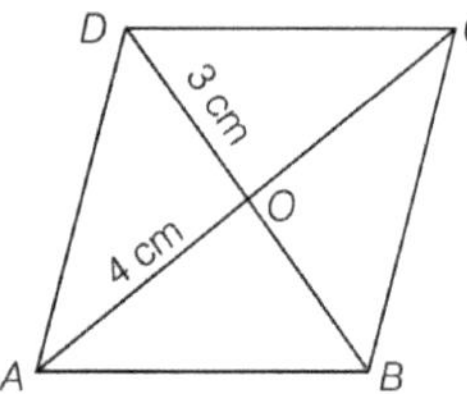

(a) 20 cm   (b) 25 cm   (c) 15 cm   (d) 17 cm

16. In $\triangle ABC$, $AB = 5$ cm, $BC = 8$ cm and $CA = 7$ cm. If D and E are respectively the mid-point of AB and BC, then the length of DE. [NCERT Exemplar]

(a) 5 cm   (b) 3.5 cm
(c) 6.5 cm   (d) 2.5 cm

17. In a parallelogram $ABCD$, diagonals AC and BD intersect at O and $AC = 6.8$ cm and $BD = 5.6$ cm. Then, the measures of OC and OD.

(a) $OC = 3.4$ cm and $OD = 3.4$ cm
(b) $OC = 2.8$ cm and $OD = 2.8$ cm
(c) $OC = 3.4$ cm and $OD = 2.8$ cm
(d) $OC = 3$ cm and $OD = 8$ cm

• **Case Based MCQs**

18. Kajal is studying in X standard, her grand-father purchase a plot, which is in a square shape (shown in figure). After visiting the land few questions came in her mind. Give answers to her questions by looking at the figure.

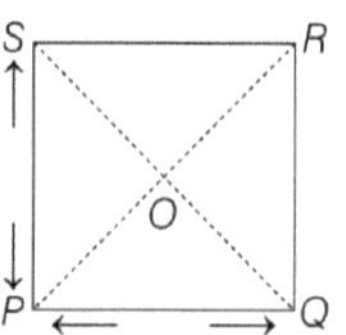

(i) Measure of $\angle QPO$

(a) 50°   (b) 45°
(c) 60°   (d) 90°

(ii) If $OP = 4$ cm, then value of OQ is

(a) 6 cm   (b) 3 cm
(c) 4 cm   (d) 7 cm

(iii) Measure of $\angle POQ$

(a) 60°   (b) 180°
(c) 90°   (d) 45°

(iv) If $OP = 10$ cm, then value of PR is

(a) 20 cm   (b) 8 cm
(c) 4 cm   (d) 5 cm

(v) Which is the correct congruence rule applicable to prove $\triangle PQO \cong \triangle PSO$

(a) SSS   (b) SSA
(c) SAS   (d) AAS

19. In the middle of Ghaziabad city, there is a Ramleela ground $WXYZ$ in the form of parallelogram, so that $WX = YZ$, $WX \parallel YZ$ and $WZ = XY$ and $WZ \parallel XY$. municipality converted this ground into rectangular form of $\triangle WPZ$ and $\triangle XYQ$. Both the triangular shape of land were covered by planting flower plants.

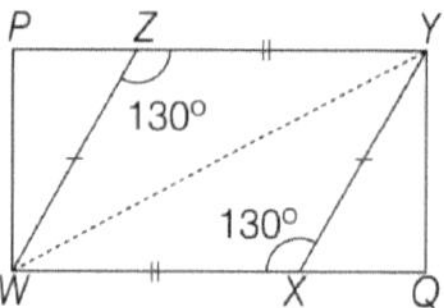

(i) The value of $\angle PZW$

(a) 60°   (b) 90°   (c) 50°   (d) 180°

(ii) The value of $\angle YQX$

(a) 90°   (b) 60°
(c) 30°   (d) None of these

(iii) $\triangle WPZ$ and $\triangle XQY$ are congruent by the criteria.

(a) SSA   (b) RHS
(c) SAS   (d) None of these

(iv) PZ is equal to which side

(a) WX (b) QX
(c) WZ (d) ZY

(v) ΔWXY and ΔYZW are congruent by which property
(a) SSS
(b) SAS
(c) RHS
(d) Both (a) and (b)

20. The sum of the four angles of a quadrilateral is $360°$.

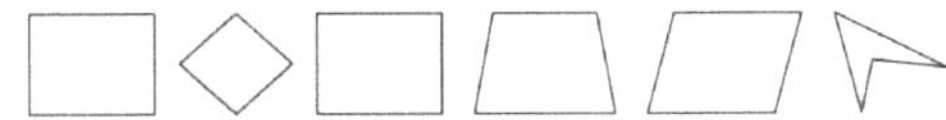

(i) The angles of quadrilateral are in the ratio $8:1:5:6$. Find the measure of each angle.
(a) $190°, 260°, 130°$ and $140°$
(b) $70°, 18°, 144°$ and $90°$
(c) $144°, 18°, 90°$ and $108°$
(d) $108°, 78°, 18°$ and $90°$

(ii) Three angles of a quadrilateral are respectively equal to $110°, 50°$ and $40°$. Find its fourth angle.
(a) $160°$
(b) $120°$
(c) $80°$
(d) $140°$

(iii) The angles of a quadrilateral are $100°, 98°$ and $92°$ respectively. Find the fourth angle.
(a) $70°$
(b) $80°$
(c) $40°$
(d) $90°$

(iv) In a quadrilateral $ABCD$, the angles A, B, C and D are in the ratio $1:2:4:5$, then the measure of each angle of a quadrilateral is
(a) $36°, 60°, 108°$ and $156°$
(b) $30°, 60°, 120°$ and $150°$
(c) $42°, 54°, 110°$ and $154°$
(d) $72°, 108°, 36°$ and $144°$

21. In a parallelogram $ABCD$, the sum of any two consecutive angles are $180°$ and opposite angles are equal. The important properties of angle of a parallelogram are
1. Opposite angles of parallelogram are equal.
2. Consecutive angles are supplementary angles to each other.

(i) In a parallelogram $ABCD$, $\angle D = 115°$, determine the measure of $\angle A$ and $\angle B$.
(a) $\angle A = 85°$ and $\angle B = 115°$
(b) $\angle A = 65°$ and $\angle B = 65°$
(c) $\angle A = 65°$ and $\angle B = 115°$
(d) $\angle A = 75°$ and $\angle B = 105°$

(ii) In the given figure, find $\angle A$ in the parallelogram $ABCD$.

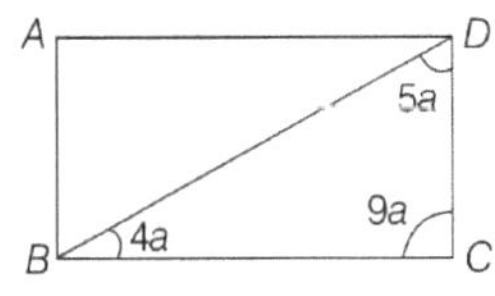

(a) $90°$
(b) $60°$
(c) $30°$
(d) $110°$

(iii) Find the value of $\angle Q$ and $\angle P$, if $\angle P = 10a$ and $\angle R = 50°$ in a parallelogram $PQRS$.
(a) $\angle Q = 50°$ and $\angle P = 130°$
(b) $\angle Q = 130°$ and $\angle P = 50°$
(c) $\angle Q = 100°$ and $\angle P = 120°$
(d) $\angle Q = 50°$ and $\angle P = 100°$

PART 2
Subjective Questions

• Short Answer Type Questions

1. The angles of a quadrilateral are in the ratio $3:5:9:13$. Find all the angles of the quadrilateral.

2. Justify your answer for the following statements.
(i) Three angles of a quadrilateral $ABCD$ are equal. Is it a parallelogram? Why or why not?
(ii) Diagonal AC and BD of a quadrilateral $ABCD$ intersect each other at O such that $OA:OC = 3:2$. Is $ABCD$ a parallelogram?
(iii) $ABCD$ is a parallelogram. If its diagonals are equal, then find the value of $\angle ABC$.
[**NCERT Exemplar**]

3. In the following figure, $ABCD$ is a rhombus. If $\angle ABC = 68°$, then determine $\angle ACD$.

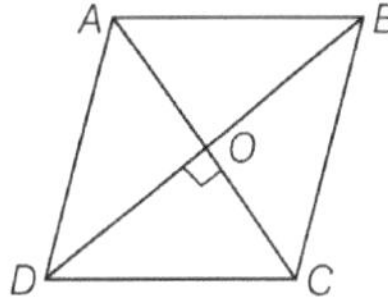

4. In the following figure, $ABCD$ is a square, diagonal BD is extended through D to E. $AD = DE$ and AE is drawn as shown in figure. What is the measure of $\angle DAE$?

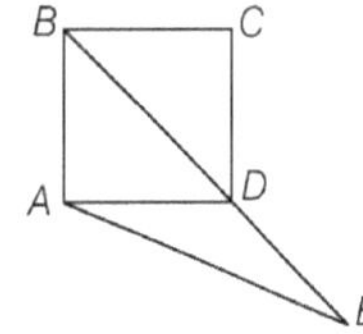

5. In a parallelogram, show that the angle bisectors of two adjacent angles intersect at right angles.

6. In the adjoining figure of rectangle $ABCD$, and $\angle CFE = 144°$. Find the measure of $\angle BEF$.

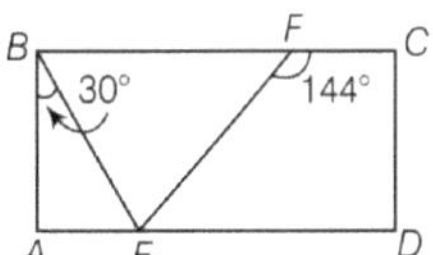

7. In the adjacent figure, $ABCD$ is a square. A line segment DX cuts the side BC at X and the diagonal AC at O, such that $\angle COD = 105°$.

Find the value of x.

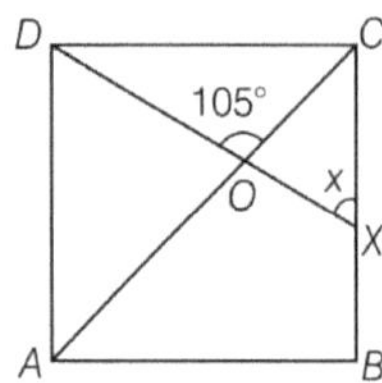

8. In a $\triangle ABC$, median AD is produced to Y such that $AD = DY$. Prove that $ABYC$ is a parallelogram.

9. In the adjoining figure, $PQRS$ is a rhombus, SQ and PR are the diagonals of the rhombus intersecting at point O. If $\angle OPQ = 35°$, then find the value of $\angle ORS + \angle OQP$.

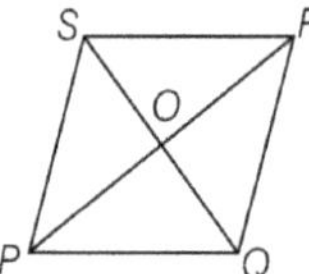

10. If $ABCD$ is a rectangle in which diagonal BD bisects $\angle B$. Show that $ABCD$ is a square. [**NCERT Exemplar**]

11. If the diagonals of a parallelogram are equal, then show that it is a rectangle.

12. Diagonal AC of a parallelogram $ABCD$ bisects $\angle A$ (see the figure). Show that

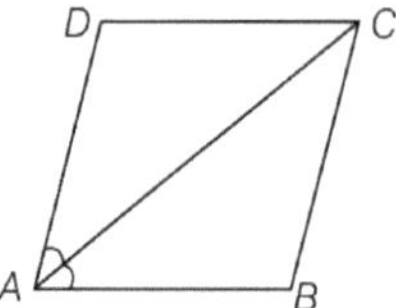

(i) it bisects $\angle C$ also.

(ii) $ABCD$ is a rhombus.

13. If P and Q are points on opposite sides AD and BC of a parallelogram $ABCD$, such that PQ passes through the point of intersection O of its diagonals AC and BD. Show that PQ is bisected at O.

14. Points X and Y lie on opposite sides AB and CD respectively of a parallelogram $ABCD$ such that $AX = CY$. Show that AC and XY bisect each other.

15. If $ABCD$ is a parallelogram and AP and CQ are perpendiculars from vertices A and C on diagonal BD (see the figure). Show that

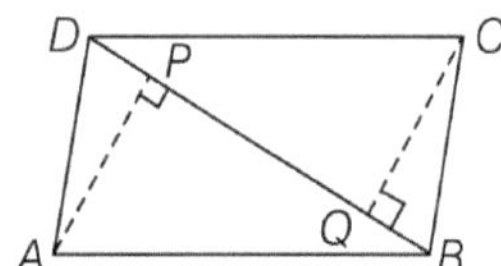

(i) $\triangle APB \cong \triangle CQD$

(ii) $AP = CQ$

16. In $\triangle ABC$, $AB = 13$ cm, $BC = 16$ cm and $AC = 8$ cm. Find the perimeter of the triangle formed by joining the mid-points of the sides of the triangle.

17. If $\triangle ABC$ is an isosceles triangle in which $AB = AC$. D and E are the mid-points of sides AB and AC and $DE = 3.5$ cm. Find the perimeter of $\triangle ABC$, when $AD = 4.5$ cm.

18. D and E are the mid-points of sides AB and AC, respectively of $\triangle ABC$. If the perimeter of $\triangle ABC = 38$ cm. Find the perimeter of $\triangle ADE$.

19. In the given figure, $ABCD$ is a parallelogram and E is the mid-point of side BC. DE and AB, when produced meet at F. Prove that $AF = 2AB$.

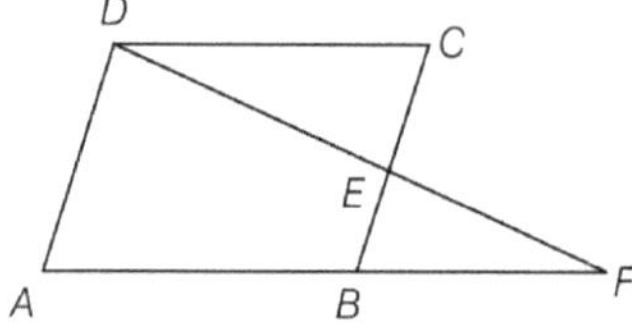

20. In the following figure, PS and RT are medians of $\triangle PQR$ and $SM \parallel RT$. Prove that $QM = \dfrac{1}{4}PQ$.

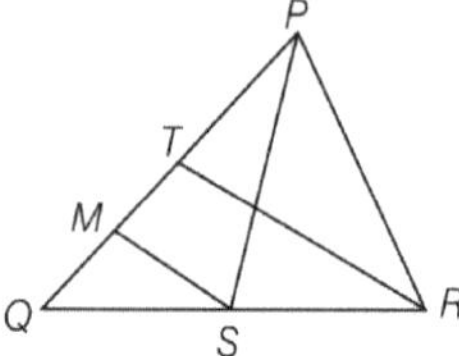

21. If P is the mid-point of the side CD of a parallelogram $ABCD$. A line through C parallel to PA intersects AB at Q and DA produced at R. Prove that (i) $DA = AR$ (ii) $CQ = QR$
[**NCERT Exemplar**]

22. If $ABCD$ is a trapezium in which $AB \parallel DC$, BD is a diagonal and E is the mid-point of AD. A line is drawn through E parallel to AB intersecting BC at F (see the figure). Show that F is the mid-point of BC.

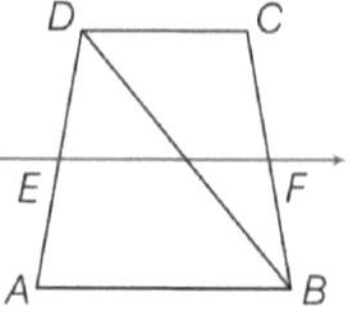

23. l, m and n are three parallel lines intersected by transversals p and q such that l, m and n cut-off equal intercepts AB and BC on p. Show that l, m and n cut-off equal intercepts DE and EF on q also.

• Long Answer Type Questions

24. In the parallelogram $ABCD$ of the given figure, $\angle PAQ$ is an obtuse angle. Two equilateral triangles ABP and ADQ are drawn outside the parallelogram. Prove that $\triangle CPQ$ is also an equilateral triangle.

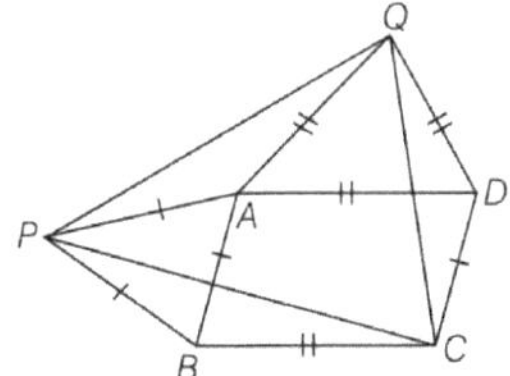

25. In the given figure, $ABCD$ is a square, if $\angle PQR = 90°$ and $PB = QC = DR$, then prove that $QB = RC, PQ = QR$ and $\angle QPR = 45°$.

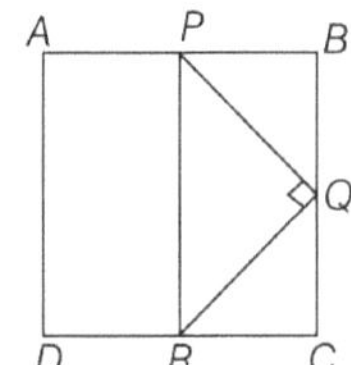

26. If PQ and RS are two equal and parallel line segments. Any point M not lying on PQ or RS is joined to Q and S lines through parallel to QM and through R parallel to SM meet at N. Prove that line segments MN and PQ are equal and parallel to each other. **[NCERT Exemplar]**

27. Show that if the diagonals of a quadrilateral are equal and bisect each other at right angles, then it is a square.

28. In the adjoining figure, $ABCD$ is a quadrilateral such that $AC = BD$ and AC and BD bisect each other at right angle. O is the intersection point of AC and BD. Show that the quadrilateral $ABCD$ is a square.

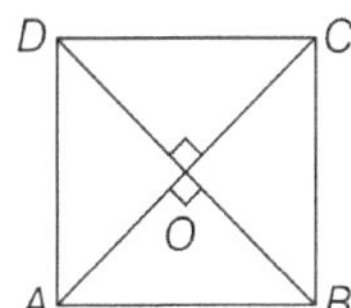

29. A square is inscribed in an isosceles right-angled triangle, so that the square and the triangle have one angle common. Show that the vertex of the square opposite the vertex of the common angle bisects the hypotenuse.

30. Two parallel lines l and m are intersected by a transversal t. Show that the quadrilateral formed by the bisectors of interior angles is a rectangle.

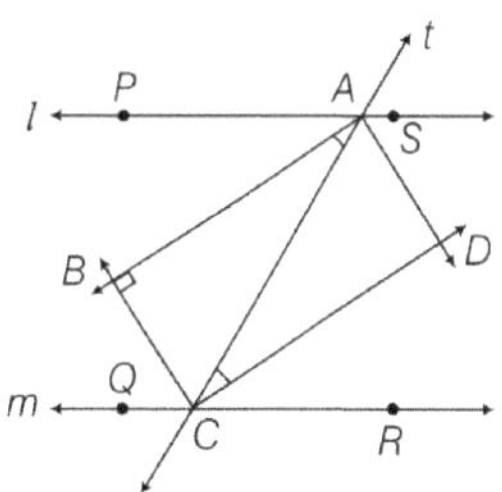

31. In the given figure, $ABCD$ is a square and $EF \parallel BD$. M is the mid-point of EF. Prove that AM bisects $\angle BAD$.

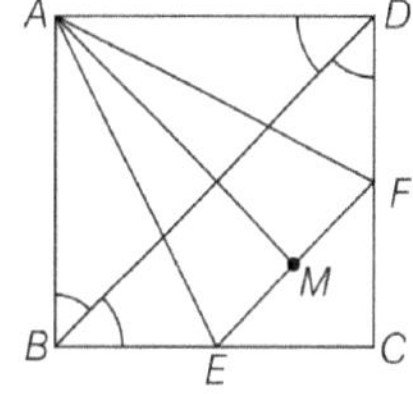

32. In the given figure, $ABCD$ is a parallelogram and $\angle DAB = 60°$. If the bisectors AP and BP of angles A and B, respectively meets at P on CD. Prove that P is the mid-point of CD.

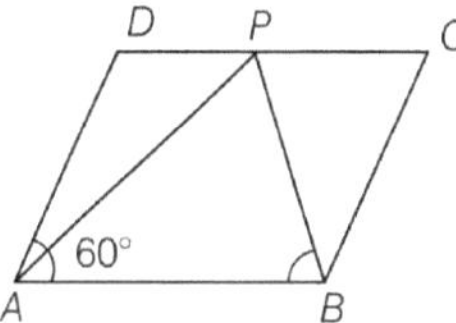

33. In the following figure, $PQRS$ is a square. M is the mid-point of PQ and $RM \perp AB$. Prove that $RA = RB$.

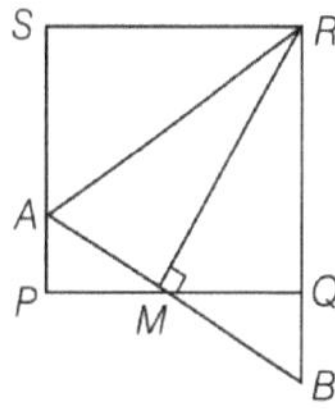

34. If E and F are respectively the mid-points of non-parallel sides AD and BC of a trapezium $ABCD$. Prove that $EF \parallel AB$ and $EF = \dfrac{1}{2}(AB + CD)$.
[NCERT Exemplar]

35. ABC is a triangle. D is a point on AB such that $AD = \dfrac{1}{4} AB$ and E is a point on AC such that $AE = \dfrac{1}{4} AC$. Prove that $DE = \dfrac{1}{4} BC$. **[NCERT Exemplar]**

36. $ABCD$ is a kite with $AB = AD$ and $CD = CB$. Prove that the figure formed by joining the mid-points of the consecutive sides is a rectangle.

37. In the adjoining figure, points A and B are on the same side of a line m, $AD \perp m$ and $BE \perp m$ and meet m at D and E, respectively. If C is the mid-point of AB, then prove that $CD = CE$.

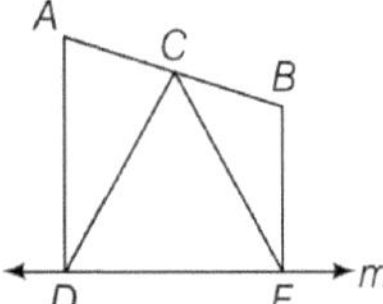

38. If $ABCD$ is a trapezium in which $AB \parallel CD$ and $AD = BC$ (see the figure). Show that

(i) $\angle A = \angle B$

(ii) $\angle C = \angle D$

(iii) $\triangle ABC \cong \triangle BAD$

(iv) Diagonal $AC =$ Diagonal BD.

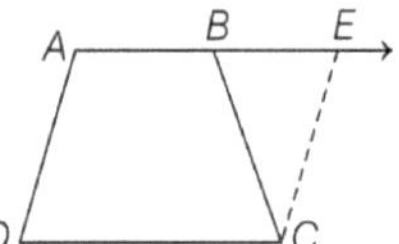

39. If $ABCD$ is a quadrilateral in which P, Q, R and S are mid-points of the sides AB, BC, CD and DA. AC is a diagonal. Show that

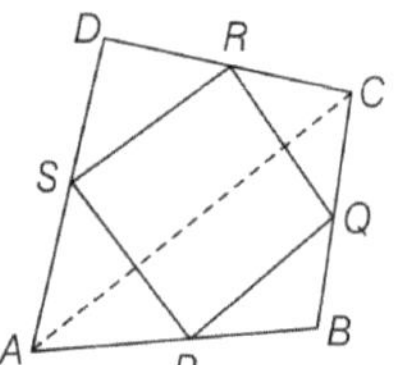

(i) $SR \parallel AC$ and $SR = \dfrac{1}{2} AC$.

(ii) $PQ = SR$.

(iii) $PQRS$ is a parallelogram.

40. If $ABCD$ is a rhombus and P, Q, R and S are the mid-points of the sides AB, BC, CD and DA, respectively. Show that the quadrilateral $PQRS$ is a rectangle.

41. $ABCD$ is a rectangle and P, Q, R and S are mid-points of the sides AB, BC, CD and DA, respectively. Show that the quadrilateral $PQRS$ is a rhombus.

42. In a parallelogram $ABCD$, E and F are the mid-points of sides AB and CD, respectively (see the figure). Show that the line segments AF and EC trisect the diagonal BD.

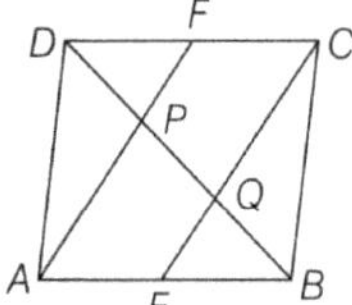

43. Show that the line segments joining the mid-points of the opposite sides of a quadrilateral bisect each other.

• Case Based Questions

44. The line segment joining the mid-points any two sides of a triangle is parallel to the third side and equal to half of its is called mid-point theorem.

Let ABC is a right angle triangular field right angle at C. A line through the mid-point M of hypotenuse AB parallel to BC intersect AC at D, as shown in figure.

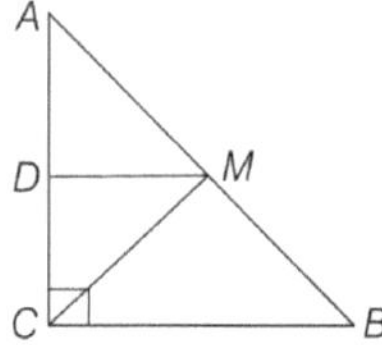

Solve the questions based on above paragraph.

(i) Show that D is the mid-point of AC in above figure.

(ii) Prove that $MD \perp AC$

(iii) Prove that $CM = MA = \dfrac{1}{2} AB$

45. In parallelogram $ABCD$, two points P and Q are taken on diagonal BD such that $DP = BQ$ (see the figure).

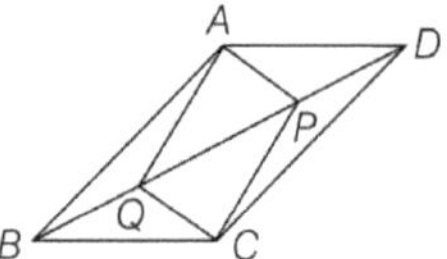

Show that

(i) $\triangle APD \cong \triangle CQB$ (ii) $AP = CQ$

(iii) $\triangle AQB \cong \triangle CPD$ (iv) $AQ = CP$

(v) $APCQ$ is a parallelogram.

46. In $\triangle ABC$ and $\triangle DEF$, $AB = DE$, $AB \parallel DE$, $BC = EF$ and $BC \parallel EF$. Vertices A, B and C are joined to vertices D, E and F, respectively (see the figure).

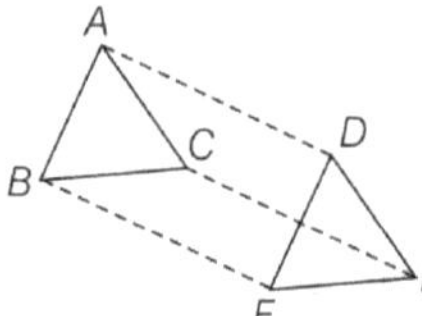

Show that

(i) quadrilateral $ABED$ is a parallelogram.

(ii) quadrilateral $BEFC$ is a parallelogram.

(iii) $AD \parallel CF$ and $AD = CF$.

(iv) quadrilateral $ACFD$ is a parallelogram.

(v) $AC = DF$

SOLUTIONS

Objective Questions

1. (c) Given, $\angle A = \angle B = 55°$

$$\angle A + \angle B + \angle C + \angle D = 360°$$

[∵ sum of all the angles of parallelogram is 360°]

$\Rightarrow 55° + 55° + \angle C + \angle D = 360°$

$\Rightarrow \quad 110° + \angle C + \angle D = 360°$

$\Rightarrow \quad \angle C + \angle D = 360° - 110°$

$\Rightarrow \quad \angle C + \angle D = 250°$

As, $\qquad \angle A = \angle B$

$\Rightarrow \qquad \angle C = \angle D$

$\therefore \qquad 2\angle C = 250°$

$\Rightarrow \qquad \angle C = 125°$

$\Rightarrow \qquad \angle D = 125°$

2. (a) Let the other two angles be $13x$ and $11x$.

Then, $50° + 70° + 13x + 11x = 360°$

[∵ angle sum property of a quadrilateral]

$\Rightarrow \quad 24x = 360° - 120° = 240°$

$\Rightarrow \qquad x = 10°$

Hence, the other two angles are

$13x = 13 \times 10° = 130°$

and $\qquad 11x = 11 \times 10° = 110°$

3. (b) Let the other three angles be $2x$, $3x$ and $7x$.

$\Rightarrow \qquad 2x + 3x + 7x + 60° = 360°$

[∵ angle sum property of a quadrilateral]

$\Rightarrow \qquad 12x = 300°$

$\Rightarrow \qquad x = \dfrac{300°}{12}$

$\Rightarrow \qquad x = 25°$

$\Rightarrow \qquad \angle S = 7x = 7 \times 25° = 175°$

4. (a) Let one of the three equal angles be $x°$.

$\Rightarrow \qquad 108° + x + x + x = 360°$

[∵ angle sum property of quadrilateral]

$\Rightarrow \qquad 3x = 360° - 108°$

$\Rightarrow \qquad 3x = 252°$

$\Rightarrow \qquad x = \dfrac{252°}{3} = 84°$

5. (d) It is a trapezium because sum of co-interior angles is 180°.

6. (c) In the given parallelogram $ABCD$, $\angle A = 40° + x$,

$\angle B = 110°$ and $\angle C = y°$

Since, in a parallelogram $ABCD$,

$$\angle A + \angle B = 180°$$

[∵ co-interior angles of a parallelogram]

$\therefore \qquad 40° + x + 110° = 180°$

$\Rightarrow \qquad x = 180° - 150° = 30° \qquad \dots(i)$

Now, also we know that in a parallelogram opposite angles are equal.

So, $\qquad \angle A = \angle C$

$\Rightarrow \qquad x + 40° = y$

$\Rightarrow \qquad 30° + 40° = y \qquad$ [using Eq. (i)]

$\Rightarrow \qquad y = 70°$

$\therefore \qquad x = 30°$ and $y = 70°$

7. (b) We know that, in a parallelogram opposite angles are equal and sum of two adjacent angles of a parallelogram is 180°.

Given, $ABCD$ is a parallelogram.

$\therefore \qquad \angle B = \angle D$ and $\angle A + \angle B = 180°$

$\Rightarrow \qquad 65° + \angle B = 180°$

$\Rightarrow \qquad \angle B = 180° - 65° = 115°$

$\Rightarrow \qquad \angle B = \angle D = 115°$

So, $\angle B + \angle D = 115° + 115° = 230°$

8. (a) Given, $AB \parallel CD$ and BC is a transversal.

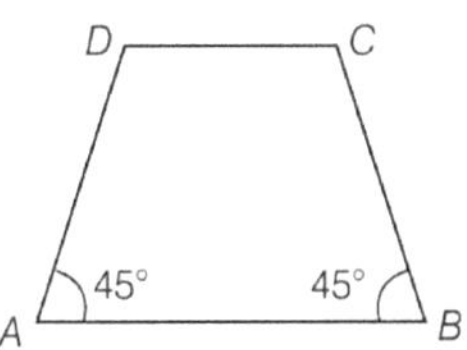

$\therefore \qquad \angle B + \angle C = 180° \quad$ [∵ consecutive interior angles]

$\Rightarrow \angle C = 180° - \angle B = 180° - 45°$

$\Rightarrow \qquad \angle C = 135°$

Similarly, $\angle A + \angle D = 180° \quad$ [∵ consecutive interior angles]

$\Rightarrow \qquad \angle D = 180° - 45°$

$\therefore \qquad \angle D = 135°$

9. (a) Given, $ABCD$ is a rectangle and $\angle AOB = 32°$

Let $\angle OCD = x$

Since, diagonal of a rectangle are equal and bisects each other.

$\therefore \qquad OC = OD$

$\Rightarrow \qquad \angle OCD = \angle ODC = x$

[∵ angles opposite to equal sides are equal]

and also $\qquad \angle AOB = \angle COD = 32°$

[∵ vertically opposite angle]

Now, in $\triangle OCD$, we get

$$\angle COD + \angle OCD + \angle ODC = 180°$$

[∵ angle sum property of triangle]

$\Rightarrow \qquad 32° + x + x = 180°$

$\Rightarrow \qquad 2x + 32° = 180°$

$\Rightarrow \qquad 2x = 180° - 32°$

$\Rightarrow \qquad 2x = 148°$

$\Rightarrow \qquad x = \dfrac{148°}{2}$

$\Rightarrow \qquad x = 74°$

Hence, $\angle OCD = 74°$

10. (c) In $\triangle ADC$, $\quad x + y + \angle ADC = 180°$

$$[\because \text{ angle sum property of a triangle}]$$

$\Rightarrow \qquad \angle ADC = 180° - (x + y) \qquad \text{...(i)}$

$\because \qquad \angle ABC = \angle ADC$

$$[\because \text{ opposite angles of a parallelogram}]$$

$\therefore \qquad z = 180° - (x + y) \qquad [\text{using Eq. (i)}]$

$\Rightarrow \qquad z + x + y = 180°$

11. (b) Given, $ABCD$ is a parallelogram in which

$$\angle ADC = 75°$$

$\therefore \qquad \angle ABC = 75°$

$$[\because \text{ in a parallelogram, opposite angles are equal}]$$

$\angle CBE = y = 180° - \angle ABC \qquad [\text{linear pair axiom}]$

$$= 180° - 75° = 105°$$

Also, $\angle x = 180° - 75° = 105°$

$$[\because \text{ since, } \angle D + \angle x = 180° \text{ as } DA \parallel CB \text{ and } DC \text{ is a transveral}]$$

$\therefore \qquad x + y = 105° + 105° = 210°$

12. (a) Given, diagonals of a quadrilateral bisect each other, so it is a parallelogram and then

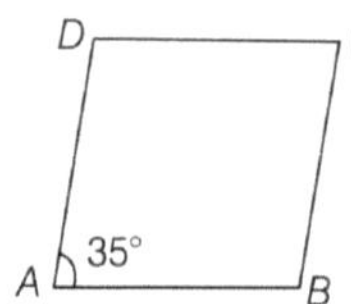

$$\angle A + \angle B = 180°$$

$$[\because \text{ consecutive interior angles of a parallelogram}]$$

$\Rightarrow \quad \angle B = 180° - \angle A = 180° - 35° = 145°$

13. (a) Given, $ABCD$ is a parallelogram and $\angle C = 55°$

$\therefore \qquad \angle A = \angle C = 55°$

$$[\text{in a parallelogram, opposite angles are equal}]$$

Also, $AEFG$ is a parallelogram.

$\therefore \qquad \angle A = \angle F = 55°$

14. (a) Let the measure of shorter side $= x$ cm

Given, longer side measure $= 9.5$ cm

and perimeter $= 32$ cm

$\Rightarrow \quad 2 \,(\text{Longer side} + \text{Shorter side}) = 32$

$$\left[\begin{array}{l} \because \text{ in a parallelogram, opposite sides are equal} \\ \Rightarrow \text{ perimeter} = \text{sum of four sides} \\ \qquad = 2(\text{longer side} + \text{shorter side}) \end{array}\right]$$

$\text{þ} \qquad 9.5 + x = \dfrac{32}{2}$

$\Rightarrow \qquad x = 16 - 9.5 \Rightarrow x = 6.5$ cm

15. (a) We know that, diagonals of a rhombus bisect each other at right angle.

In right-angled triangle $\triangle AOD$,

$$AD^2 = AO^2 + OD^2 \quad [\text{by Pythagoras theorem}]$$

$$= 4^2 + 3^2 = 25$$

$\Rightarrow \qquad AD = \sqrt{25} = 5$ cm

$\therefore \quad$ Perimeter of rhombus $= 4 \times \text{Side} = 4 \times 5 = 20$ cm

16. (b) In $\triangle ABC$, we have $AB = 5$ cm, $BC = 8$ cm and $CA = 7$ cm. Since, D and E are the mid-points of AB and BC, respectively.

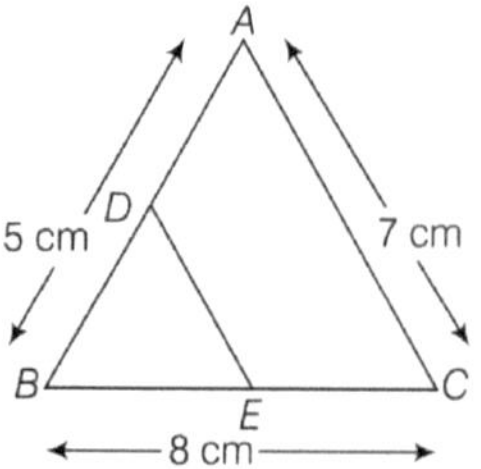

By mid-point theorem,

$$DE \parallel AC$$

and $\qquad DE = \dfrac{1}{2} AC = \dfrac{7}{2} = 3.5$ cm

$$DE = 3.5 \text{ cm}$$

17. (c) We know that, the diagonals of a parallelogram bisect each other. Therefore, O is the mid-point of diagonals AC and BD.

$\therefore \qquad OC = \dfrac{1}{2} AC = \dfrac{1}{2} \times 6.8 = 3.4$ cm

and $\qquad OD = \dfrac{1}{2} BD = \dfrac{1}{2} \times 5.6 = 2.8$ cm

18. (i) (b) $\angle QPO = 45°$

$$[\because \text{ diagonal of square bisects the angle of square}]$$

(ii) (c) $\therefore OP = OQ$

$$[\because \text{ diagonal of square bisects each other at } 90°.]$$

(iii) (c) $\angle POQ = 90°$

$$[\because \text{ diagonal of square bisects each other at } 90°]$$

(iv) (a) $PR = 20$ cm, PR is the diagonal of square and O is the intersection point i.e. $PR = 2OP$ at which diagonal bisect each other.

(v) (c) $\triangle PQO \cong \triangle PSO$

$OP = OP \qquad\qquad [\text{common line}]$

$\angle POS = \angle POQ \qquad [\because \text{ diagonal cut each other at } 90°]$

$SO = OQ \qquad [\because \text{ square diagonal bisect at centre}]$

$\therefore$ SAS property of congruence is used.

19. (i) (c) $\angle PZW = 180° - \angle WZY \qquad [\text{straight line}]$

$$= 180° - 130° = 50°$$

(ii) (a) $PWQY$ is a rectangle.

$PW = YQ \qquad [\because \text{ opposite sides of rectangle are equal}]$

$\angle WPZ = \angle XQY = 90°$

$$[\because \text{ rectangle sides intersect at } 90°]$$

$WZ = YX \qquad\qquad [\text{given}]$

$\therefore \quad PZ = QX \qquad\qquad [\text{by CPCT}]$

It is satisfy with RHS congruency. So, $\angle YQX = 90°$

(iii) (b) It is satisfy with RHS congruency as solved in part (ii).

(iv) (b) $PZ = QX$ as solved in part (ii). $\qquad [\text{by CPCT}]$

(v) (d) $WX = YZ \qquad [\because \text{ opposite sides are equal}]$

$WY = WY \qquad\qquad [\text{common}]$

$XY = WZ \qquad\qquad [\text{given}]$

$\therefore$ Proved by SSS congruency

Now, by SAS congruency

$WX = ZY$ [$\because$ opposite sides of parallelogram]

$\angle WXY = \angle WZY = 130°$ [given]

$XY = WZ$ [given]

It is satisfy with SAS congruency also.

So, both option satisfy (a) and (b).

20. (i) (c) Let the angles of quadrilateral are $8x$, x, $5x$ and $6x$.

We know that, sum of quadrilateral angles is $360°$

Then, $8x + x + 5x + 6x = 360°$

$\Rightarrow$ $20x = 360°$

$$x = \frac{360°}{20}$$

$$x = 18°$$

$$8x = 8 \times 18° = 144°$$

$$x = 18°$$

$$5x = 5 \times 18° = 90°$$

$$6x = 6 \times 18° = 108°$$

(ii) (a) Let fourth angle be x

Then, $110° + 50° + 40° + x = 360°$

     [$\because$ sum of angles of quadrilateral is $360°$]

$$200° + x = 360°$$

$\Rightarrow$ $x = 160°$

(iii) (a) Then, $100° + 98° + 92 + x = 360°$

     [$\because$ sum of angles quadrilateral is $360°$]

$$x = 70°$$

(iv) Let the angles of quadrilateral be x, $2x$, $4x$ and $5x$.

$x + 2x + 4x + 5x = 360°$

     [$\because$ sum of angles of quadrilateral is $360°$]

$$12x = 360°$$

$$x = \frac{360°}{12}$$

$$x = 30°$$

$$2x = 2 \times 30° = 60°$$

$$4x = 4 \times 30° = 120°$$

$$5x = 5 \times 30° = 150°$$

21. (i) (c) $\therefore \angle C = 180° - 115°$

     [$\because$ sum of consecutive angles is $180°$]

$$= 65°$$

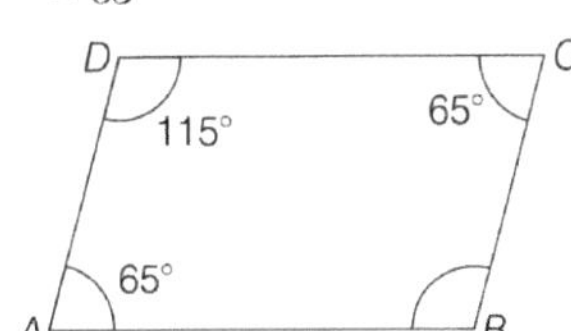

$\angle A = \angle C = 65°$

$\angle D = \angle B = 115°$ [$\because$ opposite angle's are equal]

(ii) (a) $4a + 9a + 5a = 180°$

     [$\because$ sum of angles of triangle is $180°$]

$$18a = 180°$$

$$a = \frac{180°}{18} = 10°$$

$$9a = 90°$$

$\angle C = \angle A = 90°$

     [$\because$ opposite angles of a quadrilateral are equal]

(iii) (a) $10a + 50° = 180°$

$$10a = 180° - 50°$$

$$10a = 130°$$

$$a = 13$$

$$\angle P = 10a = 130°$$

$$\angle Q = 50°$$

Subjective Questions

1. Given, the ratio of the angles of quadrilateral are

$$3 : 5 : 9 : 13$$

Let the angles of the quadrilateral are $3x$, $5x$, $9x$ and $13x$.

We know that, sum of angles of a quadrilateral is $360°$

$\therefore$ $3x + 5x + 9x + 13x = 360°$

$\Rightarrow$ $30x = 360°$

$\Rightarrow$ $x = \dfrac{360°}{30} = 12°$

$\therefore$ Angles of the quadrilateral are

$$3x = 3 \times 12 = 36°$$

$$5x = 5 \times 12 = 60°$$

$$9x = 9 \times 12 = 108°$$

and $13x = 13 \times 12 = 156°$

2. (i) It need not be a parallelogram, because we may have $\angle A = \angle B = \angle C = 80°$ and $\angle D = 120°$.

Here, $\angle B \neq \angle D$.

(ii) $ABCD$ is not a parallelogram, because diagonals of a parallelogram bisect each other.

Here, $OA \neq OC$.

(iii) As diagonals of the parallelogram $ABCD$ are equal, it is a rectangle.

Therefore, $\angle ABC = 90°$

3. Given, $ABCD$ is a rhombus.

$\Rightarrow ABCD$ is a parallelogram

$\Rightarrow$ $\angle ADC = \angle ABC = 68°$

     [$\because$ opposite angles of a parallelogram are equal]

$$\angle ODC = \frac{1}{2} \angle ADC$$

     [$\because$ diagonal DB of rhombus $ABCD$ bisects its $\angle ABC$ and $\angle ADC$]

$\Rightarrow$ $\angle ODC = \dfrac{1}{2} \times 68° = 34°$

Now, in $\triangle OCD$

$$\angle OCD + \angle ODC + \angle COD = 180°$$

     [$\because$ angle sum property of a triangle]

$\Rightarrow$ $\angle OCD + 34° + 90° = 180°$

     [$\because \angle COD = 90°$, diagonals of a rhombus bisect each other at right angles]

$\Rightarrow$ $\angle OCD + 124° = 180°$

$\Rightarrow$ $\angle OCD = 180° - 124°$

$\Rightarrow$ $\angle OCD = 56°$

or $\angle ACD = 56°$

4. Given, $ABCD$ is a square.

$\therefore \quad \angle D = 90° \Rightarrow \dfrac{1}{2} \angle D = 45°$

[∵ since, diagonal BD bisects $\angle D$]

$\Rightarrow \qquad \angle BDA = 45° \qquad\qquad ...(i)$

Also, $\quad \angle BDA + \angle ADE = 180° \qquad$ [linear pair axiom]

$\Rightarrow \qquad \angle ADE = 135° \qquad\qquad ...(ii)$

In $\triangle ADE, \qquad AD = DE \qquad\qquad$ [given]

$\therefore \qquad \angle AED = \angle DAE \qquad\qquad ...(iii)$

[∵ angles opposite to equal sides are also equal]

Now, $\angle AED + \angle DAE + \angle ADE = 180°$

[∵ angle sum property of a triangle]

$\Rightarrow \quad \angle DAE + \angle DAE + 135° = 180°$

[using Eqs. (ii) and (iii)]

$\therefore \qquad\qquad \angle DAE = 22.5°$

5. Given, $ABCD$ is a parallelogram such that angle bisectors of adjacent angles A and B intersect at point P.

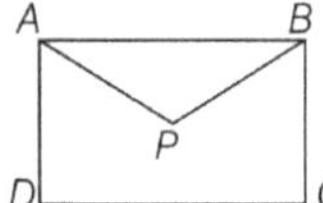

We have to show that, $\angle APB = 90°$

Here, $\qquad\qquad \angle A + \angle B = 180°$

[∵ $AD \parallel BC$ and $\angle A$ and $\angle B$ are consecutive interior angles]

$\Rightarrow \qquad \dfrac{1}{2} \angle A + \dfrac{1}{2} \angle B = 90°$

[dividing by 2 on both sides] ...(i)

But in $\triangle APB$, $\dfrac{1}{2} \angle A + \dfrac{1}{2} \angle B + \angle APB = 180°$

[∵ angle sum property of a triangle]

$\Rightarrow \qquad 90° + \angle APB = 180° \qquad$ [using Eq. (i)]

$\Rightarrow \qquad\qquad \angle APB = 90° \qquad$ **Hence proved**

6. From the figure, $\angle ABE + \angle EBF = \angle ABF$

$\Rightarrow \qquad 30° + \angle EBF = 90°$

[∵ each angles of rectangle is 90°]

$\Rightarrow \qquad\qquad \angle EBF = 60° \qquad\qquad ...(i)$

and $\quad \angle BFE + \angle CFE = 180° \qquad$ [linear pair axioms]

$\Rightarrow \qquad \angle BFE + 144° = 180° \qquad$ [∵ $\angle CFE = 144°$]

$\Rightarrow \quad \angle BFE = 180° - 144° = 36° \qquad\qquad ...(ii)$

Now, in $\triangle BEF$, $\angle EBF + \angle BFE + \angle BEF = 180°$

[∵ angle sum property of a triangle]

$\Rightarrow \qquad 60° + 36° + \angle BEF = 180°$

$\Rightarrow \qquad \angle BEF = 180° - 96° \Rightarrow \angle BEF = 84°$

7. Given, $ABCD$ is a square and $\angle COD = 105°$

We know that, the diagonal AC of square $ABCD$ will bisect the $\angle C$.

$\therefore \qquad \angle OCX = \dfrac{1}{2} \angle C = \dfrac{1}{2} \times 90° = 45° \qquad\qquad ...(i)$

Now, we have

$\qquad \angle COD + \angle COX = 180° \qquad$ [linear pair axioms]

$\Rightarrow \qquad 105° + \angle COX = 180°$

$\Rightarrow \qquad\qquad \angle COX = 75° \qquad\qquad ...(ii)$

Now, in $\triangle COX$,

$\angle COX + \angle OXC + \angle OCX = 180°$

[∵ angle sum property of a triangle]

$\Rightarrow \qquad 75° + \angle OXC + 45° = 180°$

$\Rightarrow \qquad \angle OXC = 180° - 120° = 60°$

$\therefore \qquad\qquad x = 60°$

8. AD is median.

$\therefore \qquad\qquad BD = DC$

and $\qquad\qquad AD = DY \qquad\qquad$ [given]

and $\qquad\qquad \angle BDA = \angle CDY$

[∵ diagonals AY and BC bisect each other
$\therefore ABYC$ is a parallelogram]

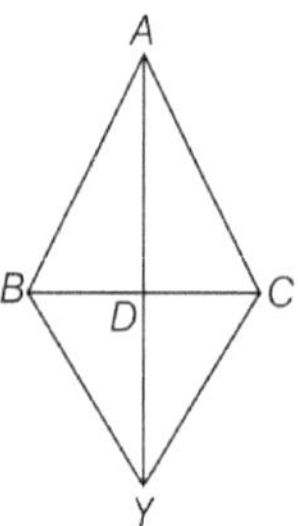

then, $\triangle ABD \cong \triangle YDC \qquad$ [by SAS congurence rule]

$\therefore \qquad AB = CY \qquad\qquad$ [by CPCT]

Similarly, $AC = BY$

So, $ABYC$ is a parallelogram.

9. Given, $PQRS$ is a rhombus $\Rightarrow PQRS$ is a parallelogram

Since, $PQ \parallel SR$ and PR is a transversal.

$\therefore \quad \angle ORS = \angle OPQ = 35° \;$ [∵ alternate interior angles] ...(i)

Also, diagonals of rhombus bisect each other at right angle.

$\therefore \qquad\qquad \angle SOR = 90° \qquad\qquad ...(ii)$

Now, in $\triangle SOR$, $\angle RSO + \angle SOR + \angle ORS = 180°$

[∵ angle sum property of triangles]

$\Rightarrow \qquad \angle RSO = 180° - \angle SOR - \angle ORS$

$\Rightarrow \qquad \angle RSO = 180° - 90° - 35° \;$ [using Eqs. (i) and (ii)]

$\Rightarrow \qquad\qquad \angle RSO = 55°$

$\Rightarrow \qquad\qquad \angle OQP = 55° \qquad\qquad ...(iii)$

[∵ alternate interior angles, since $PQ \parallel SR$ and QS is a
transversal]

From Eqs. (i) and (iii), we get

$\qquad \angle ORS + \angle OQP = 35° + 55° = 90°$

10. **Given** In a rectangle $ABCD$, diagonal BD bisects $\angle B$

Construction Join AC.

To show $ABCD$ is a square.

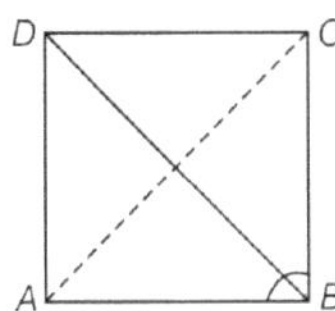

Proof In $\triangle BAD$ and $\triangle BCD$, $\angle ABD = \angle CBD$ [given]

$$\angle A = \angle C \qquad \text{[each 90°]}$$

and $\qquad\qquad BD = BD \qquad\qquad$ [common side]

$\therefore \qquad\qquad \triangle BAD \cong \triangle BCD \qquad$ [by AAS congruence rule]

Then, $AB = BC$

and $AD = DC \qquad\qquad\qquad$ [by CPCT] ...(i)

But in rectangle $ABCD$, opposite sides are equal.

$\therefore \qquad\qquad\qquad AB = DC$

and $\qquad\qquad\qquad BC = AD \qquad\qquad\qquad$ ...(ii)

From Eqs. (i) and (ii), we get $AB = BC = CD = DA$

So, $ABCD$ is a square.   **Hence proved.**

11. **Given** $ABCD$ is a parallelogram, whose diagonals AC and BD are equal, i.e. $AC = BD$.

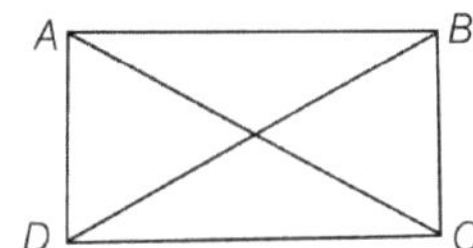

To prove $ABCD$ is a rectangle.

Proof In $\triangle ABC$ and $\triangle DCB$, we have

$$AB = CD$$

$$\text{[∵ opposite sides of parallelogram]}$$

$$BC = CB \qquad \text{[∵ common in both triangles]}$$

and $\qquad\qquad AC = BD \qquad\qquad\qquad$ [given]

$\therefore \qquad\qquad \triangle ABC \cong \triangle DCB \qquad$ [by SSS congruence rule]

So, $\qquad\qquad \angle ABC = \angle DCB \qquad\qquad$ [by CPCT] ...(i)

But $DC \parallel AB$ and transversal CB intersect them.

$\therefore \qquad\qquad \angle ABC + \angle DCB = 180°$

$$\text{[∵ since, both are interior angles on the}$$
$$\text{same side of the transversal]}$$

$\Rightarrow \qquad \angle ABC + \angle ABC = 180° \qquad$ [from Eq. (i)]

$\Rightarrow \qquad\qquad 2\angle ABC = 180°$

$\Rightarrow \qquad\qquad \angle ABC = 90° = \angle DCB$

Thus, $ABCD$ is a parallelogram and one of its angle is 90°.

Hence, $ABCD$ is a rectangle.   **Hence proved.**

12.   (i) Given, diagonal AC of a parallelogram $ABCD$ bisects $\angle A$.

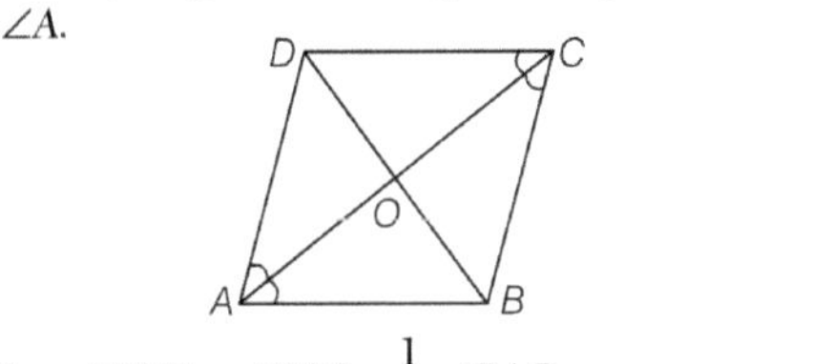

i.e. $\angle DAC = \angle BAC = \dfrac{1}{2}\angle BAD \qquad\qquad$ ...(i)

Here, $AB \parallel DC$ and AC is a transversal.

$\therefore \angle DCA = \angle BAC \qquad$ [∵ pair of alternate angles] ...(ii)

Similarly, $BC \parallel AD$ and AC is a transversal.

$\therefore \qquad\qquad \angle BCA = \angle DAC$

$$\text{[∵ pair of alternate angles] ...(iii)}$$

From Eqs. (i), (ii) and (iii), we get

$$\angle DAC = \angle BCA = \angle BAC = \angle DCA \qquad \text{...(iv)}$$

Now, $\angle BCD = \angle BCA + \angle DCA$

$$= \angle DAC + \angle BAC = \angle BAD$$

Hence, diagonal AC also bisects $\angle C$.

(ii) From Eq. (iv), $\angle DAC = \angle DCA$

$\Rightarrow \; CD = DA$

$$\text{[∵ sides opposite to equal angles are equal]}$$

But $AB = DC$ and $AD = BC$

$$\text{[∵ } ABCD \text{ is a parallelogram]}$$

$\therefore \quad AB = BC = CD = DA$

Hence, $ABCD$ is a rhombus.

13. **Given** $ABCD$ is a parallelogram, whose diagonals bisect each other at O, i.e. $OB = OD$ and $OC = OA$.

To prove PQ is bisected at O.

Proof In $\triangle ODP$ and $\triangle OBQ$,

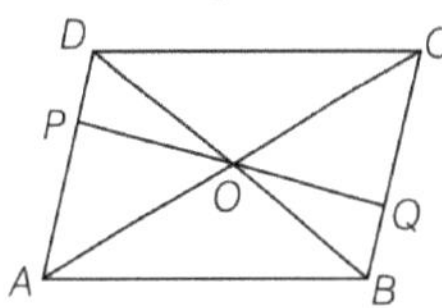

$$\angle POD = \angle BOQ \; [\because \text{vertically opposite angles}]$$

$$\angle ODP = \angle OBQ$$

$$\text{[∵ since, } AD \parallel BC \text{ and } BD \text{ is transversal]}$$

and $\qquad\qquad OD = OB \qquad\qquad\qquad$ [given]

$\therefore \qquad\qquad \triangle OBQ \cong \triangle ODP \qquad$ [by ASA congruence rule]

Then, $\qquad\qquad OQ = OP \qquad\qquad\qquad$ [by CPCT]

Hence, PQ is bisected at O.   **Hence proved.**

14. In $\triangle AOX$ and $\triangle COY$,

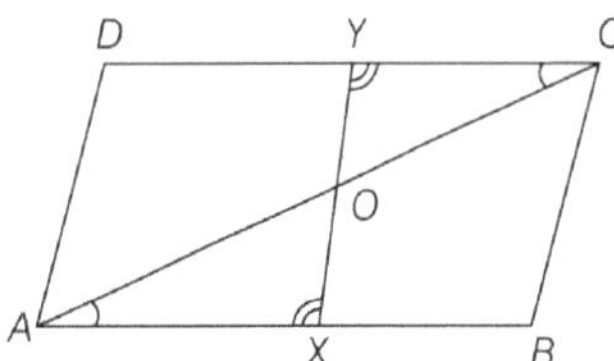

$$\angle OAX = \angle OCY$$

$$[\text{as } AB \parallel CD \Rightarrow AX \parallel CY, \text{ alternate angles are equal}]$$

$$AX = CY \qquad\qquad\qquad \text{[given]}$$

$$\angle AXO = \angle CYO \; [\because \text{alternate angles are equal}]$$

$\therefore \qquad\qquad \triangle AOX \cong \triangle COY$

$$\text{[by ASA congruence criterian]}$$

$\Rightarrow \qquad OA = OC$ and $OX = OY \qquad$ [by CPCT]

Hence, AC and XY bisect each other.

15. Given, $ABCD$ is a parallelogram and AP and CQ are perpendiculars from vertices A and C on diagonal BD.

Since, $AB \parallel DC$ and BD is a transversal.

$\therefore \qquad\qquad \angle CDB = \angle ABD \qquad\qquad\qquad$ ...(i)

(i) Now, in ΔCQD and ΔAPB, we have

$$CD = BA \quad [\because \text{sides of a parallelogram}]$$
$$\angle CQD = \angle APB = 90°$$
$$[\because \text{since, } AP \perp BD \text{ and } CQ \perp BD, \text{ given}]$$
$$\angle CDQ = \angle ABP \quad [\text{from Eq. (i)}]$$
$$\therefore \quad \Delta CQD \cong \Delta APB$$
$$[\text{by AAS congruence rule}]$$

(ii) Since, $\Delta APB \cong \Delta CQD$

$$\therefore \quad AP = CQ \quad [\text{by CPCT}] \textbf{ Hence proved.}$$

16. Using mid-point theorem,

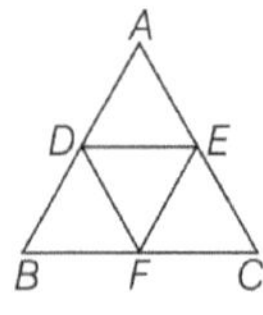

$$DF = \frac{1}{2} AC = \frac{8}{2} = 4 \text{ cm}$$
$$FE = \frac{1}{2} AB = \frac{13}{2} = 6.5 \text{ cm}$$
$$ED = \frac{1}{2} BC = \frac{16}{2} = 8 \text{ cm}$$

$\therefore$ Perimeter of $\Delta DEF = DF + FE + ED$
$$= 4 + 6.5 + 8 = 18.5 \text{ cm}$$

17. Given, ΔABC in which $AB = AC$, D and E are the mid-points of AB and AC.

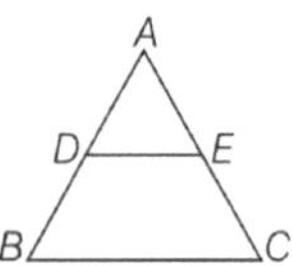

$$AD = DB = 4.5 \text{ cm}$$
Then, $\quad AB = 2 \times 4.5 = 9 \text{ cm}$
So, $\quad AB = AC = 9 \text{ cm}$

Since, D and E are the mid-points of AB and AC, respectively.

So, by mid-point theorem,
$$DE \parallel BC$$
and $\quad DE = \frac{1}{2} BC$

Then, $\quad BC = 2DE = 2 \times 3.5 = 7 \text{ cm} \quad [DE = 3.5 \text{ cm, given}]$

Now, perimeter of $\Delta ABC = AB + BC + CA$
$$= 9 + 7 + 9 = 25 \text{ cm}$$

18. Given, perimeter of $\Delta ABC = 38 \text{ cm}$

$$AB + BC + CA = 38$$

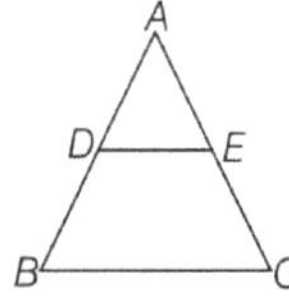

$$\Rightarrow \quad \frac{1}{2} AB + \frac{1}{2} BC + \frac{1}{2} CA = \frac{38}{2} \quad [\text{dividing both sides by 2}]$$

$$\Rightarrow \quad AD + DE + AE = 19 \text{ cm}$$
$$\left[\because \frac{1}{2} AB = AD, \frac{1}{2} CA = AE, \text{ as } D \text{ and } E \text{ are mid-points of } AB\right.$$
$$\left. \text{and } AC \text{ and } \frac{1}{2} BC = DE \text{ by mid-point theorem}\right]$$

Hence, perimeter of $\Delta ADE = 19 \text{ cm}$

19. Given $ABCD$ is a parallelogram.

$$\therefore \quad AB = CD$$
and $\quad AD = BC$

and E is the mid-point of side BC, i.e. $BE = CE$

To prove $AF = 2AB$

Proof Now, in ΔDEC and ΔFEB, we have

$$\angle DEC = \angle BEF \, [\because \text{vertically opposite angles}]$$
$$BE = CE \quad [\text{given}]$$
and $\quad \angle DCE = \angle FBE$
$$[\because \text{since, } DC \parallel AF \text{ and } BC \text{ is transversal,}$$
$$\text{so alternate interior angles}]$$

$$\therefore \quad \Delta DEC \cong \Delta FEB \quad [\text{by ASA congruence rule}]$$
So, $\quad DC = BF \quad [\text{by CPCT}] \text{ ...(i)}$
Also, we have $\quad DC = AB \quad [\text{given}] \text{ ...(ii)}$
From Eqs. (i) and (ii), we get
$$AB = BF$$
$$\therefore \quad AF = 2AB \quad \textbf{Hence proved.}$$

20. Given PS and RT are medians of ΔPQR, i.e. S and T are the mid-points of QR and PQ, respectively, i.e. $SR = QS = \frac{1}{2} QR$ and $QT = PT = \frac{1}{2} PQ$ and $SM \parallel RT$.

To prove $QM = \frac{1}{4} PQ$

Proof In ΔQTR, S is the mid-point of QR and $SM \parallel RT$. So, by converse of mid-point theorem, M is mid-point of QT.

i.e. $\quad QM = MT = \frac{1}{2} QT \quad$ ...(i)

Also, $\quad QT = \frac{1}{2} PQ \quad [\text{given}] \text{ ...(ii)}$

From Eqs. (i) and (ii), we get
$$QM = \frac{1}{2}\left(\frac{1}{2} PQ\right) \Rightarrow QM = \frac{1}{4} PQ \quad \textbf{Hence proved.}$$

21. (i) In ΔDRC

P is the mid-point of DC and $PA \parallel CR \quad [\text{given}]$

$\therefore A$ is the mid-point of DR
$$[\text{by converse of mid-point theorem}]$$

$$\Rightarrow \quad DA = AR$$

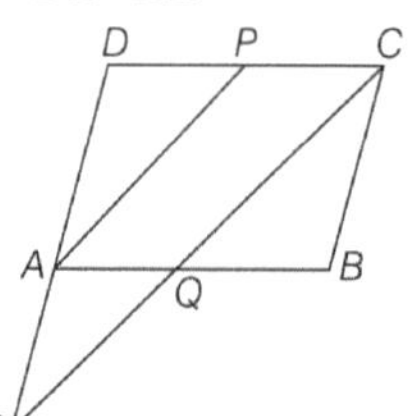

(ii) Since, $ABCD$ is a parallelogram
$\Rightarrow \qquad AB \parallel DC \Rightarrow AQ \parallel DC$
In ΔDRC, A is the mid-point of DR and $AQ \parallel DC$
$\therefore Q$ is the mid-point of RC.
$$[\text{by converse of mid-point theorem}]$$
$\Rightarrow \qquad CQ = QR \qquad\qquad$ **Hence proved.**

22. Given $ABCD$ is a trapezium in which $AB \parallel DC$, BD is a diagonal and E is mid-point of AD and a line is drawn through E parallel to AB intersecting BC at F such that $EF \parallel AB$.

To prove F is the mid-point of BC.

Proof Let EF intersects BD at P.

In ΔABD, we have $EP \parallel AB$ and E is mid-point of AD.
$$[\because EF \parallel AB] \text{ [given]}$$

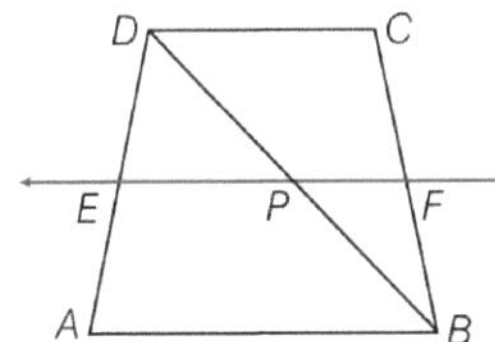

So, by converse of mid-point theorem.

We get, P is mid-point of BD.

Similarly, in ΔBCD, we have $PF \parallel CD$
$$[\because EF \parallel AB \text{ and } AB \parallel CD]$$
and P is mid-point of BD.

So, by converse of mid-point theorem, F is mid-point of BC.
$$\textbf{Hence proved.}$$

23. Given $l \parallel m \parallel n$ and $AB = BC$

To show $DE = EF$

Proof In ΔACF, B is the mid-point of AC $[\because AB = BC,$ given$]$

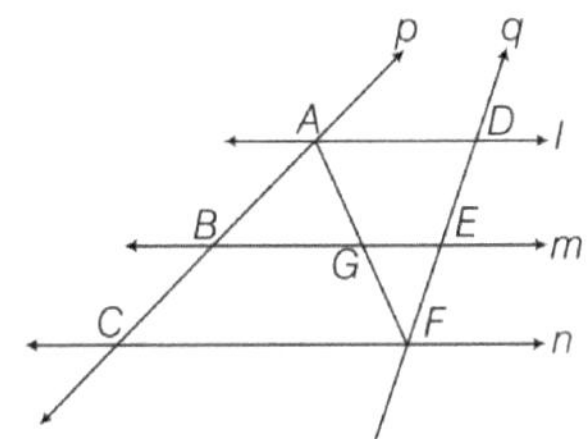

and $\qquad\qquad BG \parallel CF \qquad\qquad [\because m \parallel n,$ given$]$
By converse of mid-point theorem, G is the mid-point of AF.
Now, in ΔAFD, G is the mid-point of AF
and $\qquad\qquad GE \parallel AD \qquad\qquad [\because l \parallel m,$ given$]$
So, by converse of mid-point theorem, E is the mid-point of DF.

Then, $DE = EF$

Hence, l, m and n cut-off equal intercepts DE and EF on q also. $\qquad\qquad$ **Hence proved.**

24. Let in given parallelogram $ABCD$, $\angle ABC = x$,

So $\angle ADC = x$ and $\angle BCD = 180° - x$
$$[\because \text{opposite angles of parallelogram are same}]$$

So, $\angle PBC = x + 60°$ and $\angle QDC = x + 60° \qquad$ ... (i)

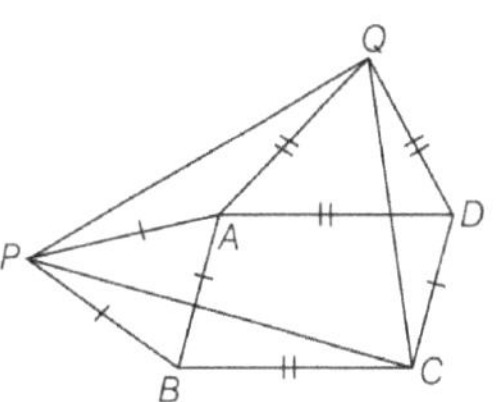

Now, in ΔPBC and ΔQDC,
$$PB = CD \qquad\qquad [\because PB = AB = CD]$$
$$BC = QD \qquad\qquad [\because BC = AD = QD]$$
and $\qquad\quad \angle PBC = \angle QDC \qquad\qquad$ [using Eq. (i)]
So, $\qquad\quad \Delta PBC \cong \Delta CDQ \qquad$ [by SAS congruence rule]
Hence $\qquad\qquad CP = CQ \qquad\qquad$ [by CPCT] ...(ii)
Also, we have
from ΔPBC, $PB = BC \Rightarrow \angle BPC = \angle BCP$
$$[\because \text{angle opposite to equal sides}]$$
$\angle PBC + \angle BPC + \angle BCP = 180°$
$$[\because \text{angle sum property of triangle}]$$
$\Rightarrow \qquad \angle PBC + 2\angle BCP = 180°$
So, $\quad \angle BCP = \dfrac{180° - x - 60°}{2} = 60° - \dfrac{x}{2}$

Similarly, from ΔQDC, we have $\angle QCD = 60° - \dfrac{x}{2}$

Therefore, $\angle PCQ = \angle BCD - \angle BCP - \angle QCD$
$$= 180° - x - \left(60° - \dfrac{x}{2}\right) - \left(60° - \dfrac{x}{2}\right) = 60° \qquad \text{... (iii)}$$

Now, in ΔCPQ, $CP = CQ \qquad\qquad$ [using Eq. (ii)]
$\Rightarrow \qquad \angle CQP = \angle CPQ \qquad$ [$\because$ angle opposite to equal sides]
$\Rightarrow \qquad \angle CPQ + \angle CQP + \angle PCQ = 180°$
$\Rightarrow \qquad \angle CPQ + \angle CPQ + 60° = 180°$
$$[\because \text{angle sum property of triangle}]$$
$\Rightarrow \qquad 2\angle CPQ = 180° - 60° \Rightarrow 2\angle CPQ = 120°$
$\Rightarrow \qquad \angle CPQ = 60°$
$\Rightarrow \angle CPQ = \angle CQP = \angle PCQ = 60°$
i.e. ΔCPQ is an equilateral triangle. $\qquad$ **Hence proved.**

25. Since, $ABCD$ is a square.
$\therefore \qquad\qquad BC = CD$
But $\qquad\qquad QC = DR \qquad\qquad$ [given]
$\Rightarrow \quad BC - QC = CD - DR \Rightarrow QB = RC \qquad$ ...(i)
Now, in ΔPBQ and ΔQCR,
$$PB = QC \qquad\qquad [\text{given}]$$
$$BQ = CR \qquad\qquad [\text{from Eq. (i)}]$$
$$\angle PBQ = \angle QCR = 90°$$
$\therefore \qquad\qquad \Delta PBQ \cong \Delta QCR \qquad$ [by SAS congruence rule]
$\Rightarrow \qquad\qquad PQ = QR \qquad\qquad$ [by CPCT]
Also, $\qquad\qquad \angle BPQ = \angle CQR$
and, $\qquad\qquad \angle BQP = \angle CRQ \qquad\qquad$ [by CPCT]
Now, since ΔPQR is an isosceles right-angled triangle.

So, $\angle PRQ + \angle QPR + \angle PQR = 180°$

$[\because$ angle sum property of a triangle]

$\Rightarrow \quad \angle QPR + \angle QPR + 90° = 180°$

$[\because$ since, ΔPQR is an isosceles triangle]

$2\angle QPR = 90°$

$\Rightarrow \quad \angle QPR = 45°$ **Hence proved.**

26. We draw the figure as per the given conditions.

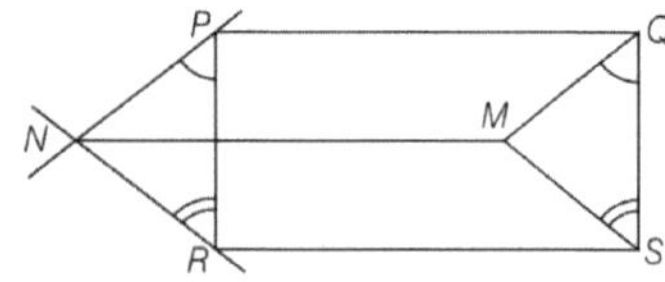

It is given that $PQ = RS$ and $PQ \parallel RS$.

Since, a pair of opposite side of a quadrilateral $PQSR$ is equal and parallel. Therefore, $PQSR$ is a parallelogram.

So, $PR = QS$ and $PR \parallel QS$ …(i)

Now, $PR \parallel QS$

Therefore, $\angle RPQ + \angle PQS = 180°$

$[\because$ interior angles on the same side of the transversal]

i.e. $\angle RPQ + \angle PQM + \angle MQS = 180°$ … (ii)

Also, $PN \parallel QM$ [by construction]

Therefore, $\angle NPQ + \angle PQM = 180°$

i.e. $\angle NPR + \angle RPQ + \angle PQM = 180°$ …(iii)

So, $\angle NPR = \angle MQS$ [from Eqs. (ii) and (iii)] …(iv)

Similarly, $\angle NRP = \angle MSQ$ …(v)

In ΔPNR and ΔQMS

$PR = QS$ [using Eq. (i)]

$\angle NPR = \angle MQS$ [using Eq. (iv)]

$\angle NRP = \angle MSQ$ [using Eq. (v)]

Therefore, $\Delta PNR \cong \Delta QMS$ [by ASA congruence rule]

So, $PN = QM$ and $NR = MS$ [by CPCT]

As, $PN = QM$ and $PN \parallel QM$, we have $PQMN$ is a parallelogram. [$\because$ since, a pair of opposite side of a quadrilateral equal and parallel]

So, $NM = PQ$ and $NM \parallel PQ$.

27. **Given** A quadrilateral $ABCD$ in which $AC = BD$ and $AC \perp BD$ such that $OA = OC$ and $OB = OD$. So, $ABCD$ is a parallelogram.

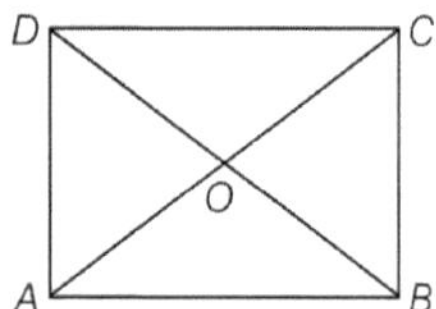

To prove $ABCD$ is a square.

Proof Let diagonals AC and BD intersect at a point O.

In ΔABO and ΔADO, we have

$BO = OD$ [given]

$AO = OA$ [common side]

$\angle AOB = \angle AOD = 90°$ [given]

$\therefore \quad \Delta ABO \cong \Delta ADO$ [by SAS congruence rule]

Then, $AB = AD$ [by CPCT]

Also, $AB = DC$ and $AD = BC$

[$\because$ opposite sides of parallelogram are equal]

$\therefore \quad AB = BC = DC = AD$ …(i)

Again, in ΔABC and ΔBAD, we have

$AB = BA$ [common side]

$AC = BD$ [given]

$BC = AD$ [from Eq. (i)]

$\therefore \quad \Delta ABC \cong \Delta BAD$ [by SSS congruence rule]

Then, $\angle ABC = \angle BAD$ [by CPCT]…(ii)

Also, $\angle ABC + \angle BAD = 180°$

[$\because$ sum of interior angles of a parallelogram]

$\angle BAD + \angle BAD = 180° \Rightarrow 2\angle BAD = 180°$

$\therefore \quad \angle ABC = \angle BAD = 90°$ [using Eq. (ii)]

Thus, $AB = BC = CD = DA$ and $\angle A = 90°$

Hence, $ABCD$ is a square. **Hence proved.**

28. Given, $ABCD$ is a quadrilateral such that $AC = BD$ and AC and BD bisect each other at right angle at point O.

$\therefore \quad OA = OB = OC = OD$ [$\because AC = BD$] …(i)

and $\angle AOB = \angle BOC = \angle COD = \angle DOA = 90°$ …(ii)

We have to show that quadrilateral $ABCD$ is a square.

Now, in ΔAOB, $OA = OB$ [given]

and $\angle AOB = 90°$ [given]

$\therefore \quad \angle OAB = \angle OBA = 45°$

[$\because$ angles opposite to equal sides are also equal]

Similarly, we can prove that

$\angle OAD = \angle ODA = 45°$

$\angle OBC = \angle OCB = 45°$

Then, $\angle A = \angle BAD = \angle BAO + \angle OAD$

$= 45° + 45°, \Rightarrow \angle A = 90°$

Similarly, $\angle B = \angle ABC = \angle OBA + \angle OBC$

$= 45° + 45° = 90°$

Also, $\angle C = 90°$ and $\angle D = 90°$

In ΔAOB and ΔCOB, $OA = OC$ [given]

$OB = OB$ [common side]

and $\angle AOB = \angle BOC$ [given]

$\therefore \quad \Delta AOB \cong \Delta COB$ [by SAS congruence rule]

Then, $AB = BC$ [by CPCT]

Similarly, we can prove that

$BC = CD$ and $CD = AD$

Thus, we get $AB = BC = CD = AD$

and $\angle A = \angle B = \angle C = \angle D = 90°$

Hence, quadrilateral $ABCD$ is a square. **Hence proved.**

29. Let $\triangle ABC$ be an isosceles right triangle, where $\angle A = 90°$ and square $ADEF$ is inscribed.

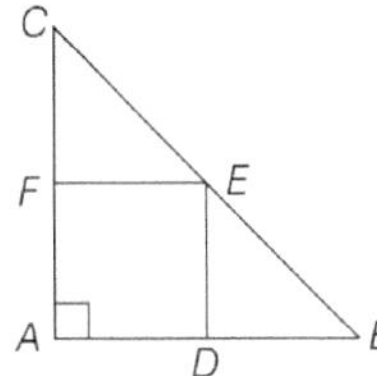

In an isosceles triangle $\triangle ABC$, $\angle A = 90°$ and
$$AB = AC \qquad \text{...(i)}$$
Since, $ADEF$ is a square.
$$\therefore \qquad AD = AF \qquad \text{...(ii)}$$
$$[\because \text{ all sides of square are equal}]$$
On subtracting Eq. (ii) from Eq. (i), we get
$$AB - AD = AC - AF$$
$$\Rightarrow \qquad BD = CF \qquad \text{...(iii)}$$
Now, In $\triangle CFE$ and $\triangle BDE$,
$$CF = BD \qquad [\text{from Eq. (iii)}]$$
$$FE = DE \qquad [\because \text{ sides of square}]$$
$$\angle CFE = \angle BDE \qquad [\because \text{ each } 90°]$$
$$\therefore \qquad \triangle CFE \cong \triangle BDE \qquad [\text{by SAS congruence rule}]$$
$$\Rightarrow \qquad CE = BE \qquad [\text{by CPCT}]$$
Thus, vertex E of the square bisects the hypotenuse BC.

30. Lines l and m are parallel, i.e. $PS \parallel QR$ and transversal t intersects PS and QR at points A and C, respectively.

The bisectors of $\angle PAC$ and $\angle ACQ$ intersect each other at B and bisectors of $\angle ACR$ and $\angle SAC$ intersect each other at D. We have to show that, quadrilateral $ABCD$ is a rectangle.

Since, $PS \parallel CR$ and t is a transversal.
$$\therefore \qquad \angle PAC = \angle ACR \qquad [\because \text{ alternate angles}]$$
$$\Rightarrow \qquad \frac{1}{2}\angle PAC = \frac{1}{2}\angle ACR$$
$$\Rightarrow \qquad \angle BAC = \angle ACD$$
These form a pair of alternate angles for lines AB and CD with AC as transversal.
So, $AB \parallel DC$
Similarly, $BC \parallel AD$
Therefore, quadrilateral $ABCD$ is a parallelogram.
Now, PS is a straight line.
So, $\angle PAC + \angle SAC = 180°$ [linear pair axiom]
$$\Rightarrow \qquad \frac{1}{2}\angle PAC + \frac{1}{2}\angle SAC = \frac{1}{2} \times 180°$$
$$\left[\text{multiply by } \frac{1}{2} \text{ on both sides}\right]$$
$$\Rightarrow \qquad \angle BAC + \angle DAC = 90°$$
$$\Rightarrow \qquad \angle BAD = 90°$$
Thus, one angle of parallelogram $ABCD$ is a right angle.
Hence, $ABCD$ is a rectangle. **Hence proved.**

31. **Given,** $ABCD$ is a square and BD is a diagonal.
$$\therefore \qquad \angle CBD = \angle CDB = \frac{1}{2} \times 90° = 45°$$
$$[\because \text{ diagonal of a square bisect each angle at the vertex}]$$
Also, $EF \parallel BD$ [given]
So, $\angle CEF = \angle CBD = 45°$ $\qquad [\because \text{ corresponding angles}]$
and $\angle CFE = \angle CDB = 45°$ $\qquad [\because \text{ corresponding angles}]$
$$\Rightarrow \qquad CE = CF$$
$$[\because \text{ sides opposite to equal angles are equal}]$$
$$\Rightarrow \qquad BC - CE = CD - CF \qquad [\because BC = CD]$$
$$\Rightarrow \qquad BE = DF \qquad \text{... (i)}$$
Now, in $\triangle ABE$ and $\triangle ADF$,
$$AB = AD \qquad [\because \text{ adjacent sides of a square}]$$
$$\angle ABE = \angle ADF \qquad [\text{each } 90°]$$
$$BE = DF \qquad [\text{from Eq. (i)}]$$
So, $\triangle ABE \cong \triangle ADF$ $\qquad [\text{by SAS congruence rule}]$
Then, $AE = AF$ $\qquad [\text{by CPCT}] \text{...(ii)}$
and $\angle BAE = \angle DAF$ $\qquad \text{...(iii)}$
Now, in $\triangle AEM$ and $\triangle AFM$,
$$AE = AF \qquad [\text{from Eq. (ii)}]$$
$$ME = MF \qquad [\because M \text{ is mid-point of } EF]$$
$$AM = AM \qquad [\text{common side}]$$
$$\therefore \qquad \triangle AEM \cong \triangle AFM \qquad [\text{by SSS congruence rule}]$$
So, $\angle EAM = \angle FAM$ $\qquad [\text{by CPCT}]\text{...(iv)}$
On adding Eqs. (iii) and (iv), we get
$$\angle BAE + \angle EAM = \angle DAF + \angle FAM$$
$$\Rightarrow \qquad \angle BAM = \angle DAM$$
i.e. AM bisects $\angle BAD$. **Hence proved.**

32. Given, $ABCD$ is a parallelogram, i.e. $AB \parallel CD$ and $AD \parallel BC$ and $\angle DAB = 60°$. AP and BP are the bisectors of $\angle A$ and $\angle B$, respectively.
$$\therefore \angle PAB = \angle DAP = \frac{1}{2}\angle DAB = \frac{1}{2} \times 60° = 30°$$
$$\Rightarrow \angle PAB = \angle DAP = 30°$$
and $\angle B = 180° - \angle A = 180° - 60° = 120°$
$$[\because \text{ co-interior angle of parallelogram}]$$
$$\Rightarrow \angle PBA = \angle CBP = \frac{1}{2} \angle B = 60°$$
We have, $AB \parallel DC$ and PA is a transversal.
$$\therefore \qquad \angle DPA = \angle PAB = 30° \qquad [\because \text{ alternate angle}] \text{...(i)}$$
Also, $\angle DAP = \angle PAB = 30°$ $\qquad [\text{given}] \text{...(ii)}$
From Eqs. (i) and (ii), we have
$$\angle DAP = \angle DPA \Rightarrow DP = DA \qquad \text{...(iii)}$$
$$[\because \text{ sides opposite to equal angles of a triangle}$$
$$\text{are also equal}]$$
Similarly, $CB = PC$ $\qquad \text{...(iv)}$
From Eqs. (iii) and (iv), we get
$$DA = CB \qquad [\because \text{ opposite sides of a parallelogram}]$$
$$\Rightarrow \quad DP = PC \qquad [\text{from Eq. (iii)}]$$
Hence, P is the mid-point of CD. **Hence proved.**

33. Given $PQRS$ is a square. M is the mid-point of PQ.

i.e. $\quad PM = MQ \quad$ and $\quad RM \perp AB$

$\therefore \quad \angle AMR = \angle BMR = 90°$

To prove $\quad RA = RB$

Proof   In ΔAMP and ΔBMQ, we have

$PM = MQ \quad\quad\quad\quad\quad\quad$ [given]

$\angle AMP = \angle BMQ \quad\quad$ [$\because$ vertically opposite angles]

and $\quad \angle APM = \angle BQM \quad\quad\quad\quad\quad$ [each 90°]

$\therefore \quad \Delta AMP \cong \Delta BMQ \quad\quad$ [by ASA congruence rule]

So, $\quad AM = MB \quad\quad\quad\quad\quad\quad$ [by CPCT] ...(i)

Now, in ΔRMA and ΔRMB, we have

$\angle AMR = \angle BMR = 90° \quad\quad\quad\quad$ [given]

$RM = RM \quad\quad\quad\quad\quad\quad$ [common side]

and $\quad AM = MB \quad\quad\quad\quad\quad\quad$ [from Eq. (i)]

$\therefore \quad \Delta RMA \cong \Delta RMB \quad\quad$ [by SAS congruence rule]

So, $\quad RA = RB \quad\quad\quad$ [by CPCT] **Hence proved.**

34. Given E and F are respectively the mid-points of non-parallel sides of AD and BC of trapezium $ABCD$.

To prove $EF \parallel AB$ and $EF = \dfrac{1}{2}(AB + CD)$

Construction Join CE and produce it to meet BA at P.

Proof   In ΔDEC and ΔAEP, we have

$\angle DEC = \angle AEP$ [$\because$ vertically opposite angles]

$\angle DCE = \angle APE$

$\quad\quad$ [$\because DC \parallel PB$ and PC is transversal, so alternate angles are equal]

$DE = AE \quad$ [$\because E$ is the mid-points of AD]

$\therefore \quad \Delta DEC \cong \Delta AEP \quad$ [by AAS congruence rule]

then, $\quad CE = PE \quad\quad\quad\quad\quad\quad$ [by CPCT]

and $\quad CD = PA \quad\quad\quad\quad\quad\quad$ [by CPCT]

Now, in ΔCPB, E is the mid-point of CP.   [$\because$ since, $CE = PE$]

and F is the mid-point of BC. $\quad\quad\quad\quad\quad$ [given]

So, by mid-point theorem

$EF \parallel PB$ and $EF = \dfrac{1}{2} PB$

$\Rightarrow \quad EF \parallel AB$ and $EF = \dfrac{1}{2}(PA + AB) = \dfrac{1}{2}(CD + AB)$

$\quad\quad\quad\quad\quad\quad\quad\quad$ [$\because PA = CD$]

Hence, $EF \parallel AB$ and $EF = \dfrac{1}{2}(AB + CD)$ **Hence proved.**

35. **Given** In ΔABC, $AD = \dfrac{1}{4} AB \quad$ and $\quad AE = \dfrac{1}{4} AC$

To prove $\quad DE = \dfrac{1}{4} BC$

Proof Let M and N be the mid-points of sides AB and AC, respectively.

By mid-point theorem,

$MN \parallel BC$

and $\quad MN = \dfrac{1}{2} BC \quad\quad\quad\quad\quad\quad$ ...(i)

We have, $\quad AM = \dfrac{1}{2} AB \quad\quad\quad\quad$ [$\because M$ is mid-point of AB]

$\Rightarrow \quad \dfrac{1}{2} AM = \dfrac{1}{4} AB \Rightarrow \dfrac{1}{2} AM = AD \quad\quad$ [$\because AD = \dfrac{1}{4} AB$]

So, D is mid-point of AM.

Similarly, $\quad AN = \dfrac{1}{2} AC \quad\quad\quad\quad$ [$\because N$ is mid-point of AC]

$\Rightarrow \dfrac{1}{2} AN = \dfrac{1}{4} AC \Rightarrow \dfrac{1}{2} AN = AE \quad\quad$ [$\because AE = \dfrac{1}{4} AC$]

So, E is mid-point of AN.

In ΔAMN, D and E are the mid-points of AM and AN, respectively.

By mid-point theorem,

$DE \parallel MN \quad$ and $\quad DE = \dfrac{1}{2} MN$

$\Rightarrow \quad\quad DE = \dfrac{1}{2}\left(\dfrac{1}{2} BC\right) \quad\quad$ [using Eq. (i)]

$\Rightarrow \quad\quad DE = \dfrac{1}{4} BC \quad\quad\quad\quad\quad$ **Hence proved.**

36. We draw the figure as shown below.

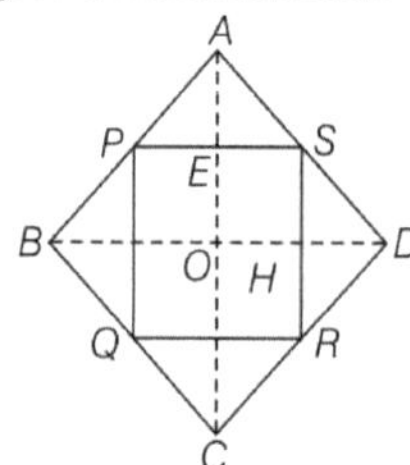

Let P, Q, R and S be the mid-points of the sides AB, BC, CD and DA respectively. Join AC and BD. Which intersects each other at O.

Now, in ΔABC, $PQ \parallel AC$ and $PQ = \dfrac{1}{2} AC \quad\quad\quad$ ...(i)

$\quad\quad\quad\quad\quad\quad\quad\quad$ [by mid-point theorem]

and in ΔACD, $RS \parallel AC$ and $RS = \dfrac{1}{2} AC \quad\quad\quad$ ...(ii)

$\quad\quad\quad\quad\quad\quad\quad\quad$ [by mid-point theorem]

From Eqs. (i) and (ii) we get,

$\quad\quad PQ \parallel RS$ and $PQ = RS$

$\quad\quad$ [$\because$ since, a pair of opposite sides equal and parallel]

So, $PQRS$ is a parallelogram

Also, $\quad\quad\quad AB = AD \quad\quad\quad\quad$ [given] ... (i)

So, A lies on the perpendicular bisector of BD further

$\quad\quad\quad\quad\quad\quad CB = CD \quad\quad\quad\quad$ [given] ...(ii)

So, C lies on the perpendicular bisector of BD. $\quad\quad$ ... (iii)

From Eqs. (ii) and (iii), AC is the perpendicular bisector of BD.

i.e. $AC \perp BD \Rightarrow \angle AOD = 90°$

Now, clearly $HS \parallel OE$ and $SE \parallel OH$

So, $SEOH$ is a parallelogram.

Hence, $\angle ESH = \angle EOH = 90°$

So, parallelogram $PQRS$ is a rectangle.   **Hence proved.**

37. Given In the given figure, $AD \perp m$ and $BE \perp m$.

Also, C is the mid-point of AB, i.e. $AC = BC$.

To prove $CD = CE$

Construction Draw $CM \perp m$ and join AE.

Proof We have, $AD \perp m, CM \perp m$ and $BE \perp m$.

$\therefore$ $\qquad\qquad AD \parallel CM \parallel BE$

In $\triangle ABE$, $\qquad CG \parallel BE$ $\qquad\qquad$ $[\because CM \parallel BE]$

and C is the mid-point of AB.

Thus, by converse of mid-point theorem, G is the mid-point of AE.

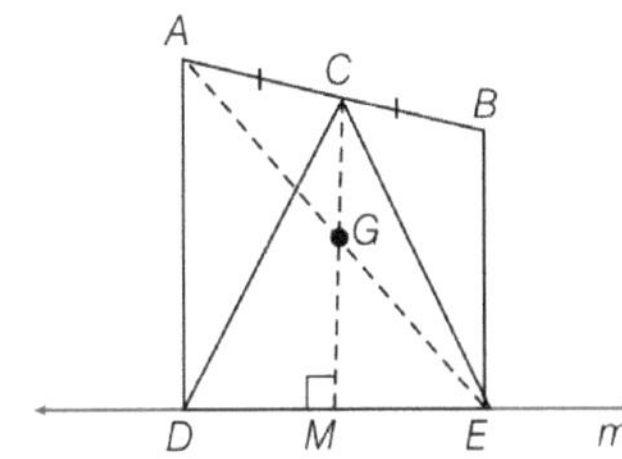

In $\triangle ADE$, G is the mid-point of AE and $GM \parallel AD$.

$\qquad\qquad\qquad\qquad\qquad\qquad\qquad$ $[\because CM \parallel AD]$

Thus, by converse of mid-point theorem, M is mid-point of DE.

In $\triangle CMD$ and $\triangle CME$,

$\qquad\qquad DM = EM$ $\quad [\because M$ is the mid-point of $DE]$

$\qquad\qquad CM = CM$ $\qquad\qquad$ [common side]

$\qquad\qquad \angle CMD = \angle CME = 90°$

$\therefore$ $\qquad\qquad \triangle CMD \cong \triangle CME$ $\quad$ [by SAS congruence rule]

So, $\qquad\qquad CD = CE$ $\qquad\qquad$ [by CPCT]

$\qquad\qquad\qquad\qquad\qquad\qquad\qquad$ **Hence proved.**

38. Given, $ABCD$ is a trapezium in which

$\qquad\qquad AB \parallel CD \quad$ and $\quad AD = BC$

Now, extend AB and draw a line through C parallel to DA intersecting AB produced at E.

$\therefore AD \parallel EC$

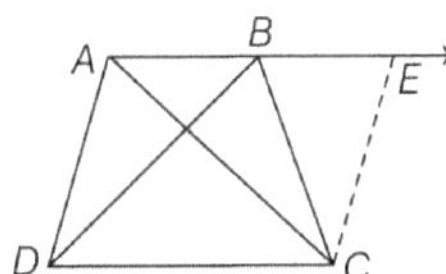

So, $ADCE$ is a parallelogram.

$\therefore$ $\quad AD = EC$ and $DC = AE$

But $\qquad\qquad AD = BC$ $\qquad\qquad$ [given]

$\therefore$ $\qquad\qquad AD = BC = EC$

$\quad$ (i) We know that, $\angle A + \angle E = 180°$

$\qquad\qquad\qquad\qquad$ $[\because$ since, interior angles on the same

$\qquad\qquad\qquad\qquad\qquad\qquad$ side of the transversal $AE]$

$\Rightarrow$ $\qquad\qquad \angle E = 180° - \angle A$

Also, $\quad BC = EC$

$\Rightarrow$ $\qquad\qquad \angle E = \angle CBE = 180° - \angle A$

But $\quad \angle ABC = 180° - \angle CBE$

$\qquad\qquad\qquad\qquad$ $[\because$ since, ABE is a straight line$]$

$\qquad\qquad = 180° - 180° + \angle A$

$\Rightarrow$ $\qquad\qquad \angle B = \angle A$ $\qquad\qquad$ ...(i)

(ii) Now, $\angle A + \angle D = 180°$

$\qquad\qquad\qquad$ $[\because$ since, interior angles on the same

$\qquad\qquad\qquad\qquad\qquad$ side of the transversal $AD]$

$\Rightarrow$ $\qquad\qquad \angle D = 180° - \angle A$

$\Rightarrow$ $\qquad\qquad \angle D = 180° - \angle B$ $\quad$ ...(ii) [from Eq. (i)]

Also, $\quad \angle C + \angle B = 180°$

$\qquad\qquad\qquad$ $[\because$ since, interior angles on the same

$\qquad\qquad\qquad\qquad\qquad$ side of the transversal $BC]$

$\Rightarrow$ $\qquad\qquad \angle C = 180° - \angle B$ $\qquad$ ...(iii)

From Eqs. (ii) and (iii), we get

$\qquad\qquad\qquad \angle C = \angle D$

(iii) Now, in $\triangle ABC$ and $\triangle BAD$, we have

$\qquad\qquad AB = BA$ $\qquad\qquad$ [common sides]

$\qquad\qquad AD = BC$ $\qquad\qquad$ [given]

$\qquad\qquad \angle A = \angle B$ $\qquad\qquad$ [from Eq. (i)]

$\therefore$ $\qquad \triangle ABC \cong \triangle BAD$ $\qquad$ [by SAS congruence rule]

(iv) Since, $\quad \triangle ABC \cong \triangle BAD$

$\therefore$ $\qquad\qquad AC = BD$ $\qquad$ [by CPCT] **Hence proved.**

39. Given P, Q, R and S are the mid-points of the sides AB, BC, CD and DA, respectively.

$\therefore$ $\quad AP = BP$, $\quad BQ = CQ$, $\quad CR = DR$

and $\quad AS = DS$

To show

$\quad$ (i) $SR \parallel AC$ and $SR = \dfrac{1}{2} AC$

$\quad$ (ii) $PQ = SR$

$\quad$ (iii) $PQRS$ is a parallelogram.

Proof

$\quad$ (i) In $\triangle ADC$, we have S is mid-point of AD and R is mid-point of DC.

$\qquad$ We know that, the line segment joining the mid-points of any two sides of a triangle is parallel to the third side and equal to half of it.

$\qquad \therefore$ $\qquad\qquad SR \parallel AC$ $\qquad\qquad$ ...(i)

$\qquad$ Also, $\qquad SR = \dfrac{1}{2} AC$ $\qquad\qquad$ ...(ii)

$\quad$ (ii) Similarly, in $\triangle ABC$, we have P is mid-point of AB and Q is the mid-point of BC.

$\qquad\qquad PQ \parallel AC$ $\qquad\qquad$ ...(iii)

$\qquad$ and $\qquad PQ = \dfrac{1}{2} AC$ $\qquad\qquad$ ...(iv)

$\qquad$ Now, from Eqs. (ii) and (iv), we get

$\qquad\qquad\qquad SR = PQ = \dfrac{1}{2} AC$ $\qquad\qquad$ ...(v)

$\quad$ (iii) From Eqs. (i) and (iii), we get

$\qquad PQ \parallel SR$ and from Eq. (v),

$\qquad\qquad\qquad PQ = SR$

$\qquad$ Since, a pair of opposite sides of a quadrilateral $PQRS$ is equal and parallel.

$\qquad$ So, $PQRS$ is a parallelogram. $\qquad$ **Hence proved.**

40. Given $ABCD$ is a rhombus and P, Q, R and S are the mid-points of the sides AB, BC, CD and DA, respectively.

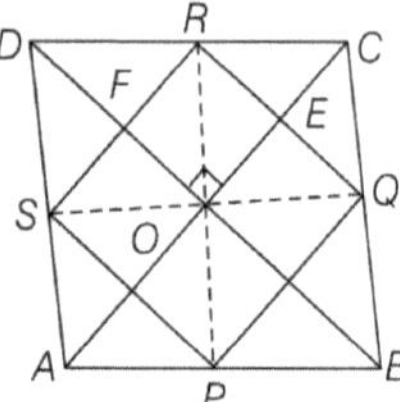

To show Quadrilateral $PQRS$ is a rectangle.

Proof By mid-point theorem.

In $\triangle ADC$, we have S and R are the mid-points of DA and CD, respectively.

$\therefore \qquad SR \parallel AC$ and $SR = \dfrac{1}{2} AC \qquad \qquad \ldots$(i)

In $\triangle ABC$, we have P and Q are the mid-points of AB and BC, respectively.

$\therefore \qquad \qquad PQ \parallel AC$

and $\qquad \qquad PQ = \dfrac{1}{2} AC \qquad \qquad \ldots$(ii)

From Eqs. (i) and (ii), we get

$\qquad \qquad PQ \parallel SR$

and $\qquad \qquad PQ = SR = \dfrac{1}{2} AC$

Since, a pair of opposite sides of a quadrilaterals $PQRS$ is equal and parallel.

So, $PQRS$ is a parallelogram.

We know that, diagonals of a rhombus bisect each other at right angles.

$\therefore \qquad \qquad \angle COD = \angle EOF = 90°$

Now, in $\triangle BCD$, R and Q are the mid-points of CD and BC, respectively.

$\qquad \qquad RQ \parallel DB \qquad$ [by mid-point theorem]

$\Rightarrow \qquad \qquad RE \parallel OF$

Also, $\qquad \qquad SR \parallel AC \qquad \qquad$ [from Eq. (i)]

$\Rightarrow \qquad \qquad FR \parallel OE$

So, $OERF$ is a parallelogram.

$\therefore \qquad \qquad \angle ERF = \angle EOF = 90°$

$\qquad \qquad$ [$\because$ opposite angles of a parallelogram are equal]

Thus, $PQRS$ is a parallelogram with $\angle R = 90°$.

Hence, $PQRS$ is a rectangle. **Hence proved.**

41. Given, $ABCD$ is a rectangle.

$\therefore \qquad \qquad \angle A = \angle B = \angle C = \angle D = 90°$

and $\qquad AD = BC,$

$\qquad \qquad AB = DC \qquad$ [$\because$ in a rectangle each angle is $90°$ and opposite sides are equal]

Also, given P, Q, R and S are mid-points of AB, BC, CD and DA, respectively.

In $\triangle ABD$, P and S are the mid-points of AB and DA, respectively.

$\therefore \qquad \qquad PS \parallel BD$ and $PS = \dfrac{1}{2} BD$

$\qquad \qquad$ [by mid-point theorem]$\ldots$(i)

and in $\triangle ACD$, R and S are the mid-points of DC and AD, respectively.

$\therefore \qquad \qquad SR \parallel AC$ and $SR = \dfrac{1}{2} AC$

$\qquad \qquad$ [by mid-point theorem]$\ldots$(ii)

In rectangle $ABCD$, $\quad AC = BD$

$\qquad \qquad$ [$\because$ since, diagonals of a rectangle are equal]

$\therefore \qquad \qquad PS = SR \quad$ [from Eqs. (i) and (ii)] $\ldots$(iii)

Now, in $\triangle ASP$ and $\triangle BQP$,

$\qquad \qquad AP = BP \qquad$ [$\because P$ is mid-point of AB]

$\qquad \qquad AS = BQ$

$\qquad \qquad$ [$\because AD = BC$ and S, Q are mid-points of AD and BC]

$\qquad \qquad \angle A = \angle B \qquad \qquad$ [each $90°$]

$\therefore \qquad \qquad \triangle ASP \cong \triangle BQP \qquad$ [by SAS congruence rule]

Then, $\qquad SP = PQ \qquad \qquad$ [by CPCT] $\ldots$(iv)

Similarly, in $\triangle RDS$ and $\triangle RCQ$, $SD = CQ$

$\qquad \qquad$ [$\because AD = BC$ and S, Q are mid-points of AD and BC]

$\qquad \qquad DR = RC \qquad \qquad$ [$\because R$ is mid-point of DC]

$\qquad \qquad \angle C = \angle D \qquad \qquad$ [each $90°$]

$\therefore \qquad \qquad \triangle RDS \cong \triangle RCQ \qquad$ [by SAS congruence rule]

Then, $\qquad SR = RQ \qquad \qquad$ [by CPCT] $\ldots$(v)

From Eqs. (iii), (iv) and (v), we get

$\qquad \qquad PS = SR = RQ = PQ$

Hence, quadrilateral $PQRS$ is a rhombus. **Hence proved.**

42. Given $ABCD$ is a parallelogram and E, F are the mid-points of sides AB and CD, respectively.

To prove Line segments AF and EC trisect the diagonal BD.

Proof Since, $ABCD$ is a parallelogram.

$\therefore \qquad AB \parallel DC$ and $AB = DC$

$\qquad \qquad$ [$\because$ opposite sides of a parallelogram]

$\Rightarrow \qquad AE \parallel FC$ and $\dfrac{1}{2} AB = \dfrac{1}{2} DC$

$\Rightarrow \qquad AE \parallel FC$ and $AE = FC$

$\qquad \qquad$ [$\because E$ and F are the mid-points of AB and CD]

Since, a pair of opposite sides of a quadrilaterals $AECF$ is equal and parallel.

So, $AECF$ is a parallelogram.

Then, $AF \parallel EC \quad \Rightarrow \quad AP \parallel EQ$ and $FP \parallel CQ$

$\qquad \qquad$ [$\because$ since, opposite sides of a parallelogram are parallel]

In $\triangle BAP$, E is the mid-point of AB and $EQ \parallel AP$, so Q is the mid-point of BP.

$\therefore \qquad BQ = PQ$ [by converse of mid-point theorem]$\ldots$(i)

Again, in $\triangle DQC$, F is the mid-point of DC and $FP \parallel CQ$.

So, P is the mid-point of DQ.

[by converse of mid-point theorem]

$\therefore \qquad QP = DP \qquad \qquad$ ...(ii)

From Eqs. (i) and (ii), we get

$$BQ = PQ = PD$$

Hence, CE and AF trisect the diagonal BD.   **Hence proved.**

43. Let $ABCD$ be a quadrilateral and P, Q, R and S be the mid-points of the sides AB, BC, CD and DA, respectively.

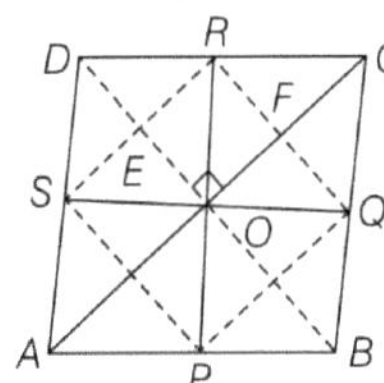

i.e. $AS = DS$, $AP = BP$, $BQ = CQ$ and $CR = DR$.

We have to show that PR and SQ bisect each other, i.e. $SO = OQ$ and $PO = OR$.

Now, in $\triangle ADC$, S and R are mid-points of AD and CD, respectively.

$\therefore \qquad SR \parallel AC \quad$ and $\quad SR = \dfrac{1}{2} AC \qquad$ ...(i)

[by mid-point theorem]

Similarly, in $\triangle ABC$, P and Q are mid-points of AB and BC, respectively.

$\therefore \qquad PQ \parallel AC \quad$ and $\quad PQ = \dfrac{1}{2} AC \qquad$ ...(ii)

[by mid-point theorem]

From Eqs. (i) and (ii), we get

$$PQ \parallel SR \quad \text{and} \quad PQ = SR = \dfrac{1}{2} AC$$

So, $PQRS$ is a parallelogram whose diagonals are SQ and PR. Also, we know that diagonals of parallelogram bisect each other. So, SQ and PR bisect each other at O, i.e. $SO = OQ$ and $PO = OR$.

[$\because$ since, a pair of opposite sides of a quadrilaterals $PQRS$ is equal and parallel]   **Hence proved.**

44. (i) In $\triangle ABC$, $BC \parallel MD$ and M is the mid-point of AB. So, D is mid-point of AC.

[by the converse of mid point theorem]

(ii) Given, $MD \parallel BC$ and CD is a transversal.

$\therefore \angle ADM = \angle ACB \qquad$ [$\because$ corresponding angles]

But, $\angle ACB = 90°$ [given]

$\therefore \quad \angle ADM = 90°$

$\Rightarrow \quad MD \perp AC$

(iii) In $\triangle ADM$ and $\triangle CDM$, we have

$DM = MD \qquad$ [$\because$ common side]

$AD = CD$

[$\because$ since, D is the mid-point of AC]

$\angle ADM = \angle MDC \qquad$ [$\because$ each equal to 90°]

$\therefore \quad \triangle ADM \cong \triangle CDM \qquad$ [by SAS congruence rule]

Then, $CM = AM \qquad \qquad$ [by CPCT] ...(i)

Also, given M is the mid-point of AB.

$\therefore \qquad AM = BM = \dfrac{1}{2} AB$

From Eqs. (i) and (ii), we get

$$CM = AM = \dfrac{1}{2} AB \qquad \textbf{Hence proved.}$$

45. Given, $ABCD$ is a parallelogram and P and Q are points on BD such that $\quad DP = BQ \qquad$ ...(i)

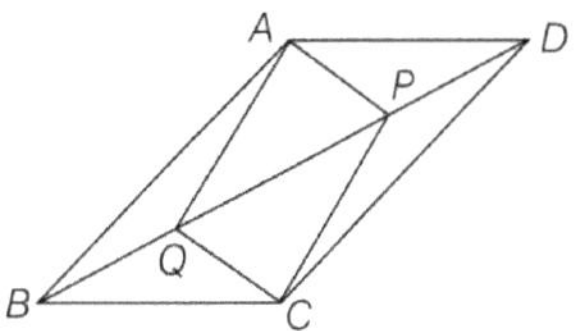

(i) We have to show,

$$\triangle APD \cong \triangle CQB$$

In $\triangle APD$ and $\triangle CQB$, we have

$DP = BQ \qquad \qquad$ [given]

$AD = BC$

[$\because$ opposite sides are equal in parallelogram]

$\angle ADP = \angle CBQ$

[$\because$ since, $AD \parallel BC$ and BD is a transversal, so alternate interior angles are equal]

$\therefore \quad \triangle APD \cong \triangle CQB \qquad$ [by SAS congruence rule]

(ii) Since, $\triangle APD \cong \triangle CQB$

$\Rightarrow \qquad AP = CQ \qquad \qquad$ [by CPCT]

(iii) We have to show,

$$\triangle AQB \cong \triangle CPD$$

Now, in $\triangle AQB$ and $\triangle CPD$, we have

$BQ = DP \qquad \qquad$ [given]

$AB = CD$

[$\because$ opposite sides of parallelogram]

$\angle ABQ = \angle CDP$

[$\because$ since, $AB \parallel CD$ and BD is a transversal, so alternate interior angles]

So, $\quad \triangle AQB \cong \triangle CPD \qquad$ [by SAS congruence rule]

(iv) Since, $\triangle AQB \cong \triangle CPD$

$\therefore \qquad AQ = CP \qquad \qquad$ [by CPCT]

(v) We have to show, $APCQ$ is a parallelogram.

Now, in $\triangle APQ$ and $\triangle CQP$, we have

$AQ = CP \qquad \qquad$ [from part (iv)]

$AP = CQ \qquad \qquad$ [from part (ii)]

$PQ = QP \qquad \qquad$ [common side]

$\therefore \qquad \triangle APQ \cong \triangle CQP \qquad$ [by SSS congruence rule]

Then, $\angle APQ = \angle CQP \qquad$ [by CPCT]

and $\qquad \angle AQP = \angle CPQ \qquad$ [by CPCT]

Now, these equal angles form a pair of alternate angles, when line segments AP and QC are intersected by a transversal PQ.

$\therefore$ $\quad\quad AP \parallel QC \quad$ and $\quad AQ \parallel PC$

Now, both pairs of opposite sides of quadrilateral $APCQ$ are parallel and equal.

Hence, $APCQ$ is a parallelogram. **Hence proved.**

46. Given, in ΔABC and ΔDEF,

$AB = DE,\ AB \parallel DE,$

$BC = EF$ and $BC \parallel EF$

(i) Now, in quadrilateral $ABED$,

$\quad AB = DE \quad$ and $\quad AB \parallel DE \quad\quad$ [given]

So, $ABED$ is a parallelogram.

$\quad$ [$\because$ since, a pair of opposite sides is equal and parallel]

(ii) In quadrilateral $BEFC$,

$\quad BC = EF \quad$ and $\quad BC \parallel EF \quad\quad$ [given]

So, $BEFC$ is a parallelogram.

$\quad$ [$\because$ since, a pair of opposite sides is equal and parallel]

(iii) Since, $ABED$ is a parallelogram.

$\therefore \quad\quad AD \parallel BE$

and $\quad AD = BE \quad\quad\quad\quad\quad\quad\quad$ ...(i)

Also, $BEFC$ is a parallelogram.

$\therefore \quad\quad CF \parallel BE$

and $\quad CF = BE \quad\quad\quad\quad\quad\quad\quad$ ...(ii)

From Eqs. (i) and (ii), we get

$\quad\quad\quad AD \parallel CF$

and $\quad\quad AD = CF$

(iv) In quadrilateral $ACFD$, we have

$\quad\quad\quad AD \parallel CF$

and $\quad\quad AD = CF \quad\quad\quad$ [from part (iii)]

So, $ACFD$ is a parallelogram.

$\quad$ [$\because$ since, a pair of opposite sides is equal and parallel]

(v) Since, $ACFD$ is a parallelogram.

$\therefore \quad\quad AC = DF$

and $\quad AC \parallel DF$

Chapter Test

Multiple Choice Questions

1. In parallelogram $ABCD$, $AB \parallel CD$, $AC \parallel BD$ and $\angle ACD = 80°$, find $x + y$

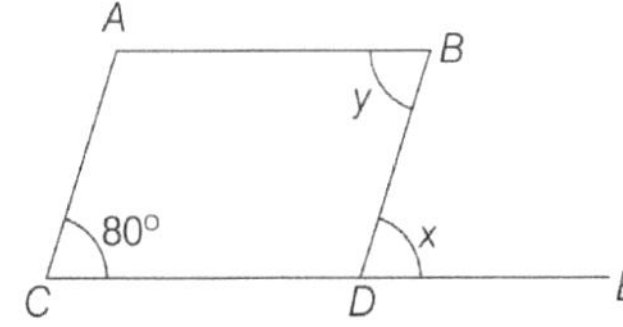

   (a) 180°   (b) 160°   (c) 170°   (d) 189°

2. In the given figure $PQRS$ is a rhombus $SO = 6$ cm and $PO = 8$ cm. Then, find the perimeter of the rhombus.

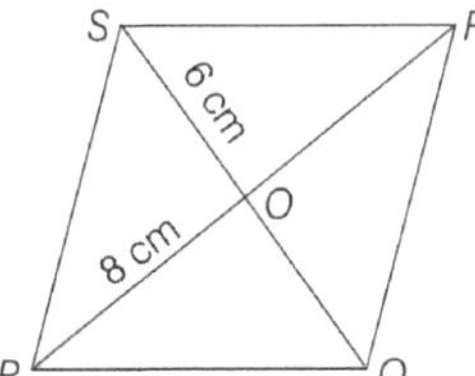

   (a) 32 cm   (b) 64 cm   (c) 40 cm   (d) 36 cm

3. D and E are the mid-points of sides AB and AC, respectively of $\triangle ABC$. If the perimeter of $\triangle ABC = 40$ cm. Find the perimeter of $\triangle ADE$.

   (a) 19   (b) 20   (c) 38   (d) 16

Case Based MCQs

4. The class teacher of IX class gave students coloured papers made by recycling of waste products in shape of quadrilateral. She asked them to make a prallelogram from its using paper folding.

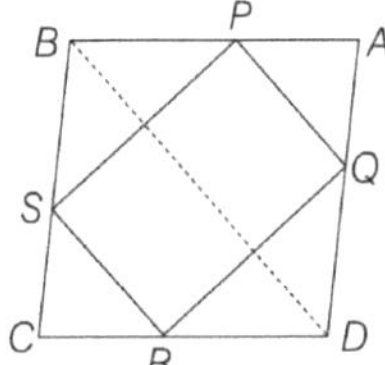

Then, teacher ask them some questions. To answer these questions, choose the correct option.

(i) How can a parallelogram be formed by using paper folding?
  (a) Joining the sides of quadrilateral
  (b) Joining the mid-points of sides of quadrilateral
  (c) Joining the vertices of quadrilateral
  (d) None of the above

(ii) Which of the following is correct condition?
  (a) $PQ = BD$ (b) $PQ = \dfrac{1}{2} BD$

  (c) $3PQ = BD$ (d) $PQ = 2BD$

(iii) Which of the following is correct condition?
  (a) $2RS = BD$

  (b) $RS = \dfrac{BD}{3}$

  (c) $RS = BD$

  (d) $RS = 2BD$

(iv) Which of the following is correct condition?
  (a) $PQ = \dfrac{SR}{2}$

  (b) $PQ = SR$

  (c) $PQ = \dfrac{SR}{3}$

  (d) $4PQ = SR$

(v) Write the formula to find the perimeter of parallelogram $PQRS$.
  (a) $PQ + QR + RS + PS$
  (b) $PQ - QR - RS + PS$
  (c) $\dfrac{PQ + QR + RS + PS}{2}$
  (d) $\dfrac{PQ + QR + RS + PS}{3}$

Short Answer Type Questions

5. A diagonal of a rectangle is inclined to the one side of the rectangle at 25°. Find the acute angle between the diagonals. **[NCERT Exemplar]**

6. In $\triangle ABC$, D, E and F are the mid-points of the sides AB, BC and AC, respectively. Then, prove that quadrilateral $DECF$ is a parallelogram.

Long Answer Type Questions

7. $ABCD$ is a parallelogram in which P and Q are mid-points of opposite sides AB and DC (given in figure). If AQ intersects DP at S and BQ intersects CP at R, show that

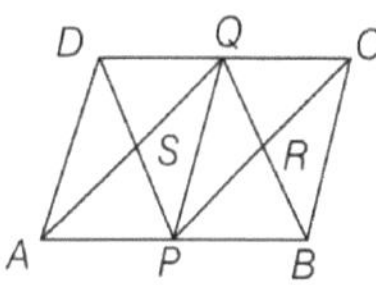

(i) $APCQ$ is a parallelogram.
(ii) $DPBQ$ is a parallelogram.
(iii) $PSQR$ is a parallelogram.

Answers

1. (b)   **2.** (c)   **3.** (b)   **4.** (i) (b) (ii) (b) (iii) (a) (iv) (b) (v) (a)

5. 50°

For Detailed Solutions

Scan the code

CHAPTER 03

Circles

In this Chapter...

- Terms Related to Circle and Angle Subtended by a Chord at a point
- Perpendicular from Centre to the Chord and Circle Passing Through Three points
- Distance of Equal Chords from the Centre
- Angle Subtended by an Arc of a Circle and Cyclic Quadrilaterals

The collection of all the points in a plane, which are at a fixed distance from a fixed point in the plane, is called a **circle**. The fixed point is called the **centre** of the circle and the fixed distance is called the **radius** of the circle or in other words, the line segment joining the centre and any point on the circle is called radius of circle. In the following figure, O is the centre and the length OP is the radius of the circle.

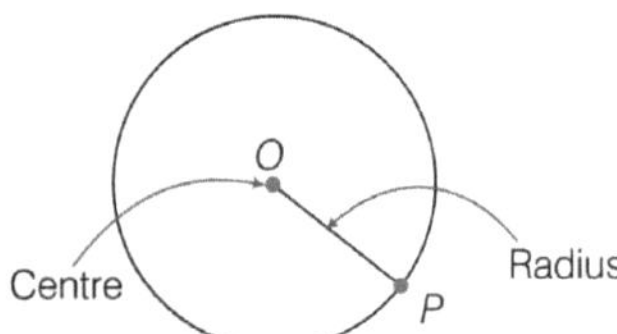

Terms Related to Circle

Chord

A line segment joining two points on the circumference of the circle is called a chord of the circle. In figure, PQ is a chord of the circle.

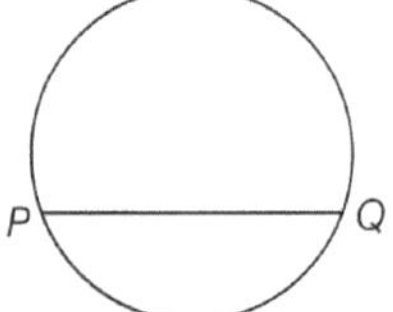

Diameter

A chord which passes through the centre of the circle is called a diameter of the circle. In figure, AB is the diameter of the circle. Diameter is the longest chord and all diameters have same length, which is equal to two times of the radius.

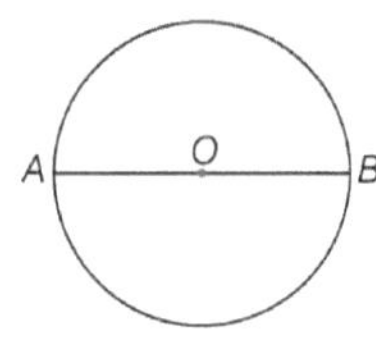

Circumference

The length of the complete circle is called its circumference.

Arc

A piece of a circle between two points on its circumference is called an arc. In other words, any part of the circumference of a circle is called an arc of that circle.

In adjoining figure, there are two pieces, one longer and the other smaller. The longer one is called the **major arc** PRQ and the smaller one is called the **minor arc** PQ. The minor arc PQ is denoted by PQ and the major arc PRQ is denoted by PRQ, where R is a point on the major arc between P and Q.

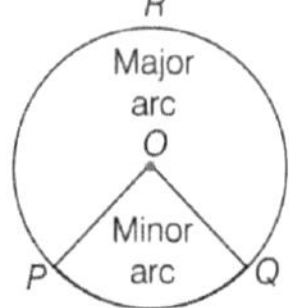

Semi-circle

A diameter of a circle divides the circle into two equal parts, i.e. into two equal arcs. Each of these two arcs is called a semi-circle.

Segment

The region between a chord and either of its arcs is called a segment of the circular region or simply a segment of the circle. This chord is called the base of the segment. The segment formed by minor arc along with chord, is called **minor segment** and the segment formed by major arc is called the **major segment**.

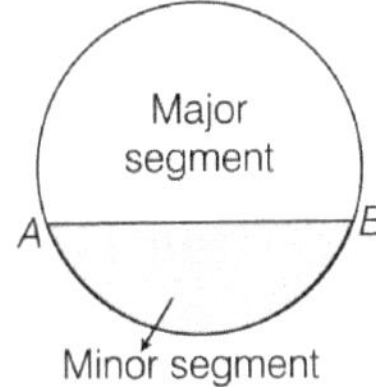

Sector

The region between an arc and the two radii joining the centre to the end points of the arc is called a sector.

Sectors are of two types – **minor sector** and **major sector**. The sector corresponding to minor arc is called minor sector and the sector corresponding to major arc is called major sector.

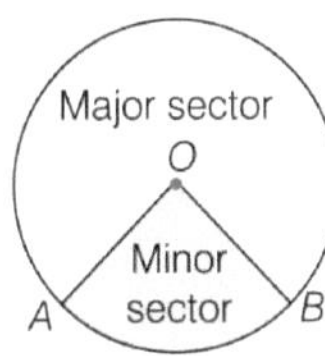

Semi-circular Region

When two arcs are semi-circles, then both segments and both sectors become same and each is known as a semi-circular region.

Angle Subtended by a Chord at a Point

We know that, if we take a line segment PQ and a point R not lying on the line PQ, then by joining PR and RQ, we get $\angle PRQ$, which is called the angle subtended by the line segment PQ. Similarly, in a circle with centre O, let AB be a chord and we take two points P and Q on the circle as shown in figure and join PA, PB, QA and QB. Then, we get $\angle APB$ and $\angle AQB$, which are called the angles subtended by the chord AB at the points P and Q, respectively. Also, $\angle AOB$ is the angle subtended by the chord AB at the centre O.

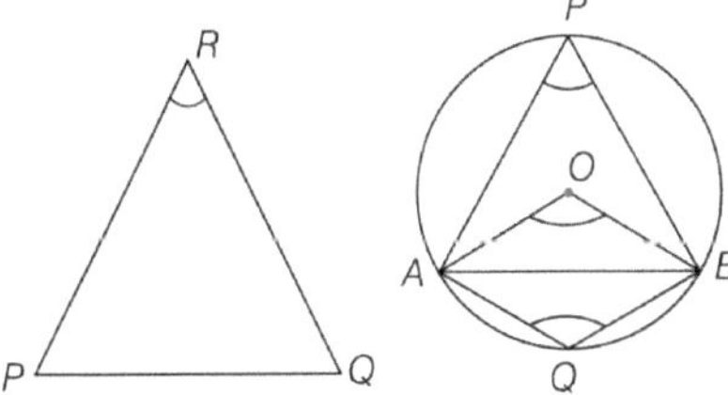

Theorem 1

Equal chords of a circle subtend equal angles at the centre.

Given A circle with centre O. AB and CD are two equal chords of the circle which subtend $\angle AOB$ and $\angle COD$ at the centre O.

To prove $\angle AOB = \angle COD$

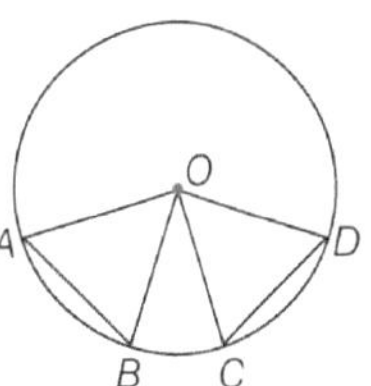

Proof In $\triangle AOB$ and $\triangle COD$,

$$OA = OC \qquad \text{[radii of same circle]}$$
$$OB = OD \qquad \text{[radii of same circle]}$$
$$AB = CD \qquad \text{[given]}$$
$$\therefore \quad \triangle AOB \cong \triangle COD \qquad \text{[by SSS congruence rule]}$$

Then, $\angle AOB = \angle COD$ [by CPCT] **Hence proved**.

Theorem 2 (Converse of Theorem 1)

If the angles subtended by the chords of a circle at the centre are equal, then the chords are equal.

Given A circle with centre O. Let AB and CD be two chords of a circle such that angles subtended by these chords at the centre O of a circle are equal i.e.

$$\angle AOB = \angle COD$$

To Prove $\qquad AB = CD$

Proof In $\triangle AOB$ and $\triangle COD$, we have

$$AO = CO \qquad \text{[radii of same circle]}$$
$$\angle AOB = \angle COD \qquad \text{[given]}$$
and $\qquad OB = OD \qquad \text{[radii of same circle]}$
$$\therefore \quad \triangle AOB \cong \triangle COD \qquad \text{[by SAS congruence rule]}$$
So, $\qquad AB = CD \qquad \text{[by CPCT]}$

Hence, chords are equal if they subtend equal angles at the centre of a circle.

Perpendicular from Centre to the Chord

In a circle, the property of a perpendicular drawn from the centre to a chord in the form of a theorem is given below

Theorem 3

The perpendicular from the centre of a circle to a chord bisects the chord.

Given AB is a chord of a circle with centre O and $OM \perp AB$.

To prove OM bisects AB,

i.e. $\qquad AM = MB$.

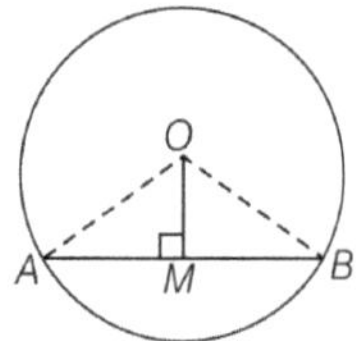

Construction Join OA and OB.

Proof In $\triangle AMO$ and $\triangle BMO$, we have

$$OA = OB \qquad \text{[radii of same circle]}$$
$$\angle AMO = \angle BMO \qquad \text{[each } 90°\text{]}$$
$$\text{and} \qquad OM = OM \qquad \text{[common sides]}$$
$$\therefore \qquad \triangle AMO \cong \triangle BMO \qquad \text{[by RHS congruence rule]}$$
$$\text{Then,} \qquad AM = MB \qquad \text{[by CPCT] } \textbf{Hence proved.}$$

Theorem 4 (Converse of theorem 1)

The line drawn through the centre of a circle to bisect a chord is perpendicular to the chord.

Given AB is a chord of a circle with centre O. A line OM is drawn through the centre O to chord AB such that M is the mid-point of AB, i.e. $AM = MB$.

To prove $OM \perp AB$.

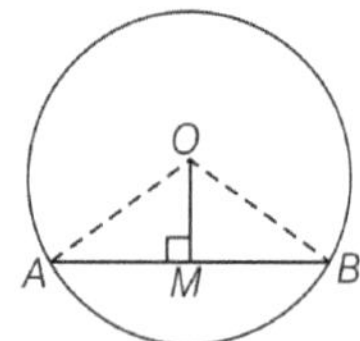

Construction Join OA and OB.

Proof In $\triangle OAM$ and $\triangle OBM$, we have

$$AM = MB \qquad [\because M \text{ is the mid-point of } AB]$$
$$OA = OB \qquad \text{[radii of same circle]}$$
$$OM = OM \qquad \text{[common sides]}$$
$$\therefore \qquad \triangle OAM \cong \triangle OBM \qquad \text{[by SSS congruence rule]}$$
$$\text{Then,} \qquad \angle OMA = \angle OMB \qquad \text{[by CPCT] ...(i)}$$

Now, AB is a straight line. So, by linear pair axiom,

$$\angle OMA + \angle OMB = 180°$$
$$\Rightarrow \qquad 2\angle OMA = 180° \qquad \text{[using Eq. (i)]}$$
$$\Rightarrow \qquad \angle OMA = \frac{180°}{2} = 90°$$

Thus, $\angle OMA = \angle OMB = 90°$

Then, $OM \perp AB$ **Hence proved.**

Distance of a Line from a Point

The length of the perpendicular from a point to a line is the distance of the line from the point.

Let AB be a line and P be a point. Since, a line has infinite number of points. So, by joining these points to P, we get infinite line segments as PL_1, PL_2, PM, PL_3, PL_4, etc. Out of these line segments, the perpendicular from P to AB say PM will be the least. This least length PM will be the distance of AB from point P.

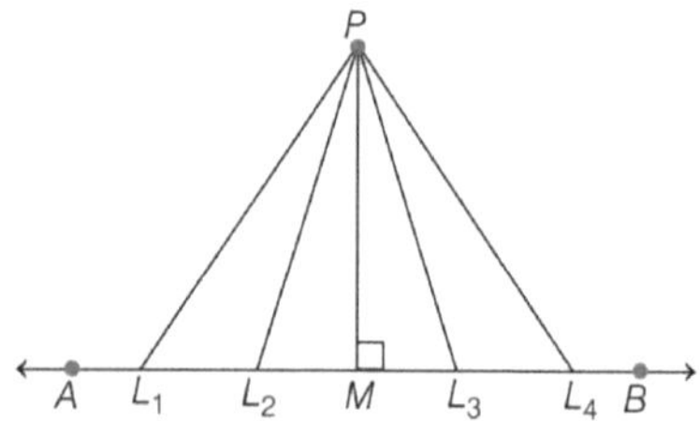

If the point lies on the line, then the distance of the line from the point is zero.

Equal Chords and Their Distances from the Centre

The longest chord of a circle is the diameter whose distance from the centre is zero because centre lies on it.

Theorem 5

Equal chords of a circle (or congruent circles) are equidistant from the centre (or centres).

Given A circle with centre O and two equal chords; AB and PQ.

To prove AB and PQ are equidistant from the centre O.

Construction Draw $OM \perp AB$ and $ON \perp PQ$. Join OA, OB, OP and OQ.

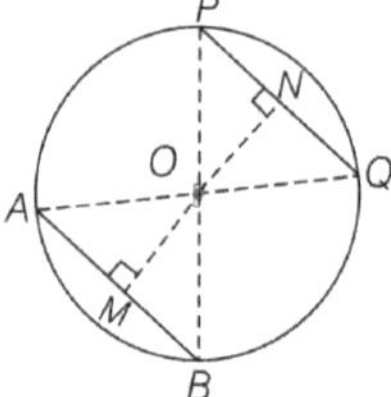

Proof We know that, a perpendicular from the centre to a chord bisects the chord.

$$\therefore \qquad AM = MB = \frac{1}{2} AB \qquad [\because OM \perp AB]$$
$$\text{and} \qquad PN = NQ = \frac{1}{2} PQ \qquad [\because ON \perp PQ]$$
$$\because \qquad \text{Chord } AB = \text{Chord } PQ \qquad \text{[given]}$$
$$\Rightarrow \qquad \frac{1}{2} AB = \frac{1}{2} PQ$$

Then, $AM = MB = PN = NQ$

Now, in $\triangle OMA$ and $\triangle ONQ$,

$$OA = OQ \qquad \text{[radii of same circle]}$$
$$AM = NQ \qquad \text{[proved above]}$$
$$\angle OMA = \angle ONQ \qquad \text{[each } 90°\text{]}$$
$$\therefore \qquad \triangle OMA \cong \triangle ONQ \qquad \text{[by RHS congruence rule]}$$
$$\text{Then,} \qquad OM = ON \qquad \text{[by CPCT]}$$

Hence, PQ and AB are equidistant from the centre O.

     Hence proved.

Congruent Arcs of a Circle

Two arcs of a circle or two arcs of congruent circles are congruent, if either of them can be superposed on the other completely.

Congruent Arcs Corresponding to Congruent Chords of a Circle

If two chords of a circle are equal, then their corresponding arcs are congruent and conversely, if two arcs are congruent, then their corresponding chords are equal.

Angle Subtended by an Arc of a Circle

We know that, a chord (other than diameter) of a circle cuts the circle into two different arcs – major arc and minor arc.

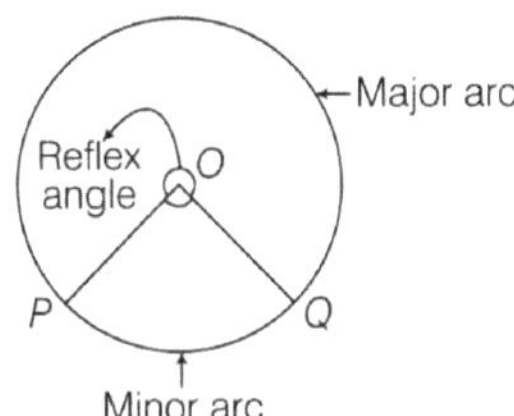

The angle subtended by an arc at the centre is defined as the angle subtended by the corresponding chord at the centre, in the sense that the minor arc subtends the angle and the major arc subtends the reflex angle.

In the given figure, the angle subtended by the minor arc PQ at O is $\angle POQ$ and the angle subtended by the major arc PQ at O is reflex $\angle POQ$.

Relation between the Angles Subtended by an Arc at the Centre and at a Point on the Circle

Let we have a circle with centre O and AB be its arc. Here, $\angle AOB$ is the angle subtended by an arc AB, (or $\overarc{AB}$) at the centre of the circle.

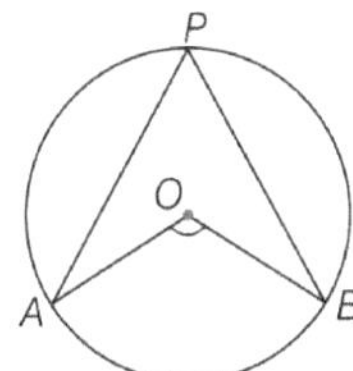

Also, $\angle APB$ is the angle subtended by arc $AB\,(\overarc{AB})$ at a point P on the remaining part of the circle (i.e. part of the circle, other than $\overarc{AB}$).

Now, there is a relation between the angles subtended by an arc at the centre and at a point on the circle which is given in the form of theorem.

Theorem 6

The angle subtended by an arc at the centre is double the angle subtended by it at any point on the remaining part of the circle.

Given A circle with centre O and let PQ be its arc. Arc PQ subtends $\angle POQ$ at the centre and $\angle PAQ$ at any point A on the remaining part of the circle.

Here, from figure, we get three cases (i) when arc PQ is minor (ii) when arc PQ is semi-circle and (iii) when arc PQ is major.

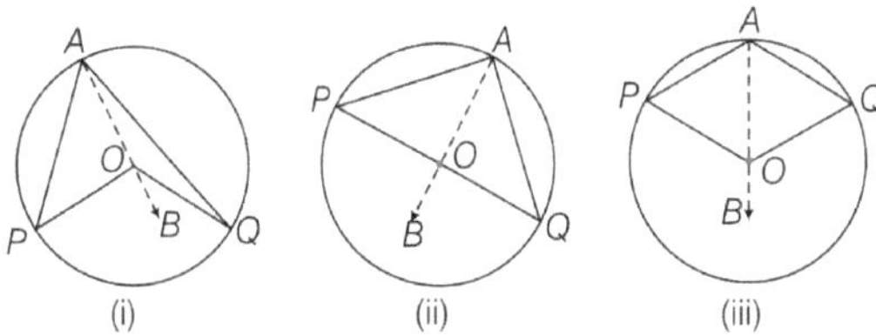

To prove $\angle POQ = 2\,\angle PAQ$ for cases (i) and (ii) and reflex $\angle POQ = 2\,\angle PAQ$ for case (iii).

Construction Join AO and extend it to a point B.

Proof We know that, exterior angle of a triangle is equal to the sum of the two interior opposite angles.

So, for $\triangle OAQ$, $\angle BOQ = \angle OAQ + \angle OQA$ ...(i)

and for $\triangle OAP$, $\angle BOP = \angle OAP + \angle OPA$ ...(ii)

Now, in $\triangle OAQ$, $\qquad OA = OQ$ [radii of same circle]

$\Rightarrow \qquad\qquad \angle OQA = \angle OAQ$

[∵ angles opposite to equal sides of a triangle are also equal]

Then, from Eq. (i), we get

$$\angle BOQ = \angle OAQ + \angle OAQ$$

$\Rightarrow \qquad\qquad \angle BOQ = 2\angle OAQ$ ...(iii)

Similarly, in $\triangle OAP$, $\angle OAP = \angle OPA$

Then, from Eq. (ii), we get

$$\angle BOP = 2\angle OAP$$ ...(iv)

On adding Eqs. (iii) and (iv), we get

$$\angle BOQ + \angle BOP = 2\angle OAQ + 2\angle OAP$$

$\Rightarrow \qquad\qquad \angle POQ = 2\,[\angle OAQ + \angle OAP]$

$\Rightarrow \qquad\qquad \angle POQ = 2\,\angle PAQ$ ...(v)

For cases (i) and (ii), we have this result and for case (iii), replace $\angle POQ$ by reflex $\angle PAQ$ in Eq. (v) we get reflex $\angle POQ = 2\angle PAQ$, as PQ is the major arc. **Hence proved.**

Note $\angle ADC = 2$ Reflex $\angle ABC$

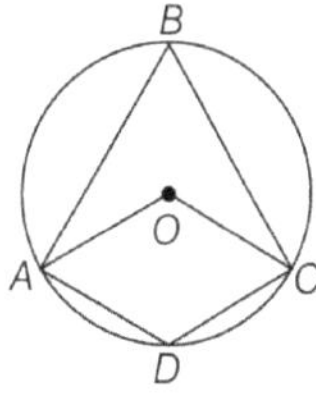

Theorem 7

Angles in the same segment of a circle are equal.

Given PQ is a chord of a circle with centre O which divides the circle in two segments and $\angle PAQ$ and $\angle PCQ$ are the angles of the same segment.

To prove $\qquad\qquad \angle PAQ = \angle PCQ$

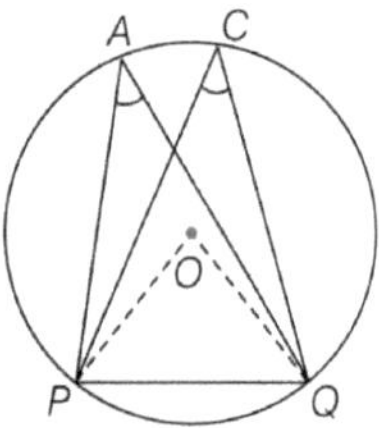

Construction Join OP and OQ.

Proof Here, minor arc PQ subtends $\angle POQ$ at the centre and $\angle PAQ$ at a point A on the remaining part of the circle.

Then, $\qquad \angle POQ = 2\angle PAQ$ $\qquad$ [by theorem 1] ...(i)

Similarly, $\quad \angle POQ = 2\angle PCQ$ $\qquad\qquad$ ...(ii)

From Eqs. (i) and (ii), we get

$$2\angle PAQ = 2\angle PCQ$$

$\Rightarrow \qquad\qquad \angle PAQ = \angle PCQ$ $\qquad$ **Hence proved.**

Theorem 8

Angle in a semi-circle is a right angle.

Given PQ is a diameter of a circle $C(O, r)$ and $\angle PRQ$ be an angle in semi-circle.

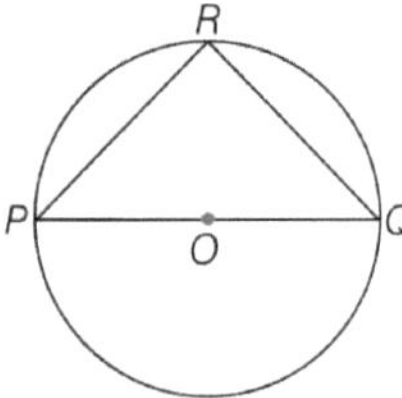

To prove $\angle PRQ = 90°$

Proof We know that, the angle subtended by an arc of a circle at its centre is twice the angle formed by the same arc at a point on the remaining part of circle.

So, $\qquad\qquad \angle POQ = 2\angle PRQ$

$\Rightarrow \qquad\qquad 180° = 2\angle PRQ$ $\qquad$ [$\because POQ$ is a straight line]

$\Rightarrow \qquad\qquad \angle PRQ = 90°$ $\quad$ [dividing by 2] $\quad$ **Hence proved.**

Cyclic Quadrilaterals

A quadrilateral $ABCD$ is called a cyclic quadrilateral, if all the four vertices A, B, C and D are concyclic, i.e. A, B, C and D lie on a circle. In figure, $ABCD$ is a cyclic quadrilateral.

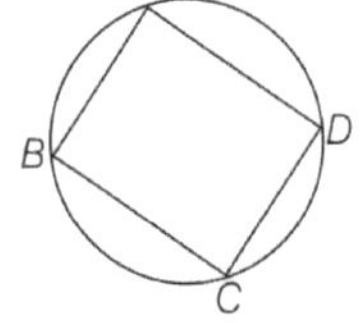

The relation between opposite angles of a cyclic quadrilateral in the form of theorem is given below.

Theorem 9

The sum of either pair of opposite angles of a cyclic quadrilateral is 180°.

Given A cyclic quadrilateral $ABCD$ inscribed in a circle with centre O.

To prove $\angle A + \angle C = \angle B + \angle D = 180°$

Construction Join OB and OD.

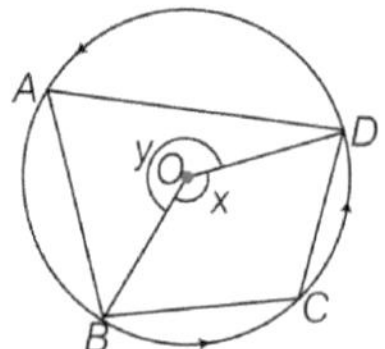

Proof Here, arc BCD subtends $\angle BOD$ at the centre and $\angle BAD$ at a point on the remaining part of circle.

Let $\qquad\qquad \angle BOD = x$

Then, $\qquad\qquad \angle A = \angle BAD = \dfrac{1}{2}x$ $\qquad$ [by theorem 1] ...(i)

Similarly, $\qquad \angle C = \angle BCD = \dfrac{1}{2}y$ $\qquad$ [by theorem 1]

$\qquad\qquad\qquad\qquad$ [say reflex $\angle BOD = y$] ...(ii)

On adding Eqs. (i) and (ii), we get

$$\angle A + \angle C = \dfrac{1}{2}x + \dfrac{1}{2}y = \dfrac{1}{2}(x+y) = \dfrac{1}{2} \times 360° = 180°$$

and $\qquad \angle B + \angle D = 360° - (\angle A + \angle C)$

$\qquad\qquad$ [$\because$ sum of angles of a quadrilateral is $360°$]

$$= 360° - 180° = 180°$$

Hence, $\angle A + \angle C = \angle B + \angle D = 180°$ $\qquad$ **Hence proved.**

Theorem 10

If the sum of a pair of opposite angles of a quadrilateral is 180°, then quadrilateral is cyclic.

Given A quadrilateral $ABCD$ in which
$$\angle A + \angle C = 180° \quad \text{or} \quad \angle B + \angle D = 180°$$

To prove $ABCD$ is a cyclic quadrilateral.

Construction Draw a circle through the points A, B and C.

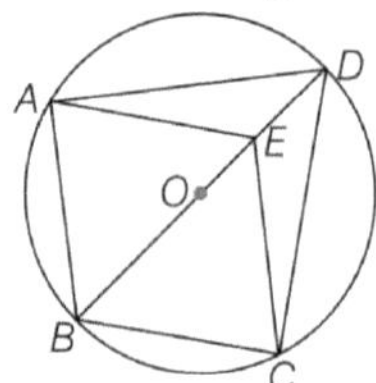

Proof Suppose, circle does not pass through the point D, then it will intersect BD at point E (or extended BD at E).

Join EC. Then, $ABCE$ is a cyclic quadrilateral.

$\therefore \qquad \angle B + \angle E = 180°$ $\qquad\qquad$ ...(i)

Also, $\quad \angle B + \angle D = 180°$ $\qquad$ [given] ...(ii)

From Eqs. (i) and (ii), we get

$$\angle B + \angle E = \angle B + \angle D$$

$\Rightarrow \qquad\qquad \angle E = \angle D$

But this is not possible unless E coincides with D.

Thus, our assumption that the point D does not lie on the circle, was wrong. So, point D lies on the circle.

Hence, $ABCD$ is a cyclic quadrilateral. $\qquad$ **Hence proved.**

Solved Examples

Example 1. In the given figure, $\angle OAB = 30°$ and $\angle OCB = 57°$. Find $\angle BOC$ and $\angle AOC$.

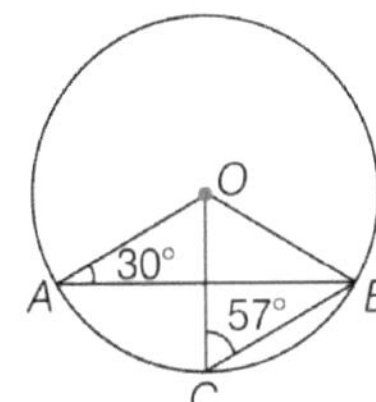

Sol. Here, $OA = OB$ [radii of same circle]

$\Rightarrow \qquad \angle OBA = \angle OAB = 30°$ ...(i)

Similarly, $\qquad \angle OCB = \angle OBC = 57°$ ...(ii)

Now, in ΔBOC, $\angle BOC + \angle OCB + \angle OBC = 180°$

$\Rightarrow \qquad \angle BOC + 57° + 57° = 180°$ [from Eq. (ii)]

$\Rightarrow \qquad \angle BOC = 180° - 114° = 66°$

In ΔAOB, $\angle AOB + \angle OAB + \angle OBA = 180°$

$\Rightarrow \qquad \angle AOB + 30° + 30° = 180°$

$\Rightarrow \qquad \angle AOB = 120°$

Now, $\angle AOC = \angle AOB - \angle BOC = 120° - 66° = 54°$

Example 2. AB is a chord of a circle having centre O. If $\angle AOB = 60°$, then prove that the chord AB is of radius length.

Sol. Let O be the centre and r be the radius of the circle.

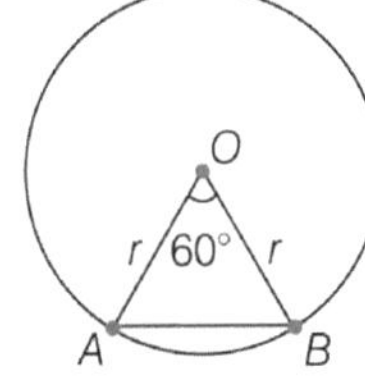

Chord AB subtends $\angle AOB = 60°$ at the centre of the circle.

Here, $\qquad OB = OA = r$ [radii of same circle]

$\Rightarrow \qquad \angle OAB = \angle OBA$

i.e. $\qquad \angle A = \angle B$ ...(i)

[$\because$ angles opposite to equal sides of a triangle are also equal]

In ΔOAB, $\angle O + \angle A + \angle B = 180°$ [angle sum property]

$\Rightarrow \qquad 60° + \angle A + \angle B = 180°$

$\Rightarrow \qquad \angle A + \angle B = 120°$ ...(ii)

From Eqs. (i) and (ii), we get

$\qquad\qquad 2\angle A = 120°$

$\Rightarrow \qquad \angle A = \dfrac{1}{2} \times 120° = 60°$

and $\qquad \angle B = 60°$

Thus, $\qquad \angle O = \angle A = \angle B = 60°$

Hence, ΔOAB is an equilateral triangle.

$\therefore \qquad AB = OA = OB = r,$

i.e. $\qquad AB = r$ **Hence proved.**

Example 3. If A, B and C are three points on a circle such that $AB = BC = CA$ and O is the centre of the circle, then find the angle subtended by the chords AB, BC and CA at the centre O.

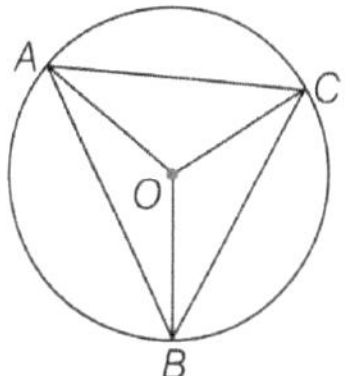

Sol. Given, three points A, B and C are on a circle such that, $AB = BC = CA$.

We know that, equal chords of a circle subtend equal angles at the centre of circle.

So, $\qquad \angle AOB = \angle BOC = \angle AOC$ ...(i)

Now, $\angle AOB + \angle BOC + \angle AOC = 360°$

         [$\because$ sum of angles at a point is 360°]

$\Rightarrow \qquad 3 \angle AOB = 360°$ [from Eq. (i)]

$\Rightarrow \qquad \angle AOB = \dfrac{360°}{3} = 120°$

Hence, angle subtended by the chords AB, BC and CA at the centre O is 120°.

Example 4. In the given figure, $AB = AC = CD$. Calculate $\angle ABC$ and $\angle BEC$.

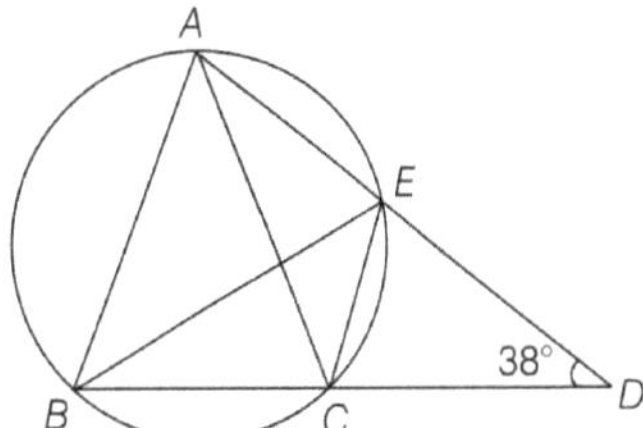

Sol. Given that, $AB = AC = CD$ and $\angle ADC = 38°$

Now, $\qquad\qquad AC = CD$

Since, equal sides have equal angles.

$\therefore \qquad \angle CAD = \angle ADC = 38°$

Let us consider ΔACD,

$\qquad \angle ACD + \angle CAD + \angle ADC = 180°$

         [$\because$ sum of all angles of a triangle is 180°]

$\Rightarrow \angle ACD + 38° + 38° = 180°$

$\Rightarrow \qquad \angle ACD = 104°$ ...(i)

Let us consider the straight line BCD,

$$\angle ACB + \angle ACD = 180° \qquad \text{[linear pair]}$$
$$\Rightarrow \quad \angle ACB + 104° = 180° \qquad \text{[from Eq. (i)]}$$
$$\Rightarrow \qquad \angle ACB = 76°$$

Now, $\qquad\qquad AB = AC$

Since, equal sides have equal angles.

$$\therefore \qquad \angle ABC = \angle ACB = 76° \qquad \ldots(ii)$$

Let us consider ΔABC,

As, sum of all angles of a triangle is $180°$.

$$\therefore \quad \angle BAC + \angle ABC + \angle ACB = 180°$$
$$\Rightarrow \qquad \angle BAC + 76° + 76° = 180° \qquad \text{[from Eq. (ii)]}$$
$$\Rightarrow \qquad \angle BAC = 180° - 152° = 28°$$

Since, angles subtended by the same chord are equal to each other.

$$\therefore \qquad \angle BEC = \angle BAC = 28°$$

Example 5. If O is the centre of a circle and points A, B, C, D, E, F, G and H are on the circle such that

$$AB = BC = CD = DE = EF = FG = GH = HA.$$
Find $\angle AOB, \angle AOC, \angle DOF$ and $\angle EOH$.

Sol. We know that, the equal chords subtends equal angles

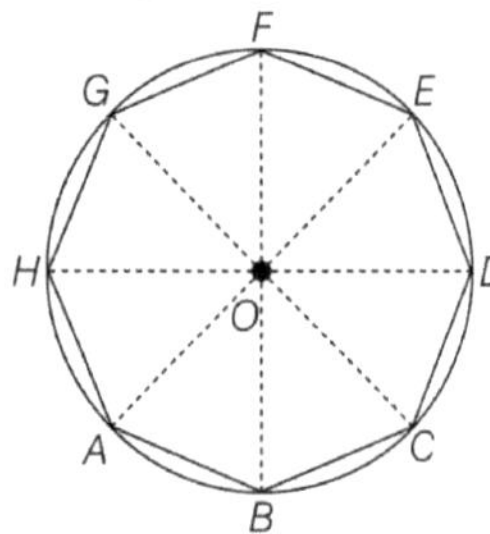

Given, $\qquad AB = BC = CD = DE = EF = FG = GH = HA$

$$\Rightarrow \qquad \angle AOB = \angle BOC = \angle COD = \angle DOE = \angle EOF$$
$$\Rightarrow \qquad \angle FOG = \angle GOH = \angle HOA$$
$$\therefore \quad 8 \times \angle AOB = 360° \Rightarrow \angle AOB = 45°$$

Now, $\angle AOC = \angle AOB + \angle BOC = 45° + 45° = 90°$

Similarly, $\angle DOF = 90°$ and $\angle EOH = 135°$

Example 6. Given, an arc say PQ of a circle. Then, complete the circle.

Sol. Given, an arc PQ of a circle and we have to complete the circle, i.e. we have to find its centre and radius.

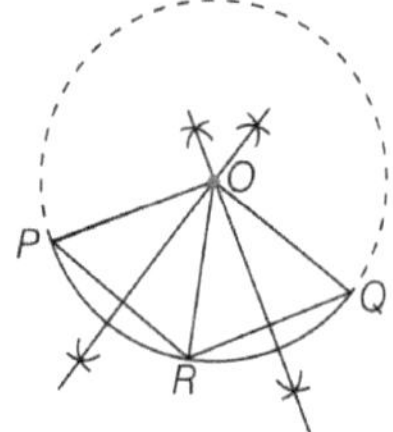

Now, take a point R on the arc PQ. Join PR and RQ and then draw perpendicular bisectors of PR and RQ which intersect at point O.

This point O is the required centre of circle and radius of circle is $PO = RO = OQ$. Now, take O as centre and PO as radius and then complete the circle.

Example 7. If the length of a chord of a circle is 16 cm and is at a distance of 15 cm from the centre of the circle, then find the radius of the circle.

Sol. It is given that $AB = 16$ cm, length of the chord is 15 cm from the centre O. To find the radius of the circle. Draw a perpendicular OP to the chord AB such that $OP = 15$ cm

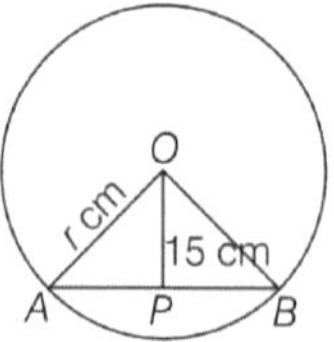

We know that, the perpendicular drawn from the centre bisects the chord.

$$\therefore \qquad\qquad AB = 2AP = 2BP$$
$$\Rightarrow \qquad\qquad AP = \frac{1}{2} AB$$

Since, $\qquad\qquad AB = 16$ cm $\qquad$ (given)

$$\Rightarrow \qquad\qquad AP = \frac{1}{2} \times 16 = 8 \text{ cm}$$

Join OA and OB.

OA and OB are the radius of the circle as it joins centre and any point in the circumference.

In right-angled triangle ΔOPA, by applying pythagoras theorem, we get

$$AP^2 + OP^2 = AO^2$$
$$\Rightarrow \qquad 8^2 + 15^2 = AO^2 \Rightarrow AO^2 = 64 + 225$$
$$\Rightarrow \qquad AO^2 = 289 \Rightarrow AO = 17 \text{ cm}$$

Thus, the radius of the circle is 17 cm.

Example 8. The circumcentre of the ΔABC is O. Prove that $\angle OBC + \angle BAC = 90°$.   **[NCERT Exemplar]**

Sol. Let $\angle OBC = \angle OCB = \theta$

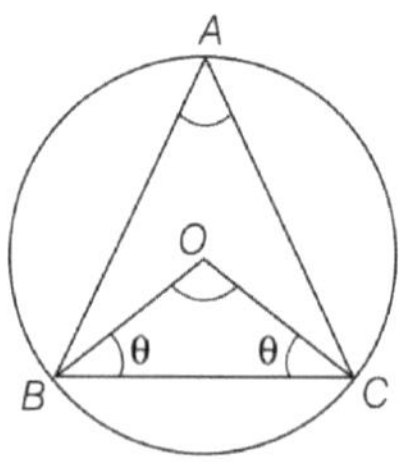

In ΔOBC,

$$\angle BOC + \angle OBC + \angle OCB = 180°$$
$$[\because \text{ sum of all angles of a triangle is } 180°]$$
$$\angle BOC + \theta + \theta = 180°$$
$$\Rightarrow \qquad \angle BOC = 180° - 2\theta$$
$$\because \qquad \angle BAC = \frac{\angle BOC}{2}$$

$[\because$ since, angle subtended at the arc is half of the angle subtended at the centre$]$

$$\therefore \qquad \angle BAC = \frac{180° - 2\theta}{2} = 90° - \theta$$
$$\angle BAC = 90° - \angle OBC$$
$$\angle OBC + \angle BAC = 90° \qquad\qquad \textbf{Hence proved.}$$

Example 9. A circle has radius $\sqrt{2}$ cm. It is divided into two segments by a chord of length 2 cm. Prove that the angle subtended by the chord at a point in major segment is 45°.   **[NCERT Exemplar]**

Sol. **Given** A circle having centre O.

Construction A chord of a circle $AB = 2$ cm, which is divided by the line OM in two equal segments.

To prove $\angle APB = 45°$

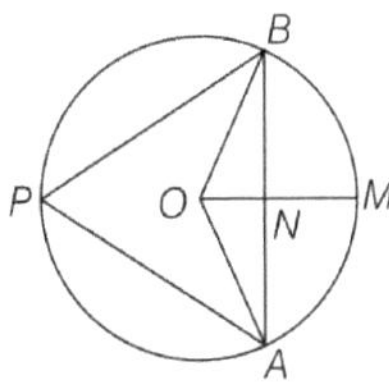

Proof Here, $AN = NB = 1$ cm

and $OA = OB = \sqrt{2}$ cm

In $\triangle ONB$, by Pythagoras theorem, we get

$$OB^2 = ON^2 + NB^2$$
$$\Rightarrow \quad (\sqrt{2})^2 = ON^2 + (1)^2$$
$$\Rightarrow \quad ON^2 = 2 - 1 = 1 \Rightarrow ON = 1$$

So, $\triangle ONB$ is an isosceles triangle.

$\because \quad \angle ONB = 90°$ [since, ON is the perpendicular bisector of the chord AB]

$\therefore \quad \angle NOB = \angle NBO = 45°$

Similarly, $\angle AON = 45°$

Now, $\angle AOB = \angle AON + \angle NOB$
$$= 45° + 45° = 90°$$

$\therefore \quad \angle APB = \dfrac{1}{2} \angle AOB$

      [$\because$ since, the angle subtended by an arc at the centre is twice the angle subtended by it at any point on the remaining part of the circle]

$\therefore \quad \angle APB = \dfrac{90°}{2} = 45°$ **Hence proved.**

Example 10. The Indian Hockey Federation organised a friendly hockey match between India and Pakistan on a circular ground. The sale proceeds of this match shall be donated to an orphanage. A rectangular turf is spread on the ground as shown in the figure.

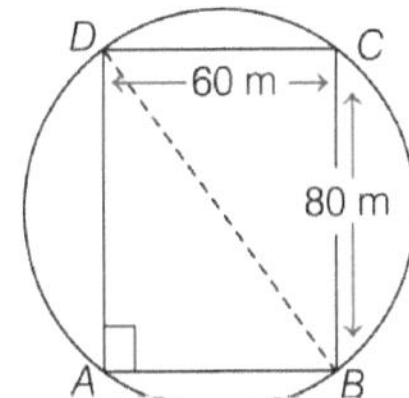

(i) Specify the name of the chord BD.

(ii) Find the radius of the stadium.

(iii) Find the area of $\triangle BCD$.

Sol. (i) As $ABCD$ is a rectangle, so each angle of a rectangle is 90°.

We know that, if any chord subtends a right angle, then the chord BD is said to be the diameter of a circle.

(ii) Diagonal of the rectangular turf
$$= \sqrt{(60)^2 + (80)^2} = \sqrt{3600 + 6400} = \sqrt{10000} = 100 \text{ m}$$

Since, rectangular turf is spread on the ground. So, its diagonal will be the diameter of the ground.

Hence, radius of circular ground $= \dfrac{100}{2} = 50$ m

(iii) Area of $\triangle BCD = \dfrac{1}{2} \times BC \times CD$
$$= \dfrac{1}{2} \times 80 \times 60 = 2400 \text{ m}^2$$

Example 11. Three students Priyanka, Sonia and David are protesting against killing innocent animals for commercial purposes in a circular park of radius 20 m. They are standing at equal distances on its boundary by holding banners in their hands.

(i) Find the distance between each of them.

(ii) Find the area of triangle inscribed in a circle.

Sol. (i) Let us assume that A, B and C be the positions of Priyanka, Sonia and David respectively on the boundary of circular park with centre O.

Draw $AD \perp BC$.

Since, the centre of the circle coincides with the centroid of the equilateral $\triangle ABC$.

$\therefore$ Radius of circumscribed circle $= \dfrac{2}{3} AD$

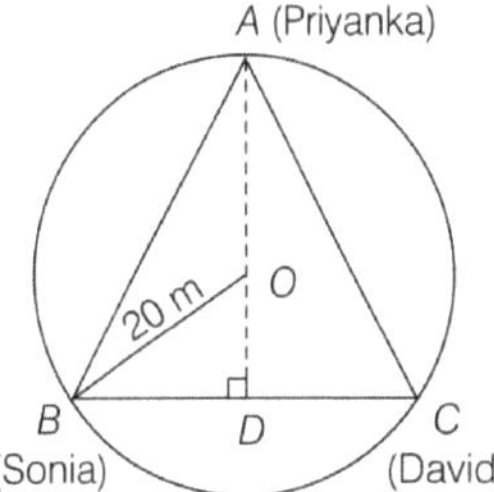

$\Rightarrow \quad 20 = \dfrac{2}{3} AD \Rightarrow AD = 20 \times \dfrac{3}{2}$

$\Rightarrow \quad AD = 30$ m

Now, $AD \perp BC$ and
let $AB = BC = CA = x$ m

$\Rightarrow BD = CD = \dfrac{1}{2} BC = \dfrac{x}{2}$

In right angle triangle $\triangle BDA$, $\angle D = 90°$

$\therefore$ By Pythagoras theorem, we have
$$AB^2 = BD^2 + AD^2$$
$$\Rightarrow \quad x^2 = \left(\dfrac{x}{2}\right)^2 + (30)^2$$

$$\Rightarrow \quad x^2 - \frac{x^2}{4} = 900$$

$$\Rightarrow \quad \frac{3}{4}x^2 = 900$$

$$\Rightarrow \quad x^2 = 900 \times \frac{4}{3}$$

$$x^2 = 1200$$

$$x = \sqrt{1200} = 20\sqrt{3}$$

Hence, distance between each of them is $20\sqrt{3}$ m.

(ii) Since, ΔABC is an equilateral triangle.

Therefore, area of $\Delta ABC = \dfrac{\sqrt{3}}{4}(\text{side})^2$

$$= \frac{\sqrt{3}}{4} \times (20\sqrt{3})^2$$

$$= \frac{\sqrt{3}}{4} \times 400 \times 3 = 300\sqrt{3}\ \text{m}^2$$

Example 12. *AB* and *AC* are two chords of a circle of radius *r* such that $AB = 2AC$. If *p* and *q* are the distances of *AB* and *AC* from the centre, then prove that $4q^2 = p^2 + 3r^2$.　　　　　　**NCERT Exemplar**

Sol. Let $AC = a$, then $AB = 2a$.

From centre *O*, perpendicular is drawn to the chords *AC* and *AB* at *M* and *N*, respectively.

$$\therefore \quad AM = MC = \frac{a}{2}$$

and $\quad AN = NB = a$

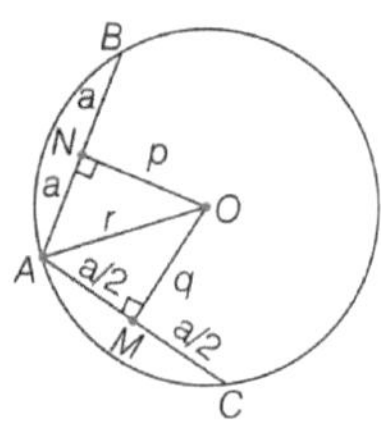

In ΔOMA and ΔONA, by Pythagoras theorem, we get

$$AO^2 = AM^2 + MO^2$$

$$\Rightarrow \quad AO^2 = \left(\frac{a}{2}\right)^2 + q^2 \qquad \ldots(i)$$

and $\quad AO^2 = AN^2 + NO^2$

$$\Rightarrow \quad AO^2 = a^2 + p^2 \qquad \ldots(ii)$$

From Eqs. (i) and (ii), we get

$$\left(\frac{a}{2}\right)^2 + q^2 = a^2 + p^2$$

$$\frac{a^2 + 4q^2}{4} = a^2 + p^2$$

$$a^2 + 4q^2 = 4a^2 + 4p^2$$

$$\Rightarrow \qquad 4q^2 = 4p^2 + 3a^2$$

$$4q^2 = p^2 + 3(a^2 + p^2)$$

$$[\because \text{ in right-angled triangle } \Delta ONA,\ r^2 = a^2 + p^2]$$

$$4q^2 = p^2 + 3r^2 \qquad \textbf{Hence proved.}$$

Example 13. In given figure, *O* is the centre of a circle and *PO* bisects $\angle APD$. Prove that $AB = CD$.

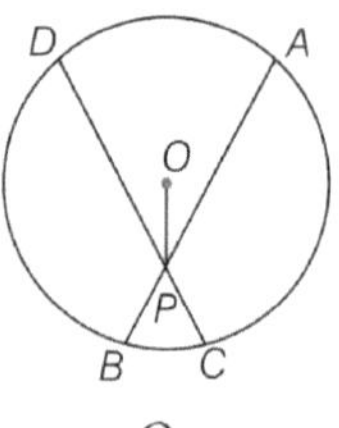

Or

If two intersecting chords of a circle make equal angles with the diameter passing through their point of intersection, then prove that the chords are equal.

Sol. Let *AB* and *CD* be two chords of a circle with centre *O* intersecting at a point *P*. *MN* is a diameter through *P* such that *MN* (or *OP*) bisects $\angle APD$, i.e. $\angle APO = \angle DPO$

To Prove $AB = CD$

Construction Draw $OE \perp AB$ and $OF \perp CD$

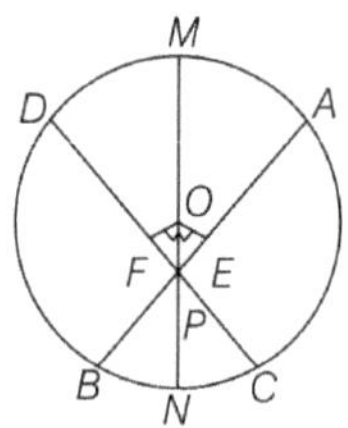

Proof In ΔOEP and ΔOFP,

$$\angle OEP = \angle OFP \qquad \text{[each 90°]}$$
$$OP = OP \qquad \text{[common sides]}$$

and $\qquad \angle OPE = \angle OPF \qquad [\because OP \text{ bisects } \angle APD]$

$$\therefore \qquad \Delta OEP \cong \Delta OFP \text{ [by AAS congruence rule]}$$

Then, $\qquad\qquad OE = OF \qquad\qquad \text{[by CPCT]}$

Thus, chords *AB* and *CD* are equidistant from the centre *O* of the circle and we know that chords of a circle which are equidistant from the centre are equal.

$$\therefore \qquad\qquad AB = CD \qquad\qquad \textbf{Hence proved.}$$

Example 14. *AB* is the diameter of the circle $C(O, r)$ and radius *OD* is perpendicular to *AB*. If there is any point *C* on arc *DB*, then find $\angle BAD$ and $\angle ACD$.

Sol. Given, circle $C(O, r)$ and $OD \perp AB$.

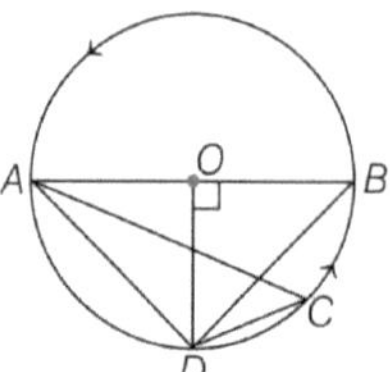

Clearly, $\quad \angle AOD = \angle BOD = 90°$

Now, arc *BD* subtends $\angle BOD$ at the centre and $\angle BAD$ at a point on the remaining part of circle.

So, $\qquad\qquad \angle BOD = 2\angle BAD \qquad\qquad \text{[by theorem 1]}$

$$\Rightarrow \qquad \angle BAD = \frac{1}{2}\angle BOD = \frac{1}{2}\times 90° = 45°$$

$$\Rightarrow \qquad \angle BAD = 45°$$

Similarly, arc AD subtends $\angle AOD$ at the centre and $\angle ACD$ at a point on the remaining part of circle.

So, $\qquad \angle AOD = 2\angle ACD$

$$\Rightarrow \qquad \angle ACD = \frac{1}{2}\angle AOD = \frac{1}{2}\times 90° = 45°$$

Example 15. Prove that, if any two chords of a circle are drawn, then the one which is nearer to the centre, is larger.

Sol. Since, the perpendicular from the centre of a circle to a chord bisects the chord.

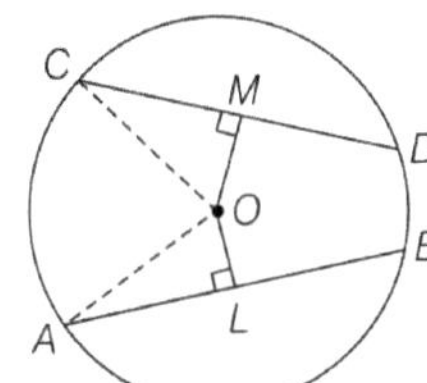

$$\therefore \quad AL = \frac{1}{2}AB \text{ and } CM = \frac{1}{2}CD$$

In right angled ΔOLA and ΔOMC, we have

$$OA^2 = OL^2 + AL^2$$

and $\qquad OC^2 = OM^2 + CM^2 \qquad$ [by Pythagoras theorem]

$$\Rightarrow \qquad AL^2 = OA^2 - OL^2 \qquad \text{...(i)}$$

and $\qquad CM^2 = OC^2 - OM^2 \qquad \text{...(ii)}$

Now, $\qquad OL < OM$

$$\Rightarrow \qquad OL^2 < OM^2 \Rightarrow -OL^2 > -OM^2$$

$\qquad\qquad\qquad\qquad$ [multiplying by $(-)$ on both sides]

$$\Rightarrow \quad OA^2 - OL^2 > OA^2 - OM^2 \text{ [adding } OA^2 \text{ on both sides]}$$

$$\Rightarrow \quad OA^2 - OL^2 > OC^2 - OM^2 \qquad [\because OA^2 = OC^2]$$

$$\Rightarrow \qquad AL^2 > CM^2 \qquad \text{[from Eqs. (i) and (ii)]}$$

$$\Rightarrow \qquad AL > CM$$

$$\Rightarrow \qquad 2AL > 2CM \text{[multiplying by 2]}$$

$$\Rightarrow \qquad AB > CD \qquad\qquad \textbf{Hence proved.}$$

Example 16. If two equal chords of a circle intersect within a circle, prove that the segments of a chord are equal to the corresponding segments of the other chord.

Sol. **Given** Let AB and CD be the two equal chords intersecting at point X.

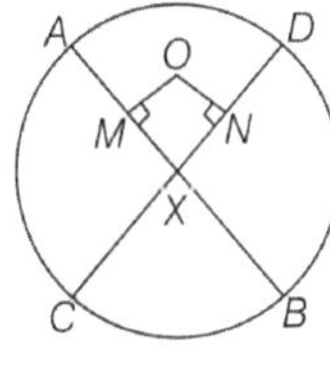

$$\Rightarrow \qquad AB = CD$$

To Prove Corresponding segments are equal, i.e. $AX = DX$ and $BX = CX$

Proof We draw $OM \perp AB$ and $ON \perp CD$

Since, perpendicular drawn from centre of a circle to a chord bisects the chord.

So, $\quad AM = BM = \frac{1}{2}AB$

and $\quad DN = CN = \frac{1}{2}CD$

As, $\qquad\qquad AB = CD$

$$\Rightarrow \qquad \frac{1}{2}AB = \frac{1}{2}CD$$

$\therefore \qquad\qquad AM = DN \qquad\qquad\qquad \text{...(i)}$

and $\qquad\qquad MB = CN \qquad\qquad\qquad \text{...(ii)}$

In ΔOMX and ΔONX,

$$\angle OMX = \angle ONX \qquad \text{[both 90°]}$$
$$OX = OX \qquad \text{[common]}$$
$$OM = ON$$

$\qquad$ [$\because AB$ and CD are equal chords and equal chords are $\qquad\qquad\qquad\qquad$ equidistant from the centre]

$\therefore \qquad\qquad \Delta OMX \cong \Delta ONX \qquad$ [RHS congruence rule]

$\Rightarrow \qquad\qquad MX = NX \qquad\qquad \text{...(iii) [by CPCT]}$

Adding Eqs. (i) and (iii), we get

$$AM + MX = DN + NX$$

$$\Rightarrow \qquad AX = DX$$

Subtracting Eq. (iii) from Eq. (ii), we get

$$BM - MX = CN - NX$$

$$\Rightarrow \qquad BX = CX$$

$\therefore \qquad AX = DX \text{ and } BX = CX \qquad\qquad \textbf{Hence proved.}$

Example 17. AB and CD are equal chords of a circle with centre O. If $OM \perp AB$ and $ON \perp CD$, then prove that $\angle OMN = \angle ONM$.

Sol. Since, two chords are equal, so both are at equidistant from the centre.

$$\therefore \qquad\qquad OM = ON$$

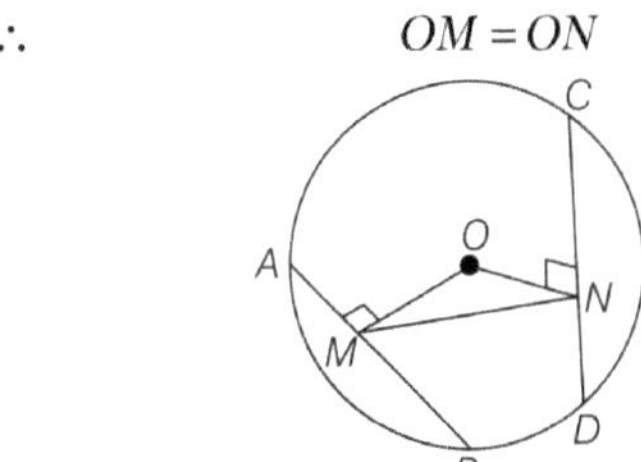

In ΔOMN, $\qquad \angle ONM = \angle OMN$

$\qquad$ [$\because$ opposite angles of equal sides are equal]

Example 18. Two equal chords AB and CD of a circle with centre O, when produced, meet at a point E as shown in figure. Prove that $BE = DE$ and $AE = CE$.

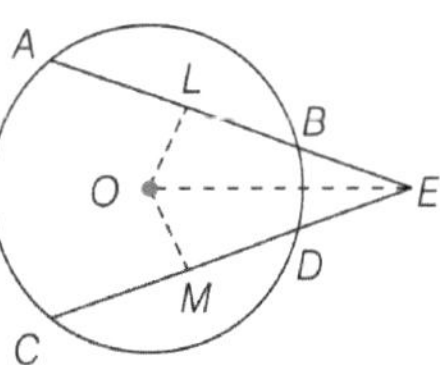

Sol. Given, $AB = CD \qquad\qquad\qquad\qquad \text{...(i)}$

In ΔOLE and ΔOME,

$$OE = OE \qquad \text{[common]}$$
$$\angle OLE = \angle OME \qquad \text{[each } 90°\text{]}$$
$$OL = OM$$
$$[\because \text{ equal chords are equidistant from centre}]$$
$$\therefore \qquad \Delta OLE \cong \Delta OME$$
$$[\text{by RHS congruence rule}]$$
$$\Rightarrow \qquad LE = ME \qquad \text{...(ii) [by CPCT]}$$

Now, $\qquad AB = CD \qquad$ (given)

$$\Rightarrow \qquad \frac{1}{2} AB = \frac{1}{2} CD$$
$$\Rightarrow \qquad BL = MD \qquad \text{...(iii)}$$

Now, subtracting Eq. (iii) from Eq. (ii),

$$LE - BL = ME - MD$$
$$\Rightarrow \qquad BE = DE \qquad \text{...(iv)}$$

Again, adding Eqs. (i) and (iv),

$$AB + BE = CD + DE$$
$$\Rightarrow \qquad AE = CE$$

Hence, $BE = DE$ and $AE = CE$.

Example 19. In the given figure, ABC is a triangle, in which $\angle BAC = 30°$. Show that the length of BC is equal to the radius of the circumcircle of ΔABC, whose centre is O.

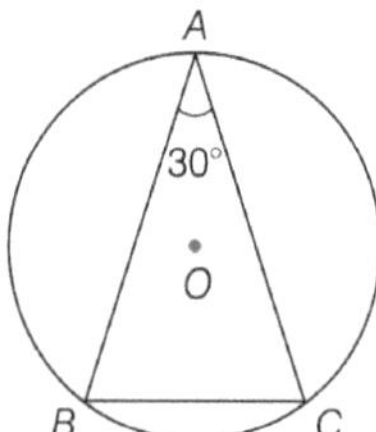

Sol. Given $\angle BAC = 30°$

Construction Draw segments OB and OC
To prove $BC = OC = OB$

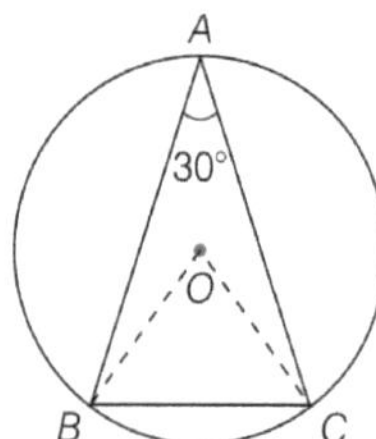

Proof Since, $\qquad \angle BAC = 30° \qquad$ [given]

$$\therefore \qquad \angle BOC = 2 \times 30° = 60° \qquad \text{...(i)}$$
$$[\because \text{ angle subtended by arc on centre} = 2 \times \text{angle subtended}$$
$$\text{by arc on circumference}]$$

Now, we know that $OB = OC = $ radius of circle = radius of circumcircle of ΔABC

$\therefore \Delta OBC$ is isosceles.

$$\Rightarrow \qquad \angle OBC = \angle OCB \qquad \text{...(ii)}$$
$$[\because \text{ angle opposite to equal sides of a triangle are equal}]$$

Now, $\angle OBC + \angle OCB + \angle BOC = 180°$
$$[\because \text{ angle sum property of triangle}]$$

$$\Rightarrow \angle OBC + \angle OCB = 180° - 60° = 120° \qquad \text{[from Eq. (i)]}$$
$$\Rightarrow \angle OBC = \angle OCB = \frac{120°}{2} = 60° \qquad \text{[from Eq. (ii)]}$$
$$\Rightarrow \angle BOC = \angle OBC = \angle OCB = 60°$$

$\therefore \Delta OBC$ is equilateral.

$$\Rightarrow BC = OB = OC = \text{radius of circumcircle of } \Delta ABC.$$

Hence proved.

Example 20. In the given figure, O is the centre of the circle, $\angle AOC = 50°$ and $\angle COB = 30°$. Find the measure of $\angle ADB$.

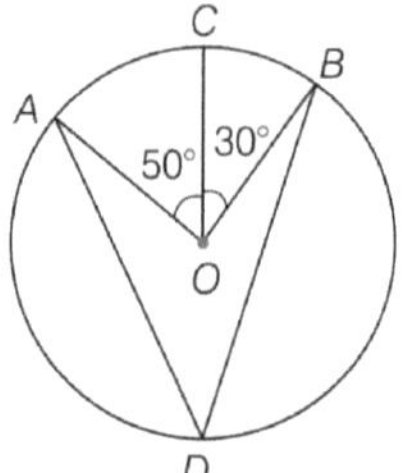

Sol. It is given that O is the centre, $\angle AOC = 50°$ and $\angle COB = 30°$

From the figure,

$$\angle AOB = \angle AOC + \angle COB$$
$$= 50° + 30°$$
$$= 80°$$

We know that, the angle at the centre of the circle is twice the angle at the circumference.

$$\Rightarrow \qquad 2\angle ADB = \angle AOB$$
$$\Rightarrow \qquad \angle ADB = \frac{1}{2} \angle AOB = \frac{1}{2} \times 80° = 40°$$

Example 21. The chord ED is parallel to the diameter AC. Determine $\angle CED$.

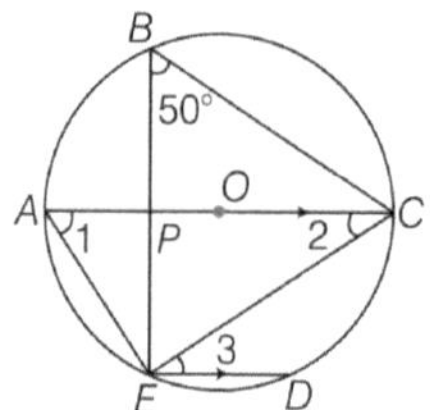

Sol. Given $ED \parallel AC$, $\angle CBE = 50°$

To find $\angle CED$

$$\angle CBE = \angle 1 \qquad [\because \text{ angles on the same segment}]$$
$$\therefore \qquad \angle 1 = 50° \qquad \text{...(i)} [\because \angle CBE = 50° \text{ (given)}]$$
$$\angle AEC = 90° \qquad \text{...(ii)} [\because \text{ angle in a semi-circle}]$$

Now, In ΔAEC,

$$\angle 1 + \angle AEC + \angle 2 = 180°$$
$$[\because \text{ angle sum property of a triangle}]$$
$$\Rightarrow \qquad 50° + 90° + \angle 2 = 180° \text{ [from Eqs. (i) and (ii)]}$$
$$\Rightarrow \qquad \angle 2 = 180° - 140° = 40° \qquad \text{...(iii)}$$

Given, $\qquad ED \parallel AC$

$$\therefore \qquad \angle 2 = \angle 3 \qquad [\because \text{ alternate interior angles}]$$
$$\Rightarrow \qquad \angle 3 = 40°$$

i.e. $\qquad \angle CED = 40°$.

Example 22. In the given figure, O is the centre of the circle. Find the value of x.

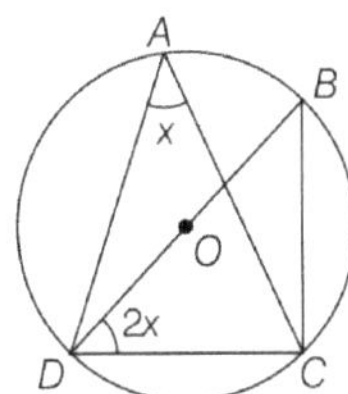

Sol. Given that O is the centre of the circle,

$\angle BDC = 2x$ and $\angle CAD = x$

Since, angles inscribed in a circle and subtended by the same chord are equal.

Here, DC is a chord.

$\therefore \quad \angle CAD = \angle CBD \Rightarrow \angle CBD = x$

Now, BD is the diameter as it passes through centre O.

$\Rightarrow \angle DCB = 90°$ [$\because$ angle in a semi-circle is a right angle]

Now, let us consider ΔBCD,

$\angle CDB + \angle DCB + \angle CBD = 180°$

           [$\because$ sum of all angles of a triangle is $180°$]

$\Rightarrow \qquad\qquad 2x + 90° + x = 180°$

$\Rightarrow \qquad\qquad 3x = 180° - 90° = 90°$

$\Rightarrow \qquad\qquad x = \dfrac{1}{3} \times 90° = 30°$

Hence, the value of x is $30°$.

Example 23. A circle with centre O and diameter COB is given. If AB and CD are parallel, then show that chord AC is equal to chord BD.

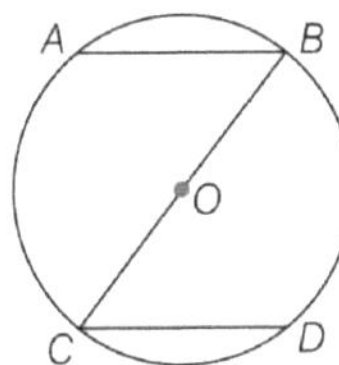

Sol. **Given** AB and CD are parallel in a circle with centre O and diameter COB.

To prove Chord $AC = $ Chord BD

Join AC and BD.

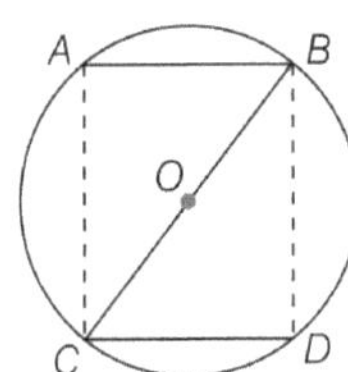

Given, COB is the diameter of circle

$\angle CAB = \angle BDC = 90°$ [$\because$ angle in a semi-circle]

Also, $AB \parallel CD$

$\Rightarrow \quad \angle ABC = \angle DCB$ ...(i) [alternate angles]

Now, $\angle ACB = 90° - \angle DCB$

$\qquad\qquad = 90° - \angle ABC$ [from Eq. (i)]

and $\angle DBC = 90° - \angle ABC$

$\Rightarrow \quad \angle ACB = \angle DBC$ ...(ii)

In ΔABC and ΔDCB,

$\qquad \angle ABC = \angle DCB$ [from Eq. (i)]

$\qquad \angle ACB = \angle DBC$ [from Eq. (ii)]

$\qquad BC = BC$ [common]

$\therefore \qquad \Delta ABC \cong \Delta DCB$ [by ASA congruency rule]

$\Rightarrow \qquad AC = BD$ [by CPCT]

Hence proved.

Example 24. In the given figure, $ABCD$ is a cyclic quadrilateral, whose side AB is a diameter of the circle through A, B, C and D. If $\angle ADC = 130°$, find $\angle BAC$

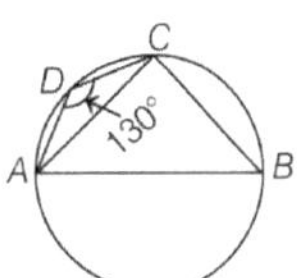

Sol. Since, $ABCD$ is a cyclic quadrilateral.

$\therefore \angle ADC + \angle ABC = 180°$

$\Rightarrow \quad 130° + \angle ABC = 180° \Rightarrow \angle ABC = 50°$

Since, $\angle ACB$ is the angle in a semi-circle.

$\therefore \qquad\qquad \angle ACB = 90°$

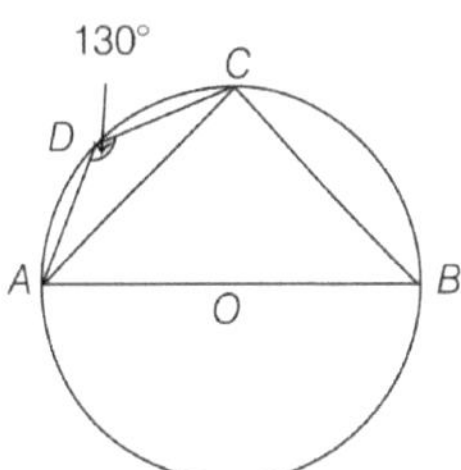

Now, in ΔABC, we have

$\angle BAC + \angle ACB + \angle ABC = 180°$

$\Rightarrow \qquad \angle BAC + 90° + 50° = 180° \Rightarrow \angle BAC = 40°$

Example 25. If diagonals of a cyclic quadrilateral are diameters of the circle through the vertices of the quadrilateral, then prove that it is rectangle.

Sol. **Given** Diagonals NP and QM of a cylic quadrilateral $NQPM$ are the diameters of circles passing through the vertices M, P, Q and N.

To Prove Quadrilateral $NQPM$ is a rectangle.

Proof Here, $ON = OP = OQ = OM$ [radii of same circle]

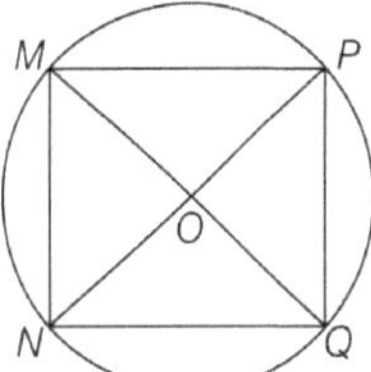

Then, $ON = OP = \dfrac{1}{2}NP$ and $OM = OQ = \dfrac{1}{2}MQ$

$\therefore \qquad NP = MQ$

Hence, the diagonals of the quadrilateral $NQPM$ are equal and bisect each other. So, quadrilateral $NQPM$ is a rectangle.

Chapter Practice

Objective Questions

• Multiple Choice Questions

1. In the given figure, O is the centre of the circle and $BA = AC$. If $\angle ABC = 50°$, then $\angle BOC$ and $\angle BDC$, respectively

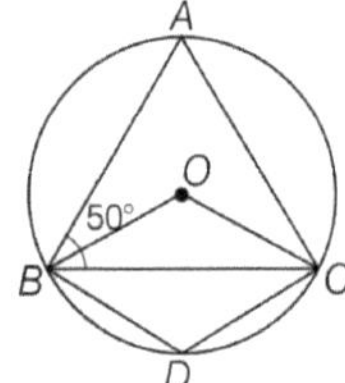

(a) 160° and 100° (b) 110° and 150°
(c) 100° and 160° (d) 150° and 110°

2. In the given figure, O is the centre of the circle and $\angle BDC = 42°$, then the value of $\angle ACB$ is

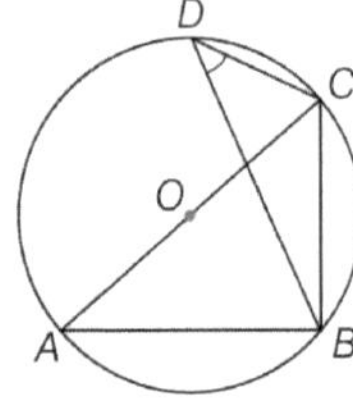

(a) 60° (b) 42° (c) 24° (d) 48°

3. In figure, if AOB is a diameter of the circle and $AC = BC$, then $\angle CAB$ is equal to
(a) 30° (b) 60° (c) 90° (d) 45°

4. In the given figure, chords AB and CD are equal. If $\angle OBA = 55°$, then find the measure of $\angle COD$.

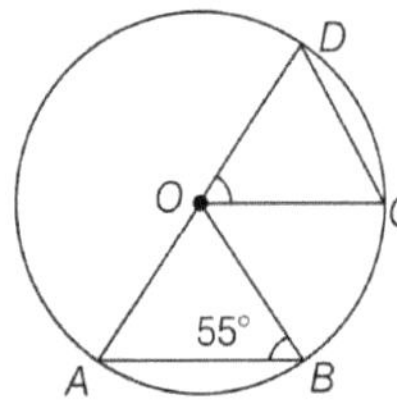

(a) 50° (b) 60° (c) 70° (d) 75°

5. In the given figure, $\angle OAB = 30°$ and $\angle OCB = 57°$, then the value of $\angle BOC + \angle AOC$ is

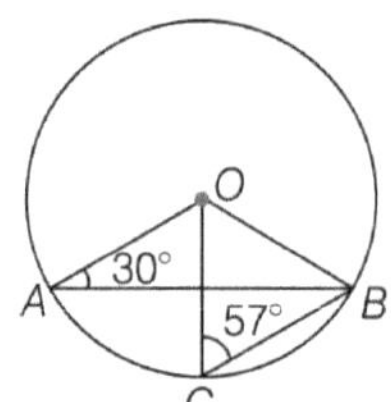

(a) 120° (b) 64°
(c) 66° (d) 57°

6. In figure, if $\angle AOB = 90°$ and $\angle ABC = 30°$, then $\angle CAO$ is equal to

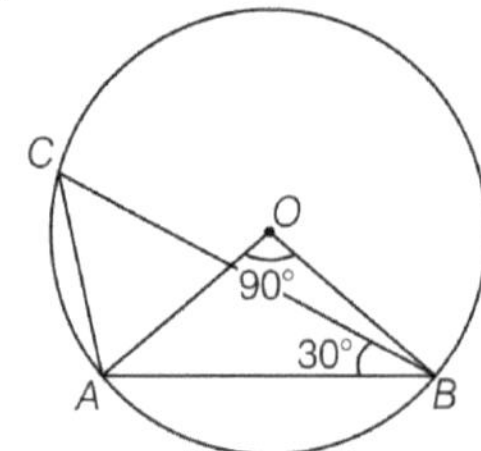

(a) 30° (b) 45°
(c) 90° (d) 60°

7. In figure, if $\angle ABC = 20°$, then $\angle AOC$ is equal to

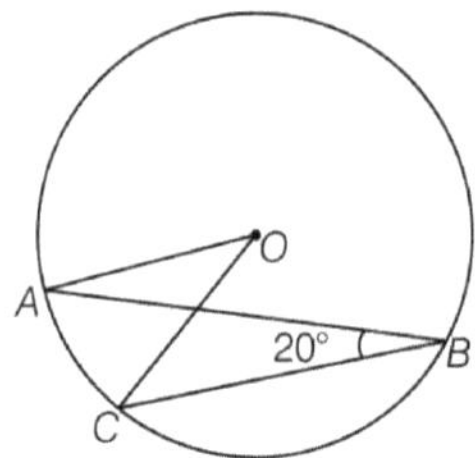

(a) 20°
(b) 40°
(c) 60°
(d) 10°

8. In figure, if $OA = 5$ cm, $AB = 8$ cm and OD is perpendicular to AB, then CD is equal to

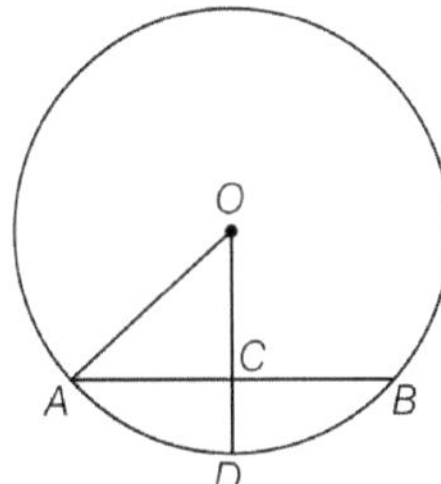

(a) 2 cm (b) 3 cm
(c) 4 cm (d) 5 cm

9. If $AB = 12$ cm, $BC = 16$ cm and AB is perpendicular to BC, then the radius of the circle passing through the points A, B and C is

(a) 6 cm (b) 8 cm
(c) 10 cm (d) 12 cm

10. Two parallel chords of a circle whose diameter is 13 cm. AB and CD are 5 cm and 12 cm, respectively. Find the distance between them, if they lie on opposite sides of the centre.

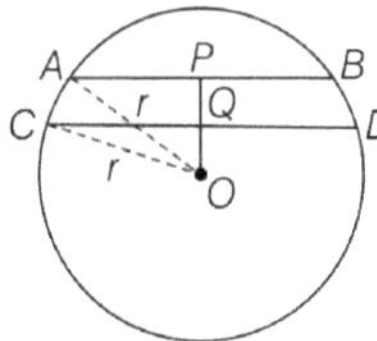

(a) 7.5 (b) 8.5 (c) 6.5 (d) 5

11. The lengths of two parallel chords of a circle are 6 cm and 8 cm. If the smaller chord is at distance 4 cm from the centre, then what is the distance of the other chord from the centre?

(a) 4 cm (b) 10 cm (c) 3 cm (d) 6 cm

12. If O is the centre of the circle, then the value of x is

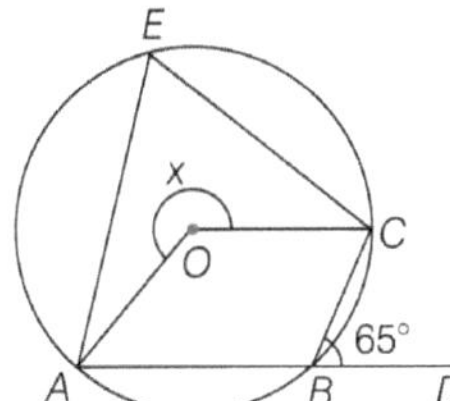

(a) 230° (b) 160°
(c) 170° (d) 220°

13. In figure, A, B and C are three points on a circle with centre O such that $\angle BOC = 30°$ and $\angle AOB = 60°$. If D is a point on the circle other than the arc ABC, then find $\angle ADC$.

(a) 45° (b) 55°
(c) 65° (d) 35°

14. In the given figure, A, B and C are three points on a circle such that the angles subtended by the chords AB and AC at the centre O are 80° and 120°, respectively. $\angle BAC$ is equal to

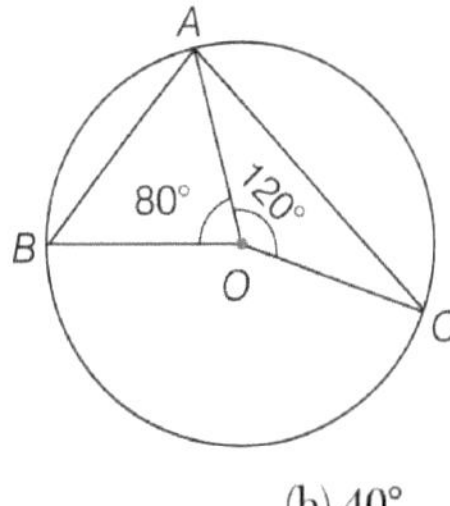

(a) 70° (b) 40°
(c) 60° (d) 80°

15. In the given figure, $\angle ACB = 40°$, then the value of $\angle OAB$ is

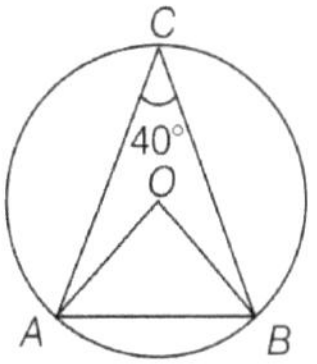

(a) 60° (b) 50°
(c) 70° (d) 100°

16. In the figure given below, O is the centre of the circle and $CD = DE = EF = GF$. If the $\angle COD = 40°$, then the reflex $\angle COG$ is

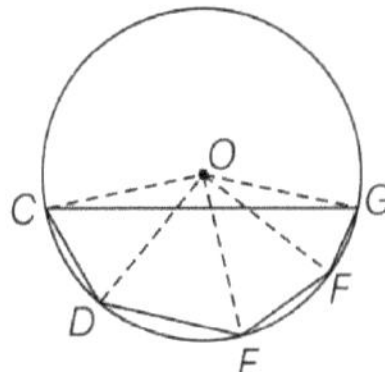

(a) 210° (b) 200°
(c) 100° (d) 110°

17. A quadrilateral $ABCD$ is inscribed in a circle such that AB is a diameter and $\angle ADC = 130°$. Then, the value of $\angle BAC$ is

(a) 50° (b) 60°
(c) 40° (d) 80°

18. In the given figure, find the value of x.

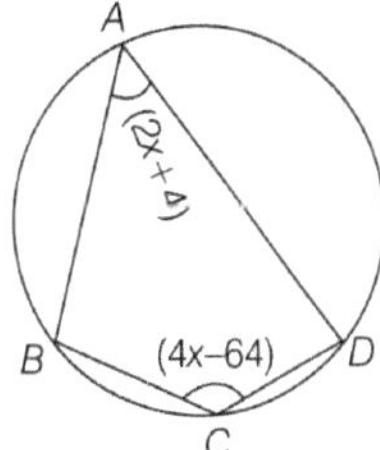

(a) 35° (b) 40° (c) 50° (d) 60°

19. In the given figure, then the value of $x + y$ is

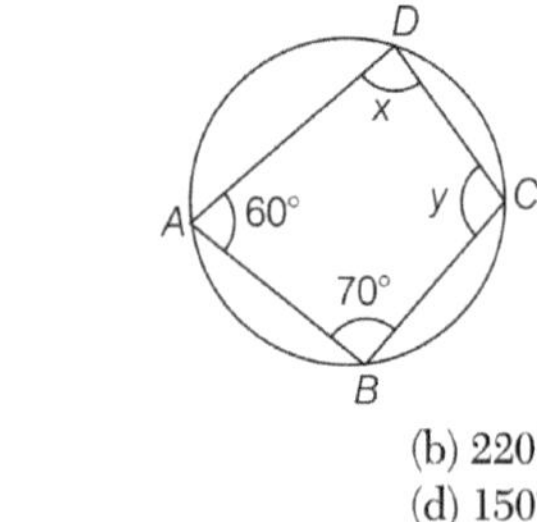

(a) 200°   (b) 220°

(c) 230°   (d) 150°

20. In the given figure, P and Q are centres of the two circles intersect at B and C. ACD is a straight line. Find the values of x, y and z.

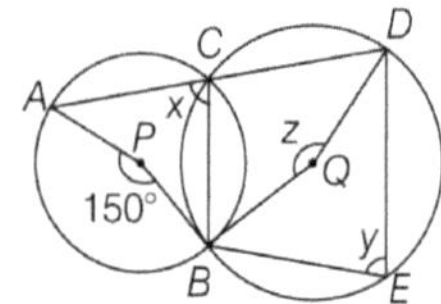

(a) $x = y = 70°$ and $z = 140°$

(b) $x = y = 150°$ and $z = 75°$

(c) $x = y = 75°$ and $z = 150°$

(d) $x = z = 150°$ and $xy = 75°$

21. In the given figure, if $\dfrac{x}{3} = \dfrac{y}{4} = \dfrac{z}{5}$, then calculate the values of x, y and z.

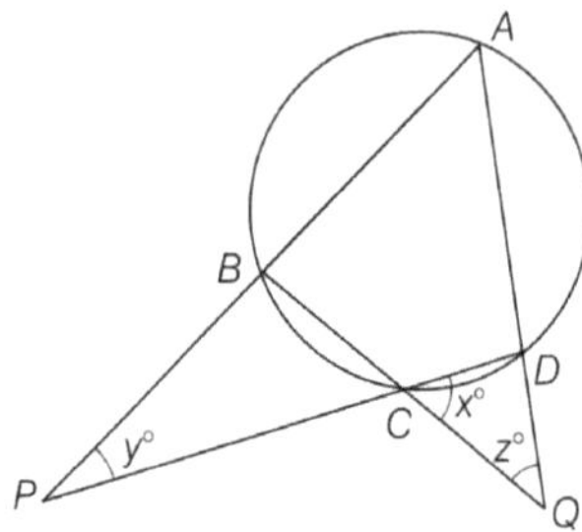

(a) $x = 36°$, $y = 48°$ and $z = 60°$

(b) $x = 48°$, $z = 36°$ and $y = 60°$

(c) $z = 48°$, $y = 36°$ and $z = 60°$

(d) $z = 60°$, $y = 36°$ and $x = 48°$

• Case Based MCQs

22. As, class VIIth A's class teacher Mr. Ram entered in the class, he told students to do some practice on circle chapter, he draws two line PQ and QR. So, that $PQ = 40$ cm and $QR = 9$ cm. He told all students to make this shape in their notebook and draw a circle passing through the three points P, Q and R.

(i) Mukesh drew PQ and QR as per fig.

(ii) He draw a perpendicular bisectors OX and OY of the line PQ and QR.

(iii) OX and OY intersect at O.

(iv) Now, taking O as a centre and OQ as radius, he draw the circle which passes through P, Q and R.

(v) He noticed that P, O and R collinear.

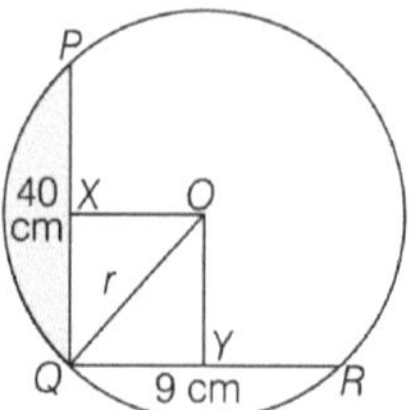

(i) What you will call the line POR?

(a) Arc   (b) Diameter

(c) Radius   (d) Chord

(ii) The measure of $\angle PQR$ is

(a) 60°   (b) 90°

(c) 45°   (d) 75°

(iii) What you will call the shaded region PAQ?

(a) Arc   (b) Sector

(c) Major Segment   (d) Minor Segment

(iv) The radius of the circle is

(a) 41 cm   (b) 40 cm

(c) 9 cm   (d) $\dfrac{41}{2}$ cm

23. Delhi government has made three new bus stopes. Situated at P, Q, R as shown in figure. Which is operated by Delhi Transport Co-operation. These three bus stopes are equidistance from each other.

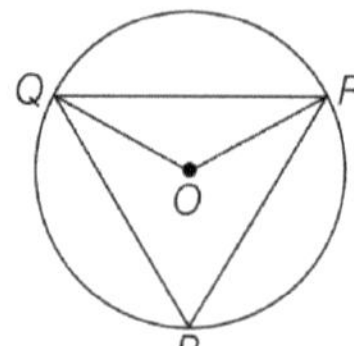

(i) Which type of ΔPQR is the given?

(a) Equilateral triangle   (b) Isosceles triangle

(c) Right-angled triangle   (d) Scalane triangle

(ii) Measure of $\angle PQR$ is

(a) 45°   (b) 60°

(c) 30°   (d) 90°

(iii) If $QR = 8$ cm, then value of $RP + PQ$ is

(a) 19   (b) 14

(c) 16   (d) 15

(iv) Measure of $\angle QOR$ is

(a) 30°   (b) 120°

(c) 110°   (d) 60°

(v) Value of $(\angle OQR + \angle ORQ)$ is

(a) 60°   (b) 30°

(c) 40°   (d) 120°

PART 2
Subjective Questions

• Short Answer Type Questions

1. If two chords of a circle with a common end-point are inclined equally to the diameter through this common end-point, then prove that the chords are equal.

2. In the given figure, the two chords AC and BC are equal and the radius OC intersects AB at M. Then, find the ratio $AM : BM$.

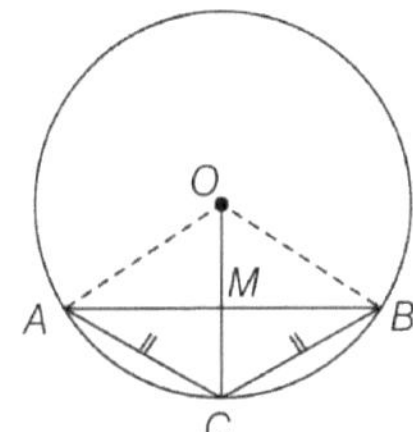

3. If arcs AXB and CYD of a circle are congruent, find the ratio of AB and CD.

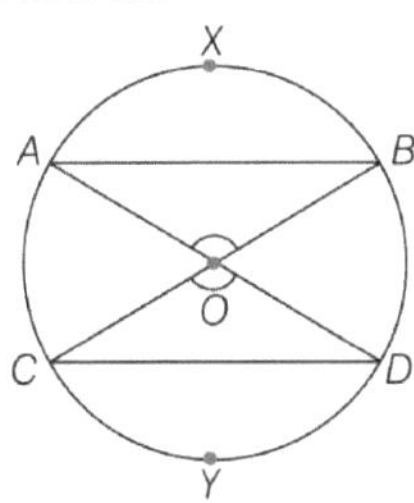

4. If AB and AC are two equal chords of a circle. Prove that the bisector of the $\angle BAC$ passes through the centre of the circle.

5. The radius of a circle is 13 cm and the length of one of its chords is 10 cm. Find the distance of the chord from the centre.

6. AD is a diameter of a circle and AB is a chord. If $AD = 34$ cm and $AB = 30$ cm, the distance of AB from the centre of the circle is.

7. Find the length of a chord of a circle which is at a distance of 6 cm from the centre of the circle. The radius of the circle is 10 cm.

8. If a line segment joining mid-points of two chords of a circle passes through the centre of the circle, Prove that the two chords are parallel.
[NCERT Exemplar]

9. In the given figure, O is the centre of the circle and the measure of arc ABC is $100°$. Determine $\angle ADC$ and $\angle ABC$.

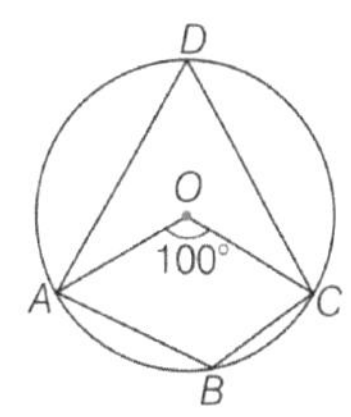

10. If O is the circumcentre of the $\triangle ABC$ and D is the mid-point of the base BC. Prove that $\angle BOD = \angle A$.

11. A chord of a circle is equal to the radius of the circle. Find the angle subtended by the chord at a point on the minor arc and also at a point on the major arc.

12. In figure, $\angle ABC = 69°$ and $\angle ACB = 31°$. Find $\angle BDC$.

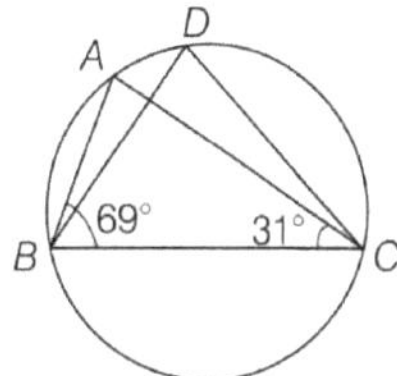

13. Prove that the rhombus, inscribed in a circle, is a square.

14. If diagonals of a cyclic quadrilateral are diameters of the circle through the vertices of the quadrilateral, then prove that it is a rectangle.

15. $ABCD$ is a cyclic quadrilateral whose diagonals intersect at a point E. If $\angle DBC = 70°$ and $\angle BAC = 30°$, then find $\angle BCD$. Further, if $AB = BC$, find $\angle ECD$.

16. In the given figure, $\angle ADC = 130°$ and chord $BC =$ chord BE. Find $\angle CBE$. **[NCERT Exemplar]**

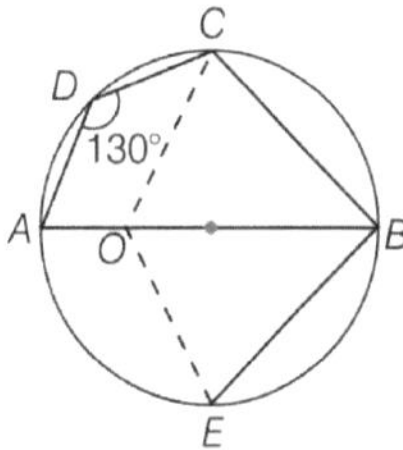

17. In the given figure, if O is the centre of a circle and $\angle ADC = 120°$, then find $\angle BAC$.

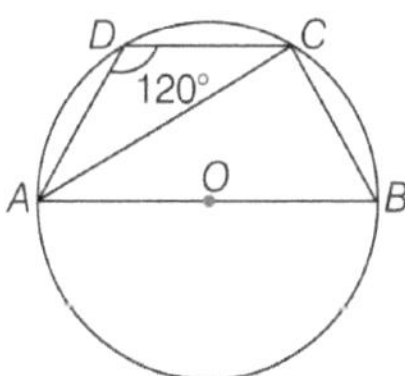

18. AB and CD are two chords of a circle such that $AB = 6$ cm, $CD = 12$ cm and $AB \| CD$. If the distance between AB and CD is 3 cm, find the radius of the circle.

19. In the following figure, equal chords AB and CD of a circle with centre O, cut at right angles at E. If M and N are the mid-points of AB and CD respectively, then prove that $OMEN$ is a square.

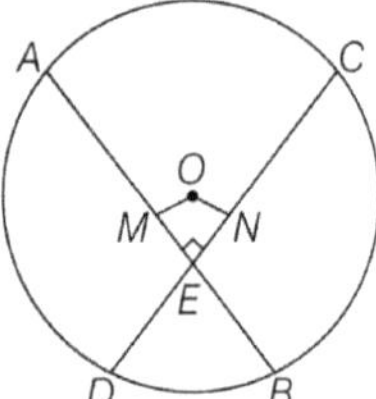

20. In the adjoining figure, O is the centre of a circle. If AB and AC are chords of the circle such that $AB = AC$, $OP \perp AB$ and $OQ \perp AC$, then prove that $PB = QC$.

21. In the given figure, $\angle BAC = 55°$, $\angle BCA = 62°$ and the altitude BE produced, meet the circle at D.

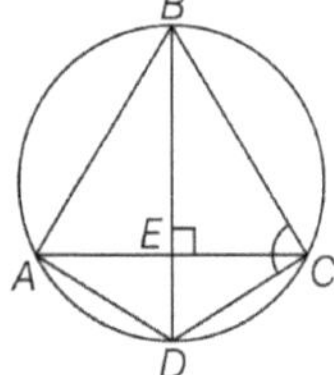

Determine

(i) $\angle ACD$ (ii) $\angle DAC$ (iii) $\angle ADB$

22. In the given figure, AB and AC are two chords of a circle whose centre is O. If $OD \perp AB$, $OE \perp AC$ and AO bisects $\angle DAE$, prove that $\triangle ADE$ is an isosceles triangle and $\angle ABC = \angle ACB$.

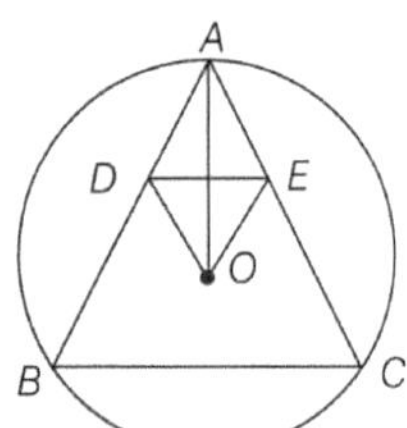

23. In the adjoining figure, C and D are points on the semi-circle inscribed on AB as diameter $\angle ABD = 75°$ and $\angle DAC = 35°$. Then, what will be the value of $\angle BDC$?

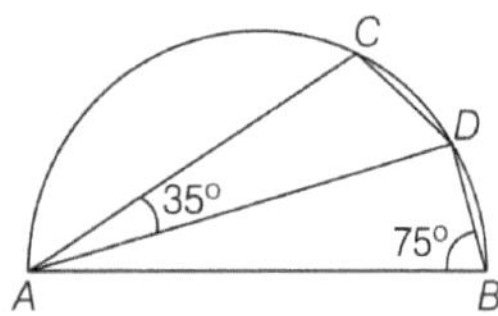

24. In the adjoining figure, AB is a diameter of the circle, CD is a chord equal to the radius of the circle. AC and BD when extended intersect at a point E. Find the value of $\angle AEB$.

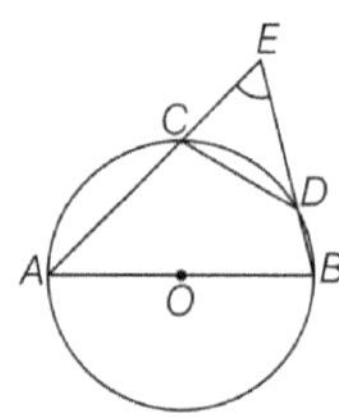

25. Prove that the quadrilateral formed (if possible) by the internal angle bisectors of any quadrilateral is cyclic.

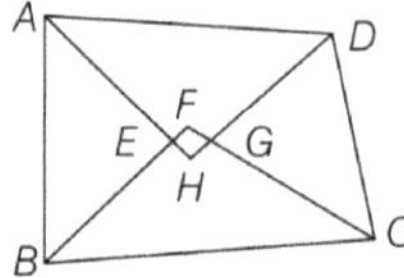

26. In the given figure, $ABCE$ is a cyclic quadrilateral and O is the centre of circle. If $\angle AEC = 110°$, then find $\angle ABC$ and $\angle ADC$.

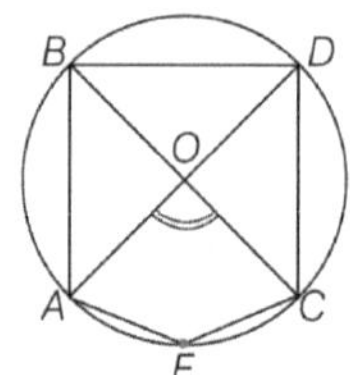

27. Three girls Reshma, Salma and Mandeep are playing a game by standing on a circle of radius 5 m drawn in a park. Reshma throws a ball to Salma, Salma to Mandeep, Mandeep to Reshma. If the distance between Reshma and Salma and between Salma and Mandeep is 6 m each, then what is the distance between Reshma and Mandeep?

28. A circular park of radius 20 m is situated in a colony. Three boys Ankur, Syed and David are sitting at equal distance on its boundary each having a toy telephone in his hand to talk each other. Find the length of the string of each phone.

29. Bisectors of $\angle A$, $\angle B$ and $\angle C$ of a $\triangle ABC$ intersect its circumcircle at D, E and F, respectively. Prove that the angles of the $\triangle DEF$ are $90° - \dfrac{1}{2} \angle A$, $90° - \dfrac{1}{2} \angle B$ and $90° - \dfrac{1}{2} \angle C$.

• Long Answer Type Questions

30. In figure, $\angle PQR = 100°$, where P, Q and R are points on a circle with centre O. Find $\angle OPR$.

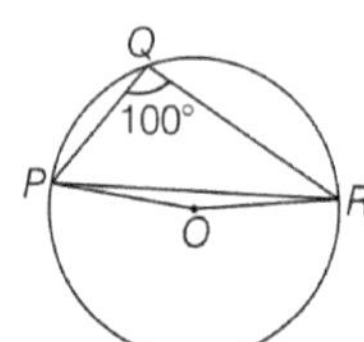

31. Two circles of radii 10 cm and 8 cm intersect and the length of the common chord is 12 cm. Find the distance between their centres.

32. In figure, *ABCD* is a cyclic quadrilateral and *O* is the centre of the circle. If $\angle BOD = 160°$, then find the measure of $\angle BPD$.

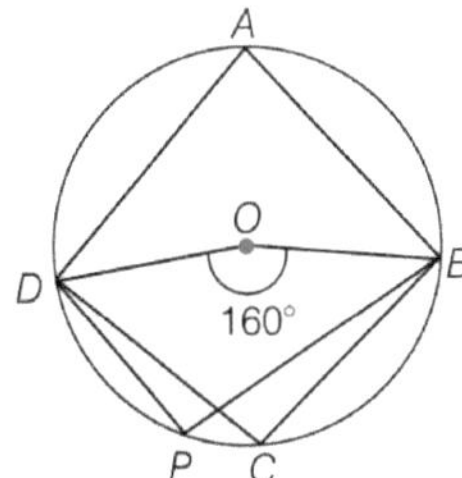

33. If *O* is the centre of the circle, then find the value of *x* in the given figure.

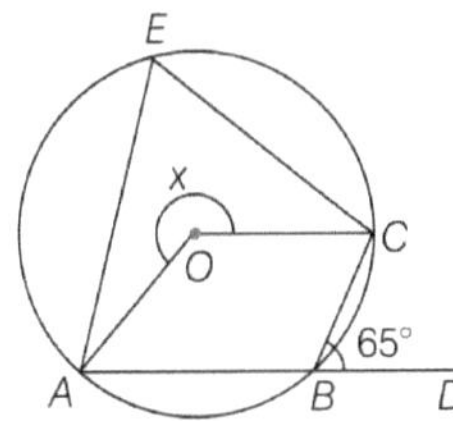

34. In the given figure *ABCD* is a cyclic quadrilateral, in which *AC* and *BD* are its diagonals. If $\angle DBC = 55°$ and $\angle BAC = 45°$, then find $\angle BCD$.

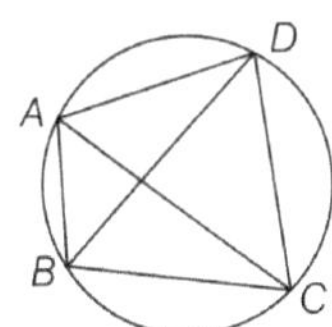

35. In the given figure, *AC* is the diameter, *AB* and *AD* are equal chords. If $\angle AED = 110°$, then find $\angle BAD$.

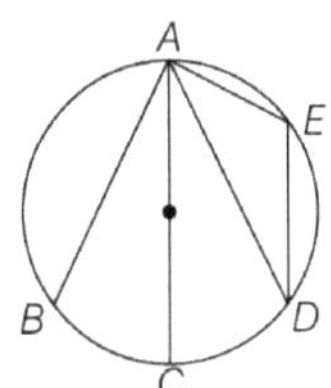

36. In the given figure, if $y = 3x$, then find the magnitude of *x*.

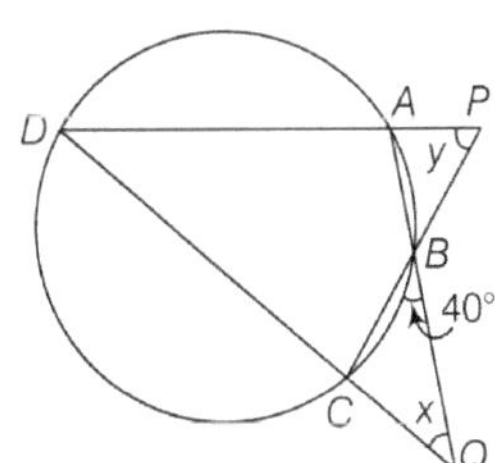

37. In the given figure, sides *AB* and *DC* of a cyclic quadrilateral *ABCD* are produced to meet at *E*. Sides *AD* and *BC* are produced to meet at *F*. If $\angle ADC = 80°$ and $\angle BEC = 50°$, then find $\angle BAD$ and $\angle CFD$.

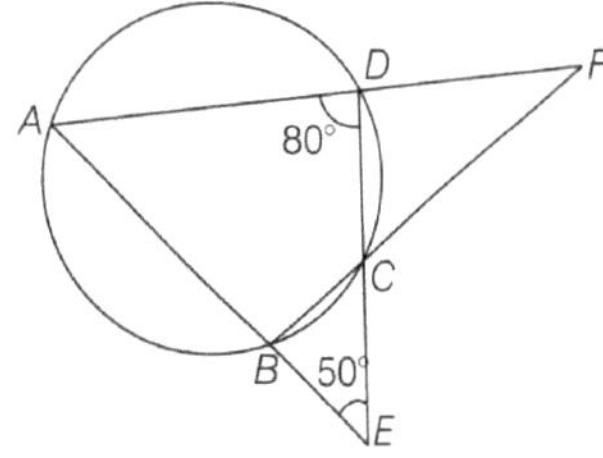

38. In a $\triangle ABC$, if $\angle A = 60°$ and the altitudes from *B* and *C* meet *AC* and *AB* at *P* and *Q*, respectively and intersect each other at *I*.

(i) Prove that *APIQ* and *PQBC* are cyclic quadrilaterals.

(ii) Find the measure of $\angle BIC$.

39. If the non-parallel sides of a trapezium are equal, then prove that it is cyclic.

40. Prove that the mid-point of the hypotenuse of a right-angled triangle is equidistant from its vertices.

● Case Based Questions

41. A circular garden as shown in the picture above. It has a different type of trees, plants and flower plants in his garden.

In the garden, there are two mango trees *A* and *B* at a distance of $AB = 10$ m. Similarly, he has two Ashoka trees at the same distance of 10 m as shown at *C* and *D*.

If *AB* subtends $\angle AOB = 140°$ at the centre *O*, the perpendicular distance of *AC* from centre is 8m. The radius of the circle is 17m.

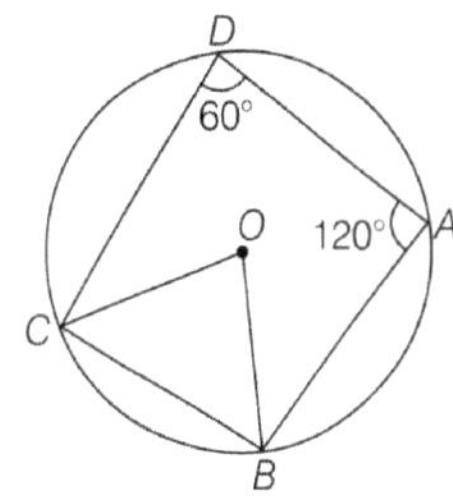

On the basis of above information, answer the following questions.

(i) What is the value of $\angle COD$?

(ii) What is the distance between tree *A* to tree *C*?

(iii) What is the value of $\angle OAB$?

(iv) What is the value of $\angle OCD$?

(v) What is the value of $\angle ODC$?

SOLUTIONS

Objective Questions

1. (a) Here, $\angle ABC = \angle ACB = 50°$

$\therefore$ $\angle BAC + \angle ABC + \angle ACB = 180°$

$\Rightarrow$ $\angle BAC + 50° + 50° = 180° \Rightarrow \angle BAC = 80°$

$\therefore$ $\angle BAC = \dfrac{1}{2} \angle BOC$

[$\because$ angle subtended by arc on centre $= 2 \times$ angle subtended by arc on circumference]

$\angle BOC = 2 \times 80° = 160°$

and $\angle ABC = \dfrac{1}{2} \angle BDC$

$\angle BDC = 2 \times 50° = 100°$

2. (d) Given, O is the centre of the circle and $\angle BDC = 42°$.
From figure, we have

$\angle ABC = 90°$

[$\because$ since, angle in a semi-circle is a right angle]

$\angle BDC = \angle BAC$

[$\because$ angles subtended by same chord are equal]

Now, in ΔABC,

$\angle ABC + \angle BAC + \angle ACB = 180°$

[by angle sum property of a triangle]

$\Rightarrow$ $90° + 42° + \angle ACB = 180°$

$\Rightarrow$ $\angle ACB = 180° - 132° = 48°$

3. (d) We know that, diameter subtends a right angle to the circle.

$\therefore$ $\angle BCA = 90°$ ...(i)

Given, $AC = BC$

$\Rightarrow$ $\angle ABC = \angle CAB$ ...(ii)

[$\because$ angles opposite to equal sides are equal]

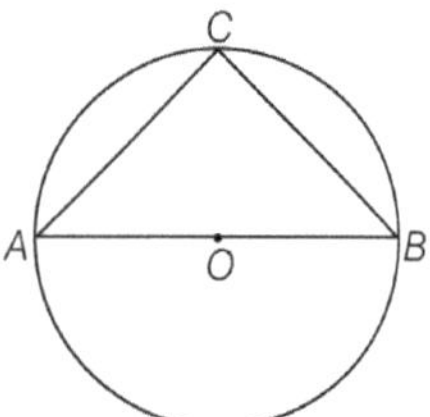

In ΔABC, $\angle CAB + \angle ABC + \angle BCA = 180°$

[by angle sum property of a triangle]

$\Rightarrow \angle CAB + \angle CAB + \angle 90° = 180°$ [from Eqs. (i) and (ii)]

$\Rightarrow$ $2\angle CAB = 180° - 90°$

$\Rightarrow$ $\angle CAB = \dfrac{90°}{2}$

$\therefore$ $\angle CAB = 45°$

4. (c) Since, $OA = OB \Rightarrow \angle OBA = \angle OAB = 55°$

$\therefore$ $\angle AOB = 180° - (55° + 55°) = 70°$

In, ΔOAB and ΔOCD,

$OA = OC$

$OB = OD$ [radii of a circle]

and $AB = CD$ [given]

$\therefore$ $\Delta OAB \cong \Delta OCD$ [by SSS congruence rule]

$\Rightarrow$ $\angle AOB = \angle COD = 70°$ [by CPCT]

5. (a) Here, $OA = OB$ [radii of same circle]

$\Rightarrow$ $\angle OBA = \angle OAB = 30°$ ...(i)

Similarly, $\angle OCB = \angle OBC = 57°$ ...(ii)

Now, in ΔBOC, $\angle BOC + \angle OCB + \angle OBC = 180°$

$\Rightarrow$ $\angle BOC + 57° + 57° = 180°$ [from Eq. (ii)]

$\Rightarrow$ $\angle BOC = 180° - 114° = 66°$

In ΔAOB, $\angle AOB + \angle OAB + \angle OBA = 180°$

$\Rightarrow$ $\angle AOB + 30° + 30° = 180°$

$\Rightarrow$ $\angle AOB = 120°$

Now, $\angle AOC = \angle AOB - \angle BOC = 120° - 66° = 54°$

$\angle BOC + \angle AOC = 66° + 54° = 120°$

6. (d) Given, $\angle AOB = 90°$ and $\angle ABC = 30°$

We know that, in a circle, the angle subtended by an arc at the centre is twice the angle subtended by it at the remaining part of the circle

$\therefore$ $\angle AOB = 2\angle ACB$

$\Rightarrow$ $90° = 2\angle ACB$ [$\because \angle AOB = 90°$, given]

$\Rightarrow$ $\angle ACB = 45°$

Also, $AO = OB$

[both are the radius of a circle]

$\Rightarrow$ $\angle ABO = \angle BAO$ ...(i)

[angles opposite to equal sides are equal]

In ΔOAB, $\angle OAB + \angle ABO + \angle BOA = 180°$

[$\because$ angle sum property of a triangle]

$\angle OAB + \angle OAB + 90° = 180°$ [from Eq. (i)]

$\Rightarrow$ $2\angle OAB = 180° - 90°$

$\Rightarrow$ $\angle OAB = \dfrac{90°}{2} = 45°$ ...(ii)

In ΔACB, $\angle ACB + \angle CBA + \angle CAB = 180°$

[$\because$ angle sum property of a triangle]

$\therefore$ $45° + 30° + \angle CAB = 180°$

$\Rightarrow$ $\angle CAB = 180° - 75° = 105°$

$\because$ $\angle CAO + \angle OAB = 105°$

$\Rightarrow$ $\angle CAO + 45° = 105°$ [from Eq. (ii)]

$\therefore$ $\angle CAO = 105° - 45° = 60°$

7. (b) Given, $\angle ABC = 20°$

We know that, angle subtended at the centre by an arc is twice the angle subtended by it at the remaining part of circle.

$\therefore$ $\angle AOC = 2\angle ABC = 2 \times 20° = 40°$

8. (a) We know that, the perpendicular from the centre of a circle to a chord bisects the chord.

$\therefore$ $AC = CB = \dfrac{1}{2} AB = \dfrac{1}{2} \times 8 = 4$ cm [$\because AB = 8$ cm, given]

$\because$ $OA = 5$ cm [given]

In right angled ΔOCA,

$AO^2 = AC^2 + OC^2$

[by Pythagoras theorem]

$\Rightarrow$ $(5)^2 = (4)^2 + OC^2$

$\Rightarrow \qquad 25 = 16 + OC^2$

$\Rightarrow \qquad OC^2 = 25 - 16 = 9$

$\Rightarrow \qquad OC = 3 \text{ cm}$

[∵ taking positive square root, because length is always positive]

$\because \qquad OA = OD \qquad$ [same radius of a circle]

$\Rightarrow \qquad OD = 5 \text{ cm}$

$\therefore \qquad CD = OD - OC = 5 - 3 = 2 \text{ cm}$

9. (c) Given, $AB = 12$ cm and $BC = 16$ cm

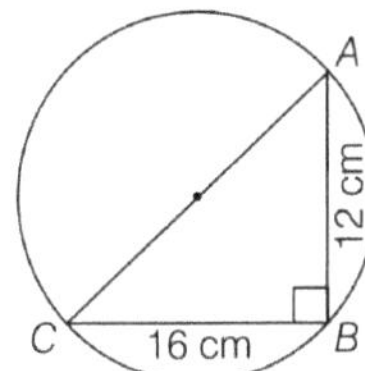

In a circle, $BC \perp AB$, it means that AC will be a diameter of circle.

[∵ diameter of a circle subtends a right angle to the circle]

Using Pythagoras theorem in right-angled triangle $\triangle ABC$,

$$AC^2 = AB^2 + BC^2$$

$\Rightarrow \qquad AC^2 = (12)^2 + (16)^2$

$\Rightarrow \qquad AC^2 = 144 + 256$

$\Rightarrow \qquad AC^2 = 400 \Rightarrow AC = \sqrt{400} = 20 \text{ cm}$

[∵ taking positive square root, because diameter is always positive]

$\therefore$ Radius of circle $= \dfrac{1}{2} AC = \dfrac{1}{2} \times 20 = 10 \text{ cm}$

Hence, the radius of circle is 10 cm.

10. (b) In $\triangle OBP$, $OP = \sqrt{(6.5)^2 - (2.5)^2} = \sqrt{36} = 6$

In $\triangle ODQ$, $OQ = \sqrt{(6.5)^2 - (6)^2} = \sqrt{6.25} = 2.5$

$\therefore \qquad BQ = 6 + 2.5 = 8.5 \text{ cm}.$

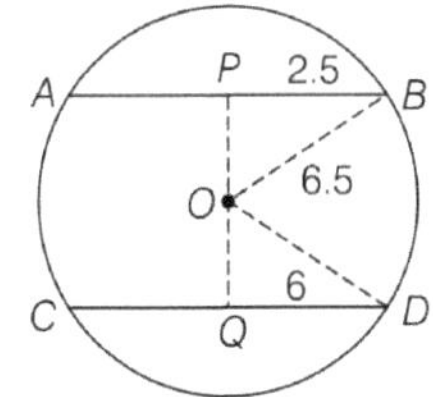

11. (c) Let PQ and RS be two parallel chords of a circle with centre O such that $PQ = 6$ cm and $RS = 8$ cm.

Let a be the radius of circle. Draw $ON \perp RS$ and $OM \perp PQ$. Since, $PQ \parallel RS$, and $ON \perp RS$ and $OM \perp PQ$. Therefore, points O, N and M are collinear.

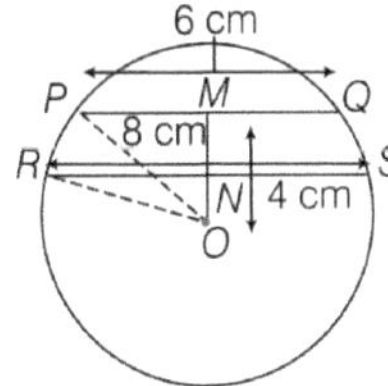

∵ $OM = 4$ cm and M and N are the mid-points of PQ and RS, respectively.

$\therefore \qquad PM = MQ = \dfrac{1}{2} PQ = \dfrac{6}{2} = 3 \text{ cm}$

and $\qquad RN = NS = \dfrac{1}{2} RS = \dfrac{8}{2} = 4 \text{ cm}$

In $\triangle OMP$, we have $OP^2 = OM^2 + PM^2$

[by Pythagoras theorem]

$\Rightarrow \quad a^2 = 4^2 + 3^2 = 16 + 9 = 25 \Rightarrow a = 5 \text{ cm}$

In $\triangle ONR$, we have $OR^2 = ON^2 + RN^2$

[by Pythagoras theorem]

$\Rightarrow \quad a^2 = ON^2 + (4)^2 \Rightarrow 25 = ON^2 + 16$

$\Rightarrow \quad ON^2 = 9 \Rightarrow ON = 3 \text{ cm}$

Hence, the distance of the chord RS from the centre is 3 cm.

12. (a) We have,

$$\angle ABC + \angle CBD = 180° \qquad \text{[linear pair axiom]}$$

$\Rightarrow \qquad \angle ABC + 65° = 180° \quad [\angle CBD = 65°, \text{ given}]$

$\Rightarrow \qquad \angle ABC = 180° - 65° = 115°$

Now, we know that,

Reflex angle $\angle AOC = 2\,\angle ABC$

[∵ since, angle subtended by an arc at the centre is double the angle subtended by it at any point on the remaining part of the circle]

$\Rightarrow \qquad x = 2 \times 115° = 230°$

Hence, the value of x is 230°.

13. (a) Here, $\angle AOC = \angle AOB + \angle BOC = 60° + 30° = 90°$

Since, arc ABC makes an angle of 90° at the centre of the circle.

$\therefore \qquad \angle ADC = \dfrac{1}{2} \angle AOC$

[∵ since, the angle subtended by an arc at the centre is double the angle subtended by it at any point on the remaining part of the circle]

$$= \dfrac{1}{2} \times 90° = 45°$$

14. (d) Here, arc BC makes $\angle BOC$ at the centre and $\angle BAC$ at a point on the remaining part of the circle.

$\therefore \qquad \angle BAC = \dfrac{1}{2} \angle BOC$

Now, $\qquad \angle BOC = 360° - (\angle AOB + \angle AOC)$

$$= 360° - (120° - 80°) = 160°$$

$\therefore \qquad \angle BAC = \dfrac{1}{2}(\angle BOC) = \dfrac{1}{2} \times 160° = 80°$

15. (b) Given, $\qquad \angle ACB = 40°$

We know that, a segment subtends an angle to the circle is half the angle subtends to the centre.

$\therefore \qquad \angle AOB = 2\angle ACB$

$\Rightarrow \qquad \angle ACB = \dfrac{\angle AOB}{2}$

$\Rightarrow \qquad 40° = \dfrac{1}{2} \angle AOB$

$\Rightarrow \qquad \angle AOB = 80° \qquad \qquad \text{...(i)}$

In $\triangle AOB$, $\qquad AO = BO$ [both are the radius of a circle]

$\Rightarrow \qquad \angle OBA = \angle OAB \qquad \qquad \text{...(ii)}$

[∵ angles opposite to the equal sides are equal]

We know that, the sum of all three angles in a triangle AOB is $180°$.

$$\therefore \quad \angle AOB + \angle OBA + \angle OAB = 180°$$
$$\Rightarrow \quad 80° + \angle OAB + \angle OAB = 180° \quad \text{[from Eqs. (i) and (ii)]}$$
$$\Rightarrow \quad 2\angle OAB = 180° - 80°$$
$$\Rightarrow \quad 2\angle OAB = 100°$$
$$\therefore \quad \angle OAB = \frac{100°}{2} = 50°$$

16. (b) Since, equal chords subtends equal angles.

$$\therefore \quad \angle COD = \angle DOE = \angle EOF = \angle FOG = 40°$$

$\therefore$ Reflex angle $\angle COG = 360° - (4 \times 40°) = 200°$

17. (c) Draw a quadrilateral $ABCD$ inscribed in a circle having centre O. Given, $\angle ADC = 130°$

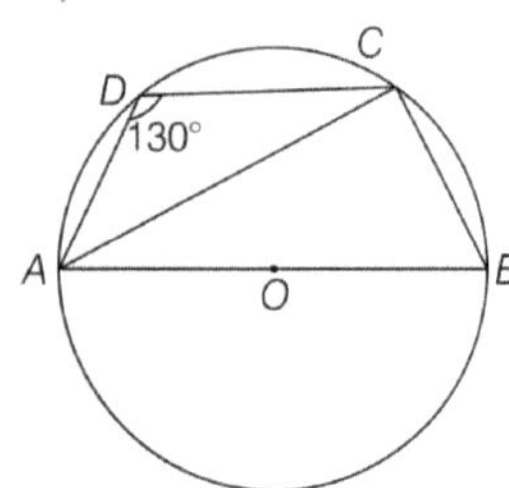

Since, $ABCD$ is a quadrilateral inscribed in a circle, therefore $ABCD$ becomes a cyclic quadrilateral.

$\because$ Since, the sum of opposite angles of a cyclic quadrilateral is $180°$.

$$\therefore \quad \angle ADC + \angle ABC = 180°$$
$$\Rightarrow \quad 130° + \angle ABC = 180° \Rightarrow \angle ABC = 50°$$

Since, AB is a diameter of a circle, then AB subtends an angle to the circle is right angle.

$$\therefore \quad \angle ACB = 90°$$

In $\triangle ABC$, $\angle BAC + \angle ACB + \angle ABC = 180°$

[by angle sum property of a triangle]

$$\Rightarrow \angle BAC + 90° + 50° = 180°$$
$$\Rightarrow \quad \angle BAC = 180° - (90° + 50°)$$
$$= 180° - 140° = 40°$$

18. (b) $2x + 4 + 4x - 64 = 180°$

[sum of opposite angles of quadrilateral is $180°$]
$$6x - 60 = 180°$$
$$x = \frac{180 + 60}{6}$$
$$x = \frac{240}{6}$$
$$x = 40°$$

19. (c) Given, $70° + x = 180°$
$$x = 110°$$

[$\because$ sum of opposite angle of cyclic quadrilateral is $180°$]
$$60° + y = 180°$$
$$y = 120°$$

[$\because$ sum of opposite angle of cyclic quadrilateral is $180°$]
$$\therefore \quad x + y = 110° + 120° = 230°$$

20. (c) Here, $\angle ACB = \dfrac{1}{2} \angle APB$

[$\because$ angle subtend by an arc at the centre is double the angle subtended by it at any point on the remaining part of circle].

$$x = \frac{1}{2} \times 150°$$
$$x = 75°$$
$$\angle BCD = 180° - 75° \quad \text{(straight angle)}$$
$$= 105°$$
$$y = 180° - 105° = 75°$$

[$\because$ opposite angle sum of cyclic quadrilateral is $180°$]
$$z = 2y$$
$$z = 2 \times 75°$$
$$z = 150°$$
$$y = x = 75°$$
$$z = 150°$$

21. (a) Let $\dfrac{x}{3} = \dfrac{y}{4} = \dfrac{z}{5} = k$ (say)

Then, $x = 3k$, $y = 4k$ and $z = 5k$

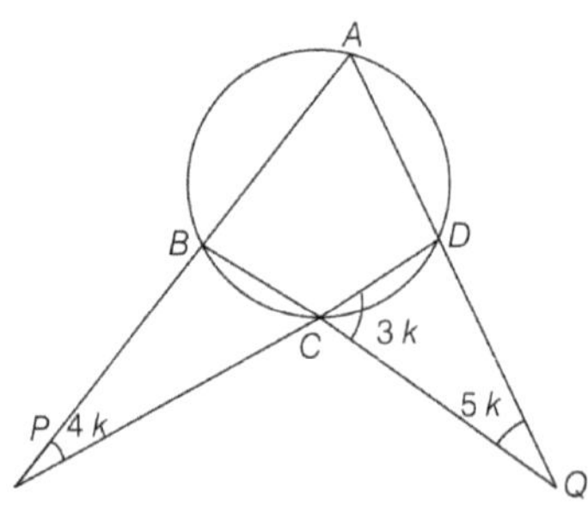

Since, $\angle DCQ = \angle BCP = 3k$ [$\because$ vertically opposite angles]

In $\triangle DCQ$, $\angle CDQ = 180° - (3k + 5k) = 180° - 8k$

By properties of cyclic quadrilateral,
$$\angle ADC + \angle CBA = 180°$$
$$180° - (180° - 8k) + \angle CBA = 180°$$
$$\Rightarrow \quad \angle CBA = 180° - 8k$$
$$\therefore \quad \angle PBC = 180° - \angle ABC$$
$$= 180° - (180° - 8k) = 8k$$

In $\triangle PBC$, $\angle P + \angle B + \angle C = 180°$
$$\therefore \quad 4k + 8k + 3k = 180°$$
$$\Rightarrow \quad k = 12°$$
$$\therefore \quad x = 36°, \ y = 48° \text{ and } z = 60°$$

22. (i) (b)

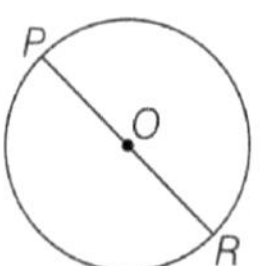

We know that, chord passes through centre called as diameter.

(ii) (b) $\angle PQR = 90°$ [$\because$ angle in semi-circle is $90°$]

(iii) (d)

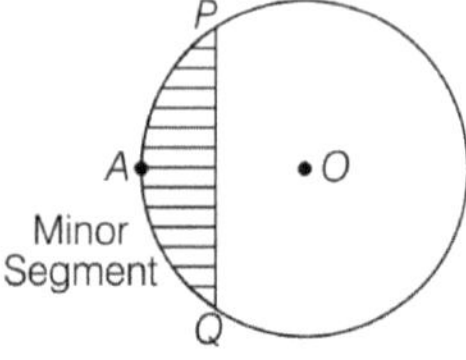

(iv) (d) In ΔPQR, using Pythagoras theorem, we get
$$PR^2 = PQ^2 + RQ^2$$
$$PR^2 = (40)^2 + (9)^2$$
$$= 1600 + 81$$
$$PR^2 = 1681$$
$$PR = 41 \qquad \text{[on taking positive square root]}$$
$\therefore$ Radius of circle is $\dfrac{41}{2}$ cm.

23. (i) (a) As, all the points are equidistance from each other, therefore the triangle given in figure is equilateral triangle.

(ii) (b) As, all sides are equal given in question, therefore it is equilateral triangle.
$$\therefore \qquad \angle PQR = 60° \qquad [\because \text{ angle of equilateral triangle}]$$

(iii) (c) $QR = 8\,\text{cm} \qquad [\because \text{ all sides of equilateral triangle are equal}]$

Then, $\quad PR = 8\,\text{cm}$
$$PQ = 8\,\text{cm}$$
$$\Rightarrow PR + PQ = 8 + 8 = 16\,\text{cm}$$

(iv) (b) $\angle QOR = 2\angle QPR$
$[\because$ the angle subtended by an arc at the centre is double the angle subtended by it at any point on the remaining part of circle.]
$$\Rightarrow \qquad \angle QPR = 60° \quad \text{[angle of equilateral triangle]}$$
$$\Rightarrow \qquad \angle QOR = 2 \times 60°$$
$$\Rightarrow \qquad \angle QOR = 120°$$

(v) (a) $\angle QOR = 120°$

$[\because$ angle subtended by the arc at the centre is double the angle subtended by it at any point on circle]
$$QO = OR \qquad \text{[radius of circle]}$$
$$\angle OQR = \angle ORQ$$
$[\because$ angle opposite to equal side]
$$\angle OQR + \angle ORQ + \angle QOR = 180°$$
$[\because$ sum of angles of triangle is 180°]
$$2x + 120 = 180°$$
$$2x = 180° - 120°$$
$$2x = 60°$$
$$x = 30°$$
$$\Rightarrow \qquad \angle OQR + \angle ORQ = 30° + 30° = 60°$$

Subjective Questions

1. In ΔOAB and ΔOCB,
$$\angle ABO = \angle CBO \qquad \text{(given)}$$
$$OB = OB \qquad \text{[common sides]}$$
and $\qquad OA = OC \qquad \text{[radii of a circle]}$
$$\therefore \qquad \Delta OAB \cong \Delta OCB \quad \text{[by SSA congruence rule]}$$
$$\Rightarrow \qquad AB = CB \qquad \text{[by CPCT]}$$

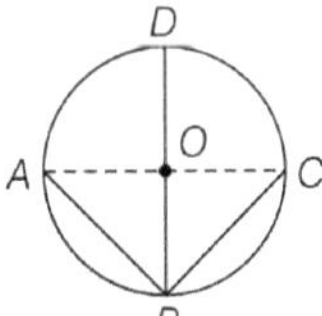

2. In ΔOAC and ΔOBC
$$OA = OB \qquad \text{[radii of a circle]}$$
$$AC = BC \qquad \text{[given]}$$
and $\qquad OC = OC \qquad \text{[common]}$
$$\therefore \qquad \Delta OAC \cong \Delta OBC \qquad \text{[by SSS congruence rule]}$$
$$\Rightarrow \qquad \angle ACO = \angle BCO \qquad \text{[by CPCT]}$$
Again, in ΔAMC and ΔBMC
$$AC = BC \qquad \text{[given]}$$
$$\angle ACM = \angle BCM \qquad \text{[proved above]}$$
and $\qquad CM = CM \qquad \text{[common]}$
$$\therefore \qquad \Delta AMC \cong \Delta BMC \qquad \text{[by SAS congruence rule]}$$
$$\Rightarrow \qquad AM = BM \qquad \text{[by CPCT]}$$
$$\Rightarrow \qquad \frac{AM}{BM} = \frac{1}{1}$$

3. Let AXB and CYD are arcs of circle whose centre and radius are O and r units, respectively.
So, $\qquad OA = OB = OC = OD = r \qquad \text{...(i)}$
$\because \qquad \text{arc } AXB \cong \text{arc } CYD$
$$\therefore \qquad \angle AOB = \angle COD \qquad \text{...(ii)}$$
[congruent arcs of a circle subtend equal angles at the centre]

In ΔAOB and ΔCOD,
$$AO = CO \qquad \text{[from Eq. (i)]}$$
$$BO = DO \qquad \text{[from Eq. (i)]}$$
and $\qquad \angle AOB = \angle COD \qquad \text{[from Eq. (ii)]}$
$$\therefore \qquad \Delta AOB \cong \Delta COD \quad \text{[by SAS congruence rule]}$$
$$\Rightarrow \qquad AB = CD \qquad \text{[by CPCT]}$$
$$\Rightarrow \qquad \frac{AB}{CD} = \frac{1}{1}$$

4. Given, AB and AC are two equal chords whose centre is O.

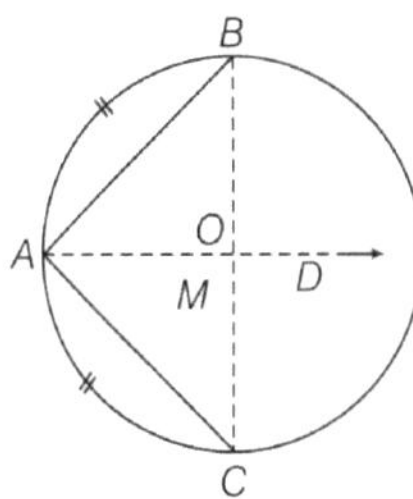

Join BC and draw bisector AD of $\angle BAC$.
In ΔBAM and ΔCAM,
$$AB = AC \qquad \text{[given]}$$
$$\angle BAM = \angle CAM \qquad \text{[given]}$$
and $\qquad AM = AM \qquad \text{[common]}$
$$\therefore \qquad \Delta BAM \cong \Delta CAM \quad \text{[by SAS congruence rule]}$$
$$\Rightarrow \qquad BM = CM \qquad \text{[by CPCT]}$$
and $\qquad \angle BMA = \angle CMA \qquad \text{[by CPCT]}$
So, $\qquad BM = CM$ and $\angle BMA = \angle CMA = 90°$
$\therefore$ AM is the perpendicular bisector of chord BC.
Hence, bisector of $\angle BAC$, i.e. AM passes through the centre O. **Hence proved.**

5. Let AB be a chord of the given circle with centre O.
Given, radius $OA = 13$ cm and $AB = 10$ cm

From O, draw $OL \perp AB$.

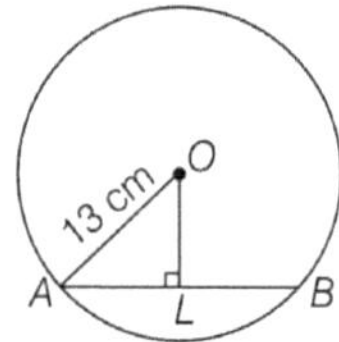

We know that, the perpendicular drawn from the centre of a circle to a chord bisects the chord.

$$\therefore \quad AL = \frac{1}{2} AB = \frac{1}{2} \times 10 = 5 \text{ cm}$$

Now, from the right-angled triangle ΔOLA,

$$OA^2 = OL^2 + AL^2 \qquad \text{[by Pythagoras theorem]}$$
$$\Rightarrow \quad 13^2 = OL^2 + 5^2$$
$$\Rightarrow \quad OL^2 = 13^2 - 5^2 = 169 - 25 = 144$$
$$\Rightarrow \quad OL = 12 \text{ cm} \qquad \text{[taking positive square root]}$$

Hence, the distance of the chord from the centre is 12 cm.

6. Given, $AD = 34$ cm and $AB = 30$ cm

In figure, draw $OL \perp AB$.

Since, the perpendicular from the centre of a circle to a chord bisects the chord.

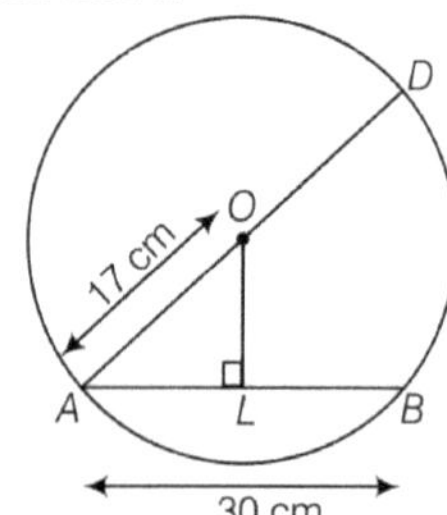

$$\therefore \quad AL = LB = \frac{1}{2} AB = 15 \text{ cm}$$

In right angled ΔOLA,

$$OA^2 = OL^2 + AL^2 \qquad \text{[by Pythagoras theorem]}$$
$$\therefore \quad (17)^2 = OL^2 + (15)^2$$
$$\Rightarrow \quad 289 = OL^2 + 225$$
$$\Rightarrow \quad OL^2 = 289 - 225 = 64$$
$$\therefore \quad OL = 8 \text{ cm}$$

[taking positive square root, because length is always positive]

Hence, the distance of the chord from the centre is 8 cm.

7. Given, radius of circle = 10 cm

Distance of chord AB from centre = 6 cm

Draw $\qquad OM \perp AB$.

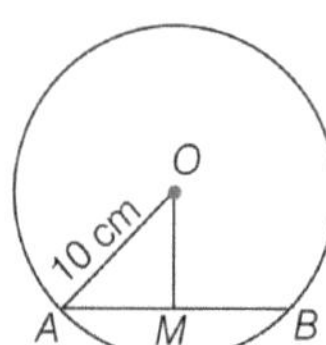

Then, by theorem 1, OM bisects the chord AB.

$$\therefore \quad AM = MB$$

In right-angled triangle ΔOMA,

$$OA = 10 \text{ cm},$$
$$OM = 6 \text{ cm}$$

Then, by Pythagoras theorem,

$$OA^2 = OM^2 + AM^2$$
$$\Rightarrow \quad 10^2 = 6^2 + AM^2$$
$$\Rightarrow \quad AM^2 = 100 - 36 = 64$$
$$\Rightarrow \quad AM = 8 \text{ cm} \qquad \text{[taking positive square root]}$$

$\therefore$ Length of the chord AB

$$= 2 \times AM$$
$$= 2 \times 8 = 16 \text{ cm}$$

8. Given AB and CD are two chords of a circle, whose centre is O and PQ is a diameter bisecting the chords AB and CD at L and M, respectively and the diameter PQ passes through the centre O of the circle.

To prove $\quad AB \parallel CD$

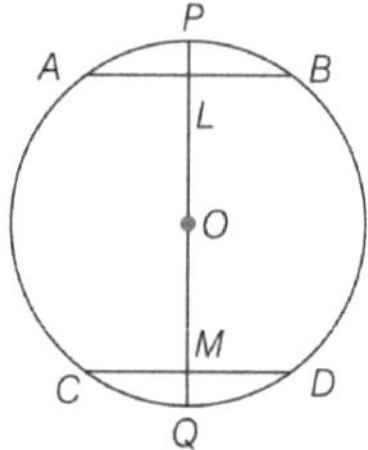

Proof Since, L is the mid-point of AB.

$$\therefore \qquad\qquad OL \perp AB$$

[$\because$ since, the line joining the centre of a circle to the mid-point of a chord is perpendicular to the chord]

$$\therefore \qquad\qquad \angle ALO = 90° \qquad\qquad \text{...(i)}$$
$$\text{Similarly,} \qquad OM \perp CD$$
$$\therefore \qquad\qquad \angle OMD = 90° \qquad\qquad \text{...(ii)}$$

From Eqs. (i) and (ii), we get

$$\angle ALO = \angle OMD \qquad\qquad \text{[each 90°]}$$

But these are alternate angles.

So, $\qquad\qquad AB \parallel CD \qquad\qquad$ **Hence proved.**

9. Given, arc ABC makes $\angle AOC = 100°$ at the centre of the circle and $\angle ADC$ at a point on the remaining part of the circle.

$$\therefore \qquad \angle ADC = \frac{1}{2}(\angle AOC) \qquad \text{[by theorem 1]}$$
$$= \frac{1}{2}(100°) = 50°$$

Similarly, $\angle ABC = \frac{1}{2}(\text{ Reflex angle } \angle AOC)$

$$\Rightarrow \qquad \angle ABC = \frac{1}{2}(360° - 100°)$$
$$= \frac{1}{2}(260°) = 130°$$

Hence, $\quad \angle ADC = 50°$

and $\qquad \angle ABC = 130°$

10. Given A circle is circumscribing a ΔABC, whose centre is O and D is mid-point of BC.

To Prove $\angle BOD = \angle A$ or $\angle BOD = \angle BAC$

Construction Join OB, OD and OC.

Proof In $\triangle BOD$ and $\triangle COD$,

$$OB = OC \quad [\because \text{radii of the same circle}]$$
$$BD = CD$$
$$[\because D \text{ is the mid-point of } BC \text{ (given)}]$$
$$OD = OD \quad [\text{common}]$$
$$\therefore \quad \triangle BOD \cong \triangle COD \ [\text{by SSS congruence rule}]$$
$$\Rightarrow \quad \angle BOD = \angle COD \quad [\text{by CPCT}]$$
$$\therefore \quad \angle BOC = 2\angle BOD \quad \text{...(i)}$$

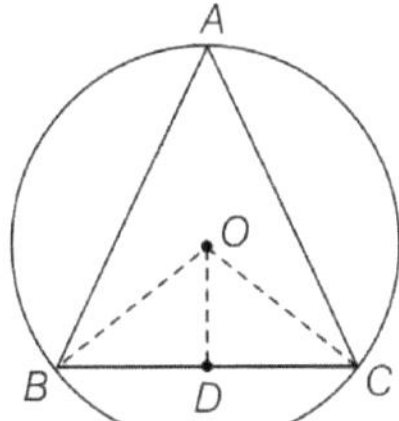

Also, $\quad \angle BAC = \dfrac{1}{2}\angle BOC$

$[\because$ since, the angle subtended by an arc at the centre is twice the angle subtended by it at any point on the remaining part of the circle$]$

$$\Rightarrow \quad \angle BAC = \dfrac{2}{2}\angle BOD$$

$[\text{from Eq. (i)}, \angle BOC = 2\ \angle BOD]$

$$\Rightarrow \quad \angle BAC = \angle BOD$$

Hence, $\angle BOD = \angle A$. **Hence proved.**

11. Let BC be a chord, which is equal to the radius.
Join OB and OC.

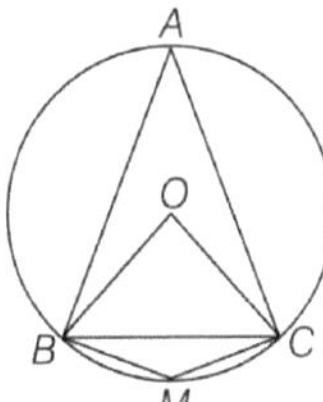

Given, $\quad BC = OB = OC \quad [\text{same radii}]$
So, $\triangle OBC$ is an equilateral triangle.

$$\therefore \quad \angle BOC = 60°$$
$$\text{Then,} \quad \angle BAC = \dfrac{1}{2}\angle BOC$$
$$= \dfrac{1}{2} \times 60° = 30°$$

$[\because$ since, the angle subtended by an arc at the centre is double the angle subtended by it at any point on the remaining part of the circle$]$

Here, $ABMC$ is a cyclic quadrilateral.

$$\therefore \ \angle BAC + \angle BMC = 180°$$

$[\because$ in a cyclic quadrilateral, the sum of any pair of opposite angles is $180°]$

$$\Rightarrow \quad \angle BMC = 180° - 30° = 150°$$

12. Here, $\quad \angle BDC = \angle BAC \quad \text{...(i)}$

$[\because$ since, the angles in the same segment are equal$]$

Now, in $\triangle ABC$, we have

$$\angle BAC + \angle ABC + \angle ACB = 180°$$

$[\because$ angle sum property of triangle$]$

$$\Rightarrow \quad \angle BAC + 69° + 31° = 180°$$
$$\Rightarrow \quad \angle BAC + 100° = 180°$$
$$\Rightarrow \quad \angle BAC = 180° - 100°$$
$$\Rightarrow \quad \angle BAC = 80°$$
$$\text{From Eq. (i),} \quad \angle BDC = 80°$$

13. Let $ABCD$ be a rhombus, inscribed in a circle.

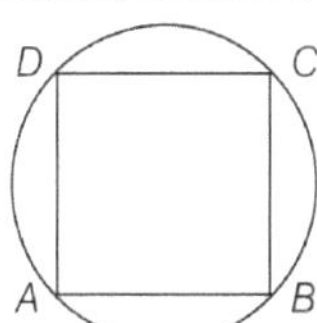

Now, $\angle BAD = \angle BCD$

$[\because$ opposite angles of a parallelogram are equal$]$

and $\angle BAD + \angle BCD = 180°$

$[\because$ pair of opposite angles in a cyclic quadrilateral are supplementary$]$

$$\therefore \quad \angle BAD = \angle BCD = \dfrac{180°}{2} = 90°$$

Similarly, the other two angles are 90° and all the sides are equal.

$\therefore ABCD$ is a square. **Hence Proved.**

14. Given Diagonals NP and QM of a cyclic quadrilateral $NQPM$ are diameters of the circle passing through the vertices M, P, Q and N.

To prove Quadrilateral $NQPM$ is a rectangle.

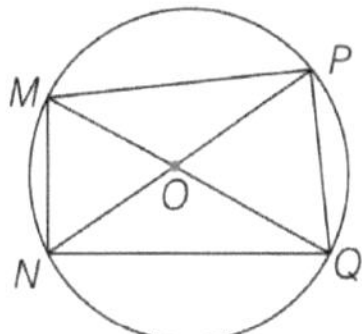

Proof Here, $ON = OP = OQ = OM \quad [\because$ radii of same circle$]$

$$\text{Then,} \quad ON = OP = \dfrac{1}{2}NP$$
$$\text{and} \quad OM = OQ = \dfrac{1}{2}MQ$$
$$\therefore \quad NP = MQ$$

Hence, the diagonals of the quadrilateral $NQPM$ are equal and bisect each other. So, quadrilateral $NQPM$ is a rectangle.

Hence proved.

15. We know that, angles in the same segment are equal.

$$\therefore \quad \angle BDC = \angle BAC$$
$$\Rightarrow \quad \angle BDC = 30°$$

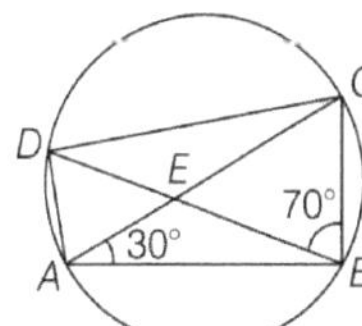

In $\triangle BCD$, we have $\angle BDC + \angle DBC + \angle BCD = 180°$

[∵ angle sum property of triangle]

$\Rightarrow 30° + 70° + \angle BCD = 180°$

[∵ $\angle DBC = 70°$ and $\angle BDC = 30°$]

$\Rightarrow \angle BCD = 180° - 30° - 70° = 80°$

If $AB = BC$, then $\angle BCA = \angle BAC = 30°$

[∵ since, angles opposite to equal sides in a triangle are equal]

Now, $\angle ECD = \angle BCD - \angle BCA$

$= 80° - 30° = 50°$

[∵ $\angle BCD = 80°$ and $\angle BCA = 30°$]

Hence, $\angle BCD = 80°$ and $\angle ECD = 50°$

16. Let we consider the points A, B, C and D formed a cyclic quadrilateral. Then, sum of opposite angles of a quadrilateral is 180°.

$\therefore \qquad \angle ADC + \angle OBC = 180°$ [∵ $\angle ABC = \angle OBC$]

$\Rightarrow \qquad 130° + \angle OBC = 180°$

$\Rightarrow \qquad \angle OBC = 180° - 130° = 50°$

Now, in $\triangle BOC$ and $\triangle BOE$,

$\qquad BC = BE$ [given]

$\qquad OC = OE$ [∵ radii of the same circle]

$\qquad OB = OB$ [common sides]

$\therefore \qquad \triangle BOC \cong \triangle BOE$ [by SSS congruence rule]

Then, $\qquad \angle OBC = \angle OBE$ [by CPCT]

$\qquad \angle OBE = \angle OBC = 50°$ [from Eq. (i)]

$\therefore \qquad \angle CBE = \angle OBC + \angle OBE$

$\qquad = 50° + 50° = 100°$

17. It is given that O is the centre of the circle and $\angle ADC = 120°$

To find $\angle BAC$,

From the figure, we can say that $ABCD$ is a cylic quadrilateral

$\Rightarrow \angle ABC + \angle ADC = 180°$

[∵ sum of opposite angles of a quadrilateral is 180°]

$\Rightarrow \qquad \angle ABC + 120° = 180°$

$\Rightarrow \qquad \angle ABC = 180° - 120° = 60°$

Now, $\angle ACB = 90°$

[∵ angle formed in a semi-circle is always 90°]

Now, let us consider $\triangle ABC$,

$\qquad \angle BAC + \angle ACB + \angle ABC = 180°$

[∵ sum of all angles of triangle is 180°]

$\Rightarrow \qquad \angle BAC + 90° + 60° = 180°$

$\Rightarrow \qquad \angle BAC = 180° - 150° = 30°$

18. We have, $AB = 6$ cm,

$CD = 12$ cm and $PM = 3$ cm

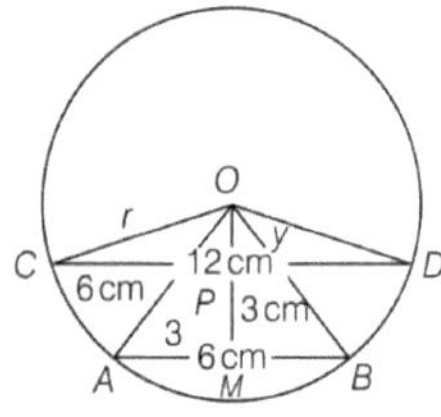

$\therefore \qquad AM = MB = 3$ cm

and $\qquad CP = PD = 6$ cm

Let $\qquad OP = y$

Also, $\qquad PM = 3$ cm [given]

$\therefore$ In $\triangle OPC$, $CP^2 + OP^2 = r^2$ ...(i)

[by Pythagoras theorem]

and In $\triangle OMA$, $AM^2 + OM^2 = r^2$ ...(ii)

$\therefore \qquad CP^2 + OP^2 = AM^2 + OM^2 = r^2$ ...(iii)

$\Rightarrow \qquad 6^2 + y^2 = 3^2 + (3+y)^2$

$\Rightarrow \qquad 36 + y^2 = 9 + 9 + y^2 + 6y$

$\Rightarrow \qquad 6y = 18 \Rightarrow y = 3$ cm

$\therefore \qquad r^2 = 6^2 + y^2 = 36 + 9 = 45$ [using Eq. (i)]

$\Rightarrow \qquad r = 3\sqrt{5}$ cm $= 6.708 = 6.71$ cm

19. Given, M and N are the mid-points of AB and CD, respectively.

$\therefore \qquad \angle OMB = \angle OND = 90°$

$\Rightarrow \qquad \angle OME = \angle ONE = 90°$

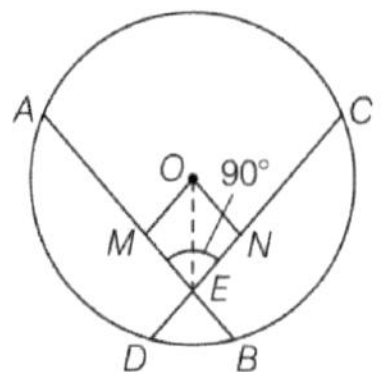

Since, equal chords of a circle are equidistant from the centre.

$\therefore \qquad OM = ON$

Thus, in $\triangle OME$ and $\triangle ONE$, we have

$\qquad OM = ON$

$\qquad \angle OME = \angle ONE$ [each 90°]

and $\qquad OE = OE$ [common sides]

$\therefore \qquad \triangle OME \cong \triangle ONE$ [by RHS congruence rule]

So, $\qquad \angle MOE = \angle NOE = 45°$ [by CPCT]

and $\qquad \angle OEM = \angle OEN = 45°$ [by CPCT]

Hence, $OMEN$ is a square.

20. **Given** AB and AC be two equal chords of circle with centre O. Also, $OP \perp AB$ at M and $OQ \perp AC$ at N.

To prove $PB = QC$

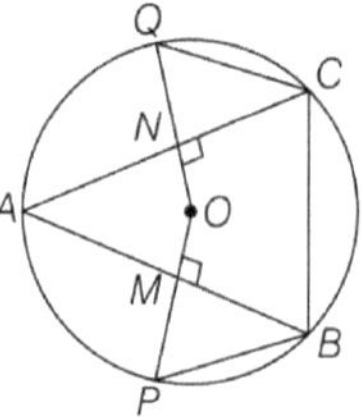

Proof We know that, the perpendicular from the centre of a circle to a chord bisects the chord.

$\therefore \qquad AM = MB = \dfrac{1}{2} AB$ [∵ $OP \perp AB$]

and $\qquad AN = NC = \dfrac{1}{2} AC$ [∵ $OQ \perp AC$]

Since, $\qquad AB = AC$

$\therefore \qquad \dfrac{1}{2} AB = \dfrac{1}{2} AC$

$\Rightarrow$ $\qquad AM = MB = AN = NC$ $\qquad$ ...(i)

Now, in ΔPMB and ΔQNC, we have

$\qquad MB = NC$ $\qquad$ [from Eq. (i)]

$\qquad \angle PMB = \angle QNC$ $\qquad$ [each 90°]

$\qquad OM = ON$ $\qquad$ ...(ii)

$\qquad$ [∵ equal chords of a circle are equidistant from the centre]

$\qquad OP = OQ$ $\qquad$ [∵ radii of same circle]...(iii)

$\Rightarrow$ $\qquad OP - OM = OQ - ON$

$\qquad$ [on subtracting Eq. (ii) from Eq. (iii)]

$\Rightarrow$ $\qquad PM = QN$

$\therefore$ $\qquad \Delta PMB \cong \Delta QNC$ $\qquad$ [by SAS congruence rule]

$\Rightarrow$ $\qquad PB = QC$ $\qquad$ [by CPCT] **Hence proved.**

21. Let us consider ΔBAE,

$\qquad \angle BEA = 90°$ and $BE \perp AE$

$\qquad \angle BAE = \angle BAC = 55°$

So, $\angle BAE + \angle BEA + \angle ABE = 180°$

$\qquad$ [∵ sum of all angles of a triangle is 180°]

$\Rightarrow \quad \angle ABE + 55° + 90° = 180°$

$\Rightarrow \angle ABE = 180° - 145° = 35°$

Now, let us consider ΔBEC,

$\qquad \angle BEC = 90°$ and $BE \perp CE$

$\qquad \angle BCE = \angle BCA = 62°$

So, $\angle BCE + \angle BEC + \angle CBE = 180°$

$\qquad$ [∵ sum of all angles of a triangle is 180°]

$\Rightarrow \quad 62° + 90° + \angle CBE = 180°$

$\Rightarrow \qquad \angle CBE = 180° - 152° = 28°$

As, angles in the same segment are equal,

$\qquad \angle ACD = \angle ABE = 35°$

$\qquad \angle DAC = \angle CBE = 28°$

$\qquad \angle ADB = \angle BCA = 62°$

22. Join OB, OC and OA.

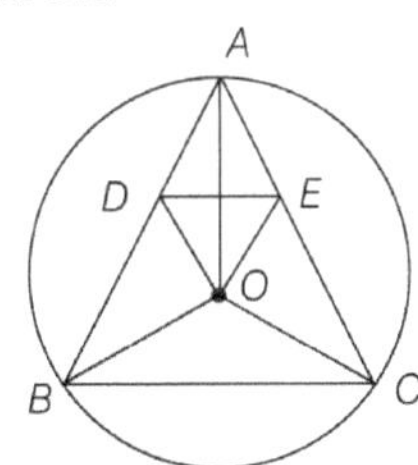

In ΔDBO and ΔECO,

$\qquad OB = OC$

$\qquad$ [∵ OB and OC are radius of circle]

$\angle ODE = \angle OEC = 90°$ $\qquad$ [as, $OD \perp AB$, $OE \perp AC$]

$\qquad OD = OE$

$\qquad$ [∵ equal angles subtends equal sides]

$\therefore \qquad \Delta DBO \cong \Delta ECO$ $\qquad$ [by SAS congruence rule]

$\Rightarrow \qquad BD = EC$ $\qquad$ ...(i) [by CPCT]

As, $OD \perp AB$,

$\therefore \qquad AD = BD$ $\qquad$ ...(ii)

As, $\qquad OE \perp AC$

$\therefore \qquad AE = EC$ $\qquad$ ...(iii)

From Eqs. (i), (ii) and (iii),

$\qquad AD = AE$

$\therefore \qquad AB = AC$

As, equal sides have equal angles.

$\therefore \qquad \angle ABC = \angle ACB$

Hence, ΔADE is an isosceles triangle. $\qquad$ **Hence proved.**

23. Since, ΔADB is a right-angled triangle, right angled at D.

$\qquad$ [∵ angle in semi-circle is 90°]

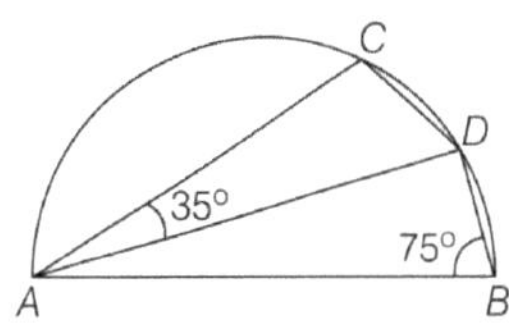

$\therefore \qquad \angle DAB = 180° - (90° + 75°)$

$\Rightarrow \qquad \angle DAB = 15°$

Also, $ABDC$ is a cyclic quadrilateral.

$\therefore \qquad \angle CAB + \angle BDC = 180°$

$\qquad$ [∵ sum of each pair of opposite angles of a cyclic quadrilateral is 180°]

$\Rightarrow \angle BDC = 180° - \angle CAB = 180° - (35° + 15°) = 130°$

24. In the given figure,

Joint OC, OD and BC.

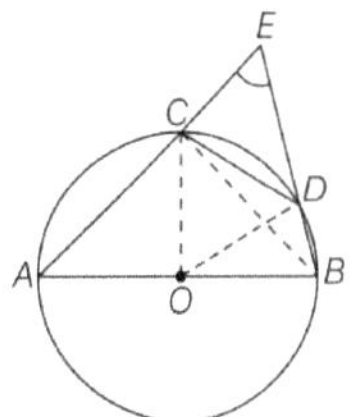

Here, $OC = OD = CD$

ΔODC is equilateral.

Therefore, $\angle COD = 60°$

Now, $\angle CBD = \dfrac{1}{2} \angle COD$

$\qquad$ [by using the theorem, the chord subtends an angle at the centre is half of the chord subtends at the circumference of circle]

This gives, $\angle CBD = 30°$

Again, $\qquad \angle ACB = 90°$

So, $\qquad \angle BCE = 180° - \angle ACB = 90°$

$\therefore \qquad \angle CEB = 90° - 30° = 60°$,

i.e. $\qquad \angle AEB = 60°$

25. Let $ABCD$ be a quadrilateral in which the angle bisectors AH, BF, CF and DH of internal angles A, B, C and D respectively form a quadrilateral $EFGH$.

To Prove $EFGH$ is a cyclic quadrilateral.

i.e. $\qquad \angle E + \angle G = 180°$ or $\angle F + \angle H = 180°$

Proof Since, $\angle FEH = \angle AEB$

$\qquad = 180° - \angle EAB - \angle EBA$

$\qquad$ [∵ in ΔAEB, $\angle EAB + \angle EBA + \angle AEB = 180°$]

$\qquad = 180° - \dfrac{1}{2} (2 \angle EAB + 2 \angle EBA)$

$$= 180° - \frac{1}{2}(\angle A + \angle B) \qquad \text{...(i)}$$

$[\because AH$ and BF are bisectors of $\angle A$ and $\angle B$ respectively]

Similarly, $\angle FGH = \angle CGD$

$$= 180° - \angle GCD - \angle GDC$$

$$= 180° - \frac{1}{2}(\angle C + \angle D) \qquad \text{...(ii)}$$

On adding Eqs. (i) and (ii), we get

$$\angle FEH + \angle FGH = 180° - \frac{1}{2}(\angle A + \angle B)$$
$$+ 180° - \frac{1}{2}(\angle C + \angle D)$$
$$= 360° - \frac{1}{2}(\angle A + \angle B + \angle C + \angle D)$$
$$= 360° - \frac{1}{2} \times 360°$$

$[\because$ sum of angles of a quadrilateral is $360°]$
$$= 360° - 180° = 180°$$

Therefore, by theorem 6, the quadrilateral $EFGH$ is cyclic.

Hence proved.

26. Given, $ABCE$ is a cylic quadrilateral and $\angle AEC = 110°$

$\therefore \qquad \angle ABC + \angle AEC = 180°$

$[\because$ sum of opposite angles of a cylic quadrilateral is $180°]$

$\Rightarrow \qquad \angle ABC + 110° = 180°$

$\Rightarrow \qquad \angle ABC = 180° - 110° = 70°$

Now, arc AC subtends both $\angle ABC$ and $\angle ADC$

$\therefore \qquad \angle ABC = \angle ADC$

$[\because$ angles at the circumference subtended by the same arc are equal]

$\Rightarrow \qquad \angle ABC = \angle ADC = 70°$

27. Let O be the centre of the circle and Reshma, Salma and Mandeep are represented by the points R, S and M, respectively. Draw $OP \perp RM$ and $ON \perp RS$.

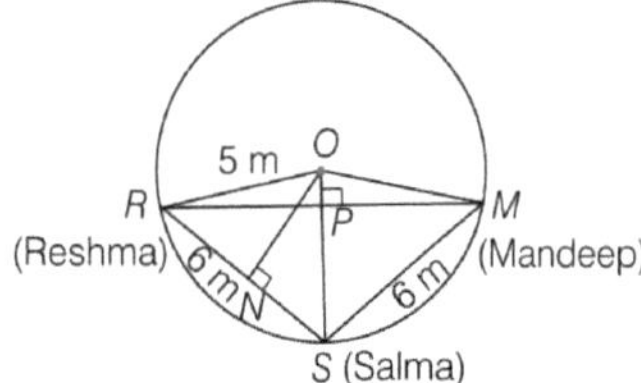

Let $RP = x$ m

Area of $\triangle ORS = \frac{1}{2} \times RP \times OS$

$[\because$ area of triangle $= \frac{1}{2} \times$ base $\times$ height]

$\Rightarrow$ Area of $\triangle ORS = \frac{1}{2} \times x \times 5 = \frac{5x}{2}$ m^2 ...(i)

In right angled $\triangle RNO$,

$$OR^2 = RN^2 + NO^2 \text{[by Pythagoras theorem]}$$

$\Rightarrow \qquad 5^2 = 3^2 + NO^2$

$[\because ON \perp RS$, therefore $RN = SN = \frac{6}{2} = 3$ m$]$

$\Rightarrow \qquad NO^2 = 25 - 9 = 16$

$\Rightarrow \qquad NO = 4$ m   [on taking positive square root]

Again, area of $\triangle ORS = \frac{1}{2} \times RS \times ON$

$$= \frac{1}{2} \times 6 \times 4 = 12 \text{ m}^2 \qquad \text{...(ii)}$$

From Eqs. (i) and (ii), we get

$$\frac{5x}{2} = 12$$

$\Rightarrow \qquad x = \frac{24}{5} = RP$

Here, P is the mid-point of RM.

$[\because$ perpendicular from centre to the chord, bisects the chord]

$\therefore \qquad RM = 2RP = 2 \times \frac{24}{5}$

$$= \frac{48}{5} = 9.6 \text{ m}$$

Hence, the distance between Reshma and Mandeep is 9.6 m.

28. Let Ankur, Syed and David be sitting on the points P, Q and R, respectively on the boundary of circular park.

Clearly, $PQ = QR = PR$, as they sitting at equal distance. Thus, $\triangle PQR$ is an equilateral triangle.

Let $\qquad PQ = QR = PR = x$ m

Now, draw altitudes PC, QD and RN from vertices to the sides of a triangle and these altitudes intersect at the centre of circle M.

$[\because$ altitudes of equilateral triangle passes through the circumcentre of the equilateral triangle.]

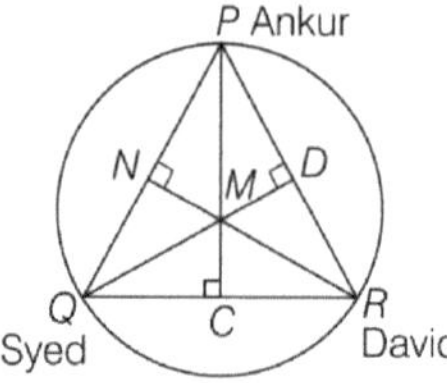

As $\triangle PQR$ is an equilateral triangle, therefore these altitudes bisect their sides.

In right angled $\triangle PCQ$,

$$PQ^2 = PC^2 + QC^2 \text{ [by Pythagoras theorem]}$$

$\Rightarrow \qquad x^2 = PC^2 + \left(\frac{x}{2}\right)^2 \qquad \left[\because QC = \frac{1}{2}QR = \frac{x}{2}\right]$

$\Rightarrow \qquad PC^2 = x^2 - \frac{x^2}{4} = \frac{3x^2}{4}$

$\therefore \qquad PC = \frac{\sqrt{3}x}{2} \qquad$ [taking positive square root]

Now, $\qquad MC = PC - PM = \frac{\sqrt{3}x}{2} - 20$

$[\because PM =$ radius $= 20$ m$]$

In right angled $\triangle QCM$, $QM^2 = QC^2 + MC^2$

[by Pythagoras theorem]

$\Rightarrow \qquad (20)^2 = \left(\frac{x}{2}\right)^2 + \left(\frac{\sqrt{3}x}{2} - 20\right)^2$

$[\because QM =$ radius $= 20$ m$]$

$$\Rightarrow \qquad 400 = \frac{x^2}{4} + \frac{3x^2}{4} - 20\sqrt{3}x + 400$$

$$\Rightarrow \qquad x^2 - 20\sqrt{3}x = 0$$

$$\Rightarrow \qquad x(x - 20\sqrt{3}) = 0$$

$$\Rightarrow \qquad x = 0 \text{ or } x - 20\sqrt{3} = 0$$

$$\Rightarrow \qquad x = 0 \text{ or } x = 20\sqrt{3}$$

But $x = 0$ is not possible, because length of side of an equilateral triangle cannot be zero.

$$\therefore \qquad x = 20\sqrt{3}\text{ m}$$

Thus, $PQ = QR = PR = 20\sqrt{3}$ m

Hence, the length of the string of each phone is $20\sqrt{3}$ m.

29. Here, $\angle EDF = \angle EDA + \angle ADF$ $\qquad$ ...(i)

Since, $\angle EDA$ and $\angle EBA$ are the angles in the same segment of the circle.

$$\therefore \angle EDA = \angle EBA = \frac{1}{2} \angle B \qquad \text{...(ii)} \; [\because EB \text{ bisects } \angle ABC]$$

Similarly, $\angle ADF$ and $\angle FCA$ are the angles in the same segment.

$$\therefore \qquad \angle ADF = \angle FCA$$
$$= \frac{1}{2} \angle C \qquad \text{...(iii)} \; [\because FC \text{ bisects } \angle C]$$

From Eq. (i),

$$\angle EDF = \frac{1}{2} \angle B + \frac{1}{2} \angle C \qquad [\text{using Eqs. (ii) and (iii)}]$$

$$\Rightarrow \qquad \angle D = \frac{\angle B + \angle C}{2}$$

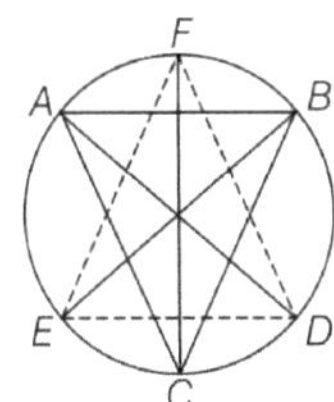

$$\text{Similarly,} \quad \angle F = \frac{\angle A + \angle B}{2}$$

$$\text{and} \qquad \angle E = \frac{\angle C + \angle A}{2}$$

$$\text{Now,} \qquad \angle D = \frac{\angle B + \angle C}{2}$$
$$= \frac{180° - \angle A}{2} \qquad [\because \angle A + \angle B + \angle C = 180°]$$

$$\text{Similarly,} \quad \angle E = \frac{180° - \angle B}{2} \qquad [\because \angle A + \angle B + \angle C = 180°]$$

$$\text{and} \qquad \angle F = \frac{180° - \angle C}{2} \qquad [\because \angle A + \angle B + \angle C = 180°]$$

$$\Rightarrow \qquad \angle D = 90° - \frac{\angle A}{2}$$

$$\angle E = 90° - \frac{\angle B}{2}$$

$$\text{and} \qquad \angle F = 90° - \frac{\angle C}{2} \qquad \textbf{Hence proved.}$$

30. Here, reflex angle $\angle POR = 2\angle PQR$
$$= 2 \times 100° = 200°$$
$$[\because \text{ since, the angle subtended by an arc at the centre is}$$
$$\text{double the angle subtended by it at any point}$$
$$\text{on the remaining part of the circle}]$$

In ΔOPR, $\qquad \angle POR = 360° - 200° = 160°$ $\qquad$ ...(i)

Again, in ΔOPR,

$$OP = OR \quad [\because \text{ radii of the same circle}]$$

$$\therefore \qquad \angle ORP = \angle OPR \qquad \text{...(ii)}$$
$$[\because \text{angles opposite to equal sides of}$$
$$\text{a triangle are also equal}]$$

Also, $\quad \angle OPR + \angle ORP + \angle POR = 180°$
$$[\text{by angle sum property of triangle}]$$

On putting the values from Eqs. (i) and (ii), we get
$$\angle OPR + \angle OPR + 160° = 180°$$
$$\Rightarrow \quad 2\angle OPR = 180° - 160° = 20°$$
$$\Rightarrow \qquad \angle OPR = \frac{20°}{2} = 10°$$

31. Let O and O' be the centres of the circles of radii 10 cm and 8 cm, respectively and PQ be their common chord of length 12 cm.

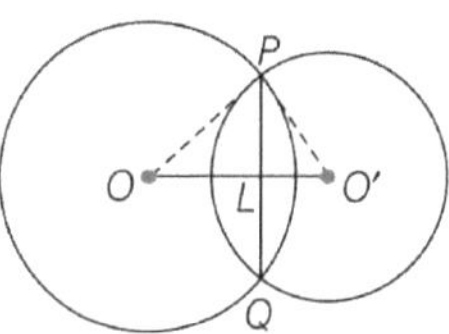

We have, $OP = 10$ cm, $O'P = 8$ cm and $PQ = 12$ cm

$$\therefore \qquad PL = \frac{1}{2} PQ = 6 \text{ cm}$$

$$[\because \text{ since, when two circles intersect at two points,}$$
$$\text{then their centres lie on the perpendicular}$$
$$\text{bisector of the common chord}]$$

In right angled ΔOLP,
$$OP^2 = OL^2 + LP^2 \qquad [\text{by Pythagoras theorem}]$$
$$\Rightarrow \qquad OL = \sqrt{OP^2 - LP^2}$$
$$[\text{taking positive square root}]$$
$$= \sqrt{10^2 - 6^2}$$
$$= \sqrt{100 - 36}$$
$$= \sqrt{64} = 8 \text{ cm}$$

Now, in right angled $\Delta O'LP$,
$$O'P^2 = O'L^2 + LP^2 \qquad [\text{by Pythagoras theorem}]$$
$$\Rightarrow \qquad O'L = \sqrt{O'P^2 - LP^2}$$
$$[\text{taking positive square root}]$$
$$= \sqrt{8^2 - 6^2}$$
$$= \sqrt{64 - 36}$$
$$= \sqrt{28}$$
$$= 5.29 \text{ cm}$$

$\therefore$ Distance between their centres, $OO' = OL + LO'$
$$= (8 + 5.29) = 13.29 \text{ cm}$$

32. We know that the angle formed at the centre of the circle is twice the angle formed at its circumferene.

$$\therefore \quad \angle BOD = 2\angle BAD$$
$$\Rightarrow \quad \angle BAD = \frac{1}{2}\angle BOD = \frac{1}{2} \times 160° = 80°$$

Since, $ABPD$ is a cylic quadrilateral.

$$\therefore \quad \angle BAD + \angle BPD = 180°$$

[∵ sum of opposite angles of a cylic quadrilateral is 180°]

$$\Rightarrow \quad 80° + \angle BPD = 180°$$
$$\Rightarrow \quad \angle BPD = 180° - 80° = 100°$$

Thus, the measure of $\angle BPD = 100°$

33. Here, ABD is a straight line.

Thus, $\quad \angle ABC + \angle CBD = 180°$ $\qquad$ [linear pair]

$$\Rightarrow \quad \angle ABC + 65° = 180°$$
$$\Rightarrow \quad \angle ABC = 180° - 65° = 115°$$

Also, $AECB$ is a cyclic quadrilateral.

Thus, $\angle AEC + \angle ABC = 180°$ (opposite angles of cylic quadrilateral are supplementary)

$$\Rightarrow \angle AEC + 115° = 180°$$
$$\Rightarrow \quad \angle AEC = 180° - 115° = 65°$$

Since, angle subtended by arc on centre is twice the angle subtended by arc on circle.

Thus, $\angle AOC = 2\angle AEC$
$$= 2 \times 65° = 130°$$

Now, $x = 360° - \angle AOC$
$$= 360° - 130° = 230°$$

34. It is given that $ABCD$ is a cyclic quadrilateral with AC and BD as diagonals, $\angle DBC = 55°$ and $\angle BAC = 45°$

To find $\angle BCD$,

From diagram,
$$\angle DAC = \angle DBC = 55°$$

[∵ angle is the same segment are equal]

Now, $\angle BAD = \angle BAC + \angle DAC$
$$= 45° + 55° = 100°$$

In cyclic quadrilateral $ABCD$,
$$\angle BAD + \angle BCD = 180°$$

[∵ sum of opposite angles of a cylic quadrilateral is 180°]

$$\Rightarrow \quad 100° + \angle BCD = 180°$$
$$\Rightarrow \quad \angle BCD = 180° - 100° = 80°$$

Thus, the value of $\angle BCD$ is 80°.

35. It is given that AC is the diameter, AB and AD are equal chords and $\angle AED = 110°$.

To find $\angle BAD$

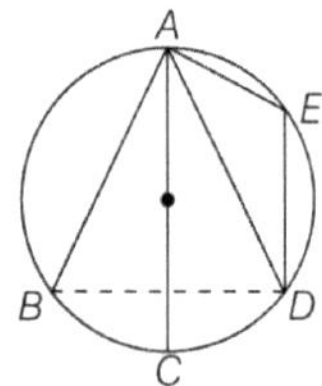

Now, let us join BD

$ABDE$ becomes a cylic quadrilateral,

$$\Rightarrow \angle AED + \angle ABD = 180°$$
$$\therefore \quad \angle ABD = 180° - 110° = 70°$$

Now, it is given that, $AB = AD$

$$\Rightarrow \quad \angle ABD = \angle ADB$$

[∵ equal sides subtend equal angles]

$$\therefore \quad \angle ADB = 70°$$

In $\triangle ABD$,
$$\angle BAD + \angle ADB + \angle DBA = 180°$$

[∵ sum of all angles of a triangle is 180°]

$$\Rightarrow \quad \angle BAD + 70 + 70° = 180°$$
$$\Rightarrow \angle BAD = 180° - 140° = 40°$$

36. Given that, $y = 3x$

As, we know that vertically opposite angles are equal.

$$\therefore \quad \angle ABP = \angle CBQ = 40°$$

Now, $ABCD$ is a cyclic quadrilateral.

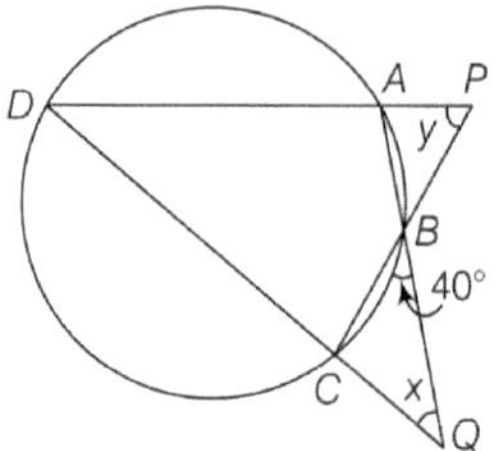

$$\therefore \quad \angle DAB + \angle BCD = 180° \qquad \ldots\text{(i)}$$

[∵ sum of opposite angles of a cylic quadrilateral is 180°]

Now, $\angle DAB = y + \angle ABP$

[∵ sum of two interior angles of a triangle is equal to the exterior angle]

$$\Rightarrow \quad \angle DAB = y + 40° \qquad \ldots\text{(ii)}$$

Similarly, $\angle BCD = x + \angle CBQ$

$$\Rightarrow \quad \angle BCD = x + 40° \qquad \ldots\text{(iii)}$$

Substituting Eqs. (ii) and (iii) in Eq. (i), we obtain

$$y + 40° + x + 40° = 180°$$
$$\Rightarrow \quad x + y + 80° = 180°$$
$$\Rightarrow \quad x + y = 180° - 80° = 100°$$
$$\Rightarrow \quad x + 3x = 100° \qquad [\because y = 3x \text{ (given)}]$$
$$\Rightarrow \quad 4x = 100°$$
$$\Rightarrow \quad x = \frac{100}{4} = 25°$$

Thus, the magnitude of x is 25°.

37. Given, $\angle ADC = 80°$ and $\angle BEC = 50°$

Now, $ABCD$ is a cyclic quadrilateral and sum of opposite angles in cyclic quadrilateral is 180°.

$$\therefore \quad \angle ABC + \angle ADC = 180°$$
$$\Rightarrow \quad \angle ABC + 80° = 180° [\because \angle ADC = 80° \text{ (given)}]$$
$$\Rightarrow \quad \angle ABC = 180° - 80° = 100°$$

Now, $\angle ABC = \angle BCE + \angle BEC$

$$\Rightarrow \quad 100° = \angle BCE + 50°$$
$$\Rightarrow \quad \angle BCE = 100 - 50° = 50°$$

Now, $\angle DCB + \angle BCE = 180°$ $\qquad$ [straight line]

$$\Rightarrow \quad \angle DCB = 180° - 50° = 130°$$

Also, $\angle DCB + \angle BAD = 180°$

[opposite angles of cylic quadrilateral]

$$\Rightarrow \quad \angle BAD = 180° - 130° = 50°$$

Now, $\angle CDA = \angle FCD + \angle CFD$ ...(i)
and, $\angle DCB = \angle FDC + \angle CFD$ ...(ii)
[exterior angle property of triangle]
Adding Eqs. (i) and (ii), we get
$\angle CDA + \angle DCB = \angle FCD + \angle CFD + \angle FDC + \angle CFD$
$\Rightarrow\ 80° + 130° = 150° + 2\angle CFD$
$\Rightarrow\ 2\angle CFD = 210° - 150°$
$\Rightarrow\ \angle CFD = 30°$
Hence, $\angle BAD = 50°$ and $\angle CFD = 30°$

38. (i)

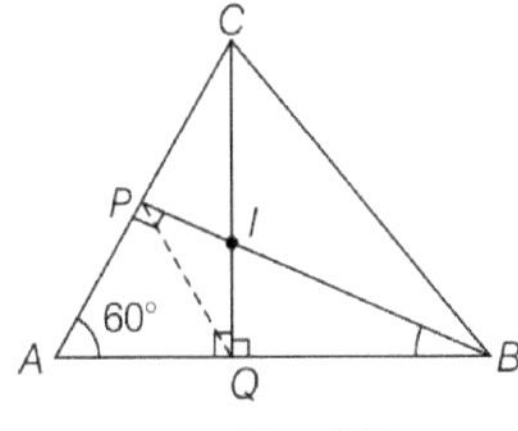

$\because\qquad\qquad \angle A = 60°$ [given]
$\angle APB = 90°$ $[\because PB \perp AC]$
and $\qquad\qquad \angle AQC = 90°$ $[\because CQ \perp AB]$
In quadrilateral $APIQ$,
$\qquad \angle P = 90°,\ \angle Q = 90°,\ \angle A = 60°$
$\therefore\quad \angle I = 360° - (90° + 90° + 60°) = 120°$ ...(i)
Now, we get $\angle P + \angle Q = 180°$
and $\qquad\qquad \angle A + \angle I = 180°$
Hence, $APIQ$ is a cyclic quadrilateral.
[since, sum of either pair of opposite angles is 180°]
Also, $\qquad \angle BPC = \angle BQC$ [each 90°]
$\therefore$ Points P, Q, B and C are concyclic.
[converse of angles in the same segment]
$\Rightarrow PQBC$ is a cyclic quadrilateral.   **Hence proved.**

(ii) From quadrilateral $APIQ$,
$\qquad\qquad \angle A + \angle I = 180°$
$\Rightarrow \qquad\qquad \angle I = 180° - \angle A$
$\qquad\qquad\qquad = 180° - 60° = 120°$
$\therefore \qquad\qquad \angle BIC = \angle PIQ = 120°$

39. Given Non-parallel sides PS and QR of a trapezium $PQRS$ are equal.
To prove $PQRS$ is a cyclic trapezium.
Construction Draw $SM \perp PQ$ and $RN \perp PQ$.

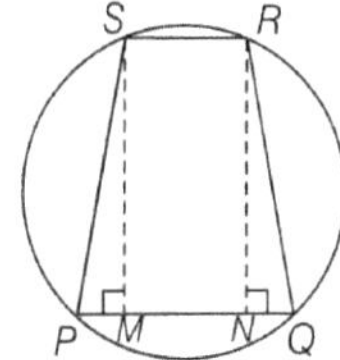

Proof In $\triangle SMP$ and $\triangle RNQ$, we have
$\qquad\qquad SP = RQ$ [given]
$\qquad\qquad \angle SMP = \angle RNQ$ [each 90°]
and $\qquad\qquad SM = RN$
[since, distance between two parallel lines is always equal]
$\therefore \qquad\qquad \triangle SMP \cong \triangle RNQ$ [by RHS congruence rule]
Then, $\qquad\qquad \angle P = \angle Q$
and $\qquad\qquad \angle PSM = \angle QRN$ [by CPCT]
Now, $\qquad\qquad \angle PSM = \angle QRN$
$\Rightarrow \qquad 90° + \angle PSM = 90° + \angle QRN$
[adding 90° both sides]
$\Rightarrow \qquad \angle MSR + \angle PSM = \angle NRS + \angle QRN$
$[\because \angle MSR = \angle NRS = 90°]$
$\Rightarrow \qquad \angle PSR = \angle QRS,$ i.e. $\angle S = \angle R$
Thus, $\qquad\qquad \angle P = \angle Q$
and $\qquad\qquad \angle R = \angle S$ ...(i)
Now, $\qquad \angle P + \angle Q + \angle R + \angle S = 360°$
$[\because$ sum of the angles of a quadrilateral is 360°]
$\Rightarrow \quad 2\angle S + 2\angle Q = 360°$ [from Eq. (i)]
$\Rightarrow \qquad \angle S + \angle Q = 180°$
Hence, $PQRS$ is a cyclic trapezium.   **Hence proved.**

40. Let $\triangle ABC$ be a right angled triangle such that $\angle BAC = 90°$.
Let O be the mid-point of the hypotenuse BC. Then, $OB = OC$, with O as centre and OB as radius, draw a circle.
Clearly, this circle passes through the points B and C. If possible, suppose this circle does not pass through A.
Let it meets BA or BA' produced at A'.
Then, $\qquad\qquad \angle BA'C = 90°$
[since, angle in a semi-circle is 90°]

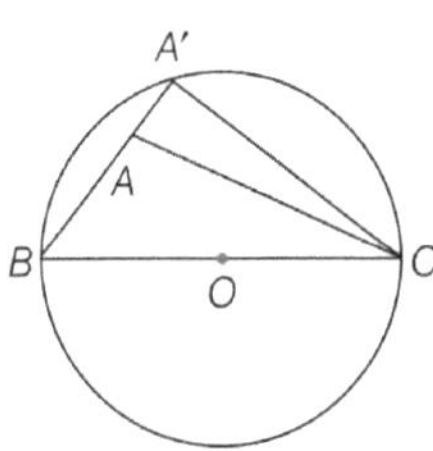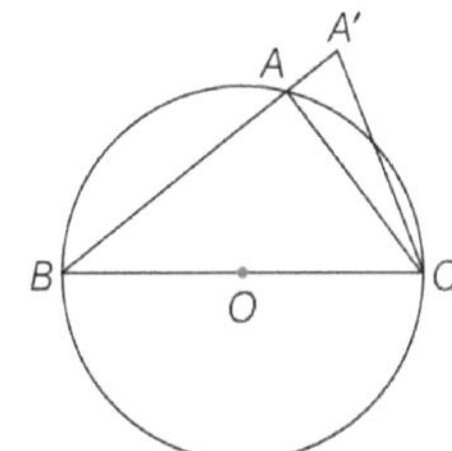

But $\qquad\qquad \angle BAC = 90°$
$\therefore \qquad\qquad \angle BA'C = \angle BAC$
This is not possible unless A coincide A'.
So, the circle which passes through B and C, also passes through A.
Consequently, $OA = OB = OC =$ Radius of the circle
Hence, the mid-point O of the hypotenuse BC of right angled $\triangle ABC$ is equidistant from its vertices.
Hence proved.

41.

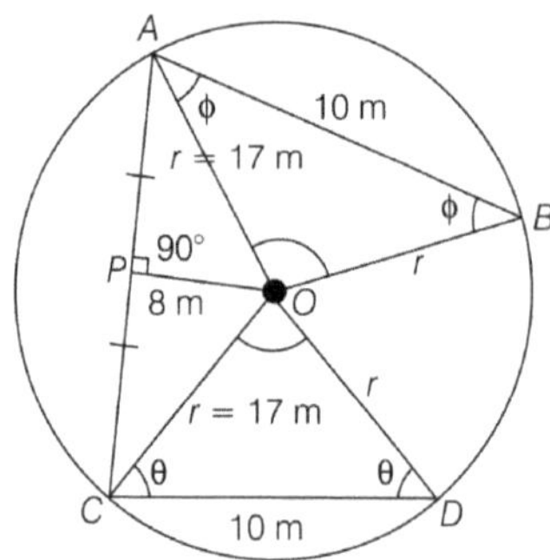

(i) $\angle OCD = \angle ODC = \theta$ [∵ angle opposite to equal side]

$\angle OAB = \angle OBA = \phi$

$\quad \theta = \phi$ [∵ angle opposite to equal side]

$OC = OA = OD = OB$ [radius of a circle]

$AB = CD = 10\,m$ [given]

$\therefore \qquad \Delta OCD \cong \Delta OBA$

$\because \qquad \Delta COD \cong \Delta BOA$

$\qquad \angle AOB = \angle COD$

$\qquad\qquad = 140°$

(ii) In ΔAOP,

$\qquad AP^2 + OP^2 = AO^2$ [by Pythagoras theorem]

$\qquad AP^2 + 8^2 = (17)^2$

$\qquad\qquad AP^2 = 225$

$\qquad\qquad AP = 15$

$\qquad AP = PC = 30\,m$

Distance between mango tree A and Ashoka tree $C = 30\,m$

In ΔCOD,

$\theta + \theta + \angle COD = 180°$

$\theta + \theta + 140° = 180°$

$2\theta + 140 = 180°$

$2\theta = 40$

$\theta = 20°$

(iii) From above solution and $\theta = \phi$

$\qquad \angle OAB = 20°$

(iv) From above solution,

$\qquad \angle OCD = 20°$

(v) From above solution

$\qquad \angle ODC = 20°$

Chapter Test

Multiple Choice Questions

1. In giving figure ABC is a cyclic triangle, as shown $\angle BAC = 70°$ then, $\angle BOC$ is

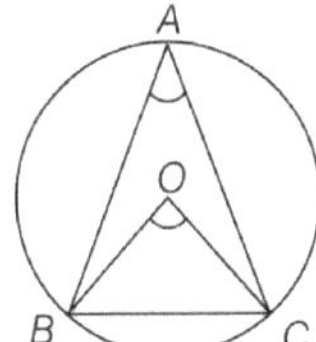

(a) 150°   (b) 35°   (c) 90°   (d) 140°

2. In the given figure, AOC is a diameter of the circle and arc $AXB = \dfrac{1}{2}$ arc BYC, then the value of $\angle BOC$. **[NCERT Exemplar]**

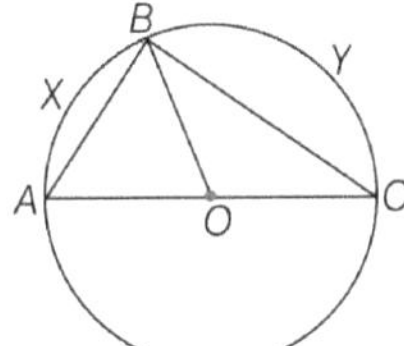

(a) 60°   (b) 50°   (c) 120°   (d) 100°

3. In figure, $ABCD$ is a cyclic quadrilateral and O is the centre of the circle. If $\angle BOD = 160°$, then the measure of $\angle BPD$ is

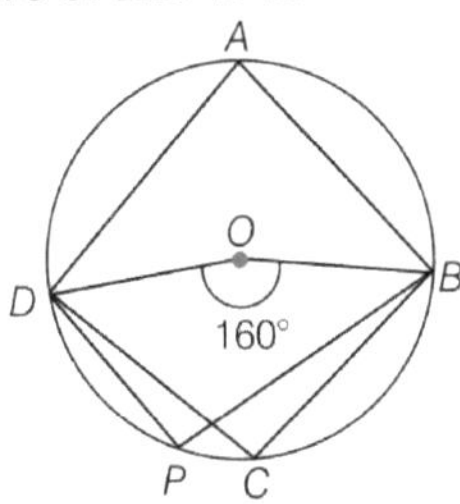

(a) 100°   (b) 150°   (c) 50°   (d) 90°

4. As shown in figure $\angle ABC = 72°$ and $\angle BCD = 75°$. Then, sum of $\angle BAD$ and $\angle ADC$ is

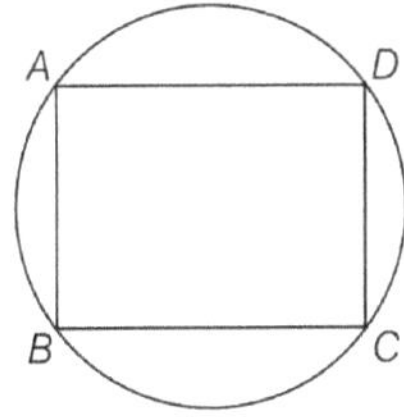

(a) 123°   (b) 214°   (c) 213°   (d) 313°

Case Based MCQs

5. There was a circular park in civil lines at Allahabad. For fencing purpose poles A, B, C and D were installed at the circumference of the park.

Mohan tied wires from A to B, B to C and C to D, he managed to measure the $\angle A = 120°$ and $\angle D = 80°$.

The point O in the middle of the park is the centre of the circle.

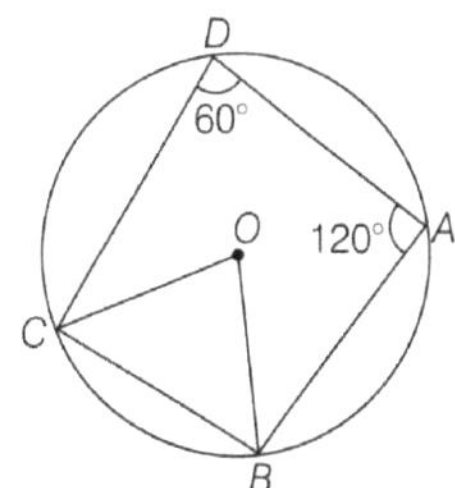

Now, answer the following questions.

(i) What is the value of $\angle ABC = ?$
(a) 80°   (b) 120°   (c) 70°   (d) 90°

(ii) What is the value of $\angle DCB$?
(a) 60°   (b) 100°   (c) 90°   (d) 70°

(iii) What is the special type of quadrilateral $ABCD$?
(a) Square   (b) Rectangle
(c) Cyclic quadrilateral   (d) Trapezium

(iv) What is the property of cyclic quadrilateral?
(a) Opposite angles are supplementary
(b) Adjacent angles are equal
(c) Opposite angles are equal
(d) None of the above

Short Answer Type Questions

6. Two congruent circles intersect each other at points A and B. Through A any line segment PAQ is drawn, so that P and Q lie on the two circles. Prove that $BP = BQ$.

7. If circles are drawn taking two sides of a triangle as diameters, then prove that the point of intersection of these circles lie on the third side.

8. Prove that a cyclic parallelogram is a rectangle.

Long Answer Type Questions

9. If $\triangle ABC$ and $\triangle ADC$ are two right angled triangles with common hypotenuse AC, then prove that $\angle CAD = \angle CBD$.

10. In any $\triangle ABC$, if the angle bisector of $\angle A$ and perpendicular bisector of BC intersect, then prove that they intersect on the circumcircle of the $\triangle ABC$.

Answers

1. (d)   2. (c)   3. (a)   4. (c)
5. (i) (b) (ii) (a) (iii) (c) (iv) (a)

For Detailed Solutions

Scan the code

CHAPTER 04

Constructions

In this Chapter...

- Some Basic Constructions of a Triangle in Different Cases
- Constructions of Triangles in Some Special Cases

Construction 1

To construct the bisector of a given angle

If an angle (say $\angle ABC$) of any measure is given to us and we have to draw the bisector of this angle, then we use the following steps of construction and its justification.

Steps of Construction

Step I First, draw the given $\angle ABC$ and draw an arc of any radius taking B as centre (say). This arc intersects BA and BC at E and D respectively.

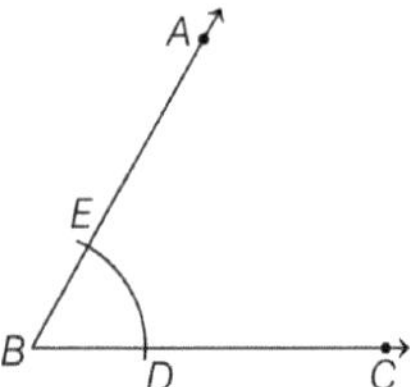

Step II Now, taking E and D as centres and with the radius more than $\dfrac{1}{2} ED$, draw two arcs which intersect each other at F (say).

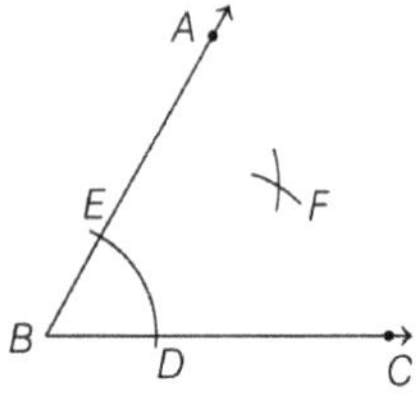

Step III Draw the ray BF, which is the required bisector of the $\angle ABC$.

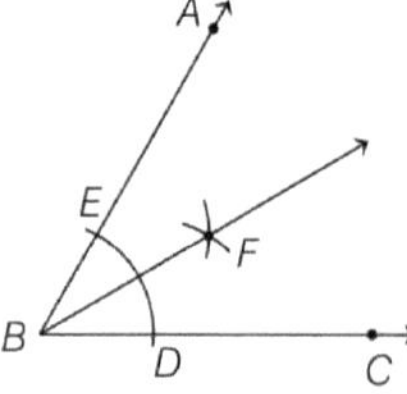

Justification   Join DF and EF.

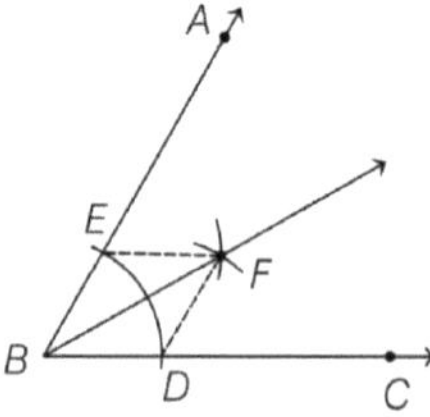

In ΔBEF and ΔBDF,

$$BE = BD \qquad \text{[radii of the same arc]}$$
$$EF = DF \qquad \text{[arcs of equal radii]}$$
$$BF = BF \qquad \text{[common sides]}$$

$\therefore \quad \Delta BEF \cong \Delta BDF \quad$ [by SSS congruence rule]

Then, $\angle EBF = \angle DBF \qquad$ [by CPCT]

Hence, BF is the bisector of a given $\angle ABC$.

Example 1. Draw the angle bisector of 60° and justify the construction.

Sol. Steps of Construction

(i) First, draw a line segment BC, and make the $\angle ABC = 60°$ and draw an arc of any radius taking B as centre (say). This arc cuts arms BA and BC at E and D, respectively.

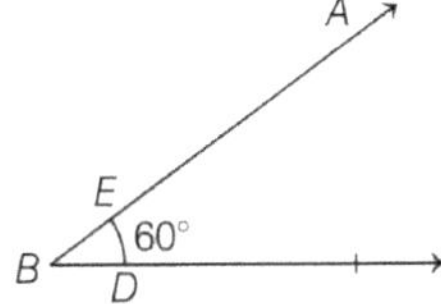

(ii) Now, taking E and D as centres and with the radius more than $\dfrac{1}{2}ED$, draw two equal arcs which cut each other at F (say).

(iii) Draw the ray BF.

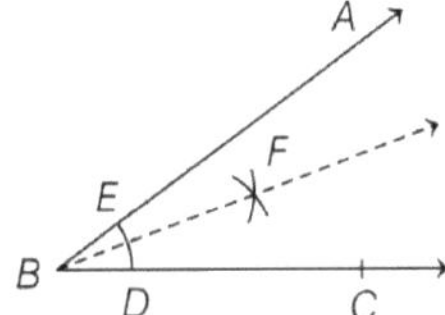

Here, BF is the angle bisector of 60°.

Justification Join EF and DF.

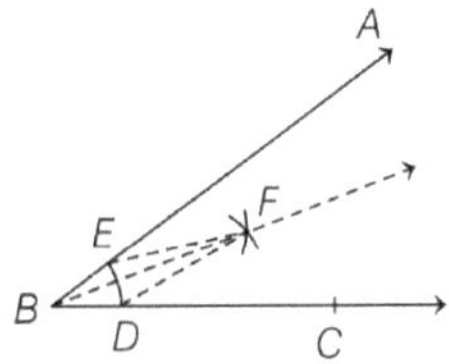

In ΔBEF and ΔBDF,

$$BE = BD \qquad \text{[radii of same arc]}$$
$$EF = DF \qquad \text{[arcs of equal radii]}$$
$$BF = BF \qquad \text{[common sides]}$$
$$\therefore \quad \Delta BEF \cong \Delta BDF \qquad \text{[by SSS congruence rule]}$$
$$\angle EBF = \angle DBF \qquad \text{[by CPCT]}$$
$$\because \quad \angle EBD = \angle EBF + \angle DBF$$
$$\text{So,} \quad \frac{\angle EBD}{2} = \angle EBF = \angle DBF$$
$$\Rightarrow \quad \frac{60°}{2} = \angle EBF = \angle DBF$$

Hence, $\angle EBF = \angle DBF = 30°$, i.e. BF is the angle bisector of $\angle ABC$.

Construction 2

To construct the perpendicular bisector of a given line segment

If a line segment of any length is given to us and we have to draw the perpendicular bisector of this line segment, then we use the following steps of construction and its justification.

Steps of Construction

Step I First, draw the given line segment, say AB. Then, taking A and B as centres and with the radius more than $\dfrac{1}{2}AB$, draw arcs on both sides of the line segment AB, which intersect each other.

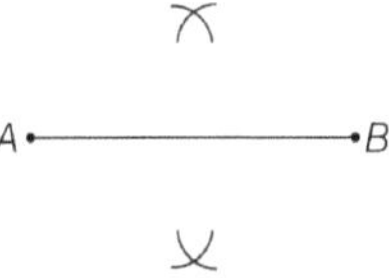

Step II Let arcs drawn in step I intersect each other at P and Q. Then, join PQ.

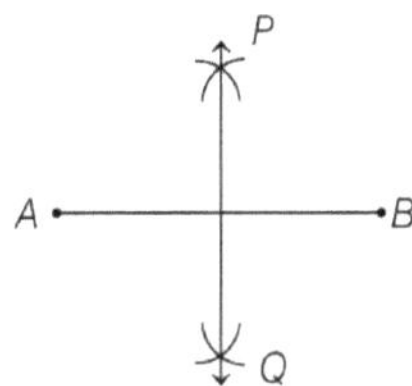

Step III PQ intersects AB at a point M (say). Then, line PMQ is the required perpendicular bisector of AB.

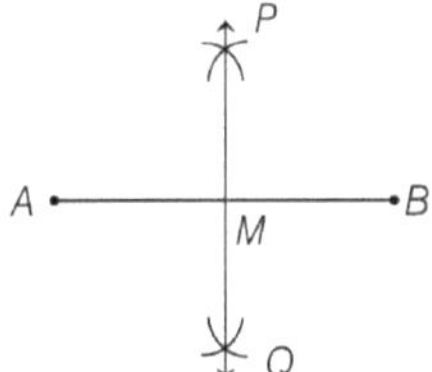

Justification

First, join AP, AQ, BP and BQ.

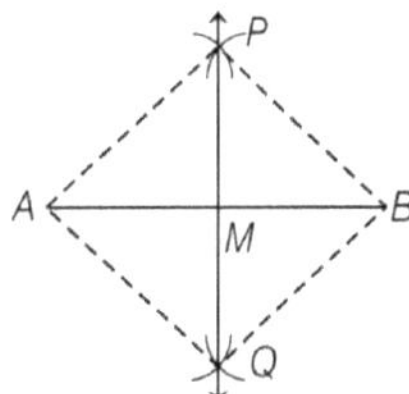

In ΔPAQ and ΔPBQ,

$$AP = BP \qquad \text{[arcs of equal radii]}$$
$$AQ = BQ \qquad \text{[arcs of equal radii]}$$
$$PQ = PQ \qquad \text{[common sides]}$$
$$\therefore \quad \Delta PAQ \cong \Delta PBQ \qquad \text{[by SSS congruence rule]}$$
$$\therefore \quad \angle APM = \angle BPM \qquad \text{[by CPCT]}$$

Now, in ΔPMA and ΔPMB,

$$AP = BP \qquad \text{[arcs of equal radii]}$$
$$PM = PM \qquad \text{[common sides]}$$
$$\angle APM = \angle BPM \qquad \text{[proved above]}$$

$\therefore$　$\Delta PMA \cong \Delta PMB$　　　[by SAS congruence rule]

$\therefore$　　$AM = BM$　　　　　　[by CPCT]

and　$\angle PMA = \angle PMB$　　　[by CPCT] ...(i)

Now,　$\angle PMA + \angle PMB = 180°$　　　　...(ii)

　　　　　　　　　　　　[linear pair axiom]

From Eqs. (i) and (ii), we get

　　　$\angle PMA = \angle PMB = 90°$

Hence, PM, i.e. PMQ is the perpendicular bisector of AB.

Example 2. Draw the perpendicular bisector of a line segment of length 8 cm and justify the construction.

Sol. **Steps of Construction**

(i) Draw line segment $AB = 8$ cm. Then, draw two arcs on both sides of the line segment AB of radius more than $\frac{1}{2} AB$ (i.e. more than 4 cm) taking A and B as centre, respectively.

(ii) Let arcs drawn in step (i) intersect each other at points P and Q.

(iii) Join PQ which intersect AB at M.

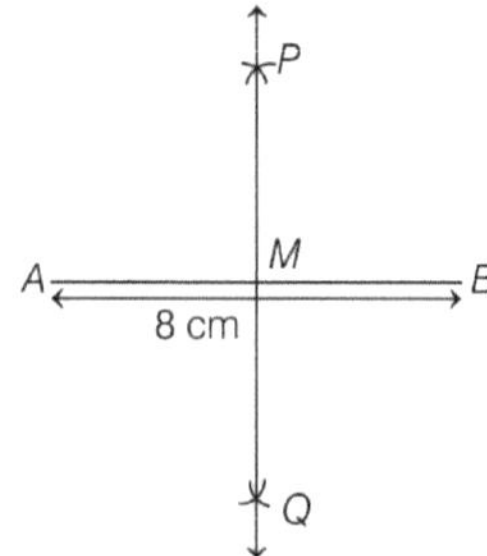

Thus, line PQ or PMQ is the required perpendicular bisector of AB.

Justification　Join AP, AQ , BP and BQ.

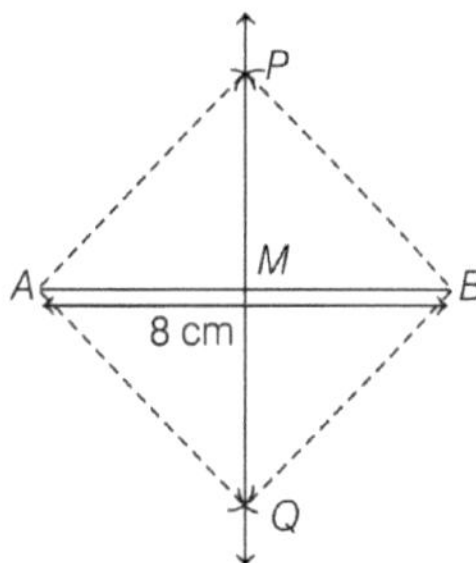

In ΔPAQ and ΔPBQ,

　　　　$AP = BP$　　　[arcs of equal radii]

　　　　$AQ = BQ$　　　[arcs of equal radii]

　　　　$PQ = PQ$　　　[common sides]

$\therefore$　　$\Delta PAQ \cong \Delta PBQ$　　[by SSS congruence rule]

$\therefore$　　$\angle APM = \angle BPM$　　[by CPCT] ...(i)

Now, in ΔPMA and ΔPMB,

　　　　$PM = PM$　　　[common sides]

　　　　$\angle APM = \angle BPM$　　　[from Eq. (i)]

　　　$AP = BP$　　　[arcs of equal radii]

$\therefore$　　$\Delta PMA \cong \Delta PMB$　　[by SAS congruence rule]

　$AM = BM$ and $\angle AMP = \angle BMP$ [by CPCT] ...(ii)

Now,　$\angle AMP + \angle BMP = 180°$　　[linear pair axiom]...(iii)

From Eqs. (ii) and (iii), we get　$\angle AMP = \angle BMP = 90°$

Hence, PMQ is the required perpendicular bisector of the given line segment AB ($= 8$ cm).

Construction 3

To construct an angle of 60° at the initial point of a given ray

Suppose, a ray AB (say) with initial point A is given and we have to draw an angle of 60° at the initial point A of AB, then we use the following steps of construction and its justification.

Steps of Construction

Step I　First, draw a ray AB with initial point A.

Step II　With some suitable radius, draw an arc of a circle taking A as centre which intersects AB at D.

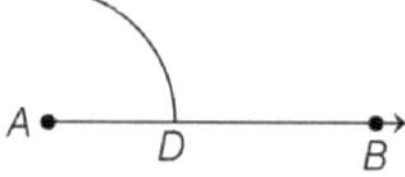

Step III　Taking D as centre, draw an arc with same radius as before to intersect previously drawn arc at a point, E (say).

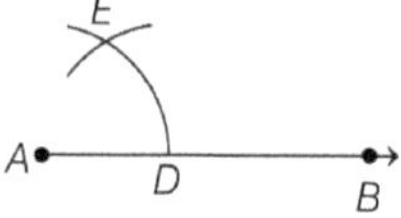

Step IV　Draw the ray AC passing through E.

　　　Then, $\angle CAB$ will be the required angle of 60°.

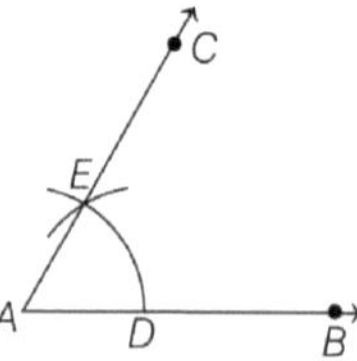

Justification　Join DE.

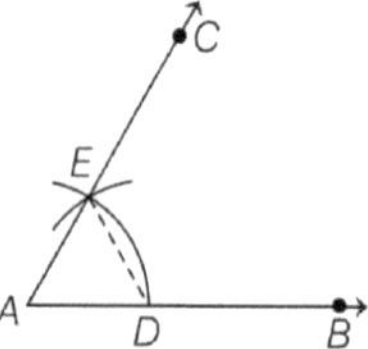

By construction, we have

　　　$AE = AD = ED$

So, ΔAED is an equilateral triangle.

Then, $\angle AED = \angle EAD = \angle ADE = 60°$

Hence, $\angle CAB = \angle EAD = 60°$

Constructions of Some more Angles Other than 60°

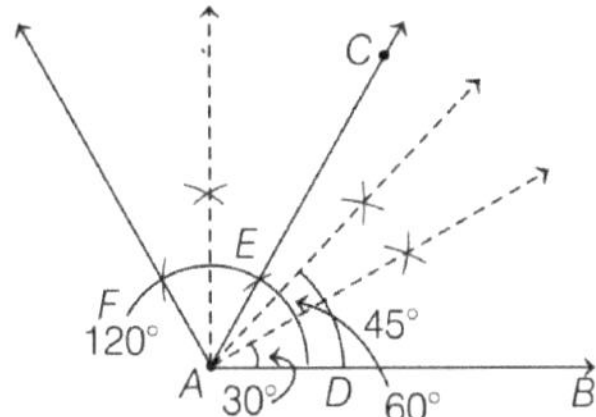

Steps of Construction

Step I To construct an angle of 30°.
- First, draw an angle of 60° and then bisect it.

Step II To construct an angle of 15°.

Since, $15° = \dfrac{30°}{2}$

- So first draw an angle of 30° and then bisect it.

Step III To construct an angle of 120°.

Since, $120° = 60° + 60°$

- So, after step III of construction 3, we take E as centre and draw an arc with same radius as before, such that it intersects the arc drawn in step II at a point, say F. On joining AF, we get the required angle of 120°.

Step IV To construct an angle of 90°.

Since, $90° = 60° + 30° = 60° + \dfrac{60°}{2}$

- So, first draw an angle of 120° with the help of above construction and then bisect the $\angle FAC$.

[see above figure]

Step V To construct an angle of 45°.

Since, $45° = \dfrac{90°}{2}$

- So, first draw an angle of 90° with the help of above construction and then bisect it to get an angle of 45°.

Example 3. Construct an angle of 150° at the initial point of a given ray and justify the construction.

Sol. Here, 150° can be written as $150° = 120° + 30°$. So, to draw an angle of 150°, we first draw an angle of 120° and then add an angle of 30°.

Steps of Construction

(i) First, draw a ray OA with initial point O.

(ii) Produce AO to A' to form ray OA'.

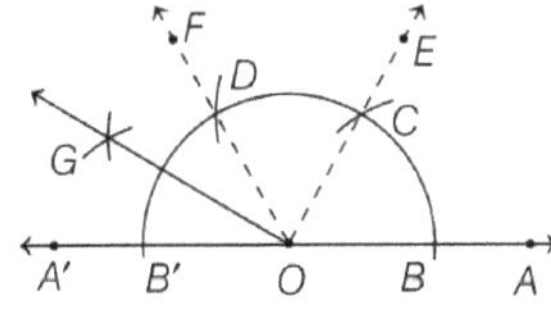

(iii) Taking O as centre and suitable radius, draw an arc of a circle which intersects OA at B and OA' at B'.

(iv) Taking B as centre and with the same radius as before, draw an arc intersecting the previously drawn arc at a point C.

(v) Taking C as centre and with the same radius as before, draw an arc intersecting the arc drawn in step (iii) at a point D.

(vi) Draw the ray OE passing through C and ray OF passing through D.

Then, $\angle EOA = 60°$, $\angle FOE = 60°$ and $\angle FOA' = 60°$

(vii) Now, taking D and B' as centres and with radius more than $\dfrac{1}{2}\, B'D$, draw two arcs to intersect each other at a point say G.

(viii) Draw the ray OG, which is the bisector of $\angle B'OF$.

Hence, $\angle GOA$ is the required angle of 150°.

Justification

$$\angle B'OG = \angle FOG = \dfrac{1}{2}\,\angle B'OF = \dfrac{1}{2}\,(60°) = 30°$$

Thus, $\angle GOA = \angle FOG + \angle FOE + \angle EOA$

$$= 30° + 60° + 60° = 150°$$

On measuring the $\angle GOA$ by protractor, we find that $\angle GOA = 150°$. Thus, the construction is justified.

Some Basic Constructions of a Triangle in Different Cases

Some basic constructions of a triangle in different cases are given below. This will be further helpful for our construction of unique triangle.

I. When two sides and angle between them are given

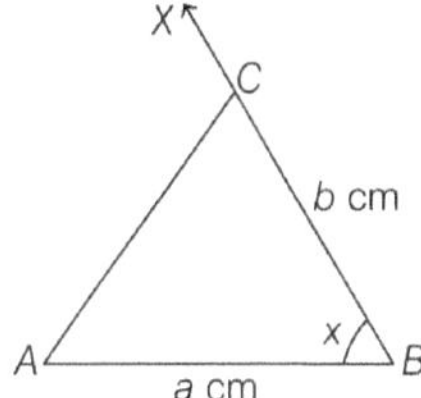

Let the two sides of ΔABC be $AB = a$ cm, $BC = b$ cm and angle between them, i.e. $\angle ABC = x$.

Steps of Construction

(i) Draw base $AB = a$ cm (say).

(ii) Draw a ray BX making an angle x at B.

(iii) Cut-off $BC = b$ cm from BX.

(iv) Join AC.

Thus, ΔABC is the required triangle.

II. When three sides of a triangle are given

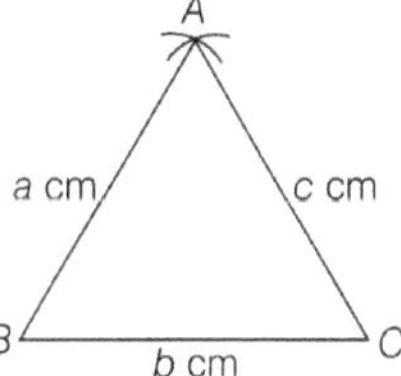

Let three sides of ΔABC be $AB = a$ cm, $BC = b$ cm and $CA = c$ cm.

Steps of Construction

(i) First, draw the base $BC = b$ cm (say).

(ii) By taking B and C as centres, draw two arcs of radius a cm and c cm respectively, which intersect each other at A.

(iii) Join AB and AC.

Thus, $\triangle ABC$ is the required triangle.

III. When one side and two angles are given

Let one side of $\triangle ABC$ be $AB = a$ cm (say) and angles be $\angle A = x$ and $\angle B = y$.

Steps of Construction

(i) Draw base $AB = a$ cm.

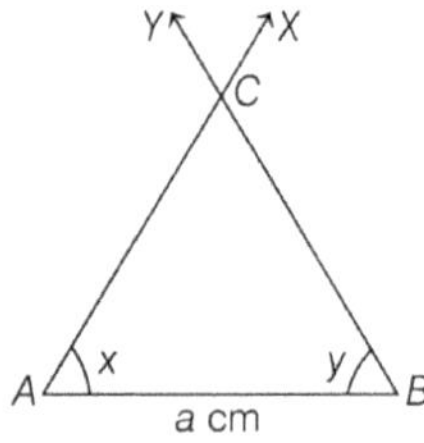

(ii) Draw two rays AX and BY making an angle x at A and y at B, which intersect each other at C.

(iii) Join AC and CB.

Thus, $\triangle ABC$ is the required triangle.

IV. When base and altitude of a triangle are given

Let the base of $\triangle ABC$ be $BC = m$ cm and altitude be n cm.

Steps of Construction

(i) Draw base $BC = m$ cm and its perpendicular bisector OQ (say), which intersects BC at P(say).

(ii) Along $PO,$ cut-off $PA = n$ cm.

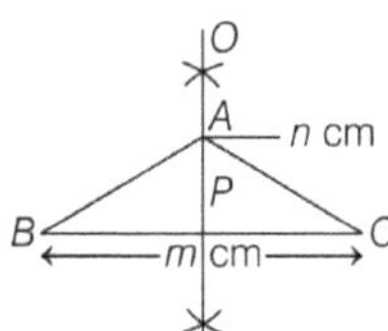

(iii) Join AB and AC. Thus, $\triangle ABC$ is the required triangle.

Constructions of Triangles in Some Special Cases

Construction 4

To construct a triangle, given its base, a base angle and sum of other two sides

Sometimes, base angle (say B), base (say BC) and sum of other two sides of a triangle (say $AB + AC$) are given to us and we have to construct the triangle (say $\triangle ABC$), then for this construction, we use the following steps of construction

Step I First, draw the given base (say BC) and make base angle (say $\angle XBC$) equal to given $\angle B$.

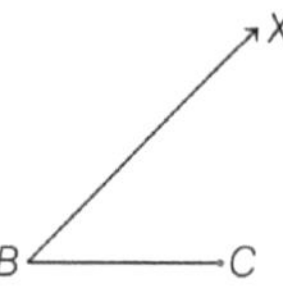

Step II Cut a line segment (say BD) equal to $AB + AC$ from the ray BX.

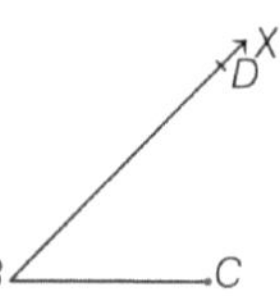

Step III Join DC.

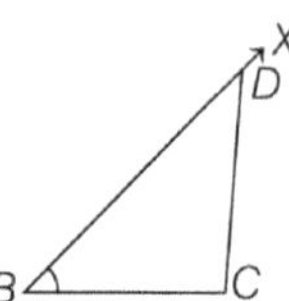

Now, we can use following two methods

Method I

Step IV Draw the perpendicular bisector of DC, say PQ.

Step V Let PQ intersects BD at a point A. Then, join AC. Thus, $\triangle ABC$ will be the required triangle.

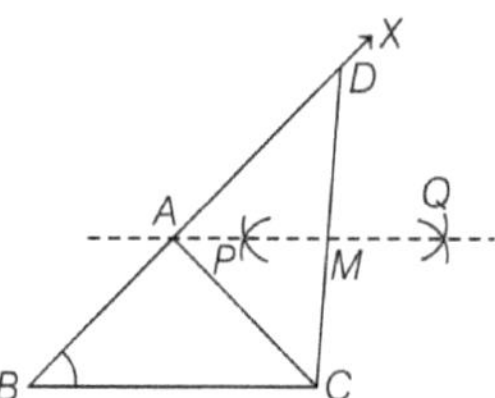

Justification

Base BC and $\angle B$ are drawn as given. Since, PQ is the perpendicular bisector of CD and A lies on it.

So, $\qquad AD = AC$

$\qquad\qquad [\because \triangle AMD \cong \triangle AMC$, by SAS congruence rule]

Now, $\qquad AB = BD - AD = BD - AC$

$\Rightarrow \qquad AB + AC = BD$

Method II

Step IV Make an $\angle DCY$ equal to $\angle BDC$ at C.

Step V Let CY intersects BX at A. Then, join AC. Thus, $\triangle ABC$ will be the required triangle.

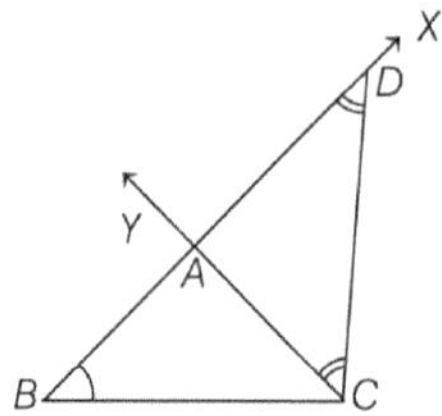

Justification

Base BC and $\angle B$ are drawn as given.

In $\triangle ACD$, $\qquad \angle ACD = \angle ADC \qquad$ [by construction]

$\therefore \qquad\qquad AD = AC \qquad\qquad\qquad$ ...(i)

[since, sides opposite to equal angles of a triangle are equal]

Now, $\qquad AB = BD - AD = BD - AC \qquad$ [$\because$ from Eq. (i)]

$\Rightarrow \quad AB + AC = BD$

Example 4. Construct a $\triangle ABC$, in which $BC = 7$ cm, $AB + AC = 13$ cm and $\angle B = 60°$ and justify it.

Sol. Given, $BC = 7$ cm, $AB + AC = 13$ cm and $\angle B = 60°$

Steps of Construction

(i) First, draw the base, $BC = 7$ cm.
Now, draw a ray BX such that $\angle XBC = \angle B = 60°$.

(ii) Here, sum of two sides $= AB + AC = 13$ cm
So, cut the line segment $BD = 13$ cm from ray BX.

(iii) Join DC.

(iv) Draw perpendicular bisector of DC, say PQ, which intersects BD at A.

(v) Now join AC.

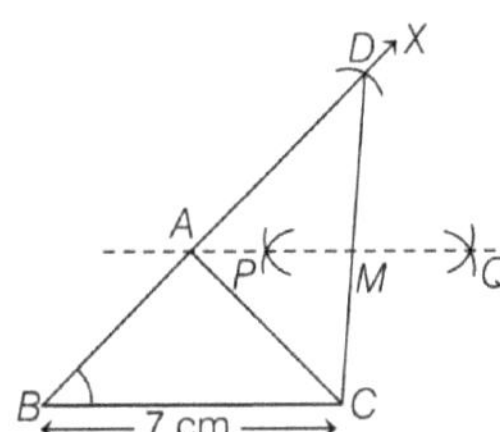

Thus, we get a $\triangle ABC$ which is the required triangle.

Justification

Base BC and $\angle B$ are drawn as given.

Since, PQ is the perpendicular bisector of CD and A lies on it.

$\therefore \qquad\qquad AD = AC \qquad\qquad\qquad$ ...(i)

[$\because \triangle AMD \cong \triangle AMC$, by SAS congruence rule]

Now, $\qquad AB = BD - AD = BD - AC \qquad$ [$\because$ from Eq. (i)]

$\Rightarrow \quad AB + AC = BD$

Thus, construction is justified.

Construction 5

To construct a triangle, given its base, a base angle and the difference of the other two sides

Sometimes, base angle (say B), base (say BC) and difference of the other two sides (say $AB - AC$ or $AC - AB$) are given to us and we have to construct the triangle (say $\triangle ABC$), then for this construction, we use the following steps according to its case.

Case I If $AB > AC$, i.e. $AB - AC$ is given.

(in other words, the side containing the base angle is greater than third side)

Steps of Construction

Step I First, draw the base BC and draw a ray BX making an $\angle XBC$ equal to given angle B.

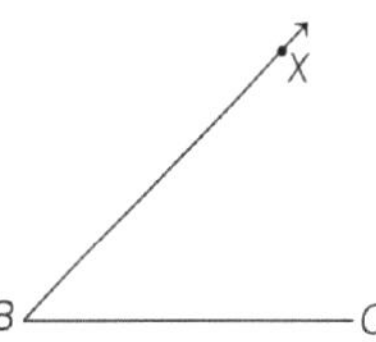

Step II Cut the line segment BD equal to given difference of sides, i.e. $AB - AC$ from the ray BX.

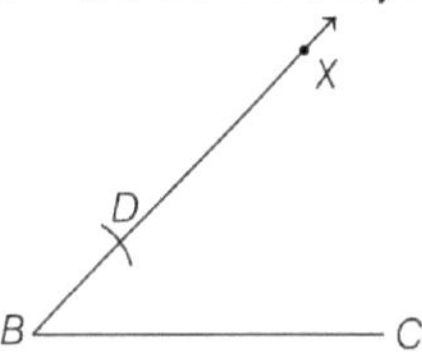

Step III Join DC and draw its perpendicular bisector say PQ, which bisects CD at M (say).

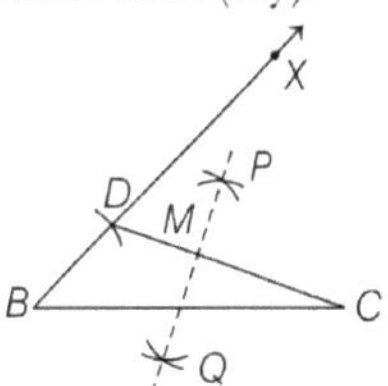

Step IV Let PQ intersects BX at a point A. Join AC.

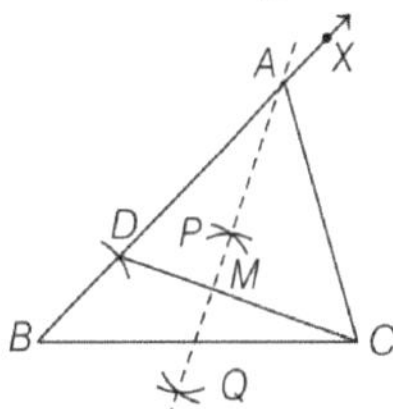

Thus, $\triangle ABC$ is the required triangle.

Justification

Base BC and $\angle B$ are drawn as given.

Since, the point A lies on the perpendicular bisector of DC.

$\therefore \qquad AD = AC$ [$\because \triangle AMD \cong \triangle AMC$, by SAS congruence rule]

So, $\quad BD = AB - AD = AB - AC$

Example 5. Construct a $\triangle ABC$, in which $BC = 10$ cm $\angle B = 45°$ and $AB - AC = 5$ cm. Give justification.

Sol. Given, $BC = 10$ cm, $\angle B = 45°$ and $AB - AC = 5$ cm

Steps of Construction

(i) First, draw the base, $BC = 10$ cm
At point B, draw a ray BX, which makes $\angle CBX = 45°$.

(ii) Here, $AB - AC = 5$ cm
$\therefore AB > AC$, i.e. The side containing the base $\angle B$ is greater than third side, so it is the case I.
Hence, cut line segment BD is equal to $AB - AC = 5$ cm from the ray BX.

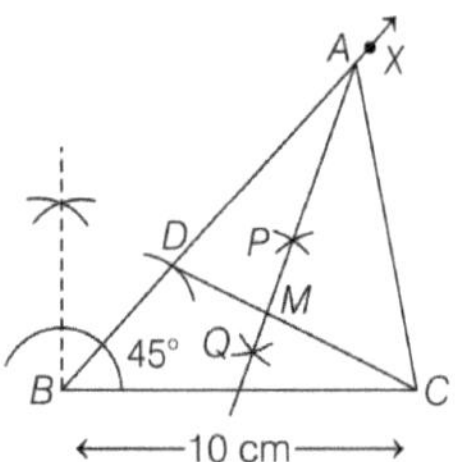

(iii) Now, join CD and draw its perpendicular bisector PQ, which bisects CD at M (say).

(iv) Let A be the intersection point of perpendicular bisector PQ and ray BX. Join AC. Thus, $\triangle ABC$ is the required triangle.

Justification

Base BC and $\angle B$ are drawn as given. Since, the point A lies on the perpendicular bisector of DC.

$\therefore \qquad AD = AC$

Now, $\qquad BD = AB - AD$

$\Rightarrow \qquad BD = AB - AC$

Thus, the construction is justified.

Case II If $AB < AC$, i.e. $AC - AB$ is given (in other words, the side containing the base angle is less than third side)

Steps of Construction

Step I First, draw the base BC and draw a ray BX making an $\angle XBC$ equal to given angle at B.

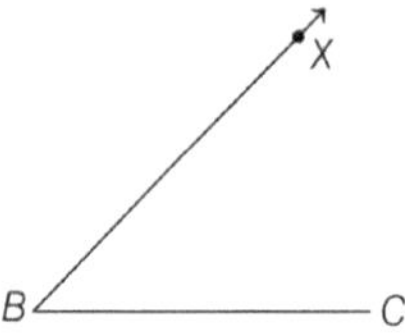

Step II Cut line segment BD equal to given difference of sides, i.e. $AC - AB$ from the ray BX extended on opposite side of base BC.

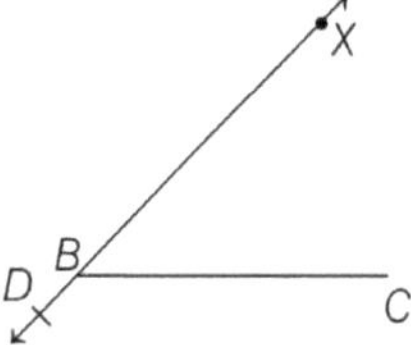

Step III Join DC and draw its perpendicular bisector, say PQ, which intersects DC at M (say).

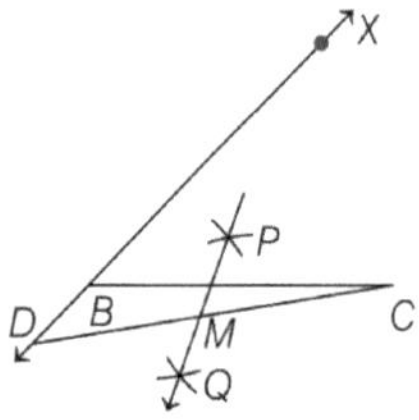

Step IV Let PQ intersects BX at a point A. Join AC.

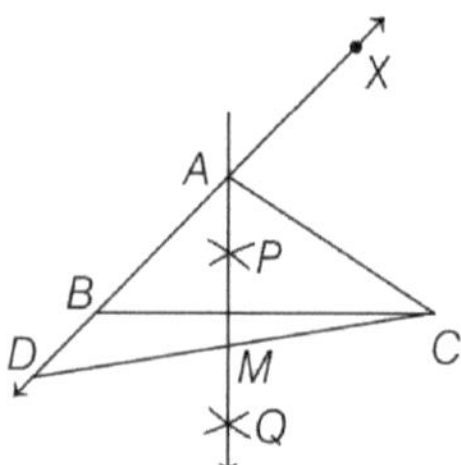

Thus, $\triangle ABC$ is the required triangle.

Justification

Base BC and $\angle B$ are drawn as given.

Since, the point A lies on the perpendicular bisector of DC.

$\therefore \qquad AD = AC$

$\qquad\qquad$ [$\because \triangle AMD \cong \triangle AMC$, by SAS congruence rule]

So, $BD = AD - AB = AC - AB$

Example 6. Construct a $\triangle PQR$, in which $QR = 6.5$ cm, $\angle Q = 60°$ and $PR - PQ = 1.5$ cm and justify it.

Sol. Given, in $\triangle PQR$, $QR = 6.5$ cm, $\angle Q = 60°$

and $\quad PR - PQ = 1.5$ cm

Steps of Construction

(i) Draw the base, $QR = 6.5$ cm.

At point Q, draw a ray QX making an $\angle XQR = 60°$.

Here, $\qquad PR - PQ = 1.5$ cm

$\therefore \qquad\qquad PR > PQ$

i.e. The side containing the base angle Q is less than third side, so it is the case II.

(ii) Cut line segment QS equal to $PR - PQ$, i.e. $QS = 1.5$ cm from the ray QX extended on opposite side of base QR.

(iii) Join SR and draw its perpendicular bisector ray AB, which intersects SR at M (say).

(iv) Let P be the intersection point of SX and perpendicular bisector AB. Then, join PR.

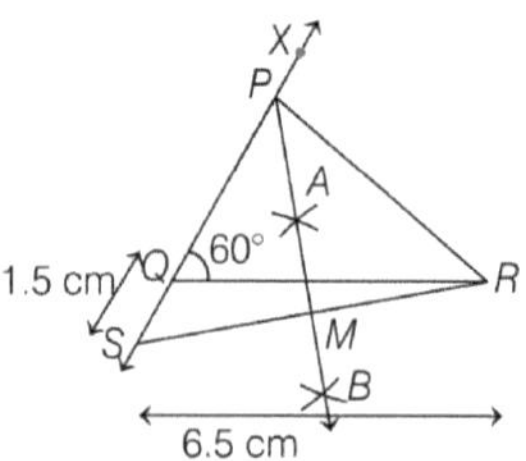

Thus, $\triangle PQR$ is the required triangle.

Justification

Base QR and $\angle Q$ are drawn as given.

Since, AB is the perpendicular bisector of SR and P lies on it.

$\therefore \qquad\qquad PS = PR$

Now, $\qquad QS = PS - PQ$

$\Rightarrow \qquad\qquad QS = PR - PQ$

Thus, construction is justified.

Chapter Practice

Objective Questions

• Multiple Choice Questions

1. Write the angle bisector of $175°$.
(a) $175°$ (b) $87.5°$
(c) $350°$ (d) $187°$

2. Can an angle of $67.5°$ be constructed?
(a) Yes, because 67.5 is multiple of 15
(b) No, because 67.5 is multiple of 15
(c) Can't say
(d) Yes, because 67.5 is not the multiple of 15

3. With the help of a ruler and a pair of compasses, it is not possible to construct an angle of
(a) $37.5°$ (b) $40°$
(c) $22.5°$ (d) $67.5°$

4. Which of the following angles cannot be constructed by using ruler and a pair of compasses only?
(a) $22\frac{1}{2}°$ (b) $45°$ (c) $70°$ (d) $90°$

5. Which of the following angles can be constructed by using ruler and a pair of compasses only?
(a) $20°$ (b) $72°$
(c) $105°$ (d) $130°$

6. Can a ΔABC be constructed, in which $BC = 6\,cm$ and $\angle C = 30°$? Then, $AC - AB$ is
(a) $7\,cm$ (b) $7.5\,cm$
(c) $4\,cm$ (d) $6.25\,cm$

7. The construction of a ΔDEF, in which $DE = 7\,cm$, $\angle D = 75°$ is possible, when $(EF - DF)$ is equal to
(a) $7.5\,cm$ (b) $7\,cm$
(c) $8\,cm$ (d) $6.5\,cm$

8. For what value of $(BC + AC)$, the construction of a ΔABC is possible, if $AB = 7\,cm$ and $\angle A = 45°$?
(a) $6.5\,cm$ (b) $7\,cm$
(c) $6.9\,cm$ (d) $7.3\,cm$

9. The construction of a ΔLMN, in which $LM = 8$ cm, $\angle L = 45°$ is possible, when $(MN + LN)$ is
(a) $6\,cm$ (b) $7\,cm$
(c) $9\,cm$ (d) $5\,cm$

10. The construction of ΔABC, given that $BC = 6\,cm$, $\angle B = 45°$ is not possible, when difference of AB and AC is equal to
(a) $6.9\,cm$ (b) $5.2\,cm$
(c) $5.0\,cm$ (d) $4.0\,cm$

11. The construction of a ΔABC, given that $BC = 3$ cm, $\angle C = 60°$ is possible, when difference of AB and AC is equal to
(a) $3.2\,cm$
(b) $3.1\,cm$
(c) $3\,cm$
(d) $2.8\,cm$

12. The construction of ΔABC, given that $BC = 6\,cm$, $\angle B = 45°$ is not possible, when difference of AB and AC is equal to
(a) $6.9\,cm$
(b) $5.2\,cm$
(c) $5\,cm$
(d) $4\,cm$

• Case Based MCQs

13. Raman is good in geometry. So, he was curious to know more about the concepts of construction. His father is a mathematician. So, he reached his knowledge nearer to father and he learn something interesting about basic of constructions as construction of angle bisector, construction of important angles with some measurement, construction of perpendicular bisector and construction of a triangle, given it base difference of the other two sides and one base angle in this chapter.

(i) With the help of a ruler and a compass, it is not possible to construct an angle of
   (a) 37.5°   (b) 73°   (c) 22.5°   (d) 67.5°

(ii) The construction of a ΔPQR, in which $QR = 5.4$ cm and $\angle Q = 60°$ is not possible, when $(PR + QR)$ is
   (a) 6 cm   (b) 6.5 cm   (c) 5 cm   (d) 7 cm

(iii) Is it possible to construct a triangle, whose sides measure 6 cm, 5 cm and 10 cm?
   (a) Yes   (b) No
   (c) Can't say   (d) Partially true or false

(iv) The construction of a ΔABC, in which $BC = 6$ cm and $\angle B = 50°$ is not possible, when $(AC - AB)$ is equal to
   (a) 5.6 cm   (b) 5 cm
   (c) 6 cm   (d) 4.8 cm

(v) In the given figure, $\angle MNO = 60°$ by the help of construction, $\angle MNA = \angle ANB + \angle BNO$ and $\angle ANB = \angle BNO$, then the measure of $\angle BNO$

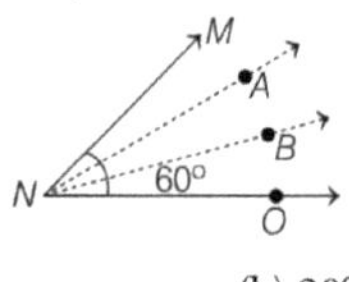

   (a) 60°   (b) 30°
   (c) 15°   (d) 45°

PART 2
Subjective Questions

• Short Answer Type Questions

1. Draw a line segment SR of length 10 cm. Divide it into 4 equal parts, using compass and ruler.

2. An angle of 37.5° can be constructed by ruler and compass. If constructed, then give its steps of construction.

3. Construct an angle of $52\frac{1}{2}°$, using ruler and compasses.

4. Draw the angle bisector of 45° and justify the construction.

5. In the given figure, $\angle MNO = 30°$ by the help of construction,
$\angle MNA = \angle ANB + \angle BNO$ and $\angle ANB = \angle BNO$.

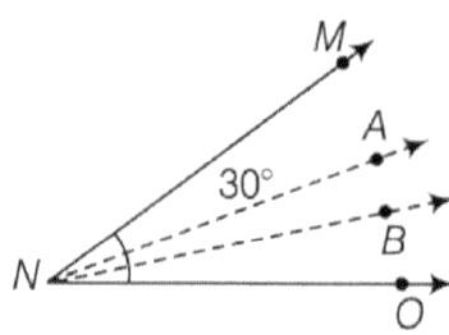

Then, find the measure of $\angle BNO$.

6. Construct a rhombus, whose diagonals are 4 cm and 6 cm in lengths and justify it.

7. Draw the perpendicular bisector of a line segment of length 7 cm and justify the construction.

8. Construct a ΔABC, given that $BC = 6.8$ cm, $\angle B = 45°$ and $\angle C = 45°$. Draw the bisectors of $\angle B$ and $\angle C$. If these bisectors meet at I, then measure $\angle BIC$.

9. Construct a pair of angle of 90° at both ends of a line segment.

10. Construct the measurement of angle $\frac{45°}{2}$ with scale and compass.

11. Construct an angle of $7\frac{1}{2}°$, using compass and ruler only.

12. Construct a right-angled triangle, whose base is 10 cm and sum of its hypotenuse and other side is 16 cm.

13. Construct an equilateral triangle one of whose altitude measures 6 cm.

14. Construct a right-angled triangle when one side is 3.5 cm and sum of other side and the hypotenuse is 5.5 cm. Also, give its justification.

15. Construct a ΔABC, when $AB = 6$ cm, $BC = 8$ cm and $AC = 7.5$ cm.

16. Construct an equilateral triangle, given its side $AB = 6$ cm and justify the construction.

17. Construct a ΔSTU in which $\angle T = 150°$, $TU = 3$ cm and $ST + US = 8$ cm.

18. Draw a ΔABC in which $BC = 3.6$ cm, $\angle B = 30°$ and $AB - AC = 1.3$ cm.

19. Construct a ΔABC, in which $BC = 7$ cm, $AB + AC = 13$ cm and $\angle B = 60°$.

20. Construct a ΔABC, in which $BC = 10$ cm, $\angle B = 45°$ and $AB - AC = 5$ cm.

21. Construct a ΔPQR, given that $QR = 3$ cm, $\angle PQR = 45°$ and $QP - PR = 2$ cm.

22. Construct a ΔPQR, in which $QR = 6.5$ cm, $\angle Q = 60°$ and $PR - PQ = 1.5$ cm and justify it.

23. Construct a triangle having sides of length 6.2 cm, 7.3 cm and 6 cm. Measure all the three angles. Bisect the smallest and the largest angles. Measure any acute angle formed by the bisecting rays at the point of intersection.

• Long Answer Type Questions

24. Construct an equilateral triangle, whose altitude is 3.2 cm. Also, give its justification.

25. Construct an isosceles ΔABC, in which base $BC = 4$ cm, sum of the perpendicular from A to BC and side $AB = 6.5$ cm.

26. Construct an angle of $90°$ at the initial point of a given ray and justify the construction.

27. Construct the angle of $105°$ and verify by measuring them by a protractor.

28. Construct an angle of $45°$ at the initial point of a given ray and justify the construction.

29. Construct a triangle, whose two sides are 6 cm and 3.3 cm and the angle opposite to the shorter side is $30°$. How many triangles can be constructed?

• Case Based Questions

30. Manoj is studying in IXth class in Government School at Mirzapur. Once he reaches his home, firstly he do a construction work, which is given by in home work.

He was trying to construct the following angles as question given in the book.

(i) Construct the angles of the following measurement by protection.
    (a) $15°$ (b) $135°$

(ii) Construct an equilateral triangle.

(iii) Justify the above question no. (ii).

SOLUTIONS

Objective Questions

1. (b) Angle bisector of $175° = \dfrac{175°}{2} = 87.5°$

2. (a) Yes, because $67.5° = \dfrac{135°}{2} = \dfrac{1}{2}(90° + 45°)$, which is a multiple of 15.

3. (b) With the help of a ruler and a pair of compasses, it is not possible to construct an angle of $40°$. Because with the help of ruler and a pair of compasses, we generate the angles $60°, 90°, 45°, 22.5°, 30°$ etc. and compass generate only the bisects of an angle.

4. (c) $70°$ cannot be constructed by using ruler and a pair of compasses only.

5. (c) $105°$ can be constructed by using ruler and a pair of compasses only.

6. (c) Yes, because the difference of any two sides of a triangle is less than the third side.

7. (d) We know that, in a triangle the difference of two sides is always less than any side
i.e. $EF - DF < DE$ or $EF - DF < 7$

8. (d) The value of $(BC + AC)$ must be greater than 7 cm. Because the sum of any two sides of a triangle is always greater than the third side.
So, the value of $(BC + AC)$ can be 7.3 cm.

9. (c) We know that, sum of two sides of a triangle is always greater than third side.
$\therefore \quad MN + LN > LM$ or $MN + LN > 8$

10. (a) Given, $BC = 6$ cm and $\angle B = 45°$
We know that, the construction of a triangle is not possible, if sum of two sides is less than or equal to the third side of the triangle.
i.e. $\quad AB + BC \le AC \Rightarrow BC \le AC - AB$
$\Rightarrow \quad\quad\quad\quad\quad 6 \le AC - AB$
So, if $AC - AB = 6.9$ cm, then construction of ΔABC with given conditions is not possible.

11. (d) $(AB - AC)$ must be less than 3 cm because the difference of any two sides of a triangle is always less than the third side.

12. (a) When we consider $AC - AB = 6.9$ cm, then the construction of a ΔABC, if $BC = 6$ cm and $\angle B = 45°$, is not possible. Because for construction, we must have
$AC - AB < BC$, i.e. $AC < AB + BC$.

13. (i) (b) With the help of a ruler and a compass, we can construct the angles $90°, 60°, 45°, 22.5°, 30°$ etc. and its bisector of an angle. So, it is not possible to construct of an angle $73°$.

(ii) (c) Triangle inequality theorem, for any triangle the sum of lengths of two sides is always greater than the length of third side.
Using this theorem, $PR + QR$ should be greater than 5.4 cm.
Option (a) as $6 > 5.4$ (correct)
Option (b) as $6.5 > 5.4$ (correct)
Option (c) as $5 > 5.4$ (not possible)
Hence, option (c) is not possible.

(iii) (a) Given, sides are 6 cm, 5 cm and 10 cm.

We know, triangle is only possible, when sum of two sides is always greater than third side.

As, $6 + 5 > 10\,cm$

Hence, triangle is possible.

(iv) (c) We know that, construction of triangle is not possible, if difference of two sides is greater than or equal to the third side of the triangle.

So, if we consider $AC - AB = 6\,cm$, then construction of ΔABC is not possible.

(v) (c) Given, $\angle MNO = 60°$

After bisector of $60°$, we get $\angle ANO = \dfrac{60°}{2}$

$\Rightarrow \angle ANO = 30°.$

Again, bisector of $\angle ANO$, we get $\angle BNO = \dfrac{30°}{2} = 15°$

Subjective Questions

1. Steps of Construction

(i) Draw a line segment $SR = 10\,cm$.

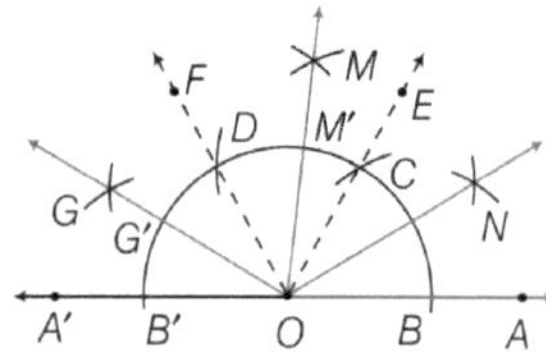

(ii) Draw a perpendicular bisector of SR, which intersects it at M.

(iii) Again, draw a perpendicular bisector of MR, which intersects it at T.

(iv) Also, draw a perpendicular bisector of MS, which intersects it at N. Thus, SR has been divided into four equal parts SN, NM, TM, RT.

2. Steps of Construction

(i) First, draw a ray OA with initial point O.

(ii) Produce AO to A' to form ray OA'.

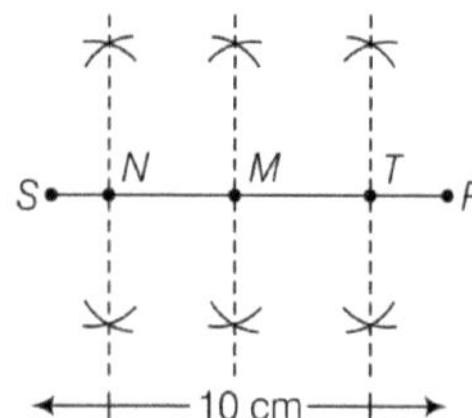

(iii) Taking O as centre and suitable radius, draw an arc of a circle, which intersects OA at B and OA' at B'.

(iv) Taking B as centre and with the same radius as before, draw an arc intersecting the previously drawn arc at a point C.

(v) Taking C as centre and with the same radius as before, draw an arc intersecting the arc drawn in step (iii) at a point D.

(vi) Draw the ray OE passing through C and ray OF passing through D.

Then, $\angle EOA = 60°$, $\angle FOE = 60°$ and $\angle FOA' = 60°$

(vii) Now, taking D and B' as centres and with radius more than $\dfrac{1}{2}\,B'D$, draw two arcs to intersect each other at a point say G.

(viii) Draw the ray OG, which is the bisector of $\angle B'OF$.

(ix) Now, taking G' and B as centres and with radius more than $\dfrac{1}{2}\,BG'$, draw two arcs to intersect each other at a point M.

$\therefore \angle MOA = \dfrac{1}{2}\,\angle GOA = \dfrac{150°}{2} = 75°$

(x) Next, taking B and M' as centres and with radius more than $\dfrac{1}{2}\,BM'$, draw two arcs to intersect each other at a point N.

$\therefore \angle NOA = \dfrac{1}{2}\,\angle MOA = \dfrac{75°}{2} = 37.5°$

Hence, $\angle NOA$ is the required angle of $37.5°$.

3. Steps of Construction

(i) First, draw a ray OA with initial point O.

(ii) Taking O as centre and any radius, draw an arc of a circle which intersects OA, say at a point B.

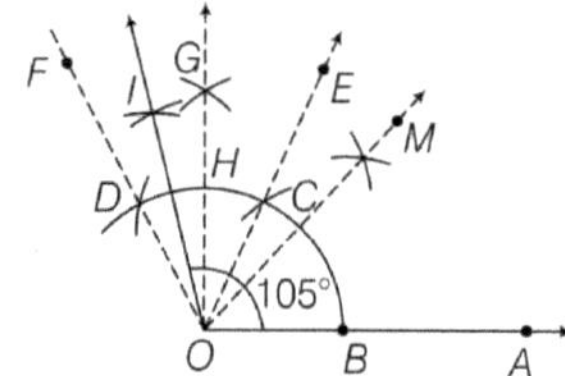

(iii) Taking B as centre and with the same radius as before, draw an arc intersecting the previously drawn arc, say at a point C.

(iv) Taking C as centre and with the same radius as before, draw an arc intersecting the arc drawn in step (ii), say at a point D.

(v) Draw the ray OE passing through C and the ray OF passing through D. Then, $\angle EOA = \angle FOE = 60°$.

(vi) Next, taking C and D as centres and with the radius more than $\dfrac{1}{2}\,CD$, draw arcs to intersect each other, say at G.

(vii) Draw the ray OG intersecting the arc drawn in step (ii) at H. This ray OG is the angle bisector of the $\angle FOE$.

i.e. $\angle FOG = \angle EOG = \dfrac{1}{2}\,\angle FOE = \dfrac{1}{2}\,(60°) = 30°$

Thus, $\angle GOA = \angle GOE + \angle EOA = 30° + 60° = 90°$

(viii) Next, taking H and D as centres and with the radius more than $\dfrac{1}{2}\,HD$, draw arcs to intersect each other, say at I.

(ix) Draw the ray OI, which is the angle bisector of the $\angle FOG$.

i.e. $\angle FOI = \angle GOI = \dfrac{1}{2}\angle FOG = \dfrac{1}{2}\,(30°) = 15°$

Thus, $\angle IOA = \angle IOG + \angle GOA = 15° + 90° = 105°$

(x) Next, taking B and D as centres and with the radius more than $\dfrac{1}{2}BD$, draw arcs to interest each other, say at

M i.e. $\angle MOA = \dfrac{1}{2}\angle FOA$

$= \dfrac{105°}{2} = 52\dfrac{1}{2}°$

4. Steps of Construction

(i) First, draw a line segment BC and make the $\angle ABC = 45°$ and draw an arc of any radius taking B as centre (say). This arc cuts arms BA and BC at E and D, respectively.

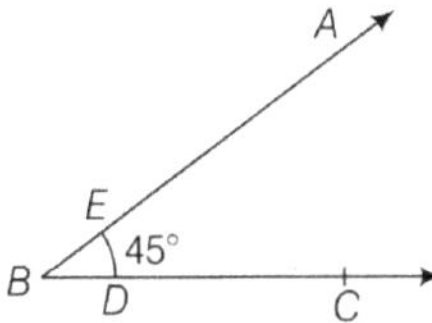

(ii) Now, taking E and D as centres and with the radius more than $\dfrac{1}{2}ED$, draw two equal arcs, which cut each other at F (say).

(iii) Draw the ray BF.

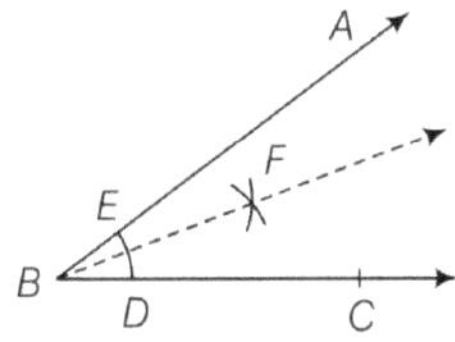

Here, BF is the angle bisector of $45°$.

Justification Join EF and DF.

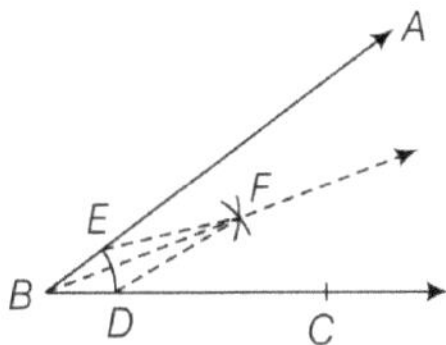

In ΔBEF and ΔBDF,

$BE = BD$ [radii of same arc]

$EF = DF$ [arcs of equal radii]

$BF = BF$ [common sides]

$\therefore \quad \Delta BEF \cong \Delta BDF$ [by SSS congruence rule]

$\angle EBF = \angle DBF$ [by CPCT]

$\because \quad \angle EBD = \angle EBF + \angle DBF$

So, $\quad \dfrac{\angle EBD}{2} = \angle EBF = \angle DBF$

$\Rightarrow \quad \dfrac{45°}{2} = \angle EBF = \angle DBF$

Hence, $\angle EBF = \angle DBF = 22\dfrac{1}{2}°$ i.e. BF is the angle bisector of $\angle ABC$.

5. Given, $\angle MNO = 30°$

After bisector of $30°$, we get $\angle ANO = \dfrac{30°}{2} = 15°$

Again, bisector of $\angle ANO$, we get

$\angle BNO = \dfrac{15°}{2} = 7\dfrac{1}{2}°$

6. We know that, all sides of a rhombus are equal and the diagonals of a rhombus are perpendicular bisectors of one another. So, to construct a rhombus, whose diagonals are 4 cm and 6 cm, use the following steps.

(i) Draw the diagonal, say $AC = 4$ cm

(ii) Taking A and C as centres and radius more than $\dfrac{1}{2}AC$, draw arcs on both sides of the line segment AC to intersect each other.

(iii) Cut both arcs intersect each other at P and Q, then join PQ.

(iv) Let PQ intersect AC at the point O. Thus, PQ is perpendicular bisector of AC.

(v) Cut off 3 cm lengths from OP and OQ, then we get points B and D.

(vi) Now, join AB, BC, CD and DA .

Thus, $ABCD$ is the required rhombus.

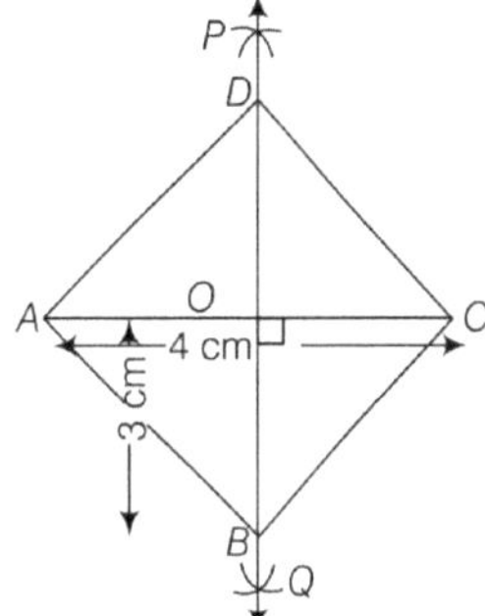

Justification

Since, D and B lie on perpendicular bisector of AC.

$DA = DC$ and $BA = BC$ ...(i)

[since, every point on perpendicular bisector of line segment is equidistant from end points of line segment]

Now, $\quad\quad \angle DOC = 90°$

Also, $\quad\quad OD = OB = 3$ cm

Thus, AC is perpendicular bisector or BD.

Therefore, $\quad\quad CD = CB$ ...(ii)

From Eqs. (i) and (ii), $AB = BC = CD = DA$

Hence, $ABCD$ is a rhombus.

7. Steps of Construction

(i) Draw line segment $AB = 7$ cm. Then, draw two arcs on both sides of the line segment AB of radius more than $\dfrac{1}{2}AB$ (i.e. more than 3.5 cm) taking A and B as centre, respectively.

(ii) Let arcs drawn in step (i) intersect each other at points P and Q.

(iii) Join PQ, which intersects AB at M.

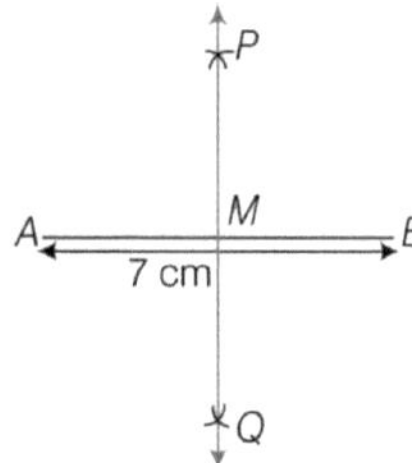

Thus, line PQ or PMQ is the required perpendicular bisector of AB.

Justification Join AP, AQ, BP and BQ.

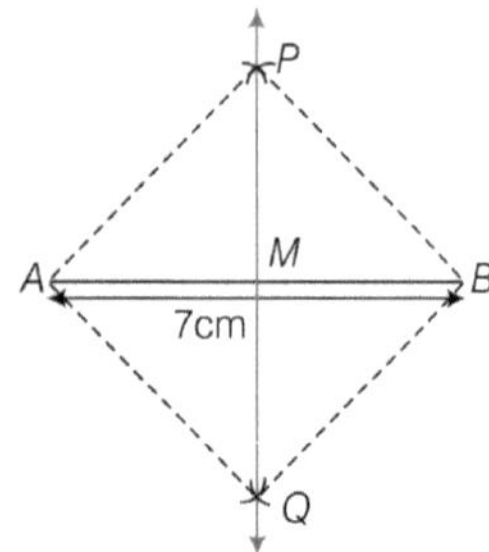

In ΔPAQ and ΔPBQ,

$$AP = BP \qquad \text{[arcs of equal radii]}$$
$$AQ = BQ \qquad \text{[arcs of equal radii]}$$
$$PQ = PQ \qquad \text{[common sides]}$$
$$\therefore \quad \Delta PAQ \cong \Delta PBQ \qquad \text{[by SSS congruence rule]}$$
$$\therefore \quad \angle APM = \angle BPM \qquad \text{[by CPCT] ...(i)}$$

Now, in ΔPMA and ΔPMB,

$$PM = PM \qquad \text{[common sides]}$$
$$\angle APM = \angle BPM \qquad \text{[from Eq. (i)]}$$
$$AP = BP \qquad \text{[arcs of equal radii]}$$
$$\therefore \quad \Delta PMA \cong \Delta PMB \qquad \text{[by SAS congruence rule]}$$
$$AM = BM \qquad \text{[by CPCT]}$$
$$\text{and} \quad \angle AMP = \angle BMP \qquad \text{[by CPCT] ...(ii)}$$
$$\text{Now,} \quad \angle AMP + \angle BMP = 180° \qquad \text{[linear pair axiom]...(iii)}$$

From Eqs. (ii) and (iii), we get

$$\angle AMP = \angle BMP = 90°$$

Hence, PMQ is the required perpendicular bisector of the given line segment AB ($= 7$ cm).

8. Steps of Construction

(i) Draw a line segment $BC = 6.8$ cm.

(ii) Draw $\angle PBC = 45°$ at point B and draw $\angle QCB = 45°$ at point C.

(iii) Mark the point of intersection of ray BP and ray CQ at A.

(iv) Now, draw the angle bisectors of $\angle ABC$ and $\angle ACB$, let them to intersect each other at point I. On measuring the $\angle BIC$, we get the value $135°$.

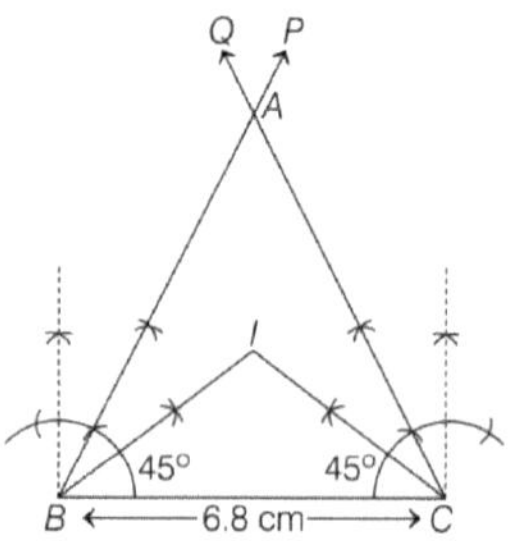

9. Steps of Construction

(i) Draw a line segment BC.

(ii) At the point B, draw a ray BA, making $\angle ABC = 60°$.

(iii) Again, draw an angle of $60°$ at the point B of ray BA such that $\angle DBA = 60°$ and $\angle DBC = 120°$.

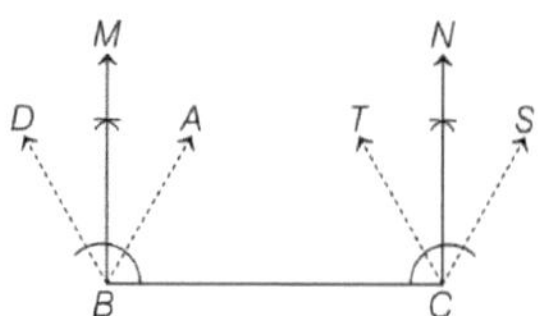

(iv) Bisect $\angle DBA$, to get $\angle MBA = 30°$.

(v) At point C, draw a ray TC, making $\angle TCB = 60°$

(vi) Again, draw an angle of $60°$ at the point C of ray CT such that $\angle SCT = 60°$ and $\angle SCB = 120°$.

(vii) Bisect $\angle SCT$, to get $\angle NCT = 30°$.

Thus, $\angle MBC = \angle NCB = 90°$ are constructed.

10. Here, $22\dfrac{1}{2}° = \dfrac{45°}{2}$. So, to draw an angle of $22\dfrac{1}{2}°$, firstly draw an angle of $90°$ and bisect it, to get an angle of $45°$. Again, bisect an angle of $45°$, to get required angle of $22\dfrac{1}{2}°$.

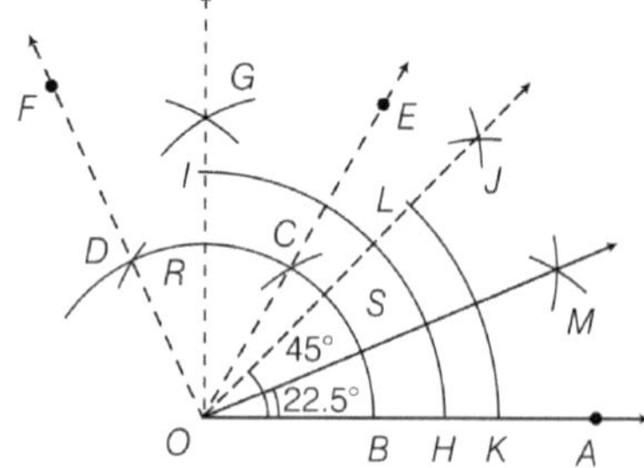

Steps of Construction

(i) First, draw a ray OA with initial point O.

(ii) Taking O as centre and suitable radius, draw an arc of a circle, which intersects OA at B.

(iii) Taking B as centre and with the same radius as before, draw an arc intersecting the previously drawn arc at point C.

(iv) Taking C as centre, draw an arc of a circle, which intersects the previous drawn arc at a point D.

(v) Draw the rays OE and OF passing through points C and D.

(vi) Taking D and C as centres, draw arcs, which intersects at point G.

(vii) Draw ray *OG*, which intersects arc *CD* at point *R*.

(viii) Again, taking *B* and *R* as centre, draw arcs, which intersect at point *J*.

(ix) Draw ray *OJ*, which intersect arc *BR* at point *S* and makes an angle 45°.

(x) Again, taking *B* and *S* as centres, draw arcs, which intersect at point *M*.

(xi) Draw ray *OM*, which makes an angle $\dfrac{45°}{2}$.

11. Steps of Construction

(i) First, draw a line segment *BC* and make the $\angle ABC = 60°$ and draw an arc of any radius, taking *B* as centre (say). This arc cut arms *BA* and *BC* at *E* and *D*, respectively.

(ii) Now, taking *E* and *D* as centres and with the radius more than $\dfrac{1}{2}ED$, draw two equal arcs, which cut each other at *P* (say).

(iii) Draw the ray *BP*.

$$\therefore \angle PBC = \dfrac{1}{2}\angle ABC = \dfrac{60°}{2} = 30°$$

(iv) Now, taking *M* and *D* as centres and with the radius more than $\dfrac{1}{2}MD$, draw two equal arcs, which cut each other at *K* (Say).

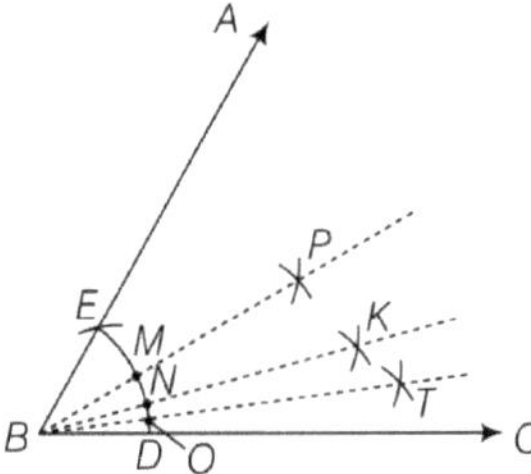

(v) Draw the ray *BK*.

$$\therefore \angle KBC = \dfrac{1}{2}\angle PBC = \dfrac{30°}{2} = 15°$$

(vi) Now, taking *N* and *D* as centres and with the radius more than $\dfrac{1}{2}ND$, draw two equal arcs, which cut each other at *T* (say).

(vii) Draw the ray *BT*.

$$\therefore \angle TBC = \dfrac{1}{2}\angle KBC$$
$$= \dfrac{15°}{2} = 7\dfrac{1}{2}°$$

Hence, $\angle TBC$ is the required angle.

12. Given, in $\triangle ABC$, base *BC* = 10 cm, $\angle B = 90°$ and *AB* + *BC* = 16 cm

Steps of Construction

(i) Draw the base *BC* = 10 cm.

(ii) At the point *B*, draw a ray *BX*, making $\angle XBC = 90°$.

(iii) Cut a line segment *BD* = *AB* + *AC* = 16 cm from the ray *BX*.

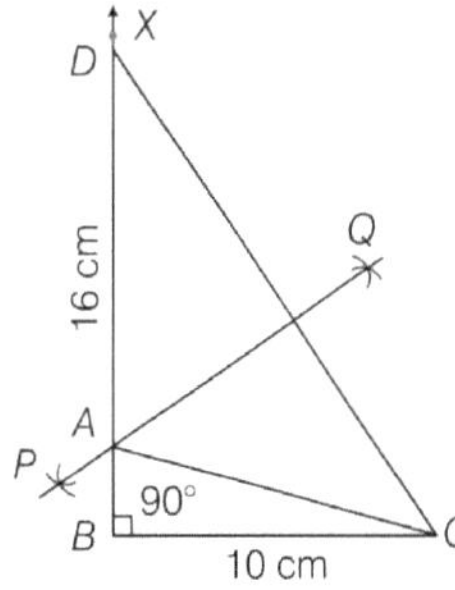

(iv) Join *DC*.

(v) Now, draw the perpendicular bisector *PQ* of *CD*, which intersects *BD* at a point *A*.

(vi) Join *AC*. Thus, $\triangle ABC$ is the required right-angled triangle.

13.

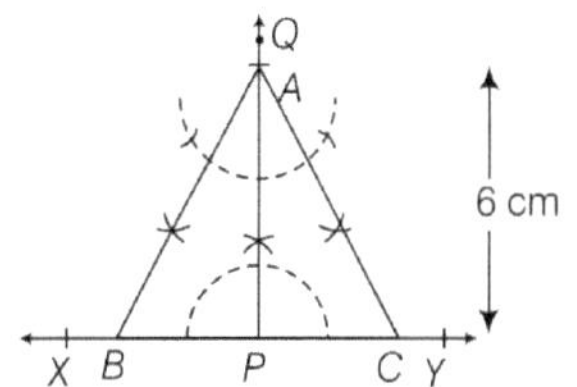

Steps of Construction

(i) Draw a line *XY*.

(ii) Take a point *P* on *XY* and draw a ray *PQ*, making $\angle QPY = 90°$.

(iii) Cut a line segment *PA* = 6 cm from the ray *PQ*.

(iv) Taking *A* as centre, draw 30° from both sides of line *AP* and this angle intersecting ray *X* and *Y* at *B* and *C*.

So, $\triangle ABC$ is the required equilateral triangle.

14. Let given right-angled triangle be $\triangle ABC$.

Then, given *BC* = 3.5 cm, $\angle B = 90°$ and sum of other side and hypotenuse i.e. *AB* + *AC* = 5.5 cm

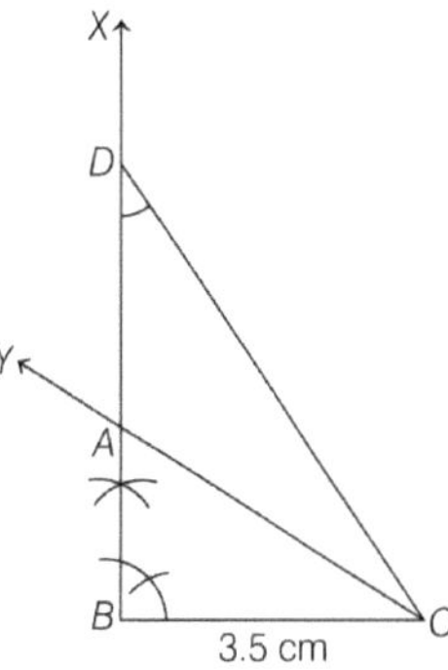

To construct $\triangle ABC$, use the following steps.

(i) Draw the base *BC* = 3.5 cm

(ii) Make an $\angle XBC = 90°$ at the point *B* of base *BC*.

(iii) Cut the line segment *BD* equal to *AB* + *AC* i.e. 5.5 cm from the ray *XB*.

(iv) Join *DC* and makes an $\angle DCY$ equal to $\angle BDC$.

(v) Let *CY* intersects *BX* at *A*.

Thus, $\triangle ABC$ is the required right-angled triangle.

Justification

Base BC and $\angle B$ are drawn as given.

In $\triangle ACD$, $\quad \angle ACD = \angle ADC$ $\qquad$ [by construction]

$\therefore \qquad\qquad AD = AC$ $\qquad\qquad$ ...(i)

$\qquad$ [sides opposite to equal angles are equal]

Now, $\qquad\quad AB = BD - AD = BD - AC$ $\quad$ [from Eq. (i)]

$\Rightarrow \qquad\qquad BD = AB + AC$

Thus, our construction is justified.

15. Steps of Construction

(i) First, draw the base $BC = 8$ cm.

(ii) By taking B and C as centres, draw two arcs of radius 6 cm and 7.3 cm, respectively, which intersect each other at A.

(iii) Join AB and AC.

Thus, $\triangle ABC$ is the required triangle.

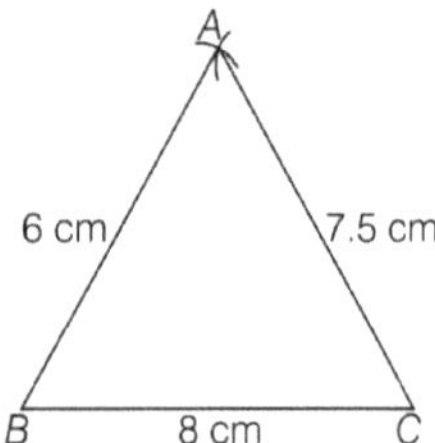

16. Steps of Construction

(i) First, draw a ray AX with initial point A.

(ii) Taking A as centre and radius (6 cm), draw an arc of a circle, which intersects AX at point B.

(iii) Taking B as centre and with the radius 6 cm, draw an arc intersecting the previously drawn arc, say at a point C.

(iv) Join AC and BC.

Thus, $\triangle ABC$ is an equilateral triangle.

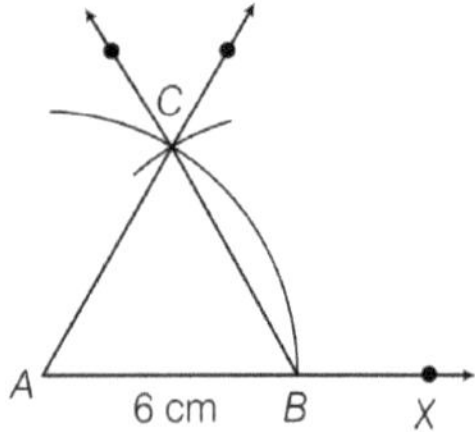

Justification

In $\triangle ABC$, $\qquad AB = BC$ $\qquad$ [radii of same circle]

$\qquad\qquad\qquad AB = AC$ $\qquad$ [radii of same circle]

$\therefore \qquad AB = BC = CA$

So, $\triangle ABC$ is an equilateral triangle.

Hence, the construction is justified.

17. Given, $TU = 3$ cm, $ST + US = 8$ cm and $\angle T = 150°$

Steps of Construction

(i) First, draw the base, $TU = 3$ cm.

Now, draw a ray TX such that $\angle XTU = \angle T = 150°$.

(ii) Here, sum of two sides $= ST + US = 8$ cm

So, cut the line segment $TD = 8$ cm from ray TX.

(iii) Join DU.

(iv) Draw perpendicular bisector of DU, say PQ, which intersects TD at S.

(v) Now, join SU. Thus, we get a $\triangle STU$, which is the required triangle.

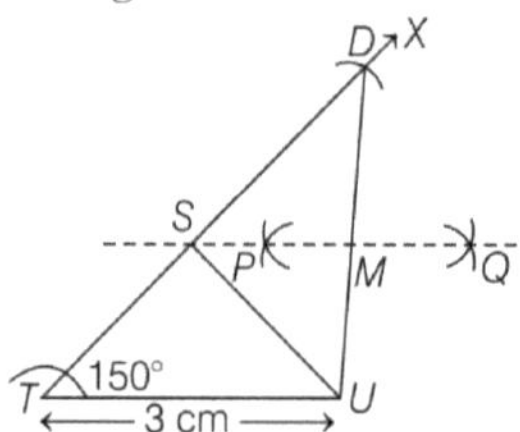

18. Given, $BC = 3.6$ cm, $\angle B = 30°$ and $AB - AC = 1.3$ cm

Steps of Construction

(i) First, draw the base, $BC = 3.6$ cm.

At point B, draw a ray BX, which makes $\angle CBX = 30°$.

(ii) Here, $AB - AC = 1.3$ cm

$\therefore AB > AC$ i.e. the side containing the base $\angle B$ is greater than third side, so it is the case I of construction S.

Hence, cut line segment BD is equal to $AB - AC = 1.3$ cm from the ray BX.

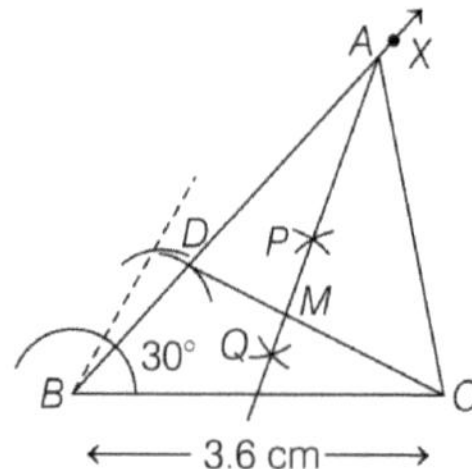

(iii) Now, join CD and draw its perpendicular bisector PQ, which bisects CD at M (say).

(iv) Let A be the intersection point of perpendicular bisector PQ and ray BX. Join AC. Thus, $\triangle ABC$ is the required triangle.

19. Given, $BC = 7$ cm, $AB + AC = 13$ cm and $\angle B = 60°$

Steps of Construction

(i) First, draw the base, $BC = 7$ cm.

Now, draw a ray BX such that $\angle XBC = \angle B = 60°$.

(ii) Here, sum of two sides $= AB + AC = 13$ cm

So, cut the line segment $BD = 13$ cm from ray BX.

(iii) Join DC.

(iv) Draw perpendicular bisector of DC, say PQ, which intersects BD at A.

(v) Now join AC. Thus, we get a $\triangle ABC$, which is the required triangle.

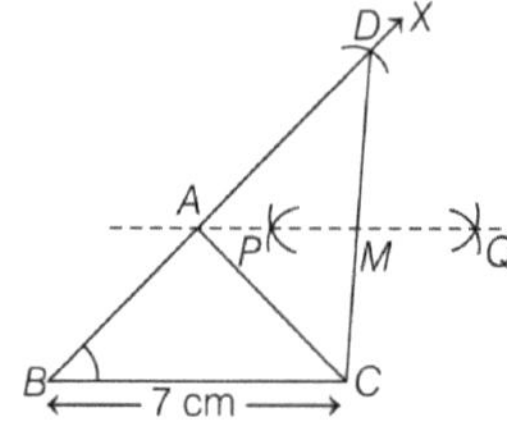

20. Given, $BC = 10$ cm, $\angle B = 45°$ and $AB - AC = 5$ cm

Steps of Construction

(i) First, draw the base, $BC = 10$ cm.

At point B, draw a ray BX, which makes an $\angle CBX = 45°$.

(ii) Here, $AB - AC = 5$ cm

$\therefore AB > AC$ i.e. the side containing the base $\angle B$ is greater than third side.

So, cut line segment BD is equal to $AB - AC = 5$ cm from the ray BX.

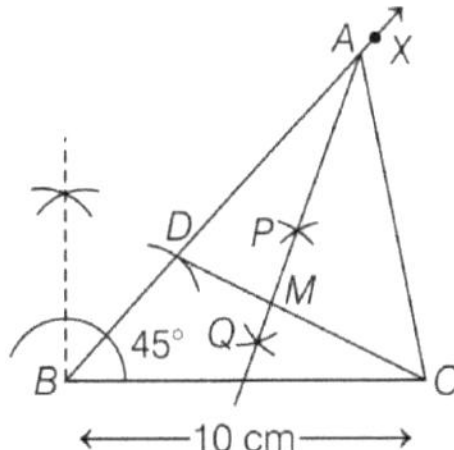

(iii) Now, join CD and draw its perpendicular bisector PQ, which bisects CD at M (say).

(iv) Let A be the intersection point of perpendicular bisector PQ and ray BX. Join AC. Thus, $\triangle ABC$ is the required triangle.

21. Given, in $\triangle PQR$, $QR = 3$ cm, $\angle PQR = 45°$

and $QP - PR = 2$ cm

To construct $\triangle PQR$, use the following steps.

(i) Draw the base QR of length 3 cm.

(ii) Make an $\angle XQR = 45°$ at point Q of base QR.

(iii) Cut the line segment $QS = QP - PR = 2$ cm from the ray QX.

(iv) Join SR and draw the perpendicular bisector of SR, say AB.

(v) Let bisector AB intersect QX at P. Join PR

Thus, $\triangle PQR$ is the required triangle.

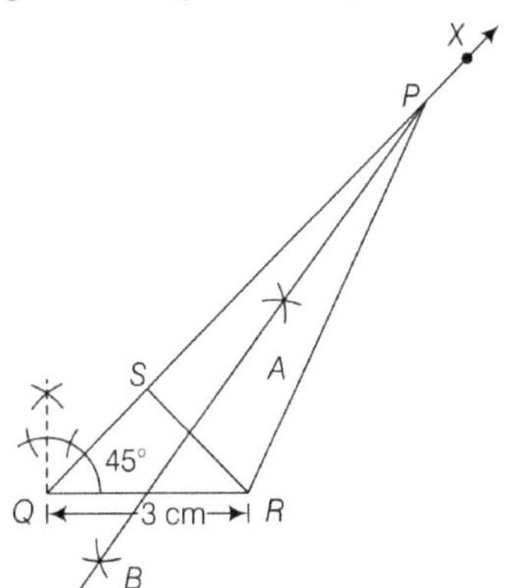

22. Given, in $\triangle PQR$, $QR = 6.5$ cm, $\angle Q = 60°$

and $PR - PQ = 1.5$ cm

Steps of Construction

(i) Draw the base, $QR = 6.5$ cm.

At point Q, draw a ray QX making an $\angle XQR = 60°$.

Here, $\qquad PR - PQ = 1.5$ cm

$\therefore \qquad\qquad PR > PQ$

i.e. The side containing the base angle $\angle Q$ is less than third side.

(ii) Cut line segment QS equal to $PR - PQ$ i.e. $QS = 1.5$ cm from the ray QX extended on opposite side of base QR.

(iii) Join SR and draw its perpendicular bisector ray AB, which intersects SR at M (say).

(iv) Let P be the intersection point of SX and perpendicular bisector AB. Then, join PR.

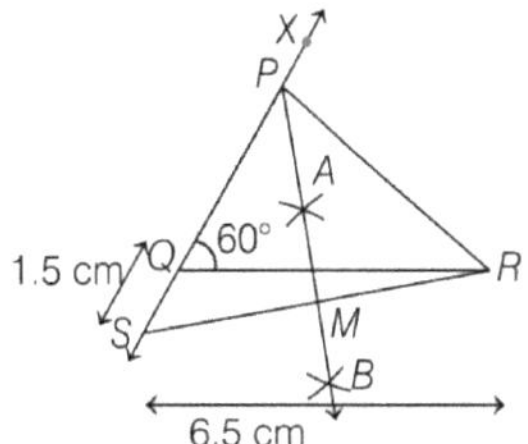

Thus, $\triangle PQR$ is the required triangle.

23. Steps of Construction

(i) Draw a line segment $AB = 6.2$ cm.

(ii) Draw an arc with A as centre and 7.3 cm as radius and draw another arc with B as centre and 6 cm as radius to intersect each other at C.

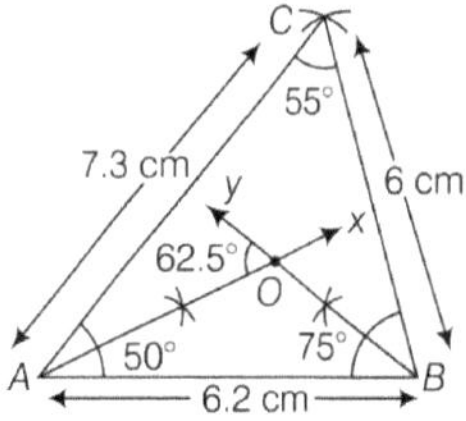

(iii) Join AC and BC. Thus, we get the required $\triangle ABC$. On measuring all the three angles, we get $\angle A = 50°$, $\angle B = 75°$ and $\angle C = 55°$.

(iv) Now, draw the angle bisector of $\angle A$ and $\angle B$, which intersect each other at O, since $\angle A$ is the smallest angle and $\angle B$ is the largest angle in $\triangle ABC$.

(v) On measuring the acute $\angle AOY$ formed by the bisecting rays AX and BY at the point of intersection O, we get $\angle AOY = 62.5°$

24. We know that, in an equilateral triangle, all sides are equal and all angles are equal i.e. each angle is of $60°$.

Given, altitude of an equilateral triangle, say $\triangle ABC$ is 3.2 cm. To construct the $\triangle ABC$, use the following steps.

(i) Draw a line PQ.

(ii) Take a point D on PQ and draw a ray $DE \perp PQ$.

(iii) Cut the line segment AD of length 3.2 cm from DE.

(iv) Make angles equal to $30°$ at A on both sides of AD, say $\angle CAD$ and $\angle BAD$, where B and C lie on PQ.

(v) Cut the line segment DC from PQ such that $DC = BD$

(vi) Join AC

Thus, $\triangle ABC$ is the required triangle.

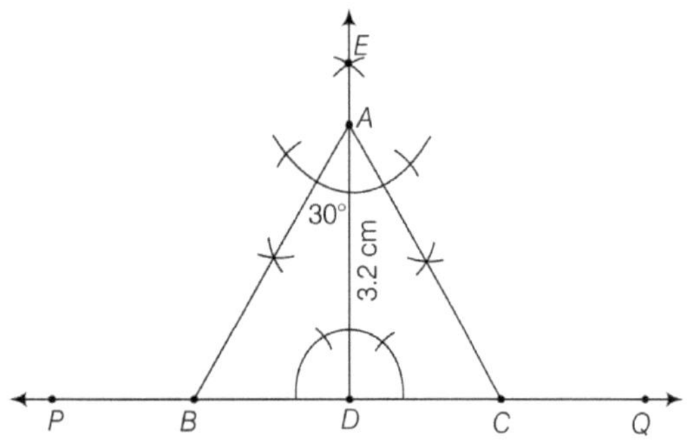

Justification

Here, $\angle A = \angle BAD + \angle CAD$

$$= 30° + 30° = 60°$$

Also, $AD \perp BC$

$\therefore$ $\angle ADB = 90°$

In $\triangle ABD$, $\angle BAD + \angle ADB + \angle DBA = 180°$

[$\because$ angle sum property of triangle]

$$30° + 90° + \angle DBA = 180°$$

[$\because \angle BAD = 30°$, by construction]

$$\angle DBA = 60°$$

Similary, $\angle DCA = 60°$

Thus, $\angle A = \angle B = \angle C = 60°$

Hence, $\triangle ABC$ is an equilateral triangle.

25. Steps of Construction

(i) Draw a line segment $BC = 4$ cm.

(ii) Draw a perpendicular bisector PQ of BC, which intersects it at M.

(iii) Cut $MN = 6.5$ cm.

(iv) Join BN.

(v) Now, draw a perpendicular bisector DE of BN, which intersects it at O and intersect MN at A.

(vi) Join AB and AC.

Thus, $\triangle ABC$ is the required triangle.

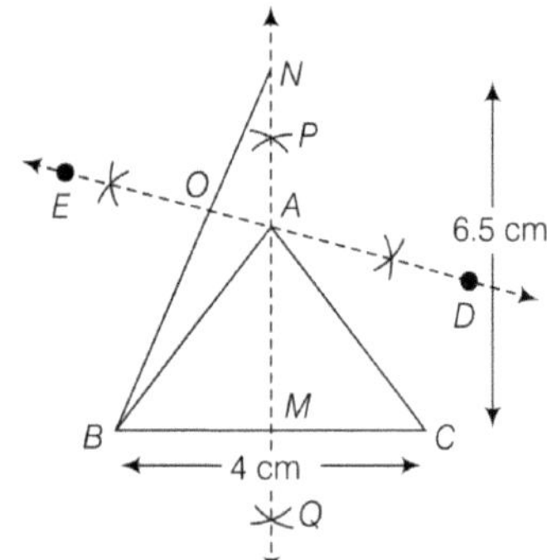

26. Steps of Construction

(i) First, draw a ray OA with initial point O.

(ii) Taking O as centre and some radius, draw an arc of a circle, which intersects OA at a point B (say).

(iii) Taking B as centre and with the same radius as before, draw an arc intersecting the previous arc at a point C (say).

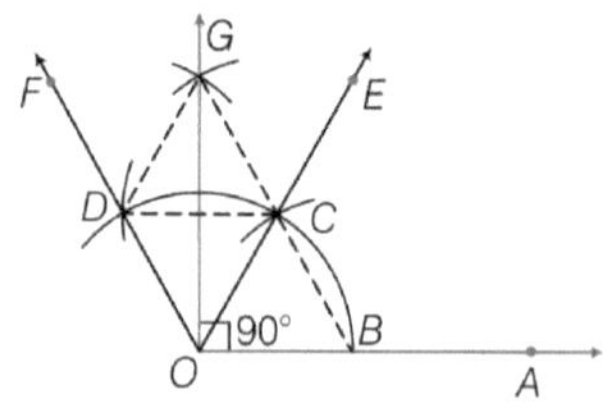

(iv) Taking C as centre and with the same radius as before, draw an arc intersecting the arc drawn in step (ii) at D (say).

(v) Draw the ray OE passing through C, then $\angle EOA = 60°$ and the ray OF passing through D, then $\angle FOE = 60°$.

(vi) Next, taking C and D as centres and with the radius more than $\dfrac{1}{2}CD$, draw arcs to intersect each other at a point G (say).

(vii) Draw the ray OG, which is the angle bisector of the $\angle FOE$.

i.e. $\angle FOG = \angle GOE = \dfrac{1}{2}\angle FOE = \dfrac{1}{2}(60°) = 30°$

Thus, $\angle GOA = \angle GOE + \angle EOA$

$$= 30° + 60° = 90°$$

Hence, $\angle GOA$ is the required angle of 90°.

Justification

(i) Join BC.

Then, $OC = OB = BC$ [by construction]

So, $\triangle COB$ is an equilateral triangle.

$\therefore$ $\angle COB = 60° = \angle EOA$ ...(i)

(ii) Join CD.

Then, $OD = OC = CD$ [by construction]

So, $\triangle DOC$ is an equilateral triangle.

$\therefore$ $\angle DOC = 60° = \angle FOE$

(iii) Join CG and DG.

In $\triangle ODG$ and $\triangle OCG$,

$$OD = OC$$ [radii of the same arc]

27. Steps of Construction

(i) First, draw a ray OA with initial point O.

(ii) Taking O as centre and any radius, draw an arc of a circle, which intersects OA, say at a point B.

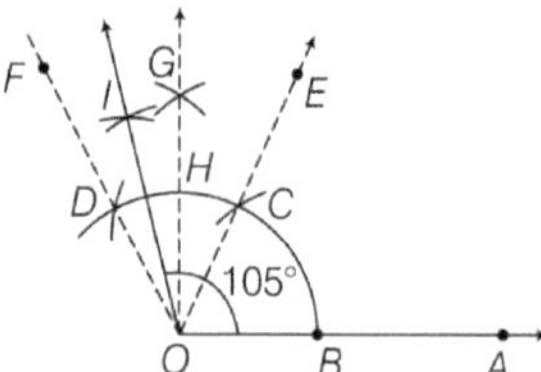

(iii) Taking B as centre and with the same radius as before, draw an arc intersecting the previously drawn arc, say at a point C.

(iv) Taking C as centre and with the same radius as before, draw an arc intersecting the arc drawn in step (ii), say at a point D.

(v) Draw the ray OE passing through C and the ray OF passing through D. Then, $\angle EOA = \angle FOE = 60°$.

(vi) Next, taking C and D as centres and with the radius more than $\dfrac{1}{2}CD$, draw arcs to intersect each other, say at G.

(vii) Draw the ray OG intersecting the arc drawn in step (ii) at H. This ray OG is the angle bisector of the $\angle FOE$.

i.e. $\angle FOG = \angle EOG = \dfrac{1}{2}\angle FOE = \dfrac{1}{2}(60°) = 30°$

Thus, $\angle GOA = \angle GOE + \angle EOA = 30° + 60° = 90°$

(viii) Next, taking H and D as centres and with the radius more than $\dfrac{1}{2}HD$, draw arcs to intersect each other, say at I.

(ix) Draw the ray OI, which is the angle bisector of the $\angle FOG$.

i.e. $\angle FOI = \angle GOI = \dfrac{1}{2}\angle FOG = \dfrac{1}{2}(30°) = 15°$

Thus, $\angle IOA = \angle IOG + \angle GOA = 15° + 90° = 105°$

On measuring the $\angle IOA$ by protractor, we find that $\angle IOA = 105°$. Thus, the construction is verified.

28. Steps of Construction

(i) First, draw a ray OA with initial point O.

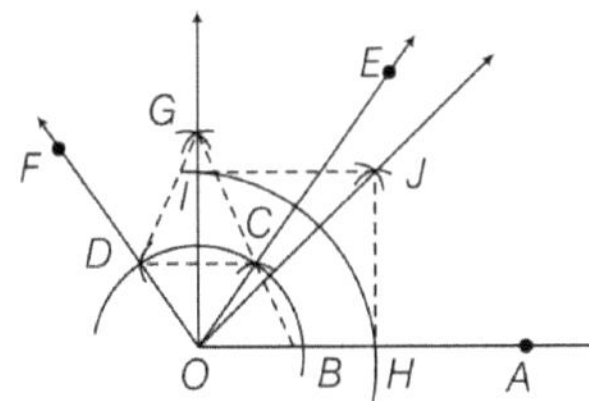

(ii) Taking O as centre and some radius, draw an arc of a circle which intersects OA, say at a point B.

(iii) Taking B as centre and with the same radius as before, draw an arc intersecting the previously drawn arc, say at a point C.

(iv) Taking C as centre and with the same radius as before, draw an arc intersecting the arc drawn in step (ii) say at D.

(v) Draw the ray OE passing through C.
Then, $\angle EOA = 60°$.

(vi) Draw the ray OF passing through D.
Then, $\angle FOE = 60°$.

(vii) Next, taking C and D as centres and with radius more than $\dfrac{1}{2}CD$, draw arcs to intersect each other, say at G.

(viii) Draw the ray OG, which is the angle bisector of the $\angle FOE$.

i.e. $\angle FOG = \angle EOG = \dfrac{1}{2}\angle FOE = \dfrac{1}{2}(60°) = 30°$

Thus, $\angle GOA = \angle GOE + \angle EOA = 30° + 60° = 90°$

(ix) Now, taking O as centre and any radius more than OB, draw an arc to intersect the rays OA and OG, say at H and I, respectively.

(x) Next, taking H and I as centres and with the radius more than $\dfrac{1}{2}HI$, draw arcs to intersect each other say at J.

(xi) Draw the ray OJ. This ray OJ is the required angle bisector of the $\angle GOA$.

Thus, $\angle GOJ = \angle AOJ = \dfrac{1}{2}\angle GOA = \dfrac{1}{2}(90°) = 45°$

Justification

(i) Join BC.
Then, $\qquad OC = OB = BC \qquad$ [by construction]
$\therefore \Delta COB$ is an equilateral triangle.
$\therefore \qquad\qquad \angle COB = 60°$
$\therefore \qquad\qquad \angle EOA = 60°$

(ii) Join CD.
Then, $\qquad OD = OC = CD \qquad$ [by construction]
$\therefore \Delta DOC$ is an equilateral triangle.
$\therefore \qquad\qquad \angle DOC = 60°$
$\therefore \qquad\qquad \angle FOE = 60°$

(iii) Join CG and DG.
In ΔODG and ΔOCG,
$\qquad OD = OC \qquad$ [radii of the same arc]
$\qquad DG = CG \qquad$ [arcs of equal radii]
$\qquad OG = OG \qquad$ [common sides]
$\therefore \qquad \Delta ODG \cong \Delta OCG$ [by SSS congruence rule]
$\therefore \qquad \angle DOG = \angle COG \qquad$ [by CPCT]
$\therefore \qquad \angle FOG = \angle EOG = \dfrac{1}{2}\angle FOE$

$\qquad\qquad\qquad = \dfrac{1}{2}(60°) = 30°$

Thus, $\qquad \angle GOA = \angle GOE + \angle EOA$
$\qquad\qquad\qquad = 30° + 60° = 90°$

(iv) Join HJ and IJ.
In ΔOIJ and ΔOHJ,
$\qquad OI = OH \qquad$ [radii of the same arc]
$\qquad IJ = HJ \qquad$ [arcs of equal radii]
$\qquad OJ = OJ \qquad$ [common sides]
$\therefore \Delta OIJ \cong OHJ \qquad$ [by SSS congruence rule]
$\therefore \angle IOJ = \angle HOJ \qquad\qquad$ [by CPCT]

$\therefore \angle AOJ = \angle GOJ = \dfrac{1}{2}\angle GOA$

$\qquad\qquad\qquad = \dfrac{1}{2}(90°) = 45°$

29. 4 triangles are possible, as shown.

Steps of Construction

(i) Draw a line segment $AB = 6$ cm.

(ii) With A as centre, make an angle of $30°$ such that $\angle XAB = 30°$.

(iii) Mark D on AX such that $AD = 3.3$ cm.

(iv) Join BD
Thus, ΔADB is the required triangle.

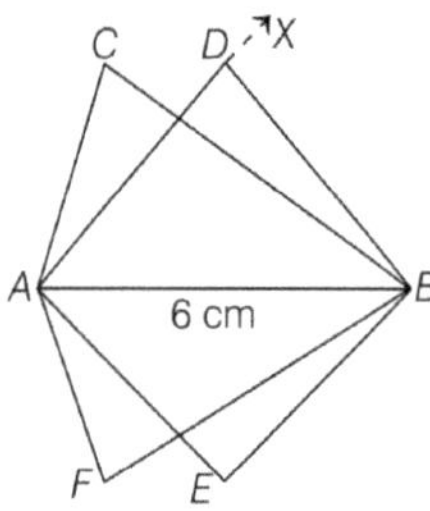

Note Similarly the remaining triangles are constructed in the mentioned procedure but only the angle differs. Instead of centre A, make an angle of $30°$ at point B. Thus, the remaining triangles are constructed upward and downward.

30. (i) (a) Here, $15° = \dfrac{30°}{2} = \dfrac{60°/2}{2} = \dfrac{60°}{4}$. So, to draw an angle of $15°$, firstly draw an angle of $60°$, then bisect it to get an angle of $30°$. Again, bisect an angle of $30°$ to get required angle of $15°$.

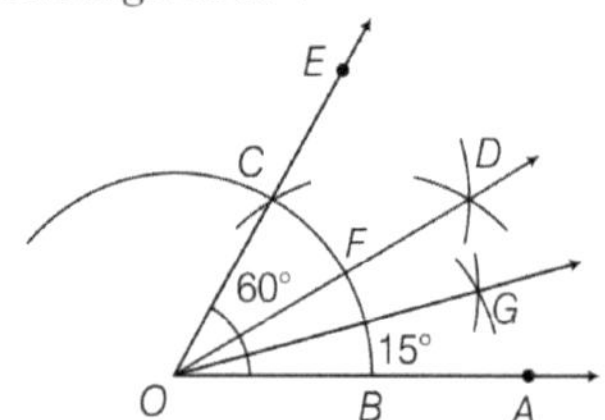

(b)

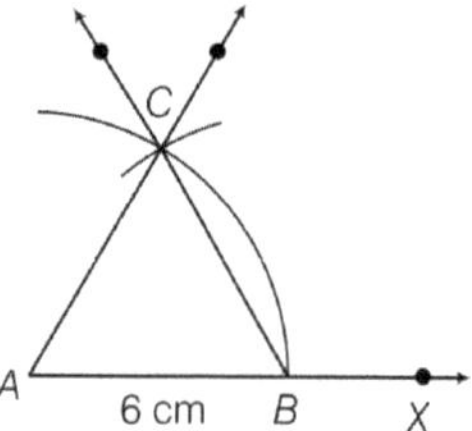

Here, $135° = 90° + 45°$. So, to draw an angle of $135°$, first draw an angle of $90°$, say $\angle AOG$ and then, draw an angle of $45°$ at the point of the ray OG (to the left side of OG), say $\angle IOG$.

Thus, $\angle IOA = \angle IOG + \angle GOA = 45° + 90° = 135°$

On measuring the $\angle IOA$ by protractor, we find that $\angle IOA = 135°$.

Thus, the construction is verified.

(ii) **Steps of Construction**

(i) First, draw a ray AX with initial point A.

(ii) Taking A as centre and some radius (say 6 cm), draw an arc of a circle, which intersects AX at point B.

(iii) Taking B as centre and with the same radius as before, draw an arc intersecting the previously drawn arc, say at a point C.

(iv) Join AC and BC.

Thus, $\triangle ABC$ is an equilateral triangle.

(iii) In $\triangle ABC$, $\qquad AB = BC \qquad$ [radii of same circle]
$$AB = AC \qquad \text{[radii of same circle]}$$
$\therefore \qquad\qquad AB = BC = CA$

So, $\triangle ABC$ is an equilateral triangle.

Hence, the construction is justified.

Chapter Test

Multiple Choice Questions

1. With the help of a ruler and compass, it is not possible to construct an angle of
(a) 120°
(b) 135°
(c) 36°
(d) 45°

2. Choose the correct answer from the given four options in the following questions.

With the help of a ruler and compass, it is possible to construct an angle of
(a) 40°
(b) 65°
(c) 37.5°
(d) 50°

3. The construction of $\triangle ABC$, in which $AB = 5$ cm, $\angle A = 60°$ is possible, when sum of BC and AC is equal to
(a) 4.6 cm
(b) 7.5 cm
(c) 3.6 cm
(d) 4.6 cm

4. The construction of $\triangle ABC$, given that $BC = 8$ cm, $\angle B = 60°$ is not possible, when the difference of AB and AC is equal to
(a) 7.3 cm
(b) 8.2 cm
(c) 7.2 cm
(d) 6.5 cm

5. The construction of a $\triangle ABC$, given that $BC = 9$ cm, $\angle C = 75°$ is possible, when the difference of AB and AC is equal to
(a) 10 cm
(b) 9.1 cm
(c) 9.6 cm
(d) 7.5 cm

Case Based MCQs

6. Banglore traffic police wants to make a traffic signal board of the shape of an equilateral triangle of side 6 cm to make the people aware of the traffic rules.

The construction of traffic signal board by taking each side as 6 cm is shown below.

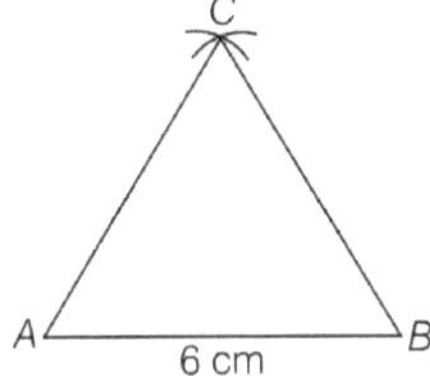

On the basis of the above information, solve the following questions.

(i) With the help of ruler and compass, which of the angle is not possible to construct it?
(a) 51°
(b) $\dfrac{45°}{2}$
(c) 30°
(d) 52.5°

(ii) The construction of a $\triangle PQR$, in which $PQ = 6.5$ cm and $\angle Q = 45°$ is not possible, when $(QR + RP)$ is
(a) 6 cm
(b) 6.8 cm
(c) 7 cm
(d) None of these

(iii) The construction of a $\triangle PQR$, in which $QR = 10$ cm, $\angle Q = 60°$ is not possible when $(PQ - PR)$ is equal to
(a) 9 cm
(b) 8 cm
(c) 11 cm
(d) 7 cm

(iv) The altitude of an equilateral $\triangle ABC$ is
(a) $4\sqrt{2}$ cm
(b) $2\sqrt{3}$ cm
(c) $\sqrt{3}$ cm
(d) $3\sqrt{3}$ cm

(v) Find the area of $\triangle ABC$ is
(a) $9\sqrt{3}$ cm^2
(b) $\dfrac{9\sqrt{3}}{4}$ cm^2
(c) $\dfrac{9\sqrt{3}}{2}$ cm^2
(d) None of these

Short Answer Type Questions

7. Construct an equilateral triangle, if its altitude is 4 cm.

8. Construct a $\triangle ABC$, in which $BC = 8$ cm, $\angle B = 45°$ and $AB - AC = 3.5$ cm.

Long Answer Type Questions

9. Construct a right-angled triangle, when one side is 6 cm and sum of other sides and the hypotenuse is 10 cm. Also, justify it.

10. Construct a rectangle, whose adjacent sides are of lengths 5 cm and 3.5 cm.

11. Construct a right-angled triangle, whose base is 12 cm and sum of its hypotenuse and other side is 18 cm.

Answers

1. (c)   *2.* (c)   *3.* (b)   *4.* (b)   *5.* (d)   *6.* (i) (a) (ii) (a) (iii) (c) (iv) (d) (v) (a)

For Detailed Solutions
Scan the code

CHAPTER 05

Surface Areas and Volumes

In this Chapter...

- Cuboid and Cube
- Right Circular Cylinder
- Right Circular Cone
- Sphere
- Hemisphere

Cuboid and Cube

A cuboid is a solid bounded by six rectangular plane surfaces. e.g. match box, brick, box, etc. are cuboid.

In a cuboid, there are 6 faces, 12 edges and 8 corners (four at bottom and four at top face) which are called **vertices**.

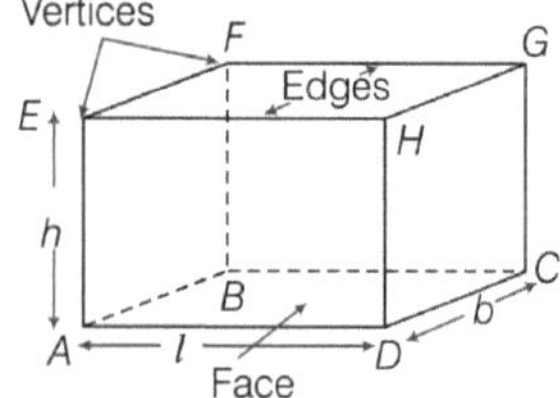

A cuboid whose length, breadth and height all are equal, is called a cube. e.g. Ice cubes, sugar cubes, dice are in cubical form.

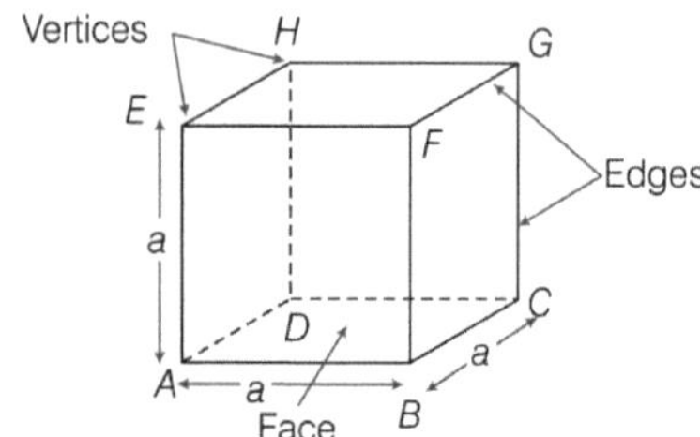

In a cube, there are 6 faces, 12 edges and 8 corners (four at bottom and four at top face) which are called **vertices**.

Surface Area of a Cuboid

Let the length of the cuboid be l units, breadth b units and height h units. Then,

(i) **Total surface area** Surface Area (SA) or Total Surface Area (TSA) of the cuboid

= Sum of areas of six rectangular faces

$= lb + lb + bh + bh + hl + hl$

$\Rightarrow$ SA or TSA $= 2(lb+bh+hl)$ sq units

i.e. SA or TSA $= 2\,($Length $\times$ Breadth

$+$ Breadth $\times$ Height $+$ Height $\times$ Length$)$

(ii) **Lateral surface area** If out of the six faces of a cuboid, we do not include the bottom and top faces, then the area of remaining four faces is called the lateral surface area of the cuboid. So,

Lateral surface area = Sum of area of four rectangular faces excluded the top and bottom faces

$= bh + bh + lh + lh = 2(l+b)h$

Lateral surface area of a cuboid $= 2(l+b)h$ sq units

or Lateral surface area of a cuboid

$=$ (Perimeter of the base) $\times$ Height

(iii) Diagonal of a cuboid $= \sqrt{l^2 + b^2 + h^2}$ units

(iv) Area of the four walls of a room $=$ Lateral surface area of a cuboid $= 2(l+b)h$.

(v) Total length of cuboid

$=$ Length of all 12 edges of the cuboid

$=$ Sum of semi-perimeter of all faces of the cuboid

$= 4(l+b+h)$ units

Surface Area of a Cube

Let each edge of the cube be 'a' units. Then,

(i) Total surface area of the cube

$=$ Sum of areas of six faces

$= 2(aa + aa + aa) = 2(a^2 + a^2 + a^2)$

$\Rightarrow$ TSA $= 6a^2$ sq units

(ii) Lateral surface area of the cube $=$ Sum of areas of four faces excluded the top and bottom faces $= 2(aa + aa)$

$\Rightarrow$ Lateral surface area $= 4a^2$ sq units

(iii) Diagonal of a cube $= \sqrt{a^2 + a^2 + a^2} = \sqrt{3a^2}$

$\Rightarrow$ Diagonal of a cube $= \sqrt{3}a$ units

Note *Total length of a cube = Length of all 12 edges of a cube =12a units, where edge of cube is a units.*

Volume of a Cuboid

Let length of the cuboid is l units, breadth is b units and height is h units, then

Volume of the cuboid $=$ Length $\times$ Breadth $\times$ Height

or Volume of the cuboid $= lbh$ cu units

Also, Volume of the cuboid $=$ Base area $\times$ Height

The unit of measurement of volume is cubic unit.

Volume of a Cube

Cube is a cuboid whose length, breadth and height are all equal. So, if one side (or edge) of a cube be a units, then Volume of cube $= l \times b \times h = a \times a \times a$

$\Rightarrow$ Volume of cube $= a^3 = (\text{Side})^3$ cu units

Surface Area of a Right Circular Cylinder

We know that, right circular cylinder is generated by revolution of a rectangular sheet about one of its side, so the area of the rectangular sheet gives us the curved surface area of the cylinder and length of the rectangular sheet is equal to the circumference of the circular base.

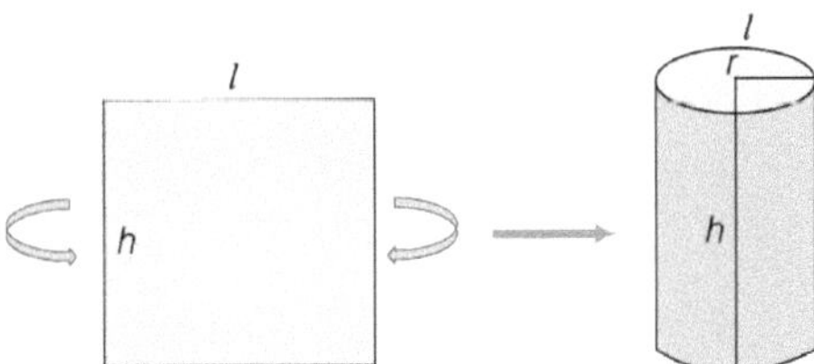

$\therefore$ Curved surface area of the cylinder

$=$ Area of rectangular sheet

$=$ Length of rectangular sheet $\times$ Height

$=$ Circumference of the base of the cylinder $\times$ Height

[$\because$ length of rectangular sheet $=$ circumference of the base]

Hence, curved surface area of cylinder $= 2\pi rh$ sq units where, circumference of the base of the cylinder $= 2\pi r$, r is the radius of the base and h is the height of the cylinder.

Total Surface Area of a Right Circular Cylinder

For total surface area of a cylinder, we also take area of both circular bases with curved surface area of the cylinder. So,

Total surface area of cylinder

$=$ Curved surface area of cylinder

$+$ Area of both circular ends

$= 2\pi rh + \pi r^2 + \pi r^2 = 2\pi rh + 2\pi r^2$

TSA of cylinder $= 2\pi r(h+r)$ sq units

where, $r =$ radius of base and $h =$ height of cylinder

Volume of a Right Circular Cylinder

We know that a right circular cylinder can be built up using circles of the same radius. Let h be the height and r be the radius of the right circular cylinder, then

Volume of the cylinder $=$ Measure of the space occupied by the cylinder

$=$ Area of circular base $\times$ Height

Volume of the cylinder $= \pi r^2 h$ cu units

Surface area of Hollow Cylinder

A solid bounded by two coaxial cylinders of the same height and different radii is called a hollow cylinder.

Let a hollow cylinder whose external and internal radii are R and r, respectively with h as height. Then,

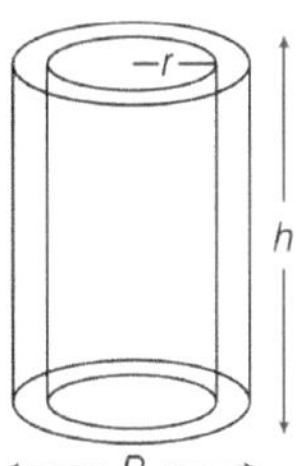

Surface area of each base $= \pi(R^2 - r^2)$ sq units

Curved surface area = External surface area
$$+ \text{ Internal surface area}$$
$$= 2\pi Rh + 2\pi rh$$
$$= 2\pi h(R + r) \text{ sq units}$$
Total surface area = Curved surface area
$$+ 2 \text{ (surface area of each base)}$$
$$= 2\pi h(R + r) + 2\pi(R^2 - r^2)$$
$$\text{TSA of hollow cylinder} = 2\pi(R + r)(h + R - r) \text{ sq units}$$

Volume of a Hollow Cylinder

For volume of the material used for making a hollow cylinder will be obtain by subtracting the interior volume from exterior volume i.e.

Volume of the material = Exterior volume − Interior volume
$$= \pi R^2 h - \pi r^2 h$$
$$\text{Volume of hollow cylinder} = \pi(R^2 - r^2)h$$

where, R and r are exterior and interior radius respectively, h is the height of that hollow cylinder.

Right Circular Cone

A right circular cone is a solid generated by revolving a line segment which passes through a fixed point and makes a constant angle with a fixed line.

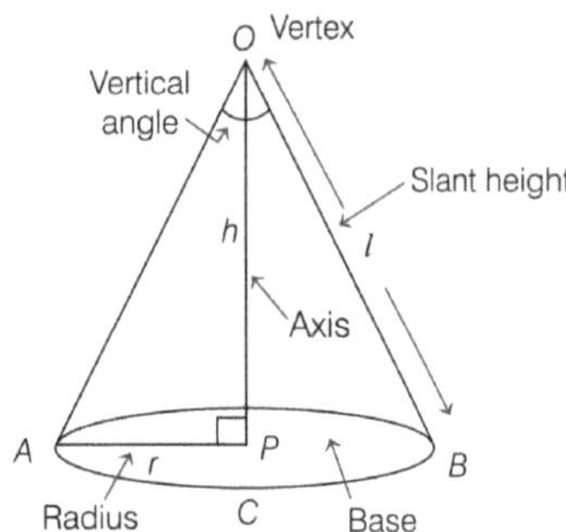

Relation between l, r and h

Let l be the slant height, r be the radius and h be the height of the cone. Then, relation between l, r and h is
$$l^2 = r^2 + h^2$$
or
$$l = \sqrt{r^2 + h^2} \text{ units}$$
$$[\text{on taking positive square root}]$$

Curved Surface Area of a Cone

For a cone having slant height 'l' and base radius 'r', the curved surface area is given by

$$\text{Curved surface area of a cone} = \frac{1}{2} l \times 2\pi r$$

$$\therefore \quad \text{Curved surface area of cone} = \pi rl \text{ sq units}$$

Total Surface Area of a Cone

If the base of the cone is to be closed, then a circular piece of paper of radius r is also required.

Total surface area of a cone = Curved surface area
$$+ \text{ Area of a base}$$
$$= \pi rl + \pi r^2$$
$$\text{TSA of a cone} = \pi r(l + r) \text{ sq units}$$

Volume of a Cone

For a cone of base radius 'r' and height 'h', then volume is given by

$$\text{Volume of a cone} = \frac{1}{3}\pi r^2 h \text{ cu units}$$

Sphere

A sphere is three-dimensional figure (solid figure) which is made up of all points in the space, which lie at a constant distance from a fixed point, called the **centre** of the sphere and the constant distance is called its **radius**.

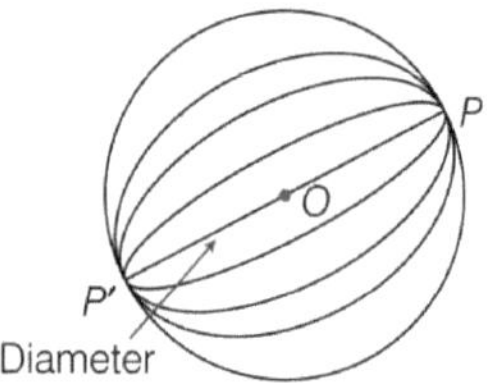

Surface Area of a Sphere

For a sphere of radius 'r', the surface area is given by

$$\text{Surface area of the sphere} = 4\pi r^2 \text{ sq units}$$

Volume of a Sphere

For a sphere of radius 'r', the volume is given by the formula

$$\text{Volume of a sphere} = \frac{4}{3}\pi r^3 \text{ cu units}$$

Hemisphere

When a plane through the centre of a sphere divides the sphere into two equal parts, then these two equal parts are called hemisphere.

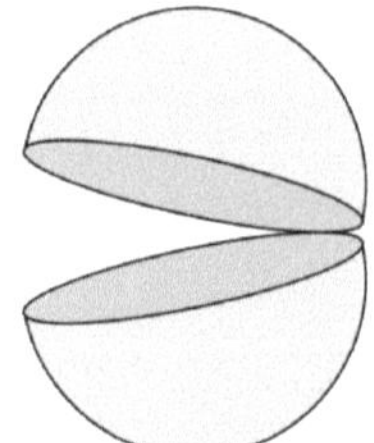

Surface Area of a Hemisphere

The surface area of a hemisphere is half the curved surface area of sphere.

So, curved surface area of hemisphere $= \dfrac{1}{2} \times 4\pi r^2$

$\Rightarrow$ Curved surface area of hemisphere $= 2\pi r^2$ sq units

where, r is the radius.

Also, area of base of the hemisphere $= \pi r^2$. So, total surface area of hemisphere

$\qquad$ = Curved surface area of a hemisphere

$\qquad\qquad\qquad$ + Area of the base of hemisphere

$\qquad = 2\pi r^2 + \pi r^2$

TSA of hemisphere $= 3\pi r^2$ sq units

where, r is the radius.

Volume of Hollow Sphere

If R and r are the external and internal radii of a hemisphere, then

Volume of hollow sphere (spherical shell)

$\qquad$ = Volume of the external sphere

$\qquad\qquad\qquad$ − Volume of the internal sphere

$$= \frac{4}{3}\pi R^3 - \frac{4}{3}\pi r^3$$

$$= \frac{4}{3}\pi (R^3 - r^3)$$

Volume of a hollow sphere

$$= \frac{4}{3}\pi (R^3 - r^3) \text{ cu units}$$

Solved Examples

Example 1. The capacity of a cuboidal tank is 50000 L of water. Find the breadth of the tank, if its length and depth are 2.5 m and 10 m, respectively.

[**NCERT Exemplar**]

Sol. Given, length (l) = 2.5 m and depth or height (h) = 10 m

Let breadth of tank be b.

Also, given capacity of a cuboidal tank

$$= \text{Volume of cuboidal tank}$$
$$= 50000 \text{ L} = \left(\frac{50000}{1000}\right) \text{m}^3 = 50 \text{ m}^3$$

$$\left[\because 1 \text{ L} = \frac{1}{1000} \text{ m}^3\right]$$

Now, volume of cuboidal tank $= 50 \text{ m}^3$

$\therefore \qquad l \times b \times h = 50$

$$[\because \text{ volume of a cuboid } (V) = lbh]$$

$\Rightarrow \qquad 2.5 \times b \times 10 = 50 \Rightarrow b = \frac{50}{25} = 2 \text{ m}$

Hence, breadth of the cuboidal tank is 2 m.

Example 2. A godown measures $40 \text{ m} \times 25 \text{ m} \times 15 \text{ m}$. Find the maximum number of wooden crates each measuring $1.5 \text{ m} \times 1.25 \text{ m} \times 0.5 \text{ m}$ that can be stored in the godown. [**NCERT Exemplar**]

Sol. Given, dimensions for godown are as

length (l) = 40 m, breadth (b) = 25 m and height (h) = 15 m

$\therefore$ Volume of the godown $= l \times b \times h = 40 \text{ m} \times 25 \text{ m} \times 15 \text{ m}$

Dimensions for each wooden crates are as

length (l_1) = 1.5 m, breadth (b_1) = 1.25 m and height (h_1) = 0.5 m

$\therefore$ Volume of each wooden crate $= l_1 \times b_1 \times h_1$
$$= 1.5 \text{ m} \times 1.25 \text{ m} \times 0.5 \text{ m}$$

Number of wooden crates

$$= \frac{\text{Volume of the godown}}{\text{Volume of one wooden crate}}$$

$$= \frac{40 \text{ m} \times 25 \text{ m} \times 15 \text{ m}}{1.5 \text{ m} \times 1.25 \text{ m} \times 0.5 \text{ m}} = \frac{15000}{0.9375} = 16000$$

Example 3. A solid cube is cut into two cuboids of equal volumes. Find the ratio of the total surface area of the given cube and that of one of the cuboids.

Sol. Let edge of the solid cube be a cm.

Then, dimensions of each of the cuboids will be a cm, a cm and $\frac{a}{2}$ cm.

$\therefore$ Total surface area of one of the cuboids

$$= 2\left(a \times a + a \times \frac{a}{2} + \frac{a}{2} \times a\right)$$

$$[\because \text{TSA of cuboid} = 2(lb + bh + hl)]$$

$$= 2\left(a^2 + \frac{a^2}{2} + \frac{a^2}{2}\right) = 4a^2 \text{ cm}^2$$

$\therefore$ Total surface area of the cube $= 6(\text{Edge})^2 = 6a^2 \text{ cm}^2$

So, ratio of the total surface area of the given cube and that of one of the cuboids

$$= \frac{6a^2}{4a^2} = \frac{3}{2} = 3:2$$

Example 4. The dimensions of a cuboid are in the ratio $1:2:3$ and its total surface area is 88 m^2. Find the dimensions of the cuboid.

Sol. Given, the dimensions of the cuboid are in the ratio $1:2:3$.

So, let the dimensions of cuboid be x m, $2x$ m and $3x$ m.

Then, total surface area $= 2(lb + bh + hl)$
$$= 2(x \times 2x + 2x \times 3x + 3x \times x)$$

But given surface area $= 88 \text{ m}^2$

$\therefore \qquad 2(x \times 2x + 2x \times 3x + 3x \times x) = 88$

$\Rightarrow \qquad 2(2x^2 + 6x^2 + 3x^2) = 88 \Rightarrow 2 \times 11x^2 = 88$

$\Rightarrow \qquad 22x^2 = 88 \Rightarrow x^2 = \frac{88}{22}$

$\Rightarrow \qquad x^2 = 4 \Rightarrow x^2 = 2^2$

$\Rightarrow \qquad x = 2 \text{ m}$

[on taking positive square root]

$\therefore \quad 2x = 2 \times 2 = 4$ m and $3x = 3 \times 2 = 6$ m

Hence, the dimensions of cuboid are 2 m, 4 m and 6 m.

Example 5. A plastic box 1.5 m long, 1.25 m wide and 65 cm deep is to be made. It is opened at the top. Ignoring the thickness of the plastic sheet, determine [**NCERT Exemplar**]

(i) the area of the sheet required for making the box.

(ii) the cost of sheet for it, if a sheet measuring 1 m^2 costs ₹ 20.

Sol. We have, a plastic box whose length (l) = 1.5 m, width (b) = 1.25 m

and depth (h) = 65 cm = $\frac{65}{100}$ = 0.65 m $\left[\because 1 \text{ cm} = \frac{1}{100} \text{ m}\right]$

Surface area of the box $= 2(lb + bh + hl)$
$$= 2(1.5 \times 1.25 + 1.25 \times 0.65 + 0.65 \times 1.5)$$
$$= 2(1.875 + 0.8125 + 0.975)$$
$$= 2(3.6625) = 7.325 \text{ m}^2$$

(i) Area of the sheet required for making the box

= Surface area of the box − Area of opened top

= $7.325 - l \times b$ [since, box is opened at the top]

= $7.325 - 1.5 \times 1.25$

= $7.325 - 1.875 = 5.45 \ \text{m}^2$

(ii) Given, cost of $1 \ \text{m}^2$ sheet = ₹ 20

∴ Cost of $5.45 \ \text{m}^2$ sheet = 20×5.45 = ₹ 109

Example 6. The dimension of a rectangular box are in the ratio $2 : 3 : 4$ and the difference between the cost of covering it with sheet of paper at the rate of ₹ 4 and ₹ 4.50 per m^2 is ₹ 416. Find the dimensions of the box.

Sol. Let the dimensions of the rectangular box be $2x$, $3x$ and $4x$ m.

∴ Surface area = $2(2x \times 3x + 3x \times 4x + 4x \times 2x)$

$$[\because \text{ surface area } = 2(lb + bh + lh)]$$

$$= 2(6x^2 + 12x^2 + 8x^2) = 2 \times 26x^2 = 52x^2$$

Cost of covering the box with sheet of paper at the rate of ₹ 4 per m^2 = ₹ $(52x^2 \times 4)$ = ₹ $208 \, x^2$.

And cost of covering the box with sheet of paper at the rate of ₹ 4.50 per m^2 = ₹ $(4.50 \times 52x^2)$ = ₹ $234x^2$

According to the question,

Difference of the cost at different rates = 416

$\Rightarrow$ $234x^2 - 208x^2 = 416 \Rightarrow 26x^2 = 416$

$\Rightarrow$ $x^2 = 16 \Rightarrow x = 4$ [on taking positive square root]

Hence, the dimension of the box are 8 m, 12 m and 16 m.

Example 7. In a cylinder, if radius is halved and height is doubled, then find its volume.

Sol. Let r be the radius and h be the height of the original cylinder.

Volume of cylinder = $\pi r^2 h$.

Volume of new cylinder = $\pi \left(\dfrac{r}{2}\right)^2 2h = \pi \dfrac{r^2}{2} h$

$$= \dfrac{1}{2} \times \text{ Volume of cylinder}$$

Hence, volume of new cylinder is halved of the original cylinder.

Example 8. The pillars of a temple are cylindrically shaped. If each pillar has a circular base of radius 20 cm and height 10 m, how much concrete mixture would be required to build 14 such pillars?

Sol. Given, radius of the base of cylinder $(r) = 20 \ \text{cm} = 0.2 \ \text{m}$

and height of the pillar $(h) = 10$ m

∴ Volume of each cylindrical shaped pillar = $\pi r^2 h$

$$= \dfrac{22}{7} \times (0.2)^2 \times 10 = \dfrac{8.8}{7} \ \text{m}^3$$

Now, required concrete mixture to make 14 such pillars

= Volume of one cylindrical pillar × 14

$$= \dfrac{8.8}{7} \ \text{m}^3 \times 14 = 17.6 \ \text{m}^3$$

Example 9. A metal pipe is 77 cm long. The inner diameter of a cross-section is 4 cm, the outer diameter being 4.4 cm (see figure). Find its

[NCERT Exemplar]

(i) inner curved surface area.

(ii) outer curved surface area.

(iii) total surface area.

Sol. Given, height of pipe $(h) = 77 \ \text{cm}$

Outer diameter $(d_1) = 4.4 \ \text{cm}$

and   inner diameter $(d_2) = 4$ cm

∴ Outer radius $(r_1) = 2.2$ cm $\left[\because \text{ radius } = \dfrac{\text{diameter}}{2}\right]$

and inner radius $(r_2) = 2 \ \text{cm}$

(i) Inner curved surface area = $2\pi r_2 h$

$$[\because \text{ curved surface area of a right circular cylinder } = 2\pi rh]$$

$$= 2 \times \dfrac{22}{7} \times 2 \times 77 = 88 \times 11 = 968 \ \text{cm}^2$$

(ii) Outer curved surface area = $2\pi r_1 h$

$$= 2 \times \dfrac{22}{7} \times 2.2 \times 77 = 44 \times 2.2 \times 11 = 1064.8 \ \text{cm}^2$$

(iii) Total surface area = Inner curved surface area

+ Outer curved surface area + Area of two bases

$$= 968 + 1064.8 + 2\pi \, (r_1^2 - r_2^2)$$

$$= 968 + 1064.8 + 2 \times \dfrac{22}{7} [(2.2)^2 - 2^2]$$

$$= 2032.8 + 2 \times \dfrac{22}{7} (4.84 - 4)$$

$$= 2032.8 + \dfrac{44}{7} \times 0.84 = 2032.8 + 44 \times 0.12$$

$$= 2032.8 + 5.28 = 2038.08 \ \text{cm}^2$$

Example 10. Circumference of the base of a cylinder, open at the top, is 132 cm. The sum of radius and height is 41 cm. Find the cost of polishing the outer surface area of cylinder at the rate ₹ 10 per dm^2 (decimetre). $\left(\text{use } \pi = \dfrac{22}{7}\right)$

Sol. Given, circumference of the base of cylinder = 132 cm

Let radius of base of cylinder be r.

∴ $2\pi r = 132$

$\Rightarrow$ $r = \dfrac{132}{2\pi} = \dfrac{132}{2 \times \dfrac{22}{7}}$

$$= \dfrac{132}{2} \times \dfrac{7}{22} = 21 \ \text{cm}$$

Let height of cylinder is h.

According to the question,

$$r + h = 41$$
$$\Rightarrow \quad h = 41 - r = 41 - 21 \qquad [\because r = 21 \text{ cm}]$$
$$= 20 \text{ cm}$$

Surface area of cylinder, whose top is open

$$= 2\pi rh + \pi r^2$$
$$= \left[2 \times \frac{22}{7} \times 21 \times 20\right] + \left[\frac{22}{7} \times (21)^2\right]$$
$$= 2640 + 1386 = 4026 \text{ cm}^2$$
$$= \frac{4026}{100} \text{ dm}^2 = 40.26 \text{ dm}^2$$

$$\left[\because (1 \text{ cm})^2 = \left(\frac{1}{10} \text{ dm}\right)^2 \Rightarrow 1 \text{ cm}^2 = \frac{1}{100} \text{ dm}^2\right]$$

$\therefore$ Total cost of polishing at the rate of ₹ 10 per dm^2

$$= 40.26 \times 10 = ₹ \, 402.60$$

Example 11. A patient in a hospital is given soup daily in a cylindrical bowl of diameter 7 cm. If the bowl is filled with soup to a height of 4 cm, then how much soup the hospital has to prepare daily to serve 250 patients?

Sol. Given, diameter of bowl $= 7$ cm

$$\therefore \quad \text{Radius}\,(r) = \frac{7}{2} \text{ cm}$$

and height of soup in bowl $(h) = 4$ cm

Capacity of the cylindrical bowl = Volume of the cylinder

$$= \pi r^2 h = \frac{22}{7} \times \frac{7}{2} \times \frac{7}{2} \times 4$$
$$= 22 \times 7 = 154 \text{ cm}^3$$

Hence, volume of soup to be prepared daily to serve 250 patients $= 154 \times 250 = 38500 \text{ cm}^3$

$$= \frac{38500}{1000} \text{ L} = 38.5 \text{ L} \qquad \left[\because 1 \text{ cm}^3 = \frac{1}{1000} \text{ L}\right]$$

Example 12. The inner diameter of a cylindrical wooden pipe is 24 cm and its outer diameter is 28 cm. The length of the pipe is 35 cm. Find the mass of the pipe, if 1 cm^3 of wood has a mass of 0.6 g.

Sol. Given, inner diameter $= 24$ cm

$$\therefore \quad \text{Inner radius}\,(r_1) = \frac{24}{2} = 12 \text{ cm and outer diameter} = 28 \text{ cm}$$

$$\therefore \quad \text{Outer radius}\,(r_2) = \frac{28}{2} = 14 \text{ cm and height}\,(h) = 35 \text{ cm}$$

Volume of cylindrical wooden pipe

$$= \text{Outer volume} - \text{Inner volume} = \pi\,(r_2^2 - r_1^2)h$$
$$= \frac{22}{7}(14^2 - 12^2) \times 35 = \frac{22}{7}(14 + 12)(14 - 12) \times 35$$
$$= 22 \times 26 \times 2 \times 5 = 5720 \text{ cm}^3$$

$\because$ Mass of 1 cm^3 of wood $= 0.6$ g

$\therefore$ Mass of 5720 cm^3 of wood $= 0.6 \times 5720$

$$= 3432 \text{ g} = \left(\frac{3432}{1000}\right) \text{ kg} = 3.432 \text{ kg}$$

$$[\because 1 \text{ kg} = 1000 \text{ g}]$$

Example 13. The students of a vidyalaya were asked to participate in a competition for making and decorating penholders in the shape of a cylinder with a base, using cardboard. Each penholder was to be of radius 3 cm and height 10.5 cm. The vidyalaya was to supply the competitors with cardboard. If there were 35 competitors, how much cardboard was required to be bought for the competition? **[NCERT Exemplar]**

Sol. Cardboard required by each competitor

$$= \text{Base area} + \text{Curved surface area of one penholder}$$
$$= \pi r^2 + 2\pi rh \qquad [\because h = 10.5 \text{ cm and } r = 3 \text{ cm, given}]$$
$$= \frac{22}{7} \times (3)^2 + 2 \times \frac{22}{7} \times 3 \times 10.5$$
$$= \frac{198}{7} + 198 = 198\left(\frac{1}{7} + 1\right) = 198 \times \frac{8}{7} \text{ cm}^2$$

For 35 competitors, required cardboard

$$= 35 \times 198 \times \frac{8}{7} = 7920 \text{ cm}^2$$

Hence, 7920 cm^2 of cardboard was required to be bought for the competition.

Example 14. Find

(i) the lateral or curved surface area of a closed cylindrical petrol storage tank that is 4.2 m in diameter and 4.5 m high.

(ii) how much steel was actually used, if $\dfrac{1}{12}$ of the steel actually used was wasted in making the tank? **[NCERT Exemplar]**

Sol. (i) Given, diameter $= 4.2$ m

$$\therefore \quad \text{Radius}\,(r) = \frac{4.2}{2} = 2.1 \text{ m and height}\,(h) = 4.5 \text{ m}$$

Curved surface area of a closed cylindrical petrol storage tank $= 2\pi rh$

$$= 2 \times \frac{22}{7} \times 2.1 \times 4.5 = 44 \times 0.3 \times 4.5 = 59.4 \text{ m}^2$$

(ii) Now, total surface area

$$= \text{Curved surface area} + 2\pi r^2$$
$$= 59.4 + 2 \times \frac{22}{7} \times (2.1)^2 = 59.4 + 27.72 = 87.12 \text{ m}^2$$

Let the actually used steel $= x$ m^2

Since, $\dfrac{1}{12}$ of the actual steel used was wasted.

Therefore, the area of the steel, which was actually used for making the tank

$$= x \text{ of } \left(1 - \frac{1}{12}\right) = \left(1 - \frac{1}{12}\right)x = \frac{11x}{12}$$

$$\therefore \quad 87.12 = \frac{11x}{12}$$

$$\Rightarrow \quad x = \frac{87.12 \times 12}{11} = \frac{1045.44}{11} = 95.04 \text{ m}^2$$

$$\therefore \quad \text{Actually used steel} = 95.04 \text{ m}^2$$

Example 15. It costs ₹ 2200 to paint the inner curved surface of a cylindrical vessel 10 m deep. If the cost of painting is at the rate of ₹ 20 per m^2, then find

(i) inner curved surface area of the vessel.

(ii) radius of the base.

(iii) capacity of the vessel.   [NCERT Exemplar]

Sol. Let r be the radius of vessel.

We have, cost to paint the inner curved surface area = ₹ 2200

Cost to paint per m^2 = ₹ 20 and height of vessel $(h) = 10$ m

$\therefore$ Inner curved surface area

$$= \frac{\text{Cost to paint the inner curved surface}}{\text{Cost of paint per m}^2}$$

$$\Rightarrow \; 2\pi rh = \frac{2200}{20} = 110 \text{ m}^2 \; \Rightarrow \; 2 \times \frac{22}{7} \times r \times 10 = 110$$

$$\Rightarrow \; r = \frac{110 \times 7}{2 \times 220} = \frac{7}{4} = 1.75 \text{ m}$$

(i) Inner curved surface area of the vessel = 110 m^2

(ii) Radius of the base is 1.75 m.

(iii) Capacity of the vessel = Volume of the vessel

$$= \pi r^2 h = \frac{22}{7} \times \frac{7}{4} \times \frac{7}{4} \times 10 = 96.25 \text{ m}^3$$

$$= 96.25 \times 1000 \text{ L} = 96.25 \text{ kL}$$

$$[\because 1 \text{ m} = 100 \text{ cm} \Rightarrow 1 \text{ m}^3 = (100)^3 \text{cm}^3, \; 1000 \text{ cm}^3 = 1 \text{ L}$$
$$\text{and } 1000 \text{ L} = 1 \text{ kL}]$$

Example 15. If the height and the radius of a cone are tripled, then find the ratio of volume of new cone and that of original cone.

Sol. Let r be the radius and h be the height of the original cone.

$$\text{Volume of original cone} = \frac{1}{3}\pi r^2 h$$

$$\text{Volume of new cone} = \frac{1}{3}\pi (3r)^2 3h = 9\pi r^2 h$$

$$\therefore \text{Required ratio} = \frac{9\pi r^2 h}{\frac{1}{3}\pi r^2 h} = \frac{27}{1} \text{ or } 27 : 1$$

Example 16. Find the capacity (in litre) of a conical vessel having height 8 cm and slant height 10 cm.

Sol. Given, height $(h) = 8$ cm

Slant height $(l) = 10$ cm

$$\therefore \; r^2 = \sqrt{l^2 - h^2} = \sqrt{(10)^2 - (8)^2} = \sqrt{100 - 64} = \sqrt{36} \Rightarrow r = 6$$

$$\therefore \text{ Capacity of vessel} = \frac{1}{3}\pi r^2 h = \left(\frac{1}{3} \times \frac{22}{7} \times 6 \times 6 \times 8\right) \text{cm}^3$$

$$= 301.71 \times \frac{1}{1000} \text{ L} = 0.3017 \text{ L} \left[\because 1 \text{cm}^3 = \frac{1}{1000}\text{L}\right]$$

Example 17. The radius and the height of a right circular cone are in the ratio $5 : 12$, respectively. If its volume is 314 m^3, then find its slant height and the radius.

Sol. Let radius of cone $= 5x$ and height of the cone $= 12x$

Given, volume of the cone = 314 m^3

$$\Rightarrow \frac{1}{3} \times 3.14 \times (5x)^2 \times (12x) = 314 \left[\because \text{ volume of cone} = \frac{1}{3}\pi r^2 h\right]$$

$$\Rightarrow \quad 314x^3 = 314 \Rightarrow x^3 = 1$$

$$\Rightarrow \qquad\qquad x = 1 \qquad \text{[on taking cube root]}$$

$\therefore$ Radius $(r) = 5$ m and height $(h) = 12$ m

Now, slant height $l = \sqrt{r^2 + h^2}$

$$= \sqrt{25 + 144} = \sqrt{169} = 13 \text{ m}$$

Hence, radius = 5 m and slant height = 13 m

Example 18. Find the ratio of the curved surface areas of two cones, if the diameters of their bases are equal and slant heights are in the ratio $3 : 4$.

Sol. Let the diameter of each cone be r.

$\therefore$ Radius of each cone $= \dfrac{r}{2}$

Also, let the slant heights of each cone be $3x$ and $4x$, respectively.

i.e. $l_1 = 3x$ and $l_2 = 4x$

Curved surface area of first cone $= \pi r l_1$

$$= \pi \times \left(\frac{r}{2}\right) \times 3x$$

and curved surface area of second cone $= \pi r l_2$

$$= \pi \times \left(\frac{r}{2}\right) \times 4x$$

$\therefore$ Required ratio of the curved surface areas

$$= \frac{\pi \times \left(\dfrac{r}{2}\right) \times 3x}{\pi \times \left(\dfrac{r}{2}\right) \times 4x} = \frac{3}{4} \text{ or } 3 : 4$$

Example 19. A conical tent is 10 m high and the radius of its base is 24 m. Find

(i) slant height of the tent.

(ii) cost of the canvas required to make the tent, if the cost of 1 m^2 canvas is ₹ 70.

Sol. We have, height $(h) = 10$ m and radius $(r) = 24$ m

(i) We know that, $l^2 = h^2 + r^2$

$$\Rightarrow \qquad\qquad l = \sqrt{r^2 + h^2}$$

$$\text{[on taking positive square root]}$$

$$\Rightarrow \qquad\qquad l = \sqrt{(24)^2 + (10)^2}$$

$$= \sqrt{576 + 100} = \sqrt{676} = 26 \text{ m}$$

Hence, the slant height of the canvas tent is 26 m.

(ii) Curved surface area of the tent $= \pi r l$

$$= \frac{22}{7} \times 24 \times 26 \text{ m}^2$$

Cost of the canvas required to make the tent, if the cost of 1 m^2 canvas is ₹ 70

$$= \frac{22}{7} \times 24 \times 26 \times 70 = ₹ 137280$$

Hence, the cost of canvas is ₹ 137280.

Example 20. The volume of a right circular cone is 9856 cm^3. If the diameter of the base is 28 cm, then find   **[NCERT Exemplar]**

(i) height of the cone.

(ii) slant height of the cone.

(iii) curved surface area of the cone.

Sol. Given, diameter of the base $(d) = 28$ cm

$$\therefore \quad \text{Radius of the base } (r) = 14 \text{ cm} \quad \left[\because \text{ radius} = \frac{\text{diameter}}{2} \right]$$

(i) Let h be the height of the cone.

Also given, volume of a right circular cone $= 9856$ cm^3

$$\therefore \qquad \frac{1}{3}\pi r^2 h = 9856$$

$$\left[\because \text{ volume of right circular cone} = \frac{1}{3}\pi r^2 h \right]$$

$$\Rightarrow \quad \frac{1}{3} \times \frac{22}{7} \times (14)^2 \times h = 9856$$

$$\Rightarrow \quad h = \frac{9856 \times 3 \times 7}{22 \times 14 \times 14} = \frac{448 \times 3}{28} = 48 \text{ cm}$$

(ii) We have, $h = 48$ cm and $r = 14$ cm

$$\therefore \qquad l = \sqrt{h^2 + r^2} = \sqrt{(48)^2 + (14)^2}$$

$$= \sqrt{2304 + 196} = \sqrt{2500}$$

$$\Rightarrow \qquad l = 50 \text{ cm}$$

Hence, slant height of the cone is 50 cm.

(iii) Curved surface area of the cone $= \pi r l$

$$= \frac{22}{7} \times 14 \times 50 = 44 \times 50 = 2200 \text{ cm}^2$$

Example 21. A bus stop is barricaded from the remaining part of the road, by using 50 hollow cones made of recycled cardboard. Each cone has a base diameter of 40 cm and height 1 m. If the outer side of each of the cones is to be painted and the cost of painting is ₹ 12 per m^2, then what will be the cost of painting all these cones?   **[NCERT Exemplar]**

(take, $\pi = 3.14$ and $\sqrt{1.04} = 1.02$)

Sol. We have, diameter $= 40$ cm

$$\therefore \quad \text{Radius } (r) = \frac{40}{2} = 20 \text{ cm}$$

$$= \frac{20}{100} \text{ m} = 0.2 \text{ m} \qquad \left[\because 1 \text{ cm} = \frac{1}{100} \text{ m} \right]$$

and height $(h) = 1$ m

We know that, $l^2 = h^2 + r^2$

$$\Rightarrow \qquad l = \sqrt{r^2 + h^2}$$

$$[\text{on taking positive square root}]$$

$$\Rightarrow \qquad l = \sqrt{(0.2)^2 + 1^2} = \sqrt{0.04 + 1}$$

$$= \sqrt{1.04} = 1.02 \text{ m} \quad [\because \sqrt{1.04} = 1.02, \text{ given}]$$

Curved surface area of a cone $= \pi r l$

$$= 3.14 \times 0.2 \times 1.02 = 0.64056 \text{ m}^2$$

Now, cost of painting per m$^2 = ₹12$

$\therefore$ Cost of painting 0.64056 m$^2 = 12 \times 0.64056 = ₹ 7.68672$

Thus, cost of painting for 1 cone $= ₹ 7.68672$

$\therefore$ Cost of painting 50 cones $= 7.68672 \times 50$

$$= 384.336 = ₹ 384.34$$

Example 22. What length of tarpaulin 3 m wide will be required to make conical tent of height 8 m and base radius 6 m? Assume that the extra length of material that will be required for stitching margins and wastage in cutting is approximately 20 cm. (take, $\pi = 3.14$)   **[NCERT Exemplar]**

Sol. Let r, h and l be the radius, height and slant height of the tent, respectively.

Given, $r = 6$ m and $h = 8$ m

We know that, $l^2 = h^2 + r^2$

$$\Rightarrow \qquad l = \sqrt{r^2 + h^2}$$

$$[\text{on taking positive square root}]$$

$$\Rightarrow \qquad l = \sqrt{(6)^2 + (8)^2} \Rightarrow l = \sqrt{36 + 64}$$

$$\Rightarrow \qquad l = \sqrt{100} = 10 \text{ m}$$

Area of the canvas used for the tent

$$= \text{Curved surface area of the cone}$$

$$= \pi r l = 3.14 \times 6 \times 10 = 188.4 \text{ m}^2$$

$\therefore$ Length of tarpaulin required

$$= \frac{\text{Area of tarpaulin required}}{\text{Width of tarpaulin}} = \frac{188.4}{3}$$

$$[\because \text{ width of tarpaulin} = 3 \text{ m, given}]$$

$$= 62.8 \text{ m}$$

The extra material required for stitching margins and cutting

$$= 20 \text{ cm} = 0.2 \text{ m} \qquad \left[\because 1 \text{ cm} = \frac{1}{100} \text{ m} \right]$$

Hence, the total length of tarpaulin required

$$= 62.8 + 0.2 = 63 \text{ m}$$

Example 23. The volume of two spheres are in the ratio 64 : 27. Find the ratio of their radii.

Sol. Let r_1 and r_2 be radii of two spheres, respectively.

Now, ratio of volumes of two sphere $= 64 : 27$

$$\Rightarrow \qquad \frac{4}{3}\pi r_1^3 : \frac{4}{3}\pi r_2^3 = 64 : 27$$

$$\Rightarrow \qquad r_1^3 : r_2^3 = 64 : 27$$

$$\Rightarrow \qquad r_1 : r_2 = 4 : 3$$

Example 24. If the radius of a sphere is doubled, then find the ratio of volume of the new sphere that of the original sphere.

Sol. Let r be the radius of original sphere.

Volume of original sphere $= \dfrac{4}{3}\pi r^3$

Volume of new sphere $= \dfrac{4}{3}\pi(2r)^3$

$\therefore$ Required ratio $= \dfrac{4/3\pi(2r)^3}{4/3\pi r^3}$

$= \dfrac{8}{1} = 8:1$

Example 25. Metallic spheres of radii 6 m, 8 m and 10 m, respectively are melted to form a single solid sphere. Find the radius of the resulting sphere.

Sol. Let r_1, r_2 and r_3 be radii of small spheres, respectively.

Let R be the radius of the resulting sphere.

Now, the sum of the volumes of three spheres is equal to volume of new spheres.

$\therefore \qquad \dfrac{4}{3}\pi\, r_1^3 + \dfrac{4}{3}\pi r_2^3 + \dfrac{4}{3}\pi r_3^3 = \dfrac{4}{3}\pi R^3$

$\Rightarrow \qquad r_1^3 + r_2^3 + r_3^3 = R^3$

$\Rightarrow \qquad 6^3 + 8^3 + 10^3 = R^3$

$\Rightarrow \qquad R^3 = 216 + 512 + 1000$

$\Rightarrow \qquad R^3 = 1728$

$\Rightarrow \qquad R = 12\,\text{m}$

Example 26. Find the volume of a sphere, whose surface area is 154 cm^2. **[NCERT Exemplar]**

Sol. Let r be the radius of the sphere.

Given, surface area of a sphere $= 154\,\text{cm}^2$

$\therefore \qquad 4\pi r^2 = 154 \qquad [\because \text{surface area of sphere} = 4\pi r^2]$

$\Rightarrow \quad 4 \times \dfrac{22}{7} \times r^2 = 154 \ \Rightarrow \ r^2 = \dfrac{154 \times 7}{22 \times 4} \ \Rightarrow \ r = \dfrac{7}{2}\,\text{cm}$

Hence, volume of a sphere $= \dfrac{4}{3}\pi\left(\dfrac{7}{2}\right)^3$

$\left[\because \text{volume of sphere} = \dfrac{4}{3}\pi r^3\right]$

$= \dfrac{4}{3} \times \dfrac{22}{7} \times \dfrac{7}{2} \times \dfrac{7}{2} \times \dfrac{7}{2} = \dfrac{11 \times 7 \times 7}{3}$

$= 179.667 = 179.67\,\text{cm}^3$

Example 27. A hemispherical bowl is made of steel, 0.25 cm thick. The inner radius of the bowl is 5 cm. Find the outer curved surface area of the bowl.
[NCERT Exemplar]

Sol. The inner radius of the hemispherical bowl $= 5$ cm.

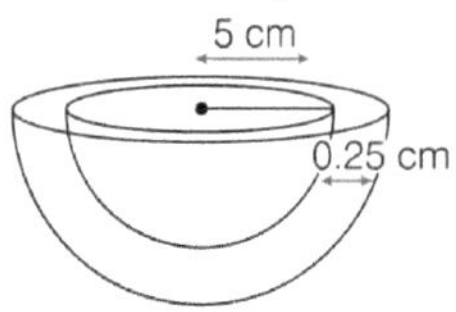

Thickness of the hemispherical bowl $= 0.25$ cm

We know that,

Outer radius of the bowl

$=$ Inner radius $+$ Thickness $= (5 + 0.25) = 5.25$ cm

Outer curved surface area of the bowl $= 2\pi r^2$

$= 2 \times \dfrac{22}{7} \times 5.25 \times 5.25 = 173.25\,\text{cm}^2$

Example 28. A hemispherical tank is made up of an iron sheet 1 cm thick. If the inner radius is 1 m, then find the volume of the iron used to make the tank. **[NCERT Exemplar]**

Sol. Given, inner radius $(r_1) = 1\,\text{m} = 100\,\text{cm}$

Thickness $= 1$ cm

$\therefore$ Outer radius $(r_2) = (100 + 1) = 101$ cm

$[\because \text{outer radius} = \text{inner radius} + \text{thickness}]$

and outer volume $= \dfrac{2}{3}\pi(101)^3\,\text{cm}^3 \qquad \left[\because \text{volume} = \dfrac{2}{3}pr^3\right]$

Inner volume $= \dfrac{2}{3}\pi(100)^3\,\text{cm}^3$

Hence, volume of the iron used to make the tank

$=$ Outer volume $-$ Inner volume

$= \dfrac{2}{3}\pi[(101)^3 - (100)^3] \qquad [\because a^3 - b^3 = (a-b)(a^2 + ab + b^2)]$

$= \dfrac{2}{3} \times \dfrac{22}{7}(101 - 100)\,[(101)^2 + 101 \times 100 + (100)^2]$

$= \dfrac{2}{3} \times \dfrac{22}{7}(10201 + 10100 + 10000) = \dfrac{44}{21}(30301)$

$= 63487.81\,\text{cm}^3 = \dfrac{63487.81}{100 \times 100 \times 100}\,\text{m}^3 \quad \left[\because 1\,\text{cm} = \dfrac{1}{100}\,\text{m}\right]$

$= 0.063\,\text{m}^3 \text{ (approx.)}$

Chapter Practice

Objective Questions

• Multiple Choice Questions

1. If A_1, A_2, A_3 denote the areas of three adjacent faces of a cuboid, then its volume is
(a) $A_1 A_2 A_3$ (b) $2 A_1 A_2 A_3$
(c) $\sqrt{A_1 A_2 A_3}$ (d) $\sqrt[3]{A_1 A_2 A_3}$

2. If dimensions of a cuboid are in the ratio $1 : 2 : 3$ and its total surface area is 88 m^2, then its volume is
(a) 48 m^3 (b) 44 m^3
(c) 40 m^3 (d) 36 m^3

3. If V is the volume of a cuboid of dimensions a, b, c and S is its surface area, then $\dfrac{2}{S}\left(\dfrac{1}{a} + \dfrac{1}{b} + \dfrac{1}{c}\right)$ equals
(a) $\dfrac{1}{V}$ (b) V (c) $\dfrac{2}{V}$ (d) $2V$

4. Find the cost of digging a cuboidal pit 8 m long, 6 m broad and 3 m deep at the rate of ₹ 30 per m^3.
                           [NCERT Exemplar]
(a) ₹ 4321   (b) ₹ 4320
(c) ₹ 4340   (d) ₹ 4220

5. Find the surface area and the length of the diagonal of a cube, if the volume of a cube is 2197 cm^3.
(a) 1035 cm^2 and 22 cm   (b) 1020 cm^2 and 22.42 cm
(c) 1014 cm^2 and 22.51 cm   (d) 1025 cm^2 and 22.50 cm

6. The total surface area of a cube is 96 cm^2. The volume of the cube is
(a) 8cm^3 (b) 512cm^3 (c) 64cm^3 (d) 27cm^3

7. Find the capacity of a cylindrical storage tank of height 4 m and base diameter 8 m.
(a) 200.14 m^3 (b) 201.14 m^3
(c) 201.18 m^3 (d) None of these

8. In a cylinder, radius is doubled and height is halved, then curved surface area will be
                           [NCERT Exemplar]
(a) halved   (b) doubled
(c) same   (d) four times

9. A rectangular paper 11 cm by 8 cm can be exactly wrapped to cover the curved surface of a cylinder of height 8 cm. Find the volume of the cylinder.
(a) 77 cm^3 (b) 78 cm^3 (c) 79 cm^3 (d) 80 cm^3

10. A cylindrical pillar is 50 cm in diameter and 3.5 m in height. Find the cost of painting the curved surface of the pillar at the rate of ₹ 12.50 per m^2.
(a) ₹ 68.75   (b) ₹ 68.70 **[NCERT Exemplar]**
(c) ₹ 68.60   (d) ₹ 68.72

11. An iron pipe 20 cm long has exterior diameter equal to 25 cm. If the thickness of the pipe is 1 cm, then find the whole surface area of the pipe.
(a) 3048 cm^2 (b) 3170 cm^2
(c) 3168 cm^2 (d) 3068 cm^2

12. The radii of two cylinders are in the ratio of $2 : 3$ and their heights are in the ratio of $5 : 3$. The ratio of their volumes is
(a) $10 : 17$ (b) $20 : 27$
(c) $17 : 27$ (d) $20 : 37$

13. How much ice-cream can be put into a cone with base radius 3.5 cm and height 12 cm?
(a) 154 cm^3 (b) 152 cm^3
(c) 162 cm^3 (d) 164 cm^3

14. The area of the curved surface of a right circular cylinder is 4400 cm^2 and the circumference of its base is 110 cm. Find the height of the cylinder.
(a) 20 cm   (b) 20.2 cm   (c) 40 cm   (d) 40.2 cm

15. The height of a cone is 15 cm. If its volume is 1570 cm^3, then find the radius of the base. (take, $\pi = 3.14$)   **[NCERT Exemplar]**
(a) 8 cm   (b) 10 cm
(c) 10.5 cm   (d) 12 cm

16. Find the radius of a sphere, whose surface area is 154 cm^2.   **[NCERT Exemplar]**
(a) 4.5 cm   (b) 3 cm
(c) 3.5 cm   (d) None of these

17. The volume of a cylinder, whose height and diameter are equal to the diameter of the sphere. The volume of a sphere is equal to [**NCERT Exemplar**]

(a) $\dfrac{1}{3}$ volume of a cylinder

(b) $\dfrac{2}{3}$ volume of a cylinder

(c) $\dfrac{3}{4}$ volume of a cylinder

(d) None of the above

18. If the radius of a sphere is $2r$, then its volume will be [**NCERT Exemplar**]

(a) $\dfrac{4}{3}\pi r^3$ cu units

(b) $4\pi r^3$ cu units

(c) $\dfrac{8\pi r^3}{3}$ cu units

(d) $\dfrac{32}{3}\pi r^3$ cu units

19. Find the total surface area of a hemisphere of radius 10 cm. (take, $\pi = 3.14$)

(a) 900 cm^2

(b) 940 cm^2

(c) 920 cm^2

(d) 942 cm^2

20. How many litres of milk can a hemispherical bowl of diameter 10.5 cm hold? [**NCERT Exemplar**]

(a) 0.300 L

(b) 0.302 L

(c) 0.402 L

(d) 0.303 L

• Case Based MCQs

21. A draughtsman planned design for a room with dimensions of 8 m, 5 m and 4 m, respectively. He also planned to make 4 windows with brown colour and 2 doors with grey colour. The room needs to be painted with Nerolac paint of red colour except for the floor and square tiles were used for flooring, as shown in the below figure.

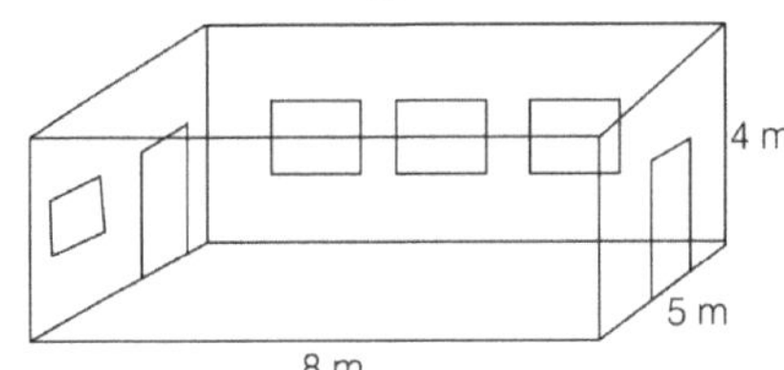

(i) The total area of the four walls is

(a) 112 m^2

(b) 212 m^2

(c) 104 m^2

(d) 412 m^2

(ii) If the area of windows and doors is 30 sq m. The area of the walls to be painted is

(a) 74 m^2

(b) 80 m^2

(c) 90 m^2

(d) 132 m^2

(iii) What is the area of the tiles to be used for flooring?

(a) 64 m^2

(b) 44 m^2

(c) 66 m^2

(d) 40 m^2

(iv) The total area of the room is (including windows and doors)

(a) 48.02 m^2

(b) 162 m^2

(c) 184 m^2

(d) 204.88 m^2

(v) What is the volume of the air in the room?

(a) 160 m^2

(b) 168 m^2

(c) 158 m^2

(d) 185 m^2

22. Mathematics teacher of a school took her 9th standard students to show Red Fort. It was a part of their Educational trip. The teacher had interest in history and she narrated the facts of Red Fort to students. Then, the teacher said in this monument, one can find combination of solid figures. There are 2 pillars which are cylindrical in shape. Also, 2 domes at the corners which are hemispherical. 7 smaller domes at the centre. Flag hoisting ceremony on Independence Day takes place near these domes.

(i) How much cloth material will be required to cover 2 big domes each of radius 7 metres? (take, $\pi = 22/7$)

(a) 375 m^2

(b) 478 m^2

(c) 616 m^2

(d) 296 m^2

(ii) If the radius of cylindrical pillar is 7 m and height is 14 m, then the volume is

(a) 1878 m^3

(b) 1656 m^3

(c) 2329 m^3

(d) 2156 m^3

(iii) Find the lateral surface area of two pillars, if height of the pillar is 7 m and radius of the base is 1.4 m.

(a) 112.3 cm^2

(b) 123.2 m^2

(c) 90 m^2

(d) 345.2 cm^2

(iv) How much is the volume of a hemisphere, if the radius of the base is 2.8 m?

(a) 46 m^3

(b) 80 m^3

(c) 98 m^3

(d) 36 m^3

(v) What is the ratio of sum of volumes of two hemispheres of radius 1 cm each to the volume of a sphere of radius 2 cm?

(a) 1 : 1

(b) 1 : 8

(c) 8 : 1

(d) 1 : 16

PART 2
Subjective Questions

• Short Answer Type Questions

1. The length, breadth and height of a cuboid are 8 m, 6 m and 4 m, respectively. Find its total surface area, diagonal and area of four walls.

2. The floor of a rectangular hall has a perimeter 250 m. If the cost of painting the four walls at the rate of ₹ 10 per m^2 is ₹ 15000, find the height of the hall. **[NCERT Exemplar]**

3. A matchbox measures $4 \, cm \times 2.5 \, cm \times 1.5 \, cm$. What will be the volume of a packet containing 12 such boxes?

4. A village, having a population of 4000, requires 150 L of water per head per day. It has a tank measuring $20 \, m \times 15 \, m \times 6 \, m$. For how many days, will the water of this tank last? **[NCERT Exemplar]**

5. The paint in a certain container is sufficient to paint an area equal to $9.375 \, m^2$. How many bricks of dimensions $22.5 \, cm \times 10 \, cm \times 7.5 \, cm$ can be painted out of this container?

6. A wall of length 10 m was to be built across an open ground. The height of the wall is 4 m and thickness of the wall is 24 cm. If this wall is to be built up with bricks, whose dimensions are $24 \, cm \times 12 \, cm \times 8 \, cm$, then how many bricks would be required?

7. A small village, having a population of 5000, requires 75 L of water per head per day. The village has got an overhead tank of measurement $40 \, m \times 25 \, m \times 15 \, m$. For how many days will the water of this tank last? **[NCERT Exemplar]**

8. A solid cube of side 12 cm is cut into eight cubes of equal volume. What will be the side of the new cube? Also, find the ratio between their surface areas.

9. The dimensions of a rectangular box are in the ratio 2 : 3 : 4 and the difference between the cost of covering it with sheet of paper at the rate of ₹ 4 and ₹ 4.50 per m^2 is ₹ 416. Find the dimensions of the box.

10. A cubical box has each edge 10 cm and another cuboidal box is 12.5 cm long, 10 cm wide and 8 cm high. **[NCERT Exemplar]**
   (i) Which box has the greater lateral surface area and by how much?
   (ii) Which box has the smaller total surface area and by how much?

11. Hameed has built a cubical water tank with lid for his house, with each outer edge 1.5 m long. He gets the outer surface of the tank excluding the base, covered with square tiles of side 25 cm. Find how much he would spend for the tiles, if the cost of the tiles is ₹ 360 per dozen?

12. Mary wants to decorate her Christmas tree. She wants to place the tree on a wooden box covered with coloured paper with picture of Santa Claus on it (see figure). She must know the exact quantity of paper to buy for this purpose. If the box has length, breadth and height as 80 cm, 40 cm and 20 cm, respectively, then how many square sheets of paper of side 40 cm would she require?

13. A storage tank is in the form of a cube. When it is full of water, the volume of water is $15.625 \, m^3$. If the present depth of water is 1.3 m, then find the volume of water already used from the tank. **[NCERT Exemplar]**

14. The ratio between the curved surface area and the total surface area of a right circular cylinder is 1 : 3. Find the ratio between the height and radius of the cylinder.

15. A river 3 m deep and 40 m wide is flowing at the rate of 2 km/h. How much water will fall into the sea in a minute?

16. Curved surface area of a right circular cylinder is $4.4 \, m^2$. If the radius of the base of the cylinder is 0.7 m, then find its height.

17. The inner diameter of a circular well is 3.5 m. It is 10 m deep. Find
   (i) its inner curved surface area.
   (ii) the cost of plastering this curved surface at the rate of ₹ 40 per m^2.

18. In a hot water heating system, there is a cylindrical pipe of length 28 m and diameter 5 cm. Find the total radiating surface area in the system. **[NCERT Exemplar]**

19. If the lateral surface area of a cylinder is 94.2 cm^2 and its height is 5 cm, then find   [**NCERT Exemplar**]
  (i) radius of its base.
  (ii) its volume. (take, $\pi = 3.14$)

20. The circumference of the base of a cylindrical vessel is 132 cm and its height is 25 cm. How many litres of water can it hold? ($1000\,\text{cm}^3 = 1\,\text{L}$)   [**NCERT Exemplar**]

21. Find the total surface area of a cone, if its slant height is 21 m and diameter of its base is 24 m.

22. The capacity of a closed cylindrical vessel of height 1 m is 15.4 L. How many square metres of metal sheet would be needed to make it?

23. A soft drink is available in two packs.
  (i) A tin can with a rectangular base of length 5 cm and width 4 cm, having a height of 15 cm.
  (ii) A plastic cylinder with circular base of diameter 7 cm and height 10 cm.
  Which container has greater capacity and by how much?

24. Parveen wanted to make a temporary shelter for her car, by making a box like structure with tarpaulin that covers all the four sides and the top of the car (with the front face as a flap, which can be rolled up). Assuming that, the stitching margins are very small and therefore negligible, how much tarpaulin would be required to make the shelter of height 2.5 m, with base dimensions 4 m $\times$ 3 m?   [**NCERT Exemplar**]

25. It is required to make a closed cylindrical tank of height 1 m and base diameter 140 cm from a metal sheet. How many square metres of the sheet are required for the same?

26. The diameter of a roller is 84 cm and its length is 120 cm. It takes 500 complete revolutions to move once over to level a playground. Find the area (in sq m) of the playground.   [**NCERT Exemplar**]

27. A cylindrical vessel of diameter 28 cm and height 12 cm is full of water. The water is emptied into a rectangular tub of length 66 cm and breadth 28 cm, then find the height of water rises in the tub.

28. A rectangular sheet of paper $44\,\text{cm} \times 18\,\text{cm}$ is rolled along its length and a cylinder is formed. Find the radius of the cylinder.

29. A cylindrical roller 2.5 m in length, 1.75 m in radius when rolled on a road, was found to cover the area of 5500 m^2. How many revolutions did it make?   [**NCERT Exemplar**]

30. Find the volume of the right circular cone with
  (i) radius 6 cm, height 7 cm.
  (ii) radius 3.5 cm, height 12 cm.

31. A school provides milk to the students daily in a cylindrical glasses of diameter 7 cm. If the glass is filled with milk upto an height of 12 cm, find how many litres of milk is needed to serve 1600 students.   [**NCERT Exemplar**]

32. The circumference of the base of 16 m high solid cone is 33 m. Find the total surface area of the cone. (take, $\pi = 22/7$)

33. Curved surface area of a cone is 308 cm^2 and its slant height is 14 cm. Find
  (i) radius of the base.
  (ii) total surface area of the cone.

34. The height and the slant height of a cone are 21 cm and 28 cm, respectively. Find the volume of the cone.

35. If the volume of a right circular cone of height 9 cm is $48\pi\,\text{cm}^3$, then find the diameter of its base.

36. Curved surface area of a cone is 308 cm^2 and its slant height is 14 cm. Find
  (i) radius of the base.
  (ii) total surface area of the cone.

37. How many metres of 5 m wide cloth will be required to make a conical tent, the radius of whose base is 3.5 m and height is 12 m?

38. If the radius of a right circular cone is halved and height is doubled, then what is the volume of new cone?

39. How many square metres of canvas is required for a conical tent, whose height is 3.5 m and the radius of the base is 12 m?   [**NCERT Exemplar**]

40. A conical tent is to accommodate 11 persons. Each person must have 4 m^2 of the space on the ground and 20 m^3 of air to breathe. Find the height of the cone.

41. The slant height and base diameter of a conical tomb are 25 m and 14 m, respectively. Find the cost of white-washing, its curved surface at the rate of ₹ 210 per 100 m^2.   [**NCERT Exemplar**]

42. A joker's cap is in the form of a right circular cone of base radius 7 cm and height 24 cm. Find the area of the sheet required to make 10 such caps.

43. A conical tent is 10 m high and the radius of its base is 24 m. Find **[NCERT Exemplar]**

(i) slant height of the tent.

(ii) cost of the canvas required to make the tent, if the cost of 1 m^2 canvas is ₹ 70.

44. A heap of wheat is in the form of a cone, whose diameter is 10.5 m and height is 3 m. Find its volume. The heap is to be covered by canvas to protect it from rain. Find the area of the canvas required.

45. Find the surface area of a sphere of diameter

(i) 14 cm   (ii) 21 cm   (iii) 3.5 m

46. Find the surface area of a sphere of radius

(i) 10.5 cm   (ii) 5.6 cm   (iii) 14 cm

47. A capsule of medicine is in the shape of a sphere of diameter 3.5 mm. How much medicine (in mm^3) is needed to fill this capsule?

[NCERT Exemplar]

48. How many balls each of radius 2 cm can be made by melting a big ball, whose radius is 8 cm?

49. Find the amount of water displaced by a solid spherical ball of diameter

(i) 28 cm   (ii) 0.21 m

50. Find the amount of water displaced by a solid spherical ball of diameter 4.2 cm, when it is completely immersed in water.

51. The diameter of the Moon is approximately one-fourth of the diameter of the Earth. Find the ratio of their surface areas.   **[NCERT Exemplar]**

52. The circumference of the edge of a hemispherical bowl is 132 cm. Find the volume of the bowl.

53. A hemispherical bowl is made from a metal sheet having thickness 0.3 cm. The inner radius of the bowl is 24.7 cm. Find the cost of polishing its outer surface at the rate of ₹ 4 per 100 cm^2. (take, $\pi = 3.14$)

54. The diameter of a metallic ball is 4.2 cm. What is the mass of the ball, if the density of the metal is 8.9 gm/cm^3?

55. Twenty seven solid iron spheres, each of radius r and surface area S are melted to form a sphere with surface area S'. Find the

(i) radius r' of the new sphere.

(ii) ratio of S and S'.

56. A shopkeeper has one spherical laddoo of radius 5 cm. With the same amount of material, how many laddoos of radius 2.5 cm can be made?

[NCERT Exemplar]

57. Two solid spheres made of the same metal have weights 5920 gm and 740 gm, respectively. Determine the radius of the larger sphere, if the diameter of the smaller one is 5 cm. **[NCERT Exemplar]**

• Long Answer Type Questions

58. The total surface area of a solid right circular cylinder is 231 cm^2. If curved surface area is 2/3rd of the total surface area, then determine the radius of its base.

59. A right circular cylinder just encloses a sphere of radius r (see figure). Find the **[NCERT Exemplar]**

(i) surface area of the sphere.

(ii) curved surface area of the cylinder.

(iii) ratio of the areas obtained in (i) and (ii).

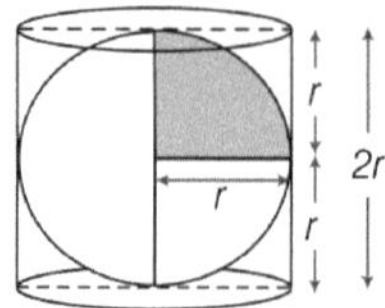

60. A solid cylinder has a total surface area of 231 m^2. Its curved surface area is $\dfrac{2}{3}$ of the total surface area. Then, find the volume of the cylinder.

61. Shanti Sweets Stall was placing an order for making cardboard boxes for packing their sweets. Two sizes of boxes were required. **[NCERT Exemplar]**

The bigger of dimensions 25 cm × 20 cm × 5 cm and the smaller of dimensions 15 cm × 12 cm × 5 cm.

For all the overlaps, 5% of the total surface area is required extra. If the cost of the cardboard is ₹ 4 for 1000 cm^2, then find the cost of cardboard required for supplying 250 boxes of each kind.

62. The cost of painting the outer curved surface of a cylinder at ₹ 1.50 per cm^2 is ₹ 660. If the height of the cylinder is 2 m. Then, find the curved surface of the base of cylinder.

63. In given figure, you see the frame of a lampshade. It is to be covered with a decorative cloth. The frame has a base diameter of 20 cm and height of 30 cm. A margin of 2.5 cm is to be given for folding it over the top and bottom of the frame. Find how much cloth is required for covering the lampshade?

[NCERT Exemplar]

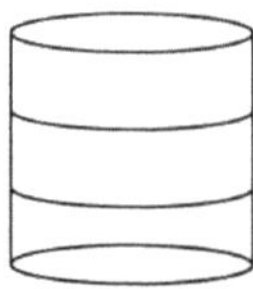

64. The students of a vidyalaya were asked to participate in a competition for making and decorating penholders in the shape of a cylinder with a base, using cardboard. Each penholder was to be of radius 3 cm and height 10.5 cm. The vidyalaya was to supply the competitors with cardboard. If there were 35 competitors, how much cardboard was required to be bought for the competition?   [**NCERT Exemplar**]

65. A lead pencil consists of a cylinder of wood with a solid cylinder of graphite filled in the interior. The diameter of the pencil is 7 mm and the diameter of the graphite is 1 mm. If the length of the pencil is 14 cm, then find the volume of the wood and that of the graphite.

66. A wooden bookshelf has external dimensions as follows.

Height $= 110$ cm, depth $= 25$ cm and

breadth $= 85$ cm (see figure).

The thickness of the plank is 5 cm everywhere. The external faces are to be polished and the inner faces are to be painted. If the rate of polishing is 20 paise per cm^2 and the rate of painting is 10 paise per cm^2, then find the total expenses required for polishing and painting the surface of the bookshelf.   [**NCERT Exemplar**]

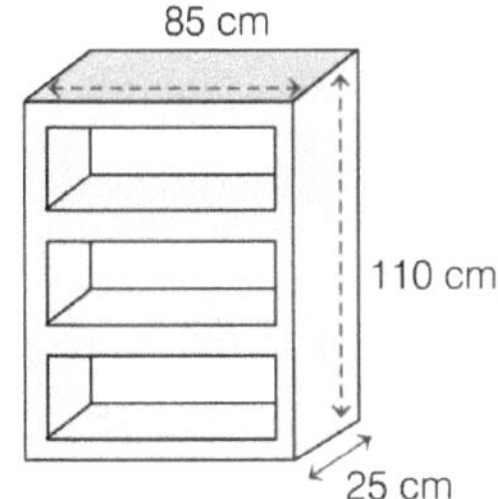

67. 30 circular plates, each of radius 14 cm and thickness 3 cm are placed one above the another to form a cylindrical solid. Find

(i) the total surface area.

(ii) volume of the cylinder, so formed.

68. The difference between outside and inside surfaces of a cylindrical metallic pipe 14 cm long is 44 cm^2. If the pipe is made of 88 cm^3 of metal. Find outer and inner radii of the pipe.

69. At a Ramzan Mela, a stall keeper in one of the food stalls has a large cylindrical vessel of the base radius 15 cm, filled upto a height of 32 cm with the orange juice. The juice is filled in small cylindrical glasses (see figure) of radius 3 cm upto a height of 8 cm and sold for ₹ 3 each.

How much money does the stall keeper receive by selling the juice completely?

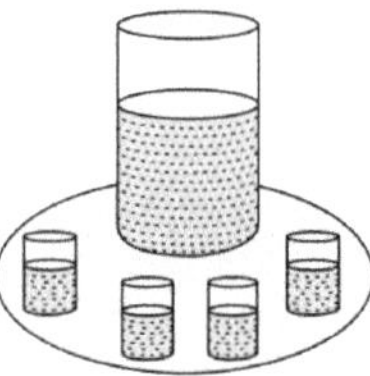

70. A corn cob (see below figure), shaped somewhat like a cone, has the radius of its broadest end as 2.1 cm and length as 20 cm. If each 1 cm^2 of the surface of the cob carries an average of four grains, then find how many grains you would find on the entire cob?

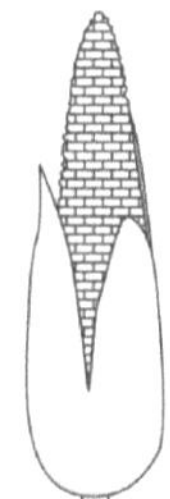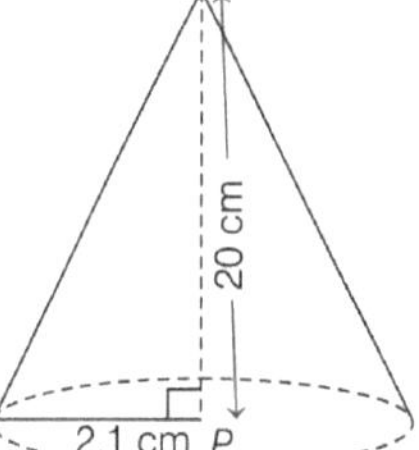

71. A cloth having an area of 165 m^2 is shaped into the form of a conical tent of radius 5 m.

(i) How many students can sit in the tent, if a student on an average occupies $\dfrac{5}{7}$ m^2 on the ground?

(ii) Find the volume of the cone.

72. A sector of a circle of radius 9 cm and central angle of 120°. It is rolled up so that the two bounding radii are joined together to form a cone.

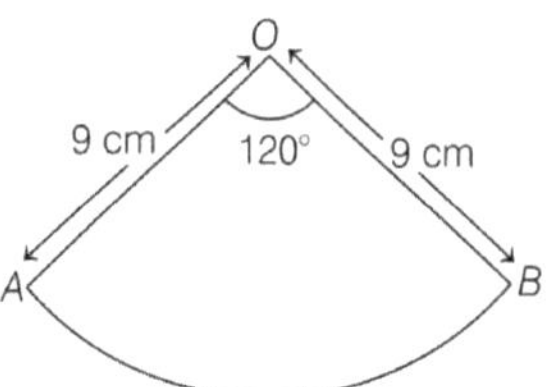

Find

(i) the slant height of the cone.

(ii) the radius of the base of the cone.

(iii) the volume of the cone.

(iv) the total surface area of the cone.

73. A copper sphere of diameter 18 cm is drawn into a wire of diameter 4 mm. Then, find the length of the wire.

74. A hemispherical dome of a building needs to be painted. If the circumference of the base of the dome is 17.6 m, then find the cost of painting it, given that cost of painting is ₹ 5 per 100 cm^2.

• Case Based Questions

75. Playground offer kids fresh air, friends, fun and exercise. But it's important to make sure that faulty equipment, improper surfaces and unsafe behaviour don't ruin the fun. In this order, Patna Nagar Nigam announced a online tender for levelling the roads of Kankarbagh Park. A contractor Vicky Saini get this work from Patna Nagar Nigam. He has a roller of diameter of 42 cm and its length is 78 cm. It takes 300 complete revolutions to move once over to level a playground.

Then, give the answer of following questions.

(i) Find the area (in m^2) covered in 1 revolution.

(ii) The area of one revolution is 5.168 m^2. Then, find the area (in m^2) of playground.

(iii) If area of playground is 3600 m^2, then find the area of one revolution.

SOLUTIONS

Objective Questions

1. (c) Let l, b and h be the length, breadth and height of the cuboid.

Then, $lb = A_1$, $bh = A_2$, $hl = A_3$ ...(i)

∴ Volume of cuboid, $V = lbh$

$\Rightarrow \qquad V^2 = l^2 b^2 h^2$ [squaring on both sides]

$= (lb)(bh)(hl)$

$= A_1 A_2 A_3$ [using Eq. (i)]

$\Rightarrow \qquad V = \sqrt{A_1 A_2 A_3}$

2. (a) Since, dimensions of the cuboid are in the ratio $1:2:3$.

So, let the dimensions of cuboid be x, $2x$ and $3x$.

Then, surface area $= 88$ m^2

$\Rightarrow \quad 2(x \times 2x + 2x \times 3x + 3x \times x) = 88$

$\Rightarrow \qquad\qquad 2 \times 11x^2 = 88$

$\Rightarrow \qquad\qquad\qquad x^2 = 4$

$\Rightarrow \qquad\qquad\qquad x = 2$

∴ Volume $= x \times 2x \times 3x = 6x^3$

$= 6 \times (2)^3 = 48$ m^3

3. (a) We have, $V = abc$ and $S = 2(ab + bc + ca)$

Now, $\dfrac{2}{S}\left(\dfrac{1}{a} + \dfrac{1}{b} + \dfrac{1}{c}\right) = \dfrac{2}{S}\left(\dfrac{bc + ca + ab}{abc}\right)$

$= \dfrac{2}{S} \times \dfrac{S}{2abc} = \dfrac{1}{abc} = \dfrac{1}{V}$

4. (b) Volume of a cuboidal pit $= l \times b \times h$

$= (8 \times 6 \times 3) = 144$ m^3

$[\because l = 8$ m, $b = 6$ m and $h = 3$ m, given$]$

$\because$ Cost of digging 1 m$^3 = ₹ 30$ [given]

∴ Cost of digging 144 m^3 cuboidal pit

$= 30 \times 144 = ₹ 4320$

5. (c) Given, volume of cube $= 2197$ cm^3

$\Rightarrow (\text{Side})^3 = 2197$ $[\because$ volume of cube $= (\text{side})^3]$

$\Rightarrow$ Side of cube $= \sqrt[3]{2197} = 13$ cm

[on taking cube root both sides]

Now, surface area of cube $= 6(\text{Side})^2$

$= 6(13)^2$ cm$^2 = 1014$ cm^2

And length of the diagonal of cube $= \sqrt{3} \times \text{Side}$

$= \sqrt{3} \times 13 = 22.517$ cm

6. (c) ∴ Surface area of a cube $= 96$ cm^2

∴ Surface area of a cube $= 6(\text{Side})^2 = 96$

$\Rightarrow \qquad\qquad (\text{Side})^2 = 16$

$\Rightarrow \qquad\qquad (\text{Side}) = 4$ cm

[taking positive square root because side is always a positive quantity]

∴ Volume of cube $= (\text{Side})^3 = (4)^3 = 64$ cm^3

Hence, the volume of the cube is 64 cm^3.

7. (b) Given, the height of cylindrical tank $= 4$ m

and diameter $= 8$ m

∴ Radius $= \dfrac{8}{2} = 4$ m

Capacity of the cylindrical tank $=$ Volume of a cylinder

$= \pi r^2 h$ $[r = $ radius and $h = $ height$]$

$= \dfrac{22}{7} \times (4)^2 \times 4 = \dfrac{22 \times 4 \times 4 \times 4}{7}$

$= \dfrac{1408}{7} = 201.14$ m^3

8. (c) Let the radius be r and height be h of a cylinder.

∴ Curved surface area of cylinder $= 2\pi rh$

We have, radius $= 2r$, height $= \dfrac{h}{2}$

New curved surface area $= 2\pi(2r) \times \dfrac{h}{2} = 2\pi rh$

Hence, the curved surface area will be same.

9. (a) Height, $h = 8$ cm

Circumference of base $=$ length of sheet $\Rightarrow 2\pi r = 11$

$\Rightarrow r = \dfrac{11 \times 7}{2 \times 22} = \dfrac{7}{4}$

∴ Volume $= \pi r^2 h = \dfrac{22}{7} \times \dfrac{7}{4} \times \dfrac{7}{4} \times 8 = 77$ cm^3

10. (a) Given, diameter = 50 cm

$$\therefore \ \text{Radius}\,(r) = \frac{50}{2 \times 100} = 0.25 \text{ m} \qquad \left[\because 1 \text{ cm} = \frac{1}{100} \text{ m}\right]$$

and height $(h) = 3.5$ m

Curved surface area of the pillar $= 2\pi rh$

$$= 2 \times \frac{22}{7} \times 0.25 \times 3.5 = 2 \times 22 \times 0.25 \times 0.5 = 5.5 \text{ m}^2$$

Now, cost of painting per m^2 = ₹ 12.50

$\therefore$ Cost of painting 5.5 m^2 = 12.50×5.5 = ₹ 68.75

11. (c) Given, length of the pipe $(h) = 20$ cm

Exterior diameter = 25 cm

$$\Rightarrow \ \text{Exterior radius}\,(R) = \frac{25}{2} = 12.5 \text{ cm}$$

Thickness of the pipe $= 1$ cm

$\therefore$ Internal radius $(r) =$ External radius – Thickness

$$= 12.5 - 1 = 11.5 \text{ cm}$$

Now, whole surface area of the pipe

$= $ (External curved surface) + (Internal curved surface)

$\qquad\qquad + \ 2$ (Area of the base of the pipe)

$= 2\pi Rh + 2\pi rh + 2(\pi R^2 - \pi r^2) = 2\pi\,(R+r)\,(h+R-r)$

$$= \left[2 \times \frac{22}{7} \times (12.5 + 11.5) \times (20 + 12.5 - 11.5)\right] \text{cm}^2$$

$$= \left[2 \times \frac{22}{7} \times 24 \times 21\right] \text{cm}^2$$

$$= 3168 \text{ cm}^2$$

12. (b) Let the radii of two cylinders be r_1 and r_2 and heights of two cylinders be h_1 and h_2.

Given, $\dfrac{r_1}{r_2} = \dfrac{2}{3}$ and $\dfrac{h_1}{h_2} = \dfrac{5}{3}$

$$\therefore \text{Ratio of volumes} = \frac{\pi r_1^2 h_1}{\pi r_2^2 h_2} = \left(\frac{r_1}{r_2}\right)^2 \left(\frac{h_1}{h_2}\right)$$

$$= \left(\frac{2}{3}\right)^2 \left(\frac{5}{3}\right) = \frac{4}{9} \times \frac{5}{3} = 20 : 27$$

Hence, the ratio of their volumes is 20 : 27.

13. (a) Given, radius $(r) = 3.5$ cm

and height $(h) = 12$ cm

Quantity of ice-cream $=$ Volume of cone $= \dfrac{1}{3}\pi r^2 h$

$$= \frac{1}{3} \times \frac{22}{7} \times (3.5)^2 \times 12 = 154 \text{ cm}^3$$

14. (c) Let r be the radius and h be the height of the cylinder.

Circumference of base, $2\pi r = 110$

Curved surface area, $2\pi rh = 4400$

$$\Rightarrow \qquad 110 \times h = 4400 \Rightarrow h = 40 \text{ cm}$$

15. (b) Let radius of the base be r cm.

Given, volume of a cone = 1570 cm^3

$$\Rightarrow \frac{1}{3}\pi r^2 h = 1570 \qquad \left[\because \text{ volume of a cone} = \frac{1}{3}\pi r^2 h\right]$$

$$\Rightarrow \frac{1}{3} \times 3.14 \times r^2 \times 15 = 1570$$

$$\Rightarrow r^2 = \frac{1570}{3.14 \times 5} = \frac{15700}{157} \ \Rightarrow r = 10 \text{ cm}$$

Hence, radius of the base is 10 cm.

16. (c) Let the radius of the sphere be r cm.

Surface area of the sphere = 154 cm^2

$$\therefore \qquad 4\pi r^2 = 154 \quad [\because \text{ surface area of a sphere} = 4\pi r^2]$$

$$\Rightarrow \qquad 4 \times \frac{22}{7} \times r^2 = 154$$

$$\Rightarrow \qquad r^2 = \frac{154 \times 7}{22 \times 4} = 12.25$$

$$\Rightarrow \qquad r = \sqrt{12.25} = 3.5 \text{ cm}$$

Hence, the radius of the sphere is 3.5 cm.

17. (b) Let the radius of the sphere and cylinder be r.

Given, height of the cylinder = diameter of the base

$$\Rightarrow \qquad h = 2r$$

According to the given condition,

Volume of sphere $= k \times$ Volume of cylinder

$$\Rightarrow \qquad \frac{4}{3}\pi r^3 = k \times \pi r^2 \times 2r$$

$$\Rightarrow \qquad k = \frac{2}{3}$$

Hence, the volume of a sphere is equal to two-third of the volume of a cylinder.

18. (d) Given, radius of a sphere = $2r$

Volume of a sphere $= \dfrac{4}{3}\pi\,(\text{radius})^3$

$$= \frac{4}{3}\pi(2r)^3 = \frac{4}{3}\pi \cdot 8r^3$$

$$= \frac{32\pi r^3}{3} \text{ cu units} \qquad\qquad [\because \text{ radius} = 2r]$$

Hence, the volume of a sphere is $\dfrac{32\pi r^3}{3}$ cu units.

19. (d) We have, radius of a hemisphere $(r) = 10$ cm

$\therefore$ Total surface area of a hemisphere $= 3\pi r^2$

$$= 3 \times 3.14 \times (10)^2 = 9.42 \times 100 = 942 \text{ cm}^2$$

20. (d) Given, diameter = 10.5 cm

$$\therefore \quad \text{Radius}\,(r) = \frac{10.5}{2} = 5.25 \text{ cm}$$

Volume of a hemisphere $= \dfrac{2}{3}\pi r^3$

$$= \frac{2}{3} \times \frac{22}{7} \times 5.25 \times 5.25 \times 5.25 = 303.1875 \text{ cm}^3$$

Quantity of milk that hemispherical bowl can hold

$$= \frac{303.1875}{1000} \text{ L} \qquad \left[\because 1 \text{ cm}^3 = \frac{1}{1000} \text{ L}\right]$$

$$= 0.303 \text{ L (approx.)}$$

21. (i) (c) Total area of four walls $= 2(l + b)h$

$$= 2(8 + 5) \times 4$$
$$= 2 \times 13 \times 4$$
$$= 104 \, \text{m}^2$$

(ii) (a) Walls painted area = Total area of four walls

$$- [\text{area of windows} + \text{area of doors}]$$
$$= [104 - 30] \, \text{m}^2$$
$$= 74 \, \text{m}^2$$

(iii) (d) Area of tiles $= l \times b$

$$= 8 \, \text{m} \times 5 \, \text{m} = 40 \, \text{m}^2$$

(iv) (c) Total area of room $= 2(lb + bh + hl)$

$$= 2(8 \times 5 + 5 \times 4 + 4 \times 8)$$
$$= 2(40 + 20 + 32)$$
$$= 2 \times 92$$
$$= 184 \, \text{m}^2$$

(v) (a) Volume of the air in the room $= lbh$

$$= 8 \times 5 \times 4 = 160 \, \text{m}^3$$

22. (i) (c) Given, radius of a dome, $r = 7$ cm

The dome is hemispherical in shape.

Then, cloth material required

$$= 2 \times \text{Surface area of hemisphere}$$
$$= 2 \times 2\pi r^2$$
$$= 4 \times \frac{22}{7} \times 7 \times 7 = 4 \times 22 \times 7 = 616 \, \text{m}^2$$

(ii) (d) Given,

radius $= 7$ m and height $= 14$ m

We know that, volume of cylinder $= \pi r^2 h$

$$\text{Volume} = \frac{22}{7} \times 7 \times 7 \times 14$$

$$\text{Volume} = 22 \times 7 \times 14 = 2156 \, \text{m}^3$$

(iii) (b) Height of each pillar, $h = 7$ m

Radius of base, $r = 1.4$ m

Lateral surface area (or curved surface area) of 2 pillars

$$= 2 \times 2\pi rh$$
$$= 4 \times \frac{22}{7} \times 1.4 \times 7 = 123.2 \, \text{m}^2$$

(iv) (a) Radius of hemisphere, $r = 2.8$ m

Then, volume of a hemisphere, $V = \frac{2}{3} \pi r^3$

$$= \frac{2}{3} \times \frac{22}{7} \times (2.8)^3 = 46 \, \text{m}^3$$

(v) (b) Volume of 2 hemispheres of radius 1 cm

$$= 2 \times \frac{2}{3} \pi r^3 = \frac{4}{3} \pi (1)^3 = \frac{4}{3} \pi \, \text{cm}^3$$

Volume of 1 sphere of radius 2 cm

$$= \frac{4}{3} \pi (r^3) = \frac{4}{3} \pi (2)^3 = \frac{32}{3} \pi \, \text{cm}^3$$

Then, required ratio $= \dfrac{\dfrac{4}{3}\pi}{\dfrac{32}{3}\pi} = \dfrac{1}{8} = 1 : 8$

Subjective Questions

1. Given, length of cuboid $(l) = 8$ m, breadth $(b) = 6$ m and height $(h) = 4$ m

$\therefore$ Total surface area of cuboid $= 2(lb + bh + hl)$

$$= 2(8 \times 6 + 6 \times 4 + 4 \times 8) = 2(48 + 24 + 32)$$
$$= 2 \times 104 = 208 \, \text{m}^2$$

Diagonal of cuboid $= \sqrt{l^2 + b^2 + h^2} = \sqrt{(8)^2 + (6)^2 + (4)^2}$

$$= \sqrt{64 + 36 + 16} = \sqrt{116} = 10.77 \, \text{m}$$

and area of the four walls of cuboid $= 2(l + b)h = 2(8 + 6) \times 4$

$$= 2 \times 14 \times 4 = 112 \, \text{m}^2$$

2. Let l, b and h be the length, breadth and height of rectangular hall, respectively.

Now, area of four walls

$$= \frac{\text{Cost of painting the four walls}}{\text{Cost of painting per m}^2}$$

$$= \frac{15000}{10} = 1500 \, \text{m}^2$$

Given, perimeter of base of the hall,

$$2(l + b) = 250 \, \text{m} \qquad \ldots(i)$$

and we have area of four walls $= 1500 \, \text{m}^2$

$$\Rightarrow \qquad 2(l + b) \times h = 1500$$

$$[\because \text{area of four walls} = 2(l + b) \times h]$$

$$\Rightarrow \qquad 250 \times h = 1500 \qquad [\text{from Eq. (i)}]$$

$$\Rightarrow \qquad h = \frac{1500}{250} = 6 \, \text{m}$$

Hence, the height of the hall is 6 m.

3. Given, dimensions of matchbox $= 4 \, \text{cm} \times 2.5 \, \text{cm} \times 1.5 \, \text{cm}$

So, length $(l) = 4 \, \text{cm}$,

breadth $(b) = 2.5 \, \text{cm}$ and height $(h) = 1.5 \, \text{cm}$.

$\therefore$ Volume of a matchbox = Volume of a cuboid (V)

$$= 4 \, \text{cm} \times 2.5 \, \text{cm} \times 1.5 \, \text{cm}$$
$$= 15 \, \text{cm}^3 \qquad [\because \text{volume of cuboid } (V) = lbh]$$

Volume of a packet containing 12 such boxes

$$= 12 \times \text{Volume of one matchbox}$$
$$= 12 \times 15 = 180 \, \text{cm}^3$$

4. Given, length $(l) = 20$ m, breadth $(b) = 15$ m and height $(h) = 6$ m

$\therefore$ Capacity of the tank = Volume of the tank

$$= lbh = (20 \times 15 \times 6) = 1800 \, \text{m}^3$$

$\because$ Water required for one person per day $= 150$ L

$\therefore$ Water required for 4000 persons per day

$$= (4000 \times 150) \, \text{L}$$
$$= \left(\frac{4000 \times 150}{1000} \right) \text{m}^3 \qquad \left[\because 1 \text{L} = \frac{1}{1000} \, \text{m}^3 \right]$$
$$= 600 \, \text{m}^3$$

Now, number of days the water will last

$$= \frac{\text{Capacity of tank}}{\text{Total water required per day}} = \frac{1800}{600} = 3$$

Hence, the water will last for 3 days.

5. Given, dimensions of a brick are
$$l = 22.5 \text{ cm}, \ b = 10 \text{ cm and } h = 7.5 \text{ cm}$$
and total surface area of container $= 9.375 \text{ m}^2$
Total surface area of a brick
$$= 2 (l \times b + b \times h + h \times l)$$
$$= 2(22.5 \times 10 + 10 \times 7.5 + 7.5 \times 22.5)$$
$$= 2(22.5 + 75 + 168.75)$$
$$= 2 \times 468.75 = 937.5 \text{ cm}^2 = \frac{937.5}{100 \times 100} \text{ m}^2$$

$$\left[\because (1 \text{ cm})^2 = \left(\frac{1}{100} \text{ m}\right)^2 \Rightarrow 1 \text{ cm}^2 = \frac{1}{100 \times 100} \text{ m}^2 \right]$$

Number of bricks that painted out of this container
$$= \frac{\text{Total area painted by container 's paint}}{\text{Total surface area of a brick}}$$
$$= \frac{9.375}{937.5} = \frac{9.375 \times 100 \times 100}{937.5} = \frac{937500}{9375} = 100$$

Hence, 100 bricks can be painted out.

6. Given, dimensions of wall are length $= 10 \text{ m} = 1000 \text{ cm}$,
thickness $= 24 \text{ cm}$ and height $= 4 \text{ m} = 400 \text{ cm}$
$\therefore$ Volume of the wall $=$ Length $\times$ Thickness $\times$ Height
$$= 1000 \times 24 \times 400 \text{ cm}^3$$

Now, each brick is a cuboid with length $= 24 \text{ cm}$,
breadth $= 12 \text{ cm}$ and height $= 8 \text{ cm}$
$\therefore$ Volume of each brick $=$ Length $\times$ Breadth $\times$ Height
$$= 24 \times 12 \times 8 \text{ cm}^3$$

Since, the cuboidal wall is built up with cuboidal bricks, so
volume of the cuboidal wall $=$ Volume of each brick
$$\times \text{ Number of bricks required}$$
$$\Rightarrow \text{Number of bricks required} = \frac{\text{Volume of the wall}}{\text{Volume of each brick}}$$
$$= \frac{1000 \times 24 \times 400}{24 \times 12 \times 8} = 4166.7$$

Hence, the wall requires 4167 bricks.

7. Given, total population of a small village $= 5000$

Water required per head per day $= 75 \text{ L}$
Volume of water required for a small village per day
$$= 5000 \times 75 = 375000 \text{ L}$$
$$= \frac{375000}{1000} \text{ m}^3 = 375 \text{ m}^3 \qquad [\because 1 \text{ m}^3 = 1000 \text{ L}]$$

Total capacity of water in overhead tank
$$= \text{Volume of overhead tank}$$
$$= 40 \times 25 \times 15 = 15000 \text{ m}^3$$

$\therefore$ Number of days
$$= \frac{\text{Total capacity of water in overhead tank}}{\text{Volume of water required for a small village per day}}$$
$$= \frac{15000}{375} = 40 \text{ days}$$

Hence, water of this tank will be last in 40 days.

8. Given, side of a solid cube $= 12 \text{ cm}$
Volume of a solid cube $= 12 \text{ cm} \times 12 \text{ cm} \times 12 \text{ cm}$
$$[\because \text{ volume of cube} = (\text{side})^3]$$
$$= 1728 \text{ cm}^3$$
The solid cube is cut into eight cubes of equal volume.
Hence, the volume of the new cube $= \dfrac{1728}{8} = 216 \text{ cm}^3$
$$\Rightarrow \qquad (\text{Side})^3 = 216 \text{ cm}^3 \qquad [\because \text{ volume of cube} = (\text{side})^3]$$
$$\Rightarrow \qquad \text{Side} = 6 \text{ cm} \qquad [\text{taking cube root}]$$
$\therefore$ Side of the new cube $= 6$ cm
Surface area of solid cube, $S_1 = 6 (\text{Side})^2 = 6 (12)^2 \text{ cm}^2$
$$\Rightarrow \qquad S_1 = 6 \times 144 = 864 \text{ cm}^2$$
Surface area of new cube, $S_2 = 6 (\text{Side})^2 = 6(6)^2$
$$\Rightarrow \qquad S_2 = 6 \times 36 = 216 \text{ cm}^2$$
$\therefore$ Required ratio $= S_1 : S_2 = 864 : 216 = 4 : 1$

9. Let the dimensions of the rectangular box be $2x$, $3x$ and
$4x$ m.
$\therefore$ Surface area $= 2(2x \times 3x + 3x \times 4x + 4x \times 2x)$
$$[\because \text{ surface area} = 2(lb + bh + lh)]$$
$$= 2(6x^2 + 12x^2 + 8x^2) = 2 \times 26x^2 = 52x^2$$

Cost of covering the box with sheet of paper at the rate of
₹ 4 per $\text{m}^2 = 52x^2 \times 4 = ₹ 208 \, x^2$.

And cost of covering the box with sheet of paper at the rate
of ₹ 4.50 per $\text{m}^2 = 4.50 \times 52x^2 = ₹ 234x^2$

According to the question,
Difference of the cost at different rate $= ₹ 416$
$$\Rightarrow 234x^2 - 208x^2 = 416 \Rightarrow 26x^2 = 416$$
$$\Rightarrow \qquad x^2 = 16 \ \Rightarrow x = 4 \ [\text{on taking positive square root}]$$

Hence, the dimensions of the box are 8 m, 12 m and 16 m.

10. Given edge of the cubical box $= 10 \text{ cm}$
For cuboidal box, length $(l) = 12.5 \text{ cm}$, breadth $(b) = 10 \text{ cm}$
and height $(h) = 8 \text{ cm}$

(i) Lateral surface area of cubical box
$$= 4l^2 = 4(10)^2 = 4 \times 100 = 400 \text{ cm}^2$$

Lateral surface area of cuboidal box
$$= 2(l + b) \times h = 2(12.5 + 10) \times 8$$
$$= 2(22.5) \times 8 = 45 \times 8 = 360 \text{ cm}^2$$

(lateral surface area of cubical box) $>$
$$(\text{lateral surface area of cuboidal box})$$
$$[\because 400 > 360]$$
$\therefore$ Required difference $= 400 - 360 = 40 \text{ cm}^2$

Hence, cubical box has 40 cm^2 more lateral surface
area.

(ii) Total surface area of cubical box
$$= 6l^2 = 6(10)^2 = 6 \times 100 = 600 \text{ cm}^2$$
Total surface area of cuboidal box
$$= 2(lb + bh + hl)$$
$$= 2(12.5 \times 10 + 10 \times 8 + 8 \times 12.5)$$
$$= 2(125 + 80 + 100) = 2 \times 305 = 610 \text{ cm}^2$$

(Area of cuboidal box) $>$ (Area of cubical box)

$$[\because 610 > 600]$$

$\therefore$ Required difference $= 610 - 600 = 10 \ \text{cm}^2$

Hence, cubical box has 10 cm^2 less total surface area.

11. Here, Hameed built a cubical water tank and covered five outer faces with square tiles. So, surface area of the tank will be equal to the product of number of tiles and area of each tile.

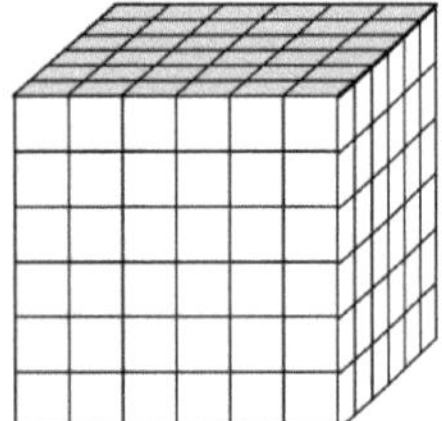

Given, edge of the cubical tank

$$= 1.5 \ \text{m} = 150 \ \text{cm}$$

$\therefore$ Surface area of the tank $= 5 \times 150 \times 150 \ \text{cm}^2$

Area of each square tile $=$ Side $\times$ Side $= 25 \times 25 \ \text{cm}^2$

Now, surface area of the tank $=$ Number of tiles required

$$\times \text{Area of each square tile}$$

$\Rightarrow$ The number of tiles required

$$= \frac{\text{Surface area of the tank}}{\text{Area of each square tile}} = \frac{5 \times 150 \times 150}{25 \times 25} = 180$$

Given, cost of 1 dozen tiles, i.e. cost of 12 tiles $= ₹ \ 360$

Then, cost of one tile $= \dfrac{360}{12} = ₹ \ 30$

$\therefore$ The cost of 180 tiles $= 180 \times 30 = ₹ \ 5400$

Hence, Hameed spends ₹ 5400 for the tiles.

12. Here, Mary wants to cover a cuboidal box with square sheets of paper. So, the quantity of paper required to cover the box will be equal to the surface area of the box.

Given, dimensions of the box are length $(l) = 80 \ \text{cm}$,

breadth $(b) = 40 \ \text{cm}$ and height $(h) = 20 \ \text{cm}$.

$\therefore$ Surface area of the box $= 2 \ (lb + bh + hl)$

$$= 2 \ (80 \times 40 + 40 \times 20 + 20 \times 80)$$

$$= 2(3200 + 800 + 1600) = 2 \times 5600 = 11200 \ \text{cm}^2$$

Dimension of square sheet of paper is 40 cm.

$\therefore$ Area of each square sheet of the paper $= 40 \times 40 = 1600 \ \text{cm}^2$

$$[\because \text{area of square} = (\text{side})^2]$$

Now, surface area of the box $=$ Number of sheets required

$$\times \text{Area of each square sheet of paper}$$

$\therefore$ Number of sheets required

$$= \frac{\text{Surface area of the box}}{\text{Area of each square sheet of paper}} = \frac{11200}{1600} = 7$$

Hence, she would require 7 square sheets of paper.

13. Let side of a cube be $= x \ \text{m}$

Volume of cubical tank $= 15.625 \ \text{m}^3$ [given]

$\Rightarrow \qquad x^3 = 15.625 \ \text{m}^3 \Rightarrow x = 2.5 \ \text{m}$

and present depth of water in cubical tank $= 1.3 \ \text{m}$

$\therefore$ Height of water used $= (2.5 - 1.3) \ \text{m} = 1.2 \ \text{m}$

Now, volume of water used $= 1.2 \times 2.5 \times 2.5 = 7.5 \ \text{m}^3$

$$= 7.5 \times 1000 = 7500 \ \text{L} \qquad [\because 1 \ \text{m}^3 = 1000 \ \text{L}]$$

Hence, the volume of water already used from the tank is 7500 L.

14. Let radius of the cylinder $= r$ and height $= h$.

Then, curved surface area of cylinder $= 2\pi r h$

and total surface area of cylinder $= 2\pi r \ (h + r)$

According to the question,

Curved surface area : Total surface area $= 1 : 3$

$$\Rightarrow \qquad \frac{2\pi r h}{2\pi r \ (h + r)} = \frac{1}{3} \quad \Rightarrow \quad \frac{h}{h + r} = \frac{1}{3}$$

$$\Rightarrow \qquad 3h = h + r \quad \Rightarrow \quad 2h = r$$

$$\Rightarrow \qquad \frac{h}{r} = \frac{1}{2} \qquad \text{or} \quad h : r = 1 : 2$$

Hence, required ratio between height and radius of the cylinder is 1 : 2.

15. Given, length $(l) = 2 \ \text{km} = (2 \times 1000) \ \text{m} = 2000 \ \text{m}$,

$$[\because 1 \ \text{km} = 1000 \ \text{m}]$$

breadth $(b) = 40 \ \text{m}$ and height $(h) = 3 \ \text{m}$

Since, the water flows at the rate of 2 km/h i.e. the water of length 2 km flows into the sea in one hour.

$\therefore$ The volume of water flowing into the sea in 1 h

$$= \text{Volume of the cuboid} = l \times b \times h$$

$$= 2000 \times 40 \times 3 = 240000 \ \text{m}^3$$

Hence, the volume of water flowing into the sea in one minute

$$= \frac{240000}{60} = 4000 \ \text{m}^3 \qquad [\because 1 \ \text{h} = 60 \ \text{min}]$$

16. Let height of cylinder be h m.

Given, radius of base $(r) = 0.7 \ \text{m}$

and curved surface area of a right circular cylinder $= 4.4 \ \text{m}^2$

$$\therefore \qquad 2\pi r h = 4.4$$

$$\Rightarrow \qquad 2 \times \frac{22}{7} \times 0.7 \times h = 4.4$$

$$\Rightarrow \qquad h = \frac{44}{44} = 1 \ \text{m}$$

Hence, the height of the right circular cylinder is 1 m.

17. We have, inner diameter $= 3.5 \ \text{m}$

$\therefore$ Inner radius $= \dfrac{3.5}{2} \ \text{m}$ and height $(h) = 10 \ \text{m}$

(i) Inner curved surface area $= 2\pi r h$

$$= 2 \times \frac{22}{7} \times \frac{3.5}{2} \times 10$$

$$= 22 \times 5 = 110 \ \text{m}^2$$

(ii) Given, cost of plastering per m^2 $= ₹ 40$

$\therefore$ Cost of plastering 110 m^2 of circular well

$$= 40 \times 110 = ₹ 4400$$

18. Given, length or height of the pipe $(h) = 28 \ \text{m}$

and diameter $= 5 \ \text{cm}$

$\therefore$ Radius $(r) = \dfrac{5}{2} = 2.5 \ \text{cm}$

$$= \frac{2.5}{100} \ \text{m} = 0.025 \ \text{m} \qquad \left[\because 1 \ \text{cm} = \frac{1}{100} \ \text{m}\right]$$

Total radiating surface area in the system

$$= \text{Curved surface area of the cylindrical pipe}$$

$$= 2\pi rh = 2 \times \frac{22}{7} \times 0.025 \times 28 = 4.4 \text{ m}^2$$

19. Let r be the radius of the base of a cylinder

We have, height $(h) = 5$ cm

and lateral surface area of a cylinder $= 94.2$ cm^2

$$\therefore \qquad 2\pi rh = 94.2$$

$$\Rightarrow \qquad 2 \times 3.14 \times r \times 5 = 94.2$$

$$\Rightarrow \qquad r = \frac{94.2}{31.4} \Rightarrow r = 3 \text{ cm}$$

(i) Hence, radius of base $(r) = 3$ cm

(ii) Volume of a cylinder $= \pi r^2 h = 3.14 \times (3)^2 \times 5$

$$= 3.14 \times 9 \times 5 = 141.3 \text{ cm}^3$$

20. Let r be the radius of a cylindrical vessel.

Given, height $(h) = 25$ cm and

circumference of the base $= 132$ cm

$$\therefore \qquad 2\pi r = 132$$

$$\Rightarrow \qquad 2 \times \frac{22}{7} \times r = 132$$

$$\Rightarrow \qquad r = \frac{132 \times 7}{22 \times 2} = 21 \text{ cm}$$

Now, volume of cylinder $= \pi r^2 h$

$$= \frac{22}{7} \times 21 \times 21 \times 25$$

$$= 34650 \text{ cm}^3 = \frac{34650}{1000} \text{ L} = 34.65 \text{ L}$$

$$\left[\because 1000 \text{cm}^3 = 1 \text{ L} \Rightarrow 1 \text{ cm}^3 = \frac{1}{1000} \text{ L} \right]$$

21. We have, slant height $(l) = 21$ m and diameter $= 24$ m

$$\therefore \text{ Radius } (r) = \frac{24}{2} = 12 \text{ m}$$

Now, total surface area of the cone $= \pi r(l + r)$

$$= \pi \times 12(21 + 12) = \pi \times 12 \times 33 = 396\pi$$

$$= 396 \times \frac{22}{7} = \frac{8712}{7} = 1244.57 \text{ m}^2$$

22. Let r be the radius of the vessel.

Given, capacity of a closed cylindrical vessel $= 15.4$ L

$$= 15.4 \times 1000 \text{ cm}^3 \qquad [\because 1 \text{L} = 1000 \text{ cm}^3]$$

$$\therefore \quad \pi r^2 h = 15400 \Rightarrow \pi r^2 \times 100 = 15400 \, [\because h = 1 \text{ m} = 100 \text{cm}]$$

$$\Rightarrow \quad r^2 = 154 \times \frac{7}{22}$$

$$\Rightarrow \quad r^2 = 7 \times 7 \Rightarrow r = 7 \text{cm}$$

Total surface area of closed cylindrical vessel

$$= 2\pi r(r + h) = 2 \times \frac{22}{7} \times 7(7 + 100)$$

$$= 44 \times 107 = 4708 \text{ cm}^2$$

$$= \left(\frac{4708}{100 \times 100} \right) \text{m}^2 \qquad \left[\because 1 \text{ cm} = \frac{1}{100} \text{ m} \right]$$

$$= 0.4708 \text{ m}^2$$

The required metal sheet is 0.4708 m^2.

23. (i) For tin can, we have, length $(l) = 5$ cm,

breadth $(b) = 4$ cm and height $(h) = 15$ cm

$$\therefore \text{Volume of cuboidal tin can} = l \times b \times h$$

$$= 5 \times 4 \times 15 = 300 \text{ cm}^3 \qquad \ldots \text{(i)}$$

(ii) For plastic cylinder, we have,

Diameter $= 7$ cm

$$\therefore \text{ Radius } (r) = \frac{7}{2} \text{ cm and height } (h) = 10 \text{ cm}$$

Then, volume of a plastic cylinder $= \pi r^2 h$

$$= \frac{22}{7} \times \frac{7}{2} \times \frac{7}{2} \times 10$$

$$= 77 \times 5 = 385 \text{ cm}^3 \qquad \ldots \text{(ii)}$$

From Eqs. (i) and (ii), we see that volume of a plastic cylinder has greater capacity and its capacity is $385 - 300 = 85 \text{ cm}^3$ more than the tin can.

24. Dimensions of shelter are

$$l = 4 \text{ m}, \ b = 3 \text{ m and } h = 2.5 \text{ m}.$$

Required area of tarpaulin to make the shelter

$$= \text{Area of 4 sides} + \text{ Area of the top of the car}$$

$$= 2(l + b) \times h + (l \times b)$$

$$= 2(4 + 3) \times 2.5 + (4 \times 3)$$

$$= (2 \times 7 \times 2.5) + 12$$

$$= 35 + 12$$

$$= 47 \text{ m}^2$$

25. Given, diameter of the base $= 140$ cm

$$\therefore \text{ Radius } (r) = \frac{140}{2} = 70 \text{ cm} = 0.70 \text{ m and height, } h = 1 \text{ m}$$

Metal sheet required to make a closed cylindrical tank

$= \text{Total surface area of right circular cylinder} = 2\pi r(h + r)$

$$= 2 \times \frac{22}{7} \times 0.7(1 + 0.7)$$

$$= 2 \times 22 \times 0.1 \times 1.7 = 7.48 \text{ m}^2$$

Hence, the sheet required to make a closed cylindrical tank is 7.48 m^2.

26. Given, diameter of a roller $= 84$ cm

$$\therefore r = \text{Radius of a roller} = \frac{84}{2} = 42 \text{ cm}$$

and length of a roller $= 120$ cm

Area covered in 1 revolution $= \text{Curved surface area of roller}$

$$= 2\pi rh = 2 \times \frac{22}{7} \times 42 \times 120$$

$$= 44 \times 720$$

$$= 31680 \text{ cm}^2 = \left(\frac{31680}{100 \times 100} \right) \text{m}^2$$

$$= 3.168 \text{ m}^2$$

$$\left[\because (1 \text{ cm})^2 = \left(\frac{1}{100} \text{m} \right)^2 \Rightarrow 1 \text{ cm}^2 = \frac{1}{100 \times 100} \text{m}^2 \right]$$

Now, area of the playground

$$= \text{Area covered in 500 complete revolutions}$$

$$= 500 \times 3.168 = 1584 \text{ m}^2$$

27. Given, diameter of vessel $= 28$ cm

$\therefore \qquad$ Radius $(r) = \dfrac{28}{2} = 14$ cm

and height of water in vessel $(h) = 12$ cm

Volume of water in the vessel $= \pi r^2 h$

$$= \dfrac{22}{7} \times 14 \times 14 \times 12 = 7392 \text{ cm}^3$$

Let h be the height of water rises in the tub.

Then, volume of water in the tub $= (66 \times 28 \times h) \text{ cm}^3$

According to the question, volume of water in vessel
$$= \text{volume of water in tub}$$

$\Rightarrow 66 \times 28 \times h = 7392 \Rightarrow h = \dfrac{7392}{66 \times 28} = 4$ cm

Hence, water rises to a height of 4 cm in the tub.

28. Given, measures of a rectangular sheet $= 44$ cm $\times 18$ cm

Here, length $= 44$ cm and breadth $= 18$ cm

Let radius of base of cylinder $= r$

On revolving it about its length, a cylinder is formed.

$\therefore$ Circumference of base of cylinder $=$ Length of sheet

$\therefore \qquad 2\pi r = 44$

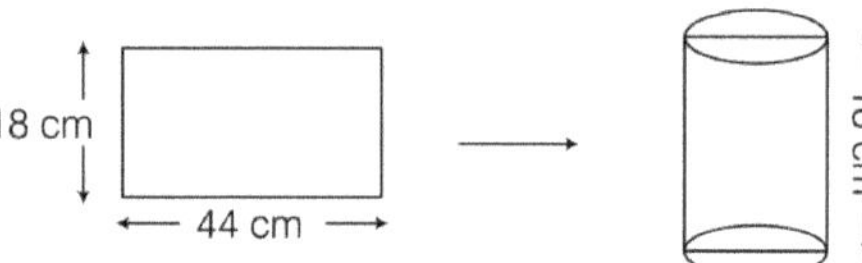

$\Rightarrow \quad 2 \times \dfrac{22}{7} \times r = 44 \quad \Rightarrow \quad r = \dfrac{44 \times 7}{2 \times 22} = 7$

Hence, radius of the cylinder is 7 cm.

29. Given, length of a cylindrical roller, $h = 2.5$ m

Radius of a cylindrical roller, $r = 1.75$ m

and total area rolled on a road by cylindrical roller $= 5500$ m^2

$\therefore$ Area rolled to cover in one revolution $=$ Curved surface area of a cylindrical roller

$$= 2\pi rh = 2 \times \dfrac{22}{7} \times 1.75 \times 2.5$$

$$= \dfrac{44 \times 4.375}{7} = \dfrac{192.5}{7} = 27.5 \text{ m}^2$$

$\therefore$ Number of revolutions rolled by a cylindrical roller

$$= \dfrac{\text{Total area rolled by a cylindrical roller}}{\text{Area rolled to cover by a cylindrical roller in one revolution}}$$

$$= \dfrac{5500}{27.5} = 200$$

Hence, the number of revolutions rolled by a cylindrical roller on a road is 200.

30. (i) Given, radius $(r) = 6$ cm and height $(h) = 7$ cm

$\therefore$ Volume of the right circular cone $= \dfrac{1}{3} \pi r^2 h$

$$= \dfrac{1}{3} \times \dfrac{22}{7} \times (6)^2 \times 7 = \dfrac{22}{3} \times 6 \times 6$$

$$= 22 \times 12 = 264 \text{ cm}^3$$

(ii) Given, radius $(r) = 3.5$ cm and height $(h) = 12$ cm

$\therefore$ Volume of right circular cone $= \dfrac{1}{3} \pi r^2 h$

$$= \dfrac{1}{3} \times \dfrac{22}{7} \times 3.5 \times 3.5 \times 12$$

$$= 88 \times 0.5 \times 3.5$$

$$= 154 \text{ cm}^2$$

31. Given, diameter of glass $= 7$ cm

Radius of glass, $r = \dfrac{7}{2}$ cm

$\therefore$ Milk contained in the cylindrical glass
$$= \text{Volume of cylindrical glass}$$

$$= \pi r^2 h = \dfrac{22}{7} \times \dfrac{7}{2} \times \dfrac{7}{2} \times 12 = 462 \text{ cm}^3$$

Now, milk required for 1600 students $= 462 \times 1600$

$$= 739200 \text{ cm}^3 = \dfrac{739200}{1000} = 739.2 \text{ L} \quad \left[\because 1 \text{ cm}^3 = \dfrac{1}{1000} \text{ L} \right]$$

Hence, 739.2 L milk is needed to serve 1600 students.

32. Circumference,

$$2\pi r = 33 \Rightarrow r = \dfrac{33 \times 7}{2 \times 22} = \dfrac{21}{4} = 5.25 \text{ m and } h = 16 \text{ m (given)}$$

$$l = \sqrt{\left(\dfrac{21}{4}\right)^2 + (16)^2}$$

$$= \sqrt{\dfrac{441}{16} + 256} = 16.84 \text{ m} \qquad [\because l^2 = r^2 + h^2]$$

Total surface area of cone $= \pi r (l + r)$

$$= \dfrac{22}{7} \times 5.25 \,(16.84 + 5.25) = 364.485 \text{ m}^2$$

33. We have, slant height $(l) = 14$ cm

Curved surface area of a cone $= 308$ cm^2

$\Rightarrow \qquad \pi r l = 308 \; [\because \text{ curved surface area of a cone } = \pi r l]$

$\Rightarrow \quad \dfrac{22}{7} \times r \times 14 = 308$

$\Rightarrow \qquad r = \dfrac{308}{22 \times 2} = 7$ cm

(i) Radius of the base $(r) = 7$ cm

(ii) Total surface area of the cone $= \pi r (r + l)$

$$= \dfrac{22}{7} \times 7(7 + 14) = 22 \times 21 = 462 \text{ cm}^2$$

34. Given, height $(h) = 21$ cm and slant height $(l) = 28$ cm

We know that, $l^2 = h^2 + r^2$

$\Rightarrow \qquad r^2 = l^2 - h^2$

$\Rightarrow \qquad r = \sqrt{l^2 - h^2}$ [on taking positive square root]

$$= \sqrt{(28)^2 - (21)^2}$$

$$= 7\sqrt{16 - 9} = 7\sqrt{7} \text{ cm}$$

Hence, volume of the cone $= \dfrac{1}{3} \pi r^2 h$

$$= \dfrac{1}{3} \times \dfrac{22}{7} \times 7\sqrt{7} \times 7\sqrt{7} \times 21 = 7546 \text{ cm}^3$$

35. Let r be the radius of the base.

Given, volume of a right circular cone $= 48\pi$ cm^3

$\therefore \qquad \dfrac{1}{3}\pi r^2 h = 48\pi$

$$\left[\because \text{ volume of a right circular cone } = \dfrac{1}{3}\pi r^2 h\right]$$

$\Rightarrow \qquad \dfrac{1}{3} \times r^2 \times 9 = 48 \qquad [\because h = 9 \text{ cm, given}]$

$\Rightarrow \qquad r^2 = 16$

$\Rightarrow \qquad r = 4$ cm $\quad$ [on taking positive square root]

Hence, diameter of the base $= 2r = 2 \times 4 = 8$ cm

36. We have, slant height $(l) = 14$ cm

Curved surface area of a cone $= 308$ cm^2

$\Rightarrow \qquad \pi r l = 308$

$$[\because \text{ curved surface area of a cone } = \pi r l]$$

$\Rightarrow \dfrac{22}{7} \times r \times 14 = 308 \Rightarrow r = \dfrac{308}{22 \times 2} = 7$ cm

(i) Radius of the base $(r) = 7$ cm

(ii) Total surface area of the cone $= \pi r(r + l)$

$$= \dfrac{22}{7} \times 7(7 + 14) = 22 \times 21 = 462 \text{ cm}^2$$

37. Given, radius $(r) = 3.5$ m

Height $(h) = 12$ m

$\therefore l = \sqrt{r^2 + h^2} = \sqrt{(3.5)^2 + 12^2} = \sqrt{156.25} = 12.5$ m

Now, length of cloth required to make conical tent

$$= \dfrac{\text{Curved surface area of conical tent}}{\text{Width of the cloth}}$$

$$[\because \text{ curved surface area of tent } = \text{ area of cloth}]$$

$$= \dfrac{\pi r l}{5} = \dfrac{\dfrac{22}{7} \times 3.5 \times 12.5}{5} = 27.5 \text{ m}$$

38. Given, radius of new cone $= \dfrac{r}{2} \qquad [\because r = \text{radius of old cone}]$

and height of new cone $= 2h \qquad [\because h = \text{height of old cone}]$

$\because \quad$ Volume of old cone $= \dfrac{1}{3}\pi r^2 h$

$\therefore \quad$ Volume of new cone $= \dfrac{1}{3}\pi \left(\dfrac{r}{2}\right)^2 (2h)$

$$= \dfrac{1}{3} \times \pi \times \dfrac{r^2}{4} \times (2h)$$

$$= \dfrac{1}{3} \times \pi \times \dfrac{r^2}{2} \times h = \dfrac{1}{2}\left(\dfrac{1}{3}\pi r^2 h\right)$$

$$= \dfrac{1}{2} \text{ (volume of old cone)}$$

Hence, volume of new cone is half of volume of old cone.

39. Given, height of a conical tent, $h = 3.5$ m and radius of the base of a conical tent, $r = 12$ m

Slant height, $l = \sqrt{h^2 + r^2} = \sqrt{(3.5)^2 + (12)^2}$

$$= \sqrt{12.25 + 144}$$

$$= \sqrt{156.25} = 12.5 \text{ m}$$

$\therefore$ Canvas required $=$ Curved surface area of the cone

(conical tent)

$$= \pi r l = \dfrac{22}{7} \times 12 \times 12.5$$

$$= 471.42 \text{ m}^2$$

Hence, the canvas required to make a conical tent is 471.42 m^2.

40. Let h be the height and r be the radius of base of the cone. Since, the tent can accommodate 11 persons and each person requires 4 m^2 of the space on the ground and 20 m^3 of air.

$\therefore$ Area of the base $= (11 \times 4) = 44$ m^2 $\ [\because$ area of base $= \pi r^2]$

$\Rightarrow \qquad \pi r^2 = 44 \text{ m}^2 \qquad\qquad \ldots\text{(i)}$

Volume of the cone $= (11 \times 20) = 220$ m^3

$\Rightarrow \qquad \dfrac{1}{3}\pi r^2 h = 220 \text{ m}^3 \qquad\qquad \ldots\text{(ii)}$

On dividing Eq. (ii) by Eq. (i), we get

$$\dfrac{\dfrac{1}{3}\pi r^2 h}{\pi r^2} = \dfrac{220}{44} \Rightarrow \dfrac{h}{3} = 5 \Rightarrow h = 15 \text{ m}$$

Hence, the height of the cone is 15 m.

41. We have, slant height $(l) = 25$ m and diameter $= 14$ m

$\therefore$ Radius $(r) = \dfrac{14}{2} = 7$ m

Curved surface area of the conical tomb $=$ Curved surface area of a cone $= \pi r l$

$$= \dfrac{22}{7} \times 7 \times 25 = 22 \times 25 = 550 \text{ m}^2$$

Given, cost of white-washing per 100 m^2 $= ₹\,210$

$\therefore$ Cost of white-washing per 1 m^2 $= ₹\,\dfrac{210}{100}$

Then, cost of white-washing 550 m^2 $= \dfrac{210 \times 550}{100} = ₹1155$

42. We have, radius $(r) = 7$ cm and height $(h) = 24$ cm

We know that, $l^2 = h^2 + r^2 \Rightarrow l = \sqrt{h^2 + r^2}$

[on taking positive square root]

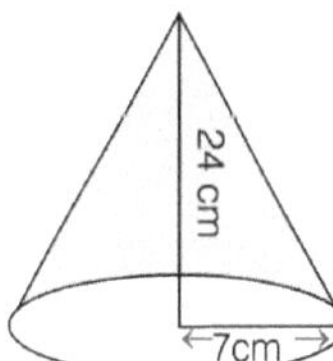

$\Rightarrow \qquad l = \sqrt{(24)^2 + 7^2} = \sqrt{576 + 49} = \sqrt{625}$

$\Rightarrow \qquad l = 25 \text{ cm}$

Curved surface area of a joker's cap

$\qquad = \text{Curved surface area of a cone} = \pi r l$

$\qquad = \dfrac{22}{7} \times 7 \times 25 = 22 \times 25 = 550 \text{ cm}^2$

$\because$ The sheet required to make 1 cap $= 550 \text{ cm}^2$

$\therefore$ The sheet required to make 10 such caps $= 550 \times 10$

$\qquad\qquad = 5500 \text{ cm}^2$

43. We have, height $(h) = 10$ m and radius $(r) = 24$ m

(i) We know that, $l^2 = h^2 + r^2 \Rightarrow l = \sqrt{r^2 + h^2}$

$\qquad\qquad$ [on taking positive square root]

$\Rightarrow l = \sqrt{(24)^2 + (10)^2} = \sqrt{576 + 100} = \sqrt{676} = 26$ m

Hence, the slant height of the canvas tent is 26 m.

(ii) Canvas required to make the tent

$\qquad = \text{Curved surface area of tent}$

$\qquad = \pi r l = \pi \times 24 \times 26 = 624\pi \text{ m}^2$

$\because$ Cost of 1 m^2 canvas $= ₹ 70$

$\therefore$ Cost of 624π m^2 canvas $= 70 \times 624\pi$

$\qquad = 70 \times 624 \times \dfrac{22}{7} = 10 \times 624 \times 22 = ₹137280$

Hence, required cost of the canvas is ₹ 137280.

44. Given, diameter $(d) = 10.5$ m, then

Radius $(r) = \dfrac{10.5}{2} = 5.25$ m and height $(h) = 3$ m

We know that, $l^2 = h^2 + r^2$

$\Rightarrow \qquad l = \sqrt{r^2 + h^2}$ [on taking positive square root]

$\qquad = \sqrt{(5.25)^2 + (3)^2}$

$\qquad = \sqrt{27.5625 + 9}$

$\qquad = \sqrt{36.5625}$

$\qquad = 6.047 = 6.05$ m

Volume of the heap of wheat cone $= \dfrac{1}{3} \pi r^2 h$

$\qquad = \dfrac{1}{3} \times \dfrac{22}{7} \times 5.25 \times 5.25 \times 3 = 86.625 \text{ m}^3$

Area of the canvas required

$\qquad = \text{Curved surface area of the heap}$

$\qquad = \pi r l = \dfrac{22}{7} \times 5.25 \times 6.05 \text{ m}^2$

$\qquad = 22 \times 0.75 \times 6.05 \text{ m}^2$

$\qquad = 99.825 \text{ m}^2$

45. (i) We have, diameter $= 14$ cm

$\therefore$ Radius $(r) = \dfrac{14}{2} = 7$ cm

$\therefore$ Surface area of a sphere $= 4\pi r^2$

$\qquad = 4 \times \dfrac{22}{7} \times 7^2$

$\qquad = 4 \times 22 \times 7$

$\qquad = 616 \text{ cm}^2$

(ii) Given, $r = \dfrac{21}{2}$ cm

$\therefore$ Surface area of sphere $= 4\pi r^2$

$\qquad = 4 \times \dfrac{22}{7} \times \dfrac{21}{2} \times \dfrac{21}{2}$

$\qquad = 22 \times 3 \times 21 = 1386 \text{ cm}^2$

(iii) Given, $r = \dfrac{3.5}{2}$ m

$\therefore$ Surface area of sphere $= 4\pi r^2$

$\qquad = \dfrac{4}{3} \times \dfrac{22}{7} \times \dfrac{3.5}{2} \times \dfrac{3.5}{2}$

$\qquad = 38.5 \text{ m}^2$

46. (i) We have, $r = $ radius of the sphere $= 10.5$ cm

$\therefore$ Surface area of a sphere $= 4\pi r^2$

$\qquad = 4 \times \dfrac{22}{7} \times 10.5 \times 10.5$

$\qquad = 88 \times 1.5 \times 10.5 = 1386 \text{ cm}^2$

(ii) Given, $r = 5.6$ cm

$\therefore$ Surface area of a sphere $= 4\pi r^2$

$\qquad = 4 \times \dfrac{22}{7} \times 5.6 \times 5.6 = 394.24 \text{ cm}^2$

(iii) Given, $r = 14$ cm

$\therefore$ Surface area of a sphere $= 4\pi r^2$

$\qquad = 4 \times \dfrac{22}{7} \times 14 \times 14$

$\qquad = 2464 \text{ cm}^2$

47. Given, diameter of capsule $= 3.5$ mm

$\therefore \qquad$ Radius $(r) = \dfrac{3.5}{2}$ mm $\qquad \left[\because \text{radius} = \dfrac{\text{diameter}}{2} \right]$

Now, volume of capsule

$\qquad = \dfrac{4}{3} \pi r^3 = \dfrac{4}{3} \times \dfrac{22}{7} \times \dfrac{3.5}{2} \times \dfrac{3.5}{2} \times \dfrac{3.5}{2}$

$\qquad = \dfrac{11 \times 0.5 \times 3.5 \times 3.5}{3} = 22.45833 = 22.46 \text{ mm}^3$

Hence, 22.46 mm^3 medicine is needed to fill this capsule.

48. Given, radius of big ball $(R) = 8$ cm

and radius of small ball $(r) = 2$ cm

$\therefore$ Volume of big ball $= \dfrac{4}{3} \pi R^3 = \dfrac{4}{3} \pi (8)^3 \text{ cm}^3$

Volume of small ball $= \dfrac{4}{3} \pi r^3 = \dfrac{4}{3} \pi (2)^3 \text{ cm}^3$

Required number of balls $= \dfrac{\text{Volume of big ball}}{\text{Volume of small ball}}$

$\qquad = \dfrac{\dfrac{4}{3} \pi (8)^3}{\dfrac{4}{3} \pi (2)^3} = \dfrac{8 \times 8 \times 8}{2 \times 2 \times 2} = 64 \text{ balls}$

49. (i) We have, diameter $(d) = 28$ cm

$\therefore$ Radius $(r) = \dfrac{28}{2} = 14$ cm $\qquad \left[\because \text{radius} = \dfrac{\text{diameter}}{2} \right]$

Amount of water displaced by a solid spherical ball

$$= \text{Volume of spherical ball} = \frac{4}{3}\pi r^3$$

$$= \frac{4}{3} \times \frac{22}{7} \times (14)^3 = \frac{4}{3} \times \frac{22}{7} \times 14 \times 14 \times 14$$

$$= 11498.67 \text{ cm}^3$$

(ii) Amount of water displaced by a solid sphere ball

$$= \text{Volume of sphere ball}$$

$$= \frac{4}{3}\pi r^3$$

$$= \frac{4}{3} \times \frac{22}{7} \times \left(\frac{0.21}{2}\right)^3$$

$$= 0.004851 \text{ m}^3$$

50. Given, diameter of a solid spherical ball $= 4.2$ cm

$\therefore$ Radius of a solid spherical ball, $r = \dfrac{4.2}{2} = 2.1$ cm

Now, volume of water displaced by a solid spherical ball, when it is completely immersed in water

$$= \text{Volume of a solid spherical ball}$$

$$= \frac{4}{3}\pi r^3 = \frac{4}{3} \times \frac{22}{7} \times (2.1)^3$$

$$= \frac{4}{3} \times \frac{22}{7} \times 2.1 \times 2.1 \times 2.1$$

$$= \frac{814.968}{21} = 38.808 = 38.81 \text{ cm}^3$$

Hence, the volume of water displaced by a solid spherical ball, when it is completely immersed in water is 38.81 cm^3.

51. Let diameter of the Earth $= d_1$

Then, diameter of the Moon $= \dfrac{1}{4} d_1$

$\therefore$ Radius of the Earth $(r_1) = \dfrac{d_1}{2}$

and radius of the Moon $(r_2) = \dfrac{d_1}{2 \times 4} = \dfrac{d_1}{8}$

Surface area of the Earth $(S_1) = 4\pi r_1^2$

$$\Rightarrow \qquad S_1 = 4\pi \left(\frac{d_1}{2}\right)^2 = \pi d_1^2$$

Surface area of the Moon,

$$S_2 = 4\pi \left(\frac{d_1}{8}\right)^2 = 4\pi \frac{d_1^2}{64} \Rightarrow S_2 = \frac{\pi d_1^2}{16}$$

$\therefore$ Required ratio, $S_1 : S_2 = \dfrac{\pi d_1^2}{1} : \dfrac{\pi d_1^2}{16} = 16 : 1$

52. Let r be the radius of hemispherical bowl.

Circumference of bowl,

$$2\pi r = 132 \Rightarrow r = \frac{132 \times 7}{2 \times 22} = 21 \text{ cm}$$

Volume of bowl $= \dfrac{2}{3}\pi r^3 = \dfrac{2}{3}\pi (21)^3$

$$= \frac{2}{3} \times \frac{22}{7} \times 21 \times 21 \times 21$$

$$= 19404 \text{ cm}^3$$

53. Given, inner radius of the hemispherical bowl $= 24.7$ cm

Thickness of metal sheet $= 0.3$ cm

Now, outer radius of the hemispherical bowl

$$= 24.7 + 0.3 = 25 \text{ cm}$$

$\therefore$ Outer surface area of the hemispherical bowl $= 2\pi r^2$

$$= 2 \times 3.14 \times (25)^2$$

$$= 157 \times 25$$

$$= 3925 \text{ cm}^2$$

Now, cost of polishing $100 \text{ cm}^2 = ₹\, 4$

$\therefore$ Cost of polishing $3925 \text{ cm}^2 = \dfrac{4 \times 3925}{100} = ₹\, 157$

54. We have, diameter $(d) = 4.2$ cm

$\therefore \qquad$ Radius $(r) = \dfrac{4.2}{2} = 2.1$ cm

Volume of the metallic ball $= \dfrac{4}{3}\pi r^3$

$$= \frac{4}{3} \times \frac{22}{7} \times (2.1)^3$$

$$= \frac{4}{3} \times \frac{22}{7} \times 2.1 \times 2.1 \times 2.1$$

$$= 88 \times 0.3 \times 0.7 \times 2.1 = 38.808 \text{ cm}^3$$

Given, the density of the metal per $\text{cm}^3 = 8.9$ gm

$\therefore$ The mass of the ball $= 38.808 \times 8.9 = 345.39$ gm

Hence, the mass of the ball is 345.39 gm.

55. (i) Given, r be the radius of each solid iron sphere and r' be the radius of new solid iron sphere, then

Volume of new sphere $= \dfrac{4}{3}\pi r'^3$

and volume of old sphere $= \dfrac{4}{3}\pi r^3$

Then, volume of 27 solid iron spheres

$$= 27 \times \text{volume of old sphere}$$

$$= 27 \times \frac{4}{3}\pi r^3 = 36\pi r^3$$

$\because$ 27 solid iron spheres are melted to form a new sphere with radius r'.

$$\therefore \qquad \frac{4}{3}\pi r'^3 = 36\pi r^3 \Rightarrow r'^3 = \frac{36 \times 3r^3}{4}$$

$$\Rightarrow \qquad (r')^3 = 27 r^3 = (3r)^3$$

$$\therefore \qquad r' = 3r \qquad\qquad \text{...(i)}$$

Radius r' of the new sphere $= 3r$

(ii) Surface area (S) of solid iron sphere $= 4\pi r^2$

Surface area (S') of new sphere $= 4\pi (r')^2$

$$= 4\pi (3r)^2 = 36\pi r^2 \qquad \text{[from Eq. (i)]}$$

$\therefore$ Required ratio $= S : S' = 4\pi r^2 : 36\pi r^2 = 1 : 9$

56. Given, radius of a spherical laddoo, $r = 5$ cm

$\therefore$ Volume of a spherical laddoo $= \dfrac{4}{3}\pi r^3 = \dfrac{4}{3}\pi (5)^3$

$$= \frac{4}{3} \times 125\pi = \frac{500}{3}\pi \text{ cm}^3$$

Now, radius of small laddoo = 2.5 cm

So, volume of small laddoo $= \dfrac{4}{3}\pi \times (2.5)^3 = \dfrac{62.5}{3}\pi$ cm^3

$\therefore$ Number of laddoos $= \dfrac{\text{Volume of laddoo}}{\text{Volume of small laddoo}}$

$= \dfrac{\dfrac{500\pi}{3}}{\dfrac{62.5\pi}{3}} = \dfrac{500}{62.5} = 8$

Hence, the number of laddoos are 8.

57. Given, weight of one solid sphere, $m_1 = 5920$ gm

and weight of another solid sphere, $m_2 = 740$ gm

Diameter of the smaller sphere $= 5$ cm

$\therefore$ Radius of the smaller sphere, $r_2 = \dfrac{5}{2}, m_2 = 740$ gm

We know that,

$$\text{Density}\,(D) = \dfrac{\text{Mass}\,(M)}{\text{Volume}\,(D)}$$

$\Rightarrow \qquad\qquad V = \dfrac{M}{D}$

$\Rightarrow \qquad\qquad V_1 = \dfrac{5920}{D}$ cm$^3 \qquad$ ...(i)

and $\qquad\qquad V_2 = \dfrac{740}{D}$ cm$^3 \qquad$ ..(ii)

On dividing Eq. (i) by Eq. (ii), we get

$$\dfrac{V_1}{V_2} = \dfrac{\dfrac{5920}{D}}{\dfrac{740}{D}}$$

$\dfrac{r_1^3}{r_2^3} = \dfrac{8}{1} \Rightarrow \dfrac{r_1^3}{\left(\dfrac{5}{2}\right)^3} = \dfrac{8}{1}$

$\dfrac{r_1^3 \times 8}{125} = \dfrac{8}{1}$

$r_1^3 = 125 \Rightarrow r_1 = 5$ cm

58. Given, total surface area of a solid right circular cylinder

$= 231$ cm^2

Now, according to the question,

Curved surface area of right circular cylinder

$= \dfrac{2}{3} \times$ Total surface area of right circular cylinder

$= \dfrac{2}{3} \times 231 = 2 \times 77 = 154$ cm^2

$\therefore$ Total surface area of right circular cylinder
$=$ Curved surface area of right circular cylinder
$\qquad\qquad\qquad\qquad + $ Area of two circular bases

$\Rightarrow 231 = 154 + 2\pi r^2 \Rightarrow 2\pi r^2 = 77$

$\Rightarrow \qquad\qquad r^2 = \dfrac{77 \times 7}{2 \times 22} = \dfrac{7 \times 7}{2 \times 2} = \left(\dfrac{7}{2}\right)^2$

$\Rightarrow \qquad\qquad r = \dfrac{7}{2} = 3.5 \quad$ [on taking positive square root]

59. Given, radius of the sphere $= r$

$\therefore$ Radius of the cylinder = Radius of the sphere $= r$

and height of the cylinder = diameter $= 2r$

(i) Surface area of the sphere $(A_1) = 4\pi r^2$

(ii) Curved surface area of the cylinder $(A_2) = 2\pi r h$

$\Rightarrow \quad A_2 = 2\pi \times r \times 2r \Rightarrow A_2 = 4\pi r^2$

(iii) Required ratio, $A_1 : A_2 = 4\pi r^2 : 4\pi r^2 = 1 : 1$

60. Let r and h be the radius and height of cylinder respectively,

Curved surface area of the cylinder

$= \dfrac{2}{3} \times$ Total surface area of the cylinder

$= \dfrac{2}{3} \times 231 = 154$ m^2

$\Rightarrow \dfrac{\text{Total surface area of the cylinder}}{\text{Curved surface area of the cylinder}} = \dfrac{231}{154}$

$\Rightarrow \qquad\qquad \dfrac{2\pi r h + 2\pi r^2}{2\pi r h} = \dfrac{3}{2}$

$\Rightarrow \qquad\qquad \dfrac{h + r}{h} = \dfrac{3}{2}$

$\Rightarrow \qquad\qquad 2h + 2r = 3h$

$\Rightarrow \qquad\qquad h = 2r \qquad$ ...(i)

$\because$ Curved surface area $= 2\pi r h = 154$

$\Rightarrow \qquad 2\pi r (2r) = 154 \qquad$ [from Eq. (i)]

Hence, required volume of the cylinder $= \pi r^2 h$

$= \dfrac{22}{7} \times \dfrac{7}{2} \times \dfrac{7}{2} \times 7$

$= \dfrac{539}{2} = 269\dfrac{1}{2}$ m^3

61. Dimensions of bigger box are

$l = 25$ cm, $b = 20$ cm and $h = 5$ cm

$\therefore$ Total surface area of the bigger box

$= 2\,(lb + bh + hl)$

$= 2(25 \times 20 + 20 \times 5 + 5 \times 25)$

$= 2(500 + 100 + 125) = 2(725) = 1450$ cm^2

Dimensions of smaller box are

$l = 15$ cm, $b = 12$ cm and $h = 5$ cm

$\therefore$ Total surface area of the smaller box

$= 2(15 \times 12 + 12 \times 5 + 5 \times 15)$

$= 2(180 + 60 + 75) = 2(315) = 630$ cm^2

Total surface area of both boxes $= 1450 + 630 = 2080$ cm^2

Area for all the overlaps $= 5\%$ of total surface area

$= 5\% \times 2080$

$= \dfrac{5}{100} \times 2080 = 104$ cm^2

Total surface area of both boxes with area of overlaps

$= 2080 + 104 = 2184$ cm^2

$\therefore$ Total surface area for such 250 boxes $= (2184 \times 250)$ cm^2

Now, cost of the cardboard for $1000 \text{ cm}^2 = ₹ 4$

Then, cost of the cardboard for $1 \text{ cm}^2 = ₹ \dfrac{4}{1000}$

$\therefore$ Cost of the cardboard for $2184 \times 250 \text{ cm}^2$

$$= \dfrac{4 \times 2184 \times 250}{1000} = ₹ 2184$$

Hence, required cost of cardboard is $₹ 2184$.

62. Given, height of the cylinder $= 2\text{m} = 200 \text{ cm}$ $[\because 1\text{m} = 100 \text{ cm}]$

The total cost of painting $= ₹ 660$

Rate of painting the outer curved surface area of the cylinder
$$= ₹ 1.50 \text{ per cm}^2$$

Total cost of painting $=$ Curved surface area of the cylinder
$$\times \text{ Rate of painting the curved surface area}$$

$\Rightarrow \qquad 660 = \text{Curved surface area} \times 1.50$

$\Rightarrow \text{Curved surface area} = \dfrac{660}{1.50} \Rightarrow 2\pi r h = 440$

$$[\because \text{ curved surface area of cylinder} = 2\pi r h]$$

$\Rightarrow 2 \times \dfrac{22}{7} \times r \times 200 = 440$

$\Rightarrow \qquad r = \dfrac{440 \times 7}{2 \times 22 \times 200}$

$\Rightarrow \qquad r = \dfrac{35}{100} \text{ cm}$

$\therefore$ Curved surface of the base of cylinder
$$= \text{Circumference of the base of cylinder} = 2\pi r$$
$$= 2 \times \dfrac{22}{7} \times \dfrac{35}{100} = 2.2 \text{ cm}$$

63. Given, diameter of the base $= 20 \text{ cm}$

$\therefore$ Radius $(r) = \dfrac{20}{2} = 10 \text{ cm}$ and height $(h) = 30 \text{ cm}$

Since, a margin of 2.5 cm is used for folding it over the top and bottom.

So, the total height of frame
$$(h_1) = 30 + 2.5 + 2.5 = 35 \text{ cm}$$

$\therefore$ Cloth required for covering the lampshade
$$= \text{Curved surface area of lampshade} = 2\pi r \,(h_1)$$
$$= 2 \times \dfrac{22}{7} \times 10 \times (35)$$
$$= \dfrac{440}{7} \times 35 = 440 \times 5 = 2200 \text{ cm}^2$$

64. Cardboard required by each competitor
$$= \text{Base area} + \text{Curved surface area of one penholder}$$
$$= \pi r^2 + 2\pi r h \qquad [\because h = 10.5 \text{ cm and } r = 3\text{cm, given}]$$
$$= \dfrac{22}{7} \times (3)^2 + 2 \times \dfrac{22}{7} \times 3 \times 10.5$$
$$= \dfrac{198}{7} + 198 = 198 \left(\dfrac{1}{7} + 1 \right) = \left(198 \times \dfrac{8}{7} \right) \text{ cm}^2$$

For 35 competitors, required cardboard
$$= 35 \times 198 \times \dfrac{8}{7} = 7920 \text{ cm}^2$$

Hence, 7920 cm^2 of cardboard was required to be bought for the competition.

65. Given, diameter of the graphite cylinder
$$= 1 \text{ mm} = \dfrac{1}{10} \text{ cm} \qquad \left[\because 1 \text{ mm} = \dfrac{1}{10} \text{ cm} \right]$$

$\therefore \qquad$ Radius $(r) = \dfrac{1}{20} \text{ cm}$ $\qquad \left[\because \text{ radius} = \dfrac{\text{diameter}}{2} \right]$

and length of the graphite $(h) = 14 \text{ cm}$

$\therefore$ Volume of the graphite cylinder $= \pi r^2 h$
$$= \left(\dfrac{22}{7} \times \dfrac{1}{20} \times \dfrac{1}{20} \times 14 \right) = 0.11 \text{ cm}^3$$

Also, diameter of the pencil $= 7 \text{ mm} = \dfrac{7}{10} \text{ cm}$

$\therefore \qquad$ Radius of the pencil $(r_1) = \dfrac{7}{20} \text{ cm}$

and length of the pencil $(h_1) = 14 \text{ cm}$

$\therefore$ Volume of the pencil
$$= \pi r_1^2 h_1 = \dfrac{22}{7} \times \dfrac{7}{20} \times \dfrac{7}{20} \times 14$$
$$= 5.39 \text{ cm}^3$$

Now, volume of wood $=$ Volume of the pencil
$$- \text{ Volume of the graphite}$$
$$= 5.39 - 0.11$$
$$= 5.28 \text{ cm}^3$$

66. We have, length $(l) = 85 \text{ cm}$, depth $(b) = 25 \text{ cm}$ and height $(h) = 110 \text{ cm}$.

$\therefore$ Area to be polished $=$ Area of four walls $+$ Area of back
$$+ \text{ Area of front beading}$$
$$= [\,2\,(110 + 85) \times 25 + 110 \times 85 + 110 \times 5 \times 2 + (75 \times 5) \times 4$$
$$= 9750 + 9350 + 1100 + 1500 = 21700 \text{ cm}^2$$

Now, cost of polishing per $\text{cm}^2 = 20 \text{ paise} = ₹ \dfrac{20}{100}$

Cost of polishing $21700 \text{ cm}^2 = \left(21700 \times \dfrac{20}{100} \right) = ₹ 4340$

Internal surface area $=$ Total surface area of 3 cuboids each of dimensions 75 cm $\times$ 30 cm $\times$ 20 cm $-$ Area of front face of 3 cuboids of dimensions 75 cm $\times$ 30 cm $\times$ 20 cm
$$= 3 \,\{2 \,(75 \times 30 + 30 \times 20 + 75 \times 20)\} - 3 \times (75 \times 30)$$
$$= 6 \,(2250 + 600 + 1500) - 6750$$
$$= 26100 - 6750 = 19350 \text{ cm}^2$$

Now, cost of painting per $\text{cm}^2 = 10 \text{ paise} = ₹ \dfrac{10}{100}$

Cost of painting $19350 \text{ cm}^2 = 19350 \times \dfrac{10}{100} = ₹ 1935$

Hence, total expenses $= 4340 + 1935 = ₹ 6275$

67. Given, radius of a circular plate, $r = 14 \text{ cm}$

Thickness of a circular plate $= 3 \text{ cm}$

Thickness of 30 circular plates $= 30 \times 3 = 90 \text{ cm}$

Since, 30 circular plates are placed one above the another to form a cylindrical solid. Then,

Height of the cylindrical solid, $h =$ Thickness of 30 circular plates $= 90 \text{ cm}$

(i) Total surface area of the cylindrical solid, so formed

$$= 2\pi r(h + r) = 2 \times \frac{22}{7} \times 14(90 + 14)$$

$$= 44 \times 2 \times 104 = 9152 \text{ cm}^2$$

Hence, the total surface area of the cylindrical solid is 9152 cm^2.

(ii) Volume of the cylinder, so formed $= \pi r^2 h$

$$= \frac{22}{7}(14)^2 \times 90 = \frac{22}{7} \times 14 \times 14 \times 90$$

$$= 22 \times 28 \times 90 = 55440 \text{ cm}^3$$

Hence, the volume of the cylinder, so formed is 55440 cm^3.

68. Let R cm and r cm be the external and internal radii of the metallic pipe, respectively.

Height/length of the pipe $(h) = 14$ cm

According to the question,

Outside surface area $-$ Inside surface area $= 44$ cm^2

$$2\pi R h - 2\pi r h = 44$$

$$\Rightarrow \quad 2 \times \frac{22}{7}(R - r) \times 14 = 44 \Rightarrow R - r = \frac{1}{2} \qquad \ldots(i)$$

Volume of the metal used for making the pipe $= 88$ cm^3

$$\pi R^2 h - \pi r^2 h = 88$$

$$\Rightarrow \frac{22}{7} \times (R + r)(R - r) \times 14 = 88$$

$$\Rightarrow \quad R + r = \frac{88}{22} \Rightarrow R + r = 4 \qquad \ldots(ii)$$

On adding Eqs. (i) and (ii), we get

$$R - r + R + r = \frac{1}{2} + 4 = 0.5 + 4 = 4.5$$

$$\Rightarrow \quad 2R = 4.5 \Rightarrow R = \frac{4.5}{20} = 2.25 \text{ cm}$$

On putting $R = 2.25$ cm in Eq. (ii), we get

$$r = 4 - 2.25 = 1.75 \text{ cm}$$

Hence, outer and inner radii of the pipe are 2.25 cm and 1.75 cm, respectively.

69. Given, radius of large cylindrical vessel $(r) = 15$ cm

and height of orange juice in large vessel $(h) = 32$ cm

$\therefore$ Volume of juice in the large vessel

$$= \pi r^2 h = \pi (15)^2 \, 32 = (\pi \times 15 \times 15 \times 32) \text{ cm}^3$$

For small cylindrical glasses, radius $(r_1) = 3$ cm

and height of juice $(h_1) = 8$ cm

$\therefore$ Volume of juice in each glass

$$= \pi r_1^2 h_1 = \pi (3)^2 \times 8 = (\pi \times 3 \times 3 \times 8) \text{ cm}^3$$

Since, small cylindrical glasses are filled with juice from large vessel.

So, volume of juice in vessel $=$ Number of glasses

$$\times \text{ Volume of juice in each glass}$$

$$\therefore \text{ Number of glasses of juice} = \frac{\text{Volume of juice in vessel}}{\text{Volume of juice in each glass}}$$

$$= \frac{\pi \times 15 \times 15 \times 32}{\pi \times 3 \times 3 \times 8} = 100$$

Now, cost of one glass juice $= ₹ 3$

$\therefore$ Cost of 100 glass juice $= 100 \times 3 = ₹ 300$

Hence, the stall keeper receive $₹ 300$ by selling the juice completely.

70. Given, radius of the broadest end $(r) = 2.1$ cm

and length $(h) = 20$ cm.

Let l be the slant height of the conical corn cob.

Then, $\quad l = \sqrt{r^2 + h^2} = \sqrt{(2.1)^2 + (20)^2}$

$$= \sqrt{4.41 + 400} = \sqrt{404.41} = 20.11 \text{ cm}$$

$\therefore$ Curved surface area of the corn cob $= \pi r l$

$$= \frac{22}{7} \times 2.1 \times 20.11$$

$$= 132.726 = 132.73 \text{ cm}^2$$

Since, the grains of corn are found on the curved surface of the corn cob.

So, total number of grains on the corn cob

$$= \text{ Curved surface area of the corn cob}$$

$$\times \text{ Number of grains of corn on 1 cm}^2$$

$$= 132.73 \times 4 = 530.92$$

So, there would be approximately 531 grains of corn on the cob.

71. (i) Given, radius of the base of a conical tent $= 5$ m

and area needs to sit a student on the ground $= \dfrac{5}{7}$ m^2

$\therefore$ Area of the base of a conical tent $= \pi r^2$

$$= \left(\frac{22}{7} \times 5 \times 5 \right) \text{ m}^2$$

Now, number of students

$$= \frac{\text{Area of the base of a conical tent}}{\text{Area needs to sit a student on the ground}}$$

$$= \frac{\dfrac{22 \times 5 \times 5}{7}}{5/7}$$

$$= \frac{22}{7} \times 5 \times 5 \times \frac{7}{5} = 110$$

Hence, 110 students can sit in the conical tent.

(ii) Given, area of the cloth to form a conical tent $= 165$ m^2

Radius of the base of a conical tent, $r = 5$ m

Curved surface area of a conical tent $=$ Area of cloth to form a conical tent

$$\Rightarrow \quad \pi r l = 165$$

$$\Rightarrow \quad \frac{22}{7} \times 5 \times l = 165$$

$$\therefore \quad l = \frac{165 \times 7}{22 \times 5} = \frac{33 \times 7}{22} = 10.5 \text{ m}$$

Now, height of a conical tent $= \sqrt{l^2 - r^2}$

$$= \sqrt{(10.5)^2 - (5)^2}$$

$$= \sqrt{110.25 - 25}$$

$$= \sqrt{85.25} = 9.23 \text{ m}$$

Volume of a cone (conical tent) $= \dfrac{1}{3}\pi r^2 h$

$$= \dfrac{1}{3} \times \dfrac{22}{7} \times 5 \times 5 \times 9.23$$

$$= \dfrac{1}{3} \times \dfrac{550 \times 9.23}{7} = \dfrac{5076.5}{7 \times 3} = 241.7 \text{ m}^3$$

Hence, the volume of the cone (conical tent) is 241.7 m^3.

72. (i) The slant height of the cone = Radius of the given sector of a circle $= 9$ cm

(ii) Let radius of base of cone be r.

$\because$ Circumference of base of the cone = Length of arc of given sector, whose central angle is $120°$.

$$\Rightarrow \quad 2\pi r = \dfrac{\theta}{360°} \times 2\pi r_1 \qquad [\because r_1 \text{ is radius of sector}]$$

$$\Rightarrow \quad 2\pi r = \dfrac{120°}{360°} \times 2\pi \times 9 = 6\pi$$

$$\Rightarrow \quad r = 3$$

$\therefore$ Radius of base of the cone is 3 cm.

(iii) Let h be the height of the cone, then $h = \sqrt{l^2 - r^2}$

$$[\text{where } l = \text{slant height}, r = \text{radius of cone}]$$

$$= \sqrt{(9)^2 - (3)^2} = \sqrt{81 - 9} = \sqrt{72} = 6\sqrt{2} \text{ cm}$$

$\therefore$ Volume of the cone $= \dfrac{1}{3}\pi r^2 h$

$$= \dfrac{1}{3}\pi (3)^2 \times 6\sqrt{2} = 18\pi\sqrt{2} \text{ cm}^3$$

(iv) Total surface area of the cone

= Area of the given sector + Area of base of the cone

$$= \dfrac{\theta}{360°} \times \pi(r_1)^2 + \pi r^2$$

$$= \dfrac{120°}{360°} \times \pi(9)^2 + \pi(3)^2$$

$$= 27\pi + 9\pi = 36\pi \text{ cm}^2$$

73. Let the length of wire be h cm.

Given, diameter of sphere $= 18$ cm

$\therefore$ Radius of sphere, $r_1 = \dfrac{18}{2} = 9$ cm $\qquad \left[\because \text{radius} = \dfrac{\text{diameter}}{2}\right]$

and diameter of wire $= 4$ mm

$\therefore$ Radius of wire, $r_2 = \dfrac{4}{2}$ mm $= 2$ mm

$$= \dfrac{2}{10} \text{ cm} \qquad \left[\because 1 \text{ mm} = \dfrac{1}{10} \text{ cm}\right]$$

Volume of sphere = Volume of wire $\qquad$ [by given condition]

$$\Rightarrow \left(\dfrac{4}{3} \times \pi \times 9 \times 9 \times 9\right) = \left(\pi \times \dfrac{2}{10} \times \dfrac{2}{10} \times h\right)$$

$$\Rightarrow \qquad \dfrac{h}{25} = 972$$

$$\left[\because \text{volume of sphere} = \dfrac{4}{3}\pi r_1^3 \text{ and volume of wire} = \pi r_2^2 h\right]$$

$\therefore \qquad h = 972 \times 25$ cm

$$= \dfrac{972 \times 25}{100} \qquad \left[\because 1\text{cm} = \dfrac{1}{100}\text{m}\right]$$

$$= 243 \text{ m}$$

Hence, the length of the wire is 243 m.

74. Let r be the radius of base of the hemispherical dome.

Since, circumference of base of the hemispherical dome

= Circumference of a circle $= 17.6$ m

$$\therefore \qquad 2\pi r = 17.6$$

$$\Rightarrow \qquad r = 2.8 \text{ m}$$

Now, curved surface area of the hemispherical dome

= Curved surface area of a hemisphere $= 2\pi r^2$

$$= 2 \times \dfrac{22}{7} \times (2.8)^2 = 49.28 \text{ m}^2$$

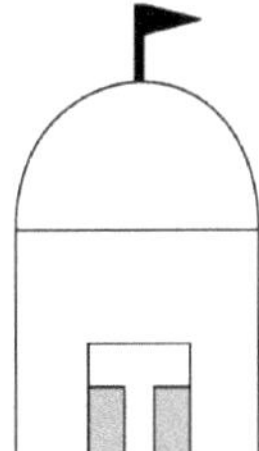

Given, cost of painting is at the rate $100 \text{ cm}^2 = ₹ 5$

$\Rightarrow$ Cost of painting $\dfrac{100}{100 \times 100} \text{ m}^2 = ₹ 5$

$\Rightarrow$ Cost of painting 1 m^2 of dome $= 5 \times 100 = ₹ 500$

$\therefore$ Total cost of painting entire hemispherical dome

$$= 500 \times 49.28 = ₹ 24640$$

75. Given,

Diameter of roller $= 42$ cm $= 0.42$ m

$\therefore$ Radius of roller $= 21$ cm $= 0.21$ m

Length of roller $= 78$ cm $= 0.78$ m

(i) Area covered in one revolution $= 2\pi r h$

$$= 2 \times \dfrac{22}{7} \times 0.21 \times 0.78 = 1.028 \text{ m}^2$$

(ii) We have,

Area of one revolution $= 5.168 \text{ m}^2$

and 300 complete revolutions to move once over to level a play ground.

Area of playground $= 300 \times 5.168$

Area of playground $= 1550.4 \text{ m}^2$

(iii) We have, area of playground $= 3600 \text{ m}^2$

Total number of revolution $= 300$

Area of one revolution $= \dfrac{\text{Area of playground}}{\text{Total number of revolution}}$

Area of one revolution $= \dfrac{3600}{300} = 12 \text{ m}^2$

Chapter Test

Multiple Choice Questions

1. The length, breadth and height of a cuboid are 8 m, 6 m and 4 m, respectively. Then, the total surface area is
(a) 256 m^2
(b) 208 m^2
(c) 198 m^2
(d) None of the above

2. A cylindrical storage tank of height 4 m and base diameter 8 m. Then, the capacity of cylinder is
(a) 201.14 m^3
(b) 183.75 m^3
(c) 219.18 m^3
(d) 311.75 m^3

3. If the volume of a right circular cone of height 9 cm is $48\pi \text{ cm}^3$, then the diameter of its base is
(a) 10 cm
(b) 16 cm
(c) 12 cm
(d) 8 cm

Case Based Questions

4. A boy has a toy, which has shape as shown below.

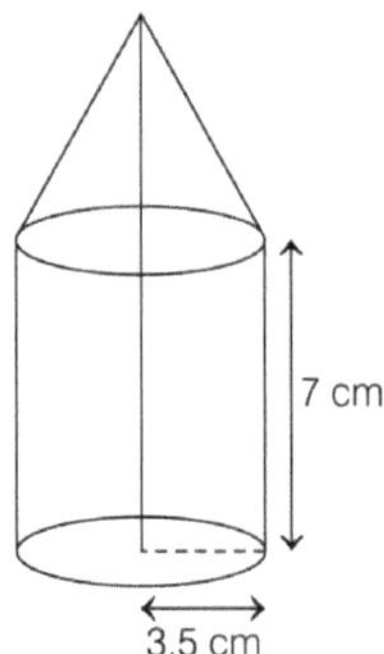

The height of the conical part is equal to radius of base of toy.

On the basis of above information, answer the following questions.

(i) Entire height of the toy is
(a) 3.5 cm   (b) 7 cm
(c) 10.5 cm   (d) 14 cm

(ii) Surface area of cylindrical part is (in cm^2)
(a) 172.5   (b) 192.5
(c) 170.5   (d) 190.5

(iii) Surface area of conical part is (in cm^2)
(a) 54.45
(b) 66.60
(c) 76.60
(d) 86.60

(iv) Total surface area of toy is (in cm^2)
(a) 246.95
(b) 249.1
(c) 239.1
(d) 229.1

(v) If the cost of painting the toy is ₹ $40/\text{cm}^2$, then total cost of painting the toy is (in ₹)
(a) 10344   (b) 9552
(c) 9878   (d) 10374

Short Answer Type Questions

5. The areas of three adjacent faces of a cuboid are x, y and z. If its volume is V, then find its volume.

6. A conical pit of top diameter 3.5 m is 12 m deep. What is its capacity (in litre)?

7. A right-angled $\triangle ABC$ with sides 5 cm, 12 cm and 13 cm is revolved about the side 12 cm. Find the volume of the solid so obtained.
[NCERT Exemplar]

Long Answer Type Questions

8. The length, breadth and height of a room are 5 m, 4 m and 3 m, respectively. Find the cost of white wasing the walls of the room and the ceiling at the rate of ₹ 7.50 per m^2.
[NCERT Exemplar]

9. A heap of wheat is in the form of a cone, whose diameter is 10.5 m and height is 3 m. Find its volume. The heap is to be covered by canvas to protect it from rain. Find the area of the canvas required.

10. A cuboidal oil tin is 30 cm × 40 cm × 50 cm. Find the cost of the tin required for making 20 such tins, if the cost of tin sheet is ₹ 20 per m^2.

11. The diameter of the Moon is approximately one-fourth of the diameter of the Earth. What fraction of the volume of the Earth is the volume of the Moon? **[NCERT Exemplar]**

Answers

1. (b)   **2.** (a)   **3.** (d)

4. (i) (c) (ii) (b) (iii) (a) (iv) (a) (v) (c)

5. $\sqrt{xyz}$ **6.** 38.5 kL   **7.** $100\pi \text{ cm}^3$

8. ₹555   **9.** 99.825 m^2

10. ₹376   **11.** $\dfrac{1}{64} V_1$

For Detailed Solutions

Scan the code

CHAPTER 06

Probability

In this Chapter...

- Experiment or Trial
- Event
- Probability – An Experimental Approach

Probability is the study of the chances of events happening. For understanding the concept of probability we have to know the some basic terms related to it.

Experiment or Trial

An operation which can produce some well-defined outcomes, is called an experiment or trial.

e.g. If a coin is tossed 20 times, then each toss is called an experiment or a trial and we get either head or tail as a result. Here, head and tail are called **outcomes**.

The experiment can be divided into two types, which are given below

1. **Random Experiment** An experiment, when repeated under identical conditions, do not produce the same outcomes every time but the outcomes produced is one out of the several possible outcomes, is known as a random or probabilistic experiment.

   e.g. Tossing a fair coin is a random experiment, because if we toss a coin, then either a head or tail will come up but if we toss a coin again and again, then the outcome each time will not be same but it will sure be either head or tail.

2. **Deterministic Experiment** An experiment, when repeated under identical conditions, produce the same result or outcomes, is known as deterministic experiment.

   e.g. Tossing an **unfair** coin having either tail or head on both sides 20 times, we get the same result.

Event

A possible outcome or combination of outcomes is called an event. e.g. Getting head in the toss of a coin is an event.

Occurrence of an Event

An event E associated to a random experiment is said to be occur (or happen) in a trial, if the outcome of trial is one of the outcomes that favours E.

e.g. If a die is rolled and the outcome of a trial is 4, then we say that each of the following events has happened (or occurred)

   (i) getting an even number.

  (ii) getting a number greater than 2.

 (iii) getting a number less than 5.

Elementary Event

An event having only one outcome of the random experiment is called an elementary event.

e.g. In tossing of a coin, the possible outcomes are Head (H) and Tail (T).

Therefore, if we define

    $E_1 = $ Getting head (H) on the upper face of the coin and

$E_2 = $ Getting tail (T) on the upper face of the coin.

Then, E_1 and E_2 are elementary events associated with the random experiment of tossing of a coin.

Compound Event

A collection of two or more elementary events associated with a random experiment is called a compound event.

e.g. In the random experiment of tossing of two coins simultaneously, if we define the event getting exactly one head, then it is a collection of elementary events (or outcomes) HT and TH. So, it is a compound event.

Probability— An Experimental Approach

If E is an event that happen when an experiment is performed, then the **experimental** or **empirical probability** of an event E is given by

$$P(E) = \frac{\text{Number of trials in which the event } E \text{ has happened}}{\text{Total number of trials}}$$

$$\text{or } P(E) = \frac{\text{Number of times in which the event } E \text{ has occurred}}{\text{Number of times the experiment has performed}}$$

Important Points Related to Probability

1. The probability of happening of an event always lies from 0 to 1, i.e. $0 \le P(E) \le 1$. In percentage, it lies from 0% to 100%.

2. If probability of an event say A is 1, i.e. $P(A) = 1$, then event A is called a **certain event** or **sure event.**

3. If probability of an event say B is 0, i.e. $P(B) = 0$, then event B is called an **impossible event.**

4. The sum of all the probabilities of all possible outcomes of an experiment is 1.

5. $P(E) + P(\text{not } E) = 1$ or $P(E) = 1 - P(\text{not } E)$

   or $P(\text{not } E) = 1 - P(E)$

6. Experimental probability of an event can never be negative.

Solved Examples

Example 1. Two coins are tossed 1000 times and the outcomes are recorded as below

Number of heads	2	1	0
Frequency	200	550	250

Based on this information, find the probability for atmost one head.   [**NCERT Exemplar**]

Sol. Given that, total number of trials = 1000

The number of trials in which atmost one head obtained
$$= 550 + 250 = 800$$
∴ The probability for atmost one head $= \dfrac{800}{1000} = \dfrac{4}{5}$

Example 2. Three coins are tossed simultaneously 150 times and it is found that 3 tails appeared 24 times, 2 tails appeared 45 times, 1 tail appeared 72 times and no tail appeared 9 times. If three coins are tossed simultaneously at random. Find the probability of getting

(i) 3 tails.   (ii) 2 tails.

(iii) 1 tail.   (iv) 0 tail.

Sol. (i) Number of trials in which 3 tails appeared = 24
$$\therefore \qquad P(A) = \dfrac{24}{150} = 0.16$$

(ii) Number of trials in which 2 tails appeared = 45
$$\therefore \qquad P(B) = \dfrac{45}{150} = 0.30$$

(iii) Number of trials in which 1 tail appeared = 72
$$\therefore \qquad P(C) = \dfrac{72}{150} = 0.48$$

(iv) Number of trials in which no tail appeared = 9
$$\therefore \qquad P(D) = \dfrac{9}{150} = 0.06$$

Example 3. Three coins are tossed simultaneously 150 times with the following frequencies of different outcomes.

Number of tails	0	1	2	3
Frequency	25	30	32	63

Compute the probability of getting

(i) atleast 2 tails.   (ii) exactly 1 tail.

Sol. As we can clearly see the table, total frequency = 150

(i) Number of atleast 2 tails = 32 + 63 = 95
$$\text{Probability of getting atleast 2 tails} = \dfrac{95}{150} = \dfrac{19}{30}$$

(ii) Probability of getting exactly 1 tail $= \dfrac{30}{150} = \dfrac{1}{5}$

Example 4. Three coins are tossed simultaneously 400 times and following frequencies of the outcomes were recorded

Outcomes	Frequencies
3 heads	103
2 heads	124
1 head	98
No head	x

(i) Find the probability of getting no head.

(ii) Find the probability of getting 1 head.

(iii) Find the probability of getting exactly 2 heads.

Sol. Given, total number of outcomes = 400

Now, outcomes for getting no head.
$$= 400 - (103 + 124 + 98) = 75$$

(i) Probability of getting no head $= \dfrac{75}{400} = \dfrac{3}{16}$

(ii) Probability of getting 1 head $= \dfrac{98}{400} = \dfrac{49}{200}$

(iii) Probability of getting exactly 2 heads $= \dfrac{124}{400} = \dfrac{31}{100}$

Example 5. A die is thrown 50 times and it shows the number 1, 23 times. Find the probability of getting a number other than 1 in the next throw of the die.

Sol. Probability of getting '1' $= \dfrac{23}{50}$

So, probability of getting a number other than 1
$$= 1 - \dfrac{23}{50} = \dfrac{50 - 23}{50} = \dfrac{27}{50}$$

Example 6. A die was rolled 200 times and the number of times 6 came up was noted. If the experimental probability calculated from this information is $\dfrac{2}{5}$, then how many times 6 came up?

Sol. Let, 6 appeared y times on die. We also know that probability of getting 6 is $\dfrac{2}{5}$.

Now, P (getting 6 on die) $= \dfrac{y}{200}$, which is same as $\dfrac{2}{5}$

So,
$$\Rightarrow \qquad \dfrac{y}{200} = \dfrac{2}{5}$$
$$\Rightarrow \qquad y = \dfrac{2}{5} \times 200 = 80$$

Hence, 6 appeared 80 times on die.

Example 7. In a survey of 364 children aged 19-36 months, it was found that 91 liked to eat potato chips. If a child is selected at random, then find the probability that he/she does not like to eat potato chips.

Sol. Total children = 364

Number of children like potato chips = 91

Number of children do not like potato chips = 364 − 91 = 273

$\therefore$ Required probability $= \dfrac{\text{Number of favourable outcomes}}{\text{Total number of outcome}}$

$= \dfrac{273}{364} = 0.75.$

Example 8. 12 packets of salt, each marked 2 kg, actually contained the following weights (in kg) of salt

1.950, 2.020, 2.060, 1.980, 2.030, 1.970,
2.040, 1.990, 1.985, 2.025, 2.000, 1.980

Out of these packets, one packet is chosen at random. What is the probability that the chosen packet contains more than 2 kg of salt?

Sol. Given that, total number of packets of salt = 12   [given]

Number of packets containing more than 2 kg of salt = 5

(i.e. 2.020, 2.060, 2.030, 2.040, 2.025)

Now, probability that the chosen packet contains more than 2 kg of salt.

$= \dfrac{\text{Number of packets containing more than 2 kg of salt.}}{\text{Total number of packets of salt}}$

$\therefore$ Required probability $= \dfrac{5}{12}$

Example 9. Teachers and students are selected at random to make two teams of 20 members each on sport day to participate in the event of 'Tug of War.' The numbers of volunteers are as follow

Teachers		Students	
Male	Female	Male	Female
12	18	20	10

Find the probability that the person chosen at random

(i) is a male teacher.   (ii) is a female student.

Sol. (i) Total number of volunteers = 12 + 18 + 20 + 10 = 60

Number of male teachers = 12

$\therefore$ Probability that the person is a male teacher

$= \dfrac{12}{60} = \dfrac{1}{5}$

(ii) Total number of volunteers = 12 + 18 + 20 + 10 = 60

Number of female students = 10

$\therefore$ Probability that the person is a female student

$= \dfrac{10}{60} = \dfrac{1}{6}$

Example 10. While working out a question on probability, it was found that there were 286 letters of English alphabet. The following was observation of occurrence of each letter

$a : 70, b : 14, e : 26, r : 40$ and $i : 36.$

Others (not including vowels) = 100

Then, find the probability of

(i) a vowel letters.

(ii) non-vowel letters.

Sol. Given, number of occurrence of letter $a = 70$

Number of occurrence of letter $b = 14$

Number of occurrence of letter $e = 26$

Number of occurrence of letter $r = 40$

Number of occurrence of letter $i = 36$

Number of occurrence of others = 100

Here, a, e and i are vowels.

(i) Number of occurrence of a, e and i

$= 70 + 26 + 36 = 132$

Total number of letters = 286

$\therefore$ P (getting a vowel) $= \dfrac{132}{286} = \dfrac{6}{13}$

(ii) Now, number of occurrence of non-vowel letters

$= 14 + 40 + 100 = 154$

$\therefore P$ (getting non-vowel letters) $= \dfrac{154}{286} = \dfrac{7}{13}$

Example 11. If the probability of winning a race of an athlete is $\dfrac{1}{6}$ less than twice the probability of losing the race, find the probability of winning the race.

Sol. Let probability of winning the race be P.

$\therefore$ Probability of losing the race $= 1 - P$

According to the statement of question, we have

$\Rightarrow$ $P\,(\text{Win}) = 2[1 - P\,(\text{Win})] - \dfrac{1}{6}$

$\Rightarrow$ $3P\,(\text{Win}) = \dfrac{11}{6}$

$\Rightarrow$ $P(\text{Win}) = \dfrac{11}{18}.$

Hence, probability of winning race is $\dfrac{11}{18}.$

Example 12. Probability of getting a blue ball is $\dfrac{2}{3}$, from a bag containing 6 blue and 3 red balls. 12 red balls are added in the bag, then find the probability of getting

(i) a blue ball.   (ii) a red ball.

Sol. Then, total number of balls in a bag = 6 + 3 = 9

After adding 12 red balls,

Total number of balls became = 9 + 12 = 21

Number of blue balls = 6

Number of red balls = 3 + 12 = 15

(i) $P(\text{getting a blue ball}) = \dfrac{\text{Number of blue balls}}{\text{Total number of balls}} = \dfrac{6}{21} = \dfrac{2}{7}$

(ii) $P(\text{getting a red ball}) = \dfrac{\text{Number of red balls}}{\text{Total number of balls}} = \dfrac{15}{21} = \dfrac{5}{7}$

Example 13. The maximum temperature in celsius of some cities on a day are given as below.

Maximum temp (in °C)	10-15	16-20	21-25	26-30	31-35	36-40
Number of cities	1	2	18	21	19	18

(i) Find the probability that maximum temperature lies between 16°C and 30°C.

(ii) Find the probability that minimum temperature is less than 25°C.

Sol. Total number of cities

$$= 1 + 2 + 18 + 21 + 19 + 18 = 79$$

Let E_1 and E_2 be the event, which show maximum temperature of cities.

(i) Number of cities whose maximum temperature lies between 16°C and 30°C $= 2 + 18 + 21 = 41$

∴ Probability that the temperature of cities lies between 16°C and 30°C $= \dfrac{41}{79}$

(ii) Number of cities whose maximum temperature is less than 25°C $= 1 + 2 + 18 = 21$

∴ Probability that the temperature of cities is less than 25°C $= \dfrac{21}{79}$

Example 14. The table shows the marks (out of 150) obtained by a student in unit tests.

Unit test	I	II	III	IV	V	VI
Marks (out of 150)	72	96	105	80	125	139

Find the probability that the student gets 80% or more in the next unit test. Also, find the probability that the student gets less than 80% marks.

Sol. The marks obtained by the student out of 150 marks $= 80\%$ of $150 = \dfrac{80}{100} \times 150 = 120$ marks

Total number of unit test in which the student get 80% or more marks $= 2$

Probability that the student gets 80% or more marks in the next unit test $= \dfrac{2}{6} = \dfrac{1}{3}$

Probability that the student gets less than 80% marks

$$= 1 - \dfrac{1}{3} = \dfrac{2}{3}$$

Example 15. The table shows the number of people visiting the 'Good-living pavilion' in a trade fair during different times of the day.

Time	Number of people
9 am - 11 am	175
11 am - 1 pm	125
1 pm - 3 pm	225
3 pm - 5 pm	200
5 pm - 7 pm	120

Find the probability that the randomly chosen person visited the pavilion

(i) after 1 pm but before 5 pm.

(ii) between 9 am to 1 pm.

(iii) after 5 pm.

(iv) between 3 pm and 5 pm.

Sol. Total number of people visited

$$= 175 + 125 + 225 + 200 + 120 = 845$$

(i) Number of people visited after 1 pm before 5 pm

$$= 225 + 200 = 425$$

Probability that the people visited after 1 pm before 5 pm $= \dfrac{425}{845} = 0.50$

(ii) Number of persons, who visited the pavilion between 9 am to 1 pm $= 175 + 125 = 400$

∴ Required probability $= \dfrac{400}{845} = 0.473$

(iii) Number of people visited after 5 pm $= 120$

∴ Required probability $= \dfrac{120}{845} = 0.142$

(iv) Number of people visited between 3 pm and 5 pm

$$= \dfrac{200}{845} = 0.236$$

Chapter Practice

Objective Questions

● Multiple Choice Questions

1. A coin is tossed 100 times and head appears 46 times. Now, if we toss a coin at random, then the probability of getting a tail is

(a) $\dfrac{23}{50}$ (b) $\dfrac{27}{50}$ (c) $\dfrac{28}{50}$ (d) $\dfrac{26}{50}$

2. Two coins are tossed 1000 times and the outcomes are recorded as below.

Number of heads	2	1	0
Frequency	200	550	350

Based on this information, the probability for atmost one head is

(a) $\dfrac{1}{5}$ (b) $\dfrac{1}{4}$ (c) $\dfrac{9}{10}$ (d) $\dfrac{3}{4}$

3. Three coins are tossed simultaneously 200 times with the following frequencies of different outcomes.

Outcome	3 heads	2 heads	1 head	No head
Frequency	23	72	77	28

If the three coins are simultaneously tossed again, then the probability of 2 heads coming up is

(a) $\dfrac{3}{25}$ (b) $\dfrac{6}{25}$ (c) $\dfrac{9}{25}$ (d) $\dfrac{8}{25}$

4. In 50 throws of a die, the outcomes were noted as under.

Outcome	1	2	3	4	5	6
Number of items	8	9	6	7	12	8

A die is thrown at random. What is the probability of getting an even number?

(a) $\dfrac{12}{25}$ (b) $\dfrac{3}{50}$

(c) $\dfrac{1}{8}$ (d) $\dfrac{1}{2}$

5. A die is thrown 250 times and the outcomes are noted as given below.

Outcomes	1	2	3	4	5	6
Frequency	65	40	42	25	33	45

If a die is thrown at random, then the probabilities of getting 1 and 5 are respectively

(a) 0.26 and 0.132 (b) 0.21 and 0.139
(c) 0.20 and 0.139 (d) 0.11 and 0.112

6. On one page of a telephone directory, there were 200 telephone number. The frequency distribution of their unit place digit (e.g. in the number 25828573 the unit's place digit is 3) is given in the following table.

Digit	0	1	2	3	4	5	6	7	8	9
Frequency	22	26	22	22	20	10	14	28	16	20

Without looking at the page, the pencil is placed on one of these numbers i.e. the number is chosen at random. What is the probability that the digit in its unit place is 6?

(a) 0.01 (b) 0.03 (c) 0.05 (d) 0.07

7. To know the opinion of the students about the subject statistics, a survey of 200 students was conducted. The data is recorded in the following table.

Opinion	Number of students
Like	135
Dislike	65

Find the probability that a student chosen at random

(i) likes statistics, (ii) does not like it.

(a) $\dfrac{27}{40}$ and $\dfrac{13}{40}$ (b) $\dfrac{17}{40}$ and $\dfrac{13}{40}$ (c) $\dfrac{22}{4}$ and $\dfrac{11}{5}$ (d) $\dfrac{7}{5}$ and $\dfrac{27}{40}$

8. On one page of a directory, there are 160 telephone numbers. The frequency distribution of the unit place digit is given as under.

Unit place digit	Frequency
0	19
1	16
2	18
3	21
4	14
5	11
6	15
7	16
8	13
9	17

From this page, one of the numbers is chosen at random. What is the probability that the unit place digit in the chosen number is 6?

(a) $\dfrac{2}{5}$ (b) $\dfrac{3}{32}$ (c) $\dfrac{3}{80}$ (d) $\dfrac{29}{32}$

9. In a cricket match, if a batsman hits a boundary 8 times out of 40 balls, he plays. Then, the probability that he didn't hit a boundary, is

(a) 0.2   (b) 0.4   (c) 0.6   (d) 0.8

10. 80 bulbs are selected at random from a lot and their life time (in hours) is recorded in the form of a frequency table given below.

Life time (in hours)	300	500	700	900	1100
Frequency	10	12	23	25	10

One bulb is selected at random from the lot. The probability that its life is 1150 h, is

(a) $\dfrac{1}{80}$ (b) $\dfrac{7}{16}$

(c) 0   (d) 1

11. Refer to Q. 10. The probability that bulbs selected randomly from the lot has life less than 900 h, is

(a) $\dfrac{11}{40}$ (b) $\dfrac{5}{16}$

(c) $\dfrac{7}{16}$ (d) $\dfrac{9}{16}$

12. A Mathematics book contains 250 pages. A page is selected at random. What is the probability that the number on the page selected is a perfect square?

(a) $\dfrac{4}{25}$ (b) $\dfrac{3}{50}$

(c) $\dfrac{7}{50}$ (d) $\dfrac{9}{50}$

13. The maximum temperature in celsius of some cities on a day are given as below.

Maximum temperature (in °C)	10-15	16-20	21-25	26-30	31-35	36-40
Number of cities	1	2	18	21	19	18

The probability that maximum temperature lies between 16°C and 30°C, is

(a) $\dfrac{41}{79}$ (b) $\dfrac{56}{81}$ (c) $\dfrac{21}{53}$ (d) $\dfrac{1}{10}$

14. In a survey of 364 children aged (19-36) months, it was found that 91 liked to eat potato chips. If a child is selected at random, the probability that he/she does not like to eat potato chips, is

(a) 0.25   (b) 0.50   (c) 0.75   (d) 0.80

15. In a sample study of 642 people, it was found that 514 people have a high school certificate. If a person is selected at random, the probability that the person has a high school certificate, is

(a) 0.5   (b) 0.6   (c) 0.7   (d) 0.8

16. In a medical examination of students of a class, the following blood groups are recorded.

Blood group	A	AB	B	O
Number of students	10	13	12	5

A student is selected at random from the class. The probability that he/she has blood group B, is

(a) $\dfrac{1}{4}$ (b) $\dfrac{13}{40}$ (c) $\dfrac{3}{10}$ (d) $\dfrac{1}{8}$

• Case Based MCQs

17. Anil went to shop to purchase a child's game along with parent. He selected one child's game, which has 9 circles of which 3 are blue and rest are red, and 10 squares of which 5 are blue and rest are red. While checking the game, one piece is lost at random.

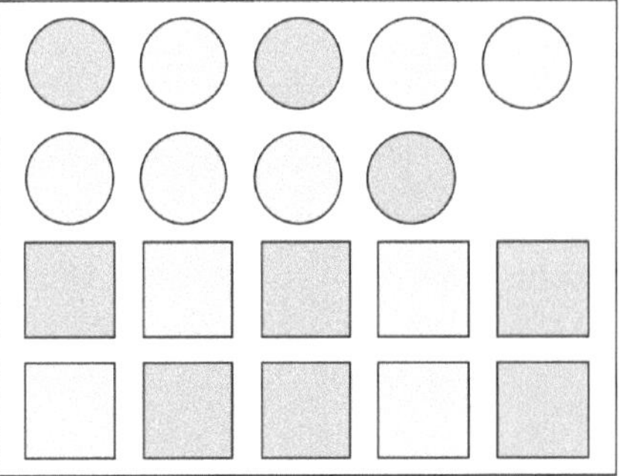

(i) How many circles are of red colour and how many squares are of red colour?
   (a) 5, 4   (b) 4, 5
   (c) 6, 5   (d) 8, 6

(ii) Find the probability that lost piece is square.
   (a) $\dfrac{4}{9}$ (b) $\dfrac{5}{9}$
   (c) $\dfrac{1}{3}$ (d) $\dfrac{10}{19}$

(iii) Find the probability that lost piece is circles.
   (a) $\dfrac{4}{19}$ (b) $\dfrac{5}{19}$
   (c) $\dfrac{9}{19}$ (d) $\dfrac{5}{18}$

(iv) Find the probability that lost piece is square of blue colour.
   (a) $\dfrac{4}{19}$ (b) $\dfrac{5}{19}$
   (c) $\dfrac{1}{3}$ (d) $\dfrac{5}{18}$

(v) Find the probability that lost piece is circles of red colour.
   (a) $\dfrac{6}{19}$ (b) $\dfrac{5}{19}$
   (c) $\dfrac{1}{13}$ (d) $\dfrac{5}{18}$

18. Rajni runs a handicraft shop in chandani chowk in Delhi. She makes beautiful necklaces using colourful beads, which she keeps in a potli. Today she prepared 18 necklaces, but could not make the 19th necklace, as she had no yellow beads left. She counted the beads and found that there were 8 red, 6 green and 14 blue beads remaining in her potli. Her little daughter Lily requested for a bead. Rajni decides to take out one bead from her potli for Lily.

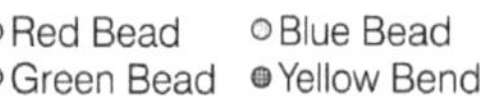

(i) Find the probability that she draws a green bead.
   (a) 3/11   (b) 3/7
   (c) 11/14   (d) 3/14

(ii) Find the probability that the bead drawn by her is not blue.
   (a) 3/11   (b) 3/7
   (c) $\dfrac{1}{2}$ (d) $\dfrac{2}{3}$

(iii) Find the probability that she draws either a green or a blue bead.
   (a) 5/7   (b) 5/12
   (c) 7/12   (d) 3/14

(iv) Find the probability that she draws neither a red nor a green bead.
   (a) 3/14   (b) 1/3
   (c) 3/7   (d) 1/2

(v) Which of the followings is an impossible event?
   (a) The bead drawn is not red
   (b) The bead drawn is neither red nor blue
   (c) The bead drawn is either red or green or blue
   (d) The bead drawn is yellow

19. One day, during games period four friends A, B, C and D planned to play game using number cards. They prepared 25 numbered cards with labelled 1 to 25 and then, they put all the number cards in the empty chalk box available in the classroom. In this game, every friend was asked to pick the card randomly and after each draw, card was replaced back in the chalk box.

1	2	3	4	5
6	7	8	9	10
11	12	13	14	15
16	17	18	19	20
21	22	23	24	25

(i) Find the probability, first boy pick the card and he get the card with an odd number.
   (a) $\dfrac{1}{4}$ (b) $\dfrac{10}{25}$ (c) $\dfrac{13}{25}$ (d) $\dfrac{12}{25}$

(ii) If the card drawn in first case is replaced and the second boy draws a card. What is the probability getting a composite number?
   (a) $\dfrac{3}{5}$ (b) $\dfrac{4}{5}$ (c) $\dfrac{7}{8}$ (d) $\dfrac{9}{11}$

(iii) If the card drawn is not replaced in the second draw, what is the probability that he goes a multiple of 3 greater than 4?
   (a) $\dfrac{1}{11}$ (b) $\dfrac{7}{20}$ (c) $\dfrac{6}{19}$ (d) $\dfrac{5}{19}$

(iv) For a sure event A, $P(A) = ?$
   (a) 1   (b) 0
   (c) −1   (d) 2

(v) If all cards drawn are replaced, then what is the probability of getting a multiple 3 and 5?
   (a) $\dfrac{1}{2}$ (b) $\dfrac{1}{5}$
   (c) $\dfrac{1}{20}$ (d) $\dfrac{1}{18}$

PART 2
Subjective Questions

• Short Answer Type Questions

1. Cards marked with the numbers 2 to 101 are placed in a box and mixed thoroughly. One card is drawn from this box. Find the probability that the number on the card is

   (i) an even number.   (ii) a number less than 14.

  (iii) a number, which is a perfect square.

2. The record of a weather station shows that out of the past 250 consecutive days, its weather forecast were correct 175 times.

   (i) What is the probability that on a given day, it was correct?

  (ii) What is the probability that it was not correct on a given day?

3. A company selected 4000 households at random and surveyed them, to find out a relationship between income level and the number of television sets in a home. The information, so obtained is listed in the following table.

Monthly income (in ₹)	Number of televisions/households			
	0	**1**	**2**	**Above 2**
< 10000	20	80	10	0
10000-14999	10	240	60	0
15000-19999	0	380	120	30
20000-24999	0	520	370	80
25000 and above	0	1100	760	220

Find the probability

   (i) of a household earning ₹ 10000-₹ 14999 per year and having exactly one television.

  (ii) of a household earning ₹ 25000 and more per year owning 2 televisions.

4. Activity Ask all the students in your class to write a 3-digit number. Choose any student from the room at random. What is the probability that the number written by her/him is divisible by 3? Remember that a number is divisible by 3, if the sum of its digit is divisible by 3.

5. In a particular section of class IX, 40 students were asked about the month of their birth and the following graph was prepared for the data so obtained.

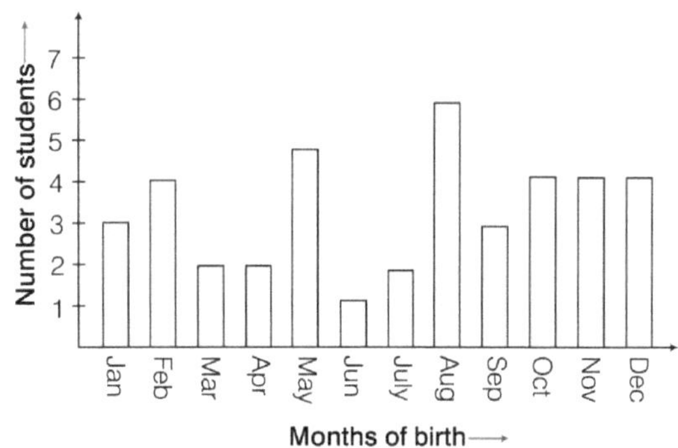

Find the probability that a student of the class was born in August.

6. A teacher wanted to analyse the performance of two sections of students in a mathematics test of 100 marks. Looking at their performances, she found that a few students got under 20 marks and a few got 70 marks or above. So, she decided to group them into intervals of varying sizes as follows,

0-20, 20-30, ..., 60-70, 70-100. Then, she formed the following table.

Marks	Number of students
0-20	7
20-30	10
30-40	10
40-50	20
50-60	20
60-70	15
70-above	8
Total	**90**

   (i) Find the probability that a student obtained less than 20% in the mathematics test.

  (ii) Find the probability that a student obtained marks 60 or above.

7. The probabilities of a student getting A, B, C and D grades are 0.35, 0.25, 0.35 and 0.05.

Then, find the probability that

   (i) a student gets atmost grade C.

  (ii) a student gets atleast grade C.

8. Bulbs are packed in cartons each containing 40 bulbs, seven hundred cartons were examined for defective bulbs and the results are given in the following table.

Number of defective bulbs	0	1	2	3	4	5	6	More than 6
Frequency	400	180	48	41	18	8	3	2

One carton was selected at random. What is the probability that it has

(i) no defective bulb?

(ii) defective bulbs from 2-6?

(iii) defective bulbs less than 4?

9. Activity Note the frequency of two-wheelers, three-wheelers and four-wheelers going past during a time interval, in front of your school gate. Find the probability that any one vehicle out of the total vehicles you have observed is a two-wheeler?

Types of Vehicles	Frequency
Two-Wheelers	550
Three-Wheelers	250
Four-Wheelers	80

10. On one page of a telephone directory, there were 200 telephone numbers. The frequency distribution of their unit place digit (e.g. in the number 25828573, the unit place digit is 3) is given in table.

Digit	0	1	2	3	4	5	6	7	8	9
Frequency	22	26	22	22	20	10	14	28	16	20

Without looking at the page, the pencil is placed on one of these numbers i.e. the number is chosen at random. What is the probability that the digit in its unit place is 6?

11. The distance (in km) of 40 engineers from their residence to their place of work were found as follows.

5	3	10	20	25	11	13	7	12	31
19	10	12	17	18	11	32	17	16	2
7	9	7	8	3	5	12	15	18	3
12	14	2	9	6	15	15	7	6	12

What is the empirical probability that an engineer lives

(i) less than 7 km from her place of work?

(ii) more than or equal to 7 km from her place of work?

(iii) within $\dfrac{1}{2}$ km from her place of work?

12. A recent survey found that the ages of workers in a factory as follows.

Age (in years)	20-29	30-39	40-49	50-59	60 and above
Number of workers	38	27	86	46	3

If a person is selected at random, find the probability that the person is

(i) 40 yr or more.

(ii) under 40 yr.

(iii) having age from 30-39 yr.

(iv) under 60 but over 39 yr.

13. A tyre manufacturing company kept a record of the distance covered before a tyre needed to be replaced. The table shows the results of 1000 cases.

Distance (in km)	Less than 4000	4000 to 9000	9001 to 14000	More than 14000
Frequency	20	210	325	445

If you buy a tyre of this company, what is the probability that

(i) it will need to be replaced before it has covered 4000 km?

(ii) it will last more than 9000 km?

(iii) it will need to be replaced after it has covered somewhere between 4000 km and 14000 km?

14. 80 bulbs are selected at random from a lot and their lifetime is recorded in the form of a frequency table given below.

Lifetime (in hours)	300	500	700	900	1100
Frequency	10	15	23	25	7

A bulb is chosen at random from the lot. What is the probability that the bulb chosen has lifetime less than 900 h?

15. If the difference between the probability of success and failure of an event is 5 / 19. Find the probability of success and failure of the event.

16. In a cricket match, a batswoman hits a boundary 6 times out of 30 balls she plays. Find the probability that she did not hit a boundary.

17. The distances (in km) of 40 students from their residences to the school are given below.

4, 19, 7, 13, 3, 10, 9, 14, 10, 12, 7, 2, 20, 13, 8, 9, 15, 19, 3, 5, 10, 10, 5, 15, 15, 11, 11, 15, 7, 16, 15, 7, 12, 16, 18, 6, 20, 2, 3, 2

Find the probability that a student selected at random

(i) lives at a distance atmost 15 km from their school.

(ii) lives within 1 km from their school.

• Long Answer Type Questions

18. Two coins are tossed simultaneously 300 times and it is found that two heads appeared 135 times, one head appeared 111 times and no head appeared 54 times. If two coins are tossed at random, what is the probability of getting

(i) 2 heads?

(ii) 1 head?

(iii) 0 head?

19. A die is thrown 250 times and the outcomes are noted as given below.

Outcomes	1	2	3	4	5	6
Frequency	65	40	42	25	33	45

If a die is thrown at random, then find the probability of getting

(i) 1   (ii) 2   (iii) 3

(iv) 4   (v) 5   (vi) 6

20. Two dice are thrown simultaneously 500 times. Each time the sum of two numbers appearing on their tops is noted and recorded, as given in the following table.

Sum	Frequency
2	14
3	30
4	42
5	55
6	72
7	75
8	70
9	53
10	46
11	28
12	15

If the dice are thrown once more, then what is the probability of getting a sum

(i) 3?

(ii) more than 10?

(iii) less than or equal to 5?

(iv) between 8 and 12?

21. The percentage of marks obtained by a student in the monthly unit tests are given below.

Unit test	I	II	III	IV	V
Percentage of marks obtained	58	74	76	62	85

Find the probability that the student gets

(i) a first class i.e. atleast 60% marks.

(ii) marks between 70% and 80%.

(iii) a distinction i.e. 75% or above.

(iv) less than 65% marks.

22. 1500 families with 2 children each were selected randomly and the following data were recorded.

Number of girls in a family	2	1	0
Number of families	475	814	211

Compute the probability of a family, chosen at random having

(i) 2 girls.   (ii) 1 girl.   (iii) no girl.

Also, check whether the sum of these probabilities is 1.

23. Over the past 200 working days, the number of defective parts produced by a machine is given in the following table.

Number of defective parts	Days
0	50
1	32
2	22
3	18
4	12
5	12
6	10
7	10
8	10
9	8
10	6
11	6
12	2
13	2

Determine the probability that tomorrow's output will have

(i) no defective part.

(ii) atleast one defective part.

(iii) not more than 5 defective parts.

(iv) more than 13 defective parts.

24. Given below is the frequency distribution of daily wages (in ₹) of 30 workers in a certain factory.

Daily wages (in ₹)	110-130	130-150	150-170	170-190	190-210	210-230	230-250
Number of workers	3	4	5	6	5	4	3

A worker is selected at random. Find the probability that his wages is

(i) less than ₹ 150.

(ii) atleast ₹ 210.

(iii) more than or equal to ₹ 150 but less than ₹ 210.

(iv) in the interval ₹ 190-₹ 250.

25. The percentage of marks obtained by a student in monthly unit test are given below.

Unit test	I	II	III	IV	V
Percentage of marks	70	72	65	68	85

Find the probability that the student gets

(i) more than 70% marks.

(ii) more than 90% marks.

26. A survey of 200 people was conducted about their preference of visiting various pavilion during trade fair.

Pavilion	Good living	Delhi pavilion	Toy pavilion	Defence pavilion
Number of people	95	45	40	20

Find the probability that a randomly selected person visited

(i) both good living and delhi pavilion.

(ii) only the defence pavilion.

(iii) only the toy pavilion.

(iv) both toy pavilion and defence pavilion.

27. Fifty seeds were selected at random from each of 5 bags of seeds and were kept under standardised conditions favourable to germination. After 20 days, the number of seeds which had germinated in each collection were counted and recorded as follows.

Bags	1	2	3	4	5
Number of seeds germinated	40	48	42	39	41

What is the probability of germination of

(i) more than 40 seeds in a bag?

(ii) 49 seeds in a bag?

(iii) more than 35 seeds in a bag?

28. A tyre manufacturing company kept a record of the distance covered before a tyre was replaced.

Distance (in km)	More than 1500	1100-1500	700-1100	300-700	Less than 300
Number of tyres	250	150	120	200	80

If you buy a tyre of this company, what is the probability that

(i) it will need a replacement before it has covered 700 km?

(ii) it will last more than 1100 km?

(iii) it will need to be replaced between 300 km to 1500 km?

(iv) it will need to be replaced after 1500 km?

• Case Based Questions

29. Insurance is a means of protection from financial loss. It is a form of risk management, primarily used to hedge against the risk of a contingent on uncertain loss. For insurance awareness, an insurance company selected 2000 drivers at random in a particular city, find a relationship between age and accidents. The data obtained is given in the following table.

Age of drivers (in year)	Accidents in one year				
	0	1	2	3	over 3
18-29	440	160	110	61	35
30-50	505	125	60	22	18
Above 50	306	45	35	15	9

Answer the following questions.

(i) Find the probability of the following events for a driver chosen at random from the city being (18-29) yr of age and having exactly 3 accidents in one year.

(ii) Find the probability of the following events for a driver chosen at random from the city being (30-50) yr of age and having one or more accidents in one year.

(iii) Find the probability of the following events for a driver chosen at random from the city having no accidents in one year.

SOLUTIONS

Objective Questions

1. (b) Given, a coin is tossed 100 times, therefore total number of trials = 100

Also, head appears 46 times.

Now, tail appears $100 - 46 = 54$ times

$\therefore P(\text{getting a tail}) = \dfrac{54}{100} = \dfrac{27}{50}$

2. (c) The total number of coins tossed, $n(S) = 1000$

Number of outcomes in which atmost one head,
$n(E) = 550 + 350 = 900$

$\therefore$ Probability for atmost one head $= \dfrac{n(E)}{n(S)} = \dfrac{900}{1000} = \dfrac{9}{10}$

Hence, the probability for atmost one head is $\dfrac{9}{10}$.

3. (c) In tossing of three coins, getting two heads comes out 72 times i.e. $n(E) = 72$

The total number of tossed three coins $n(S) = 200$

$\therefore$ Probability of 2 heads coming up $= \dfrac{n(E)}{n(S)} = \dfrac{72}{200} = \dfrac{9}{25}$

4. (a) Given,

Total number of thrown a die $= 50$

Number of trials getting an even number $= 9 + 7 + 8 = 24$

$\therefore$ Required probability

$= \dfrac{\text{Number of trials}}{\text{Total number of throws}}$

$= \dfrac{24}{50} = \dfrac{12}{25}$

5. (a) Here, a die is thrown 250 times.

So, total number of trials $= 250$

In a random throw of a die, let E_1 and E_2 be the events of getting 1 and 5, respectively.

Here, frequency of outcomes 1 is 65, i.e. 1 occurs on a die 65 times.

$\therefore \quad P(\text{getting } 1) = P(E_1) = \dfrac{\text{Number of times 1 occur}}{\text{Total number of trials}}$

$= \dfrac{65}{250} = 0.26$

and here 5 occurs on a die 33 times.

$\therefore P(\text{getting } 5) = P(E_5) = \dfrac{\text{Number of times 5 occurs}}{\text{Total number of trials}}$

$= \dfrac{33}{250} = 0.132$

6. (d) Here, 200 telephone numbers are given on one page of a telephone directory.

$\therefore$ Total number of selected telephone numbers $= 200$

The frequency of digit 6 at unit place is 14 i.e. in 14 telephone numbers 6 is at unit place.

$\therefore$ Required probability

$= \dfrac{\text{Frequency of 6}}{\text{Total number of selected telephone numbers}}$

$= \dfrac{14}{200} = 0.07$

7. (a) Total number of students, $n(S) = 200$

  (i) The number of students who like Statistics, $n(E) = 135$

$\therefore$ The probability, that the student like Statistics

$= \dfrac{n(E)}{n(S)} = \dfrac{135}{200} = \dfrac{27}{40}$

  (ii) The number of students who does not like Statistics,
$n(F) = 65$

$\therefore$ The probability, that the student does not like

Statistics $= \dfrac{n(F)}{n(S)} = \dfrac{65}{200} = \dfrac{13}{40}$

8. (b) Total number of cases given is 160.

Total number of trials on which 6 occurs at unit place $= 15$

then, required probability $= \dfrac{15}{160} = \dfrac{3}{32}$

9. (d) Let A denote the event that the batsman did not hit a boundary, we have total number of trials $= 40$

Number of trials, in which the event A happened

$= 40 - 8 = 32$

$\therefore \qquad P(A) = \dfrac{32}{40} = \dfrac{4}{5} = 0.8$

10. (c) Total bulb in a lot, $n(S) = 80$

Number of bulbs, whose life time is 1150 h, $n(E) = 0$

$\therefore$ Probability that its life time is 1150 h $= \dfrac{n(E)}{n(S)} = \dfrac{0}{80} = 0$

Hence, the probability that its life time is 1150 h is 0.

11. (d) Total number of bulbs in a lot, $n(S) = 80$

Number of bulbs, whose life time is less than 900 h,

$n(E) = 10 + 12 + 23 = 45$

$\therefore$ Probability that bulbs has life time less than 900 h $= \dfrac{n(E)}{n(S)}$

$= \dfrac{45}{80} = \dfrac{9}{16}$

Hence, the probability that bulb has life time less than 900 h is $9/16$.

12. (b) $\because$ Total number of pages $= 250$ [given]

Now, numbers on the page, which are perfect square are 1, 4, 9, 16, 25, 36, 49, 64, 81, 100, 121, 144, 169, 196, 225.

So, the total number on the pages, which are perfect square

$= 15$

$\therefore$ Required probability $= \dfrac{15}{250} = \dfrac{3}{50}$.

13. (a) Total number of cities $= 1 + 2 + 18 + 21 + 19 + 18 = 79$

Let E be the event, which show maximum temperature of cities.

Number of cities, whose maximum temperature lies between 16°C and 30°C $= 2 + 18 + 21 = 41$

∴ Probabilities that the temperature of cities lies between 16°C and 30°C $= \dfrac{41}{79}$

14. (c) Total number of survey children's age from 19-36 months, $n(S) = 364$

In those of them 91 out of them liked to eat potato chips.

∴ Number of children, who do not like to eat potato chips,
$$n(E) = 364 - 91 = 273$$

∴ Probability that he/she does not like to eat potato chips
$$= \dfrac{n(E)}{n(S)} = \dfrac{273}{364} = 0.75$$

Hence, the probability that he/she does not like to eat potato chips is 0.75.

15. (d) The total number of people in sample study, $n(S) = 642$.

The number of people, who have high school certificate, $n(E) = 514$.

So, the probability that the person selected has a high school certificate
$$= \dfrac{n(E)}{n(S)}$$
$$= \dfrac{514}{642} = 0.8$$

Hence, the probability that the person has a high school certificate is 0.8.

16. (c) Total number of students in a medical examination, $n(S) = 40$

Number of persons, who have B blood group, $n(E) = 12$

∴ Probability that he/she has blood group B $= \dfrac{n(E)}{n(S)} = \dfrac{12}{40}$
$$= \dfrac{3}{10}$$

Hence, the probability that he/she has blood group B is 3/10.

17. (i) (c) Total number of circles $= 9$

Total number of red colour circles $= 9 -$ blue colour circles

Total number of blue colour circles $= 9 - 3 = 6$

Number of red colour squares $= 10 - 5 = 5$

(ii) (d) $n(E) = 10$
$$n(S) = 9 + 10 = 19$$
$$\therefore \; P(E) = \dfrac{n(E)}{n(S)} = \dfrac{10}{19}$$

(iii) (c) $n(E) = 9$
$$n(S) = 9 + 10 = 19$$
$$\therefore \; P(E) = \dfrac{n(E)}{n(S)} = \dfrac{9}{19}$$

(iv) (b) $n(E) = 10 - 5 = 5$
$$n(S) = 9 + 10 = 19$$
$$\therefore \; P(E) = \dfrac{5}{19}$$

(v) (a) $n(E) = 9 - 3 = 6$
$$n(S) = 9 + 10 = 19$$
$$\therefore \; P(E) = \dfrac{6}{19}$$

18. (i) (d) Total number of beads in the potli $= 8 + 6 + 14 = 28$

Number of green beads in the potli $= 6$

∴ Required probability
$$= \dfrac{\text{Number of green beads in potli}}{\text{Total number of beads in the potli}}$$
$$= \dfrac{6}{28} = \dfrac{3}{14}$$

(ii) (c) Number of beads not blue in the potli
$$= 28 - 14 = 14$$
∴ Required probability $= \dfrac{14}{28} = \dfrac{1}{2}$

(iii) (a) Number of blue and green beads in the potli
$$= 14 + 6 = 20$$
∴ Required probability
$$= \dfrac{\text{Number of blue and green beads in potli}}{\text{Total number of beads in the potli}} = \dfrac{20}{28} = \dfrac{5}{7}$$

(iv) (d) Number of beads neither green nor red bead in the potli
$$= 28 - (8 + 6) = 14$$
Number of blue beads in the potli $= 14$

∴ Required probability $= \dfrac{14}{28} = \dfrac{1}{2}$

(v) (d) The bead drawn is yellow.

19. (i) (c) Number of possible outcomes $= 25$

Number of favourable outcomes
$$= [1, 3, 5, 7, 9, 11, 13, 15, 17, 19, 21, 23, 25] \text{ i.e. } 13$$
$$\therefore P(\text{odd number}) = \dfrac{13}{25}$$

(ii) (a) ∴ Number of favourable outcomes
$$= [4, 6, 8, 9, 10, 12, 14, 15, 16, 18, 20, 21, 22, 24, 25]$$
i.e. 15
$$\therefore P(\text{composite number}) = \dfrac{15}{25} = \dfrac{3}{5}$$

(iii) (d) Number of possible outcomes $= 20 - 1 = 19$

Favourable outcomes $= 6, 9, 12, 15, 18$ i.e. 5
$$\therefore P(\text{multiple of 3 greater than 4}) = \dfrac{5}{19}$$

(iv) (a) A sure event is an event, which always happens. The probability of a sure event has the value of 1.

(v) (c) Number of possible outcomes $= 20$

Favourable cases $= 15$ i.e. 1
$$P(\text{multiple of 3 and 5}) = \dfrac{1}{20}$$

Subjective Questions

1. Since, the cards are marked from 2 to 101.

Therefore, total number of cards = 100

  (i) There are 50 cards marked with even numbers from 2 to 101.

$$\therefore\ P\,(\text{getting an even number}) = \frac{50}{100} = \frac{1}{2}$$

Hence, the probability of getting even number card is $\frac{1}{2}$.

  (ii) There are 12 cards on which marked numbers are less than 14.

$$\therefore\ P\ (\text{getting a number less than 14}) = \frac{12}{100} = \frac{3}{25}$$

Hence, the probability that the number on card is less than 14, is $\frac{3}{25}$.

  (iii) The numbers from 2 to 101, which are perfect square, are 4, 9, 16, 25, 36, 49, 64, 81, 100. i.e. Squares of 2, 3, 4, 5, 6, 7, 8, 9 and 10, respectively.

Total number of cards having a number, which is a perfect square = 9

$$\therefore\ P\ (\text{getting a number, which is a perfect square}) = \frac{9}{100}$$

Hence, the probability that the number marked on the card, which is a perfect square, is $\frac{9}{100}$.

2. Total number of days for which the weather forecast record is available = 250

  (i) Here, 175 times the weather forecast were correct.

$\therefore$ Number of days, when the forecasts was correct = 175

Hence, required probability $= \dfrac{175}{250} = 0.7$

  (ii) Probability that forecast was not correct on a given day

= 1 – Probability that forecast was correct on a given day

= 1 – 0.7 = 0.3

Alternate Method

Number of days, when the forecast was not correct

= Total number of days

       – Number of days, when forecast was correct

= 250 – 175 = 75

Hence, required probability $= \dfrac{75}{250} = 0.3$

3. The total number of the households selected by the company, $n(S) = 4000$

  (i) Number of households earning ₹ 10000 - ₹ 14999 per year and having exactly one television, $n(E_1) = 240$

$$\therefore\ \text{Required probability} = \frac{n(E_1)}{n(S)} = \frac{240}{4000}$$

$$= \frac{6}{100} = \frac{3}{50} = 0.06$$

Hence, the probability of a household earning ₹ 10000 - ₹ 14999 per year and having exactly one television is 0.06.

  (ii) Number of households earning ₹ 25000 and more per year owning 2 televisions, $n(E_2) = 760$

$$\therefore\text{Required probability} = \frac{n(E_2)}{n(S)}$$

$$= \frac{760}{4000} = 0.19$$

Hence, the probability of a household earning ₹ 25000 and more per year owning 2 televisions is 0.19.

4. Suppose, there are 40 students in a class.

$\therefore$ The probability of selecting any of the student $= \dfrac{40}{40} = 1$

A three digit number start from 100 to 999

Total number of three digit numbers = 999 – 99 = 900

$\therefore$ Multiple of 3 in three digit numbers = {102, 105, ..., 999}

$\therefore$ Number of multiples of 3 in three digit numbers

$$= \frac{900}{3} = 300$$

i.e. $n(E) = 300$

$\therefore$ The probability that the number written by her/him is

divisible by $3 = \dfrac{n(E)}{n(S)} = \dfrac{300}{900} = \dfrac{1}{3}$

5. Total number of students in class IX, $n(S) = 40$

Number of students born in the month of August, $n(E) = 6$

$\therefore$ Probability, that the students of the class was born in

August $= \dfrac{n(E)}{n(S)} = \dfrac{6}{40} = \dfrac{3}{20}$

6.   (i) Total number of students in a class, $n(S) = 90$

The number of students less than 20% lies in the interval 0-20.

i.e. $n(E) = 7$

$\therefore$ The probability, that a student obtained less than 20%

in the mathematics test $= \dfrac{n(E)}{n(S)} = \dfrac{7}{90}$

  (ii) The number of students obtained marks 60 or above lies in the marks interval 60-70 and 70-above

i.e. $n(F) = 15 + 8 = 23$

$\therefore$ The probability that a student obtained marks 60 or

above $= \dfrac{n(F)}{n(S)} = \dfrac{23}{90}$

7. Let E_1, E_2, E_3 and E_4 denote the events getting grade A, B, C and D, respectively.

Then, $P(E_1) = 0.35,\ P(E_2) = 0.25,$

$\qquad P(E_3) = 0.35$ and $P(E_4) = 0.05$

  (i) A student, who gets atmost grade C, can also get grade D.

$\therefore\ P$ (getting atmost grade C)

$\qquad = P(\text{getting grade } C) + P\ (\text{getting grade } D)$

$\qquad = 0.35 + 0.05 - 0.40$

Hence, the probability that a student gets atmost grade C is 0.40.

(ii) A student, who gets atleast grade C, can also get grades A and B.

$\therefore P$ (getting atleast grade C)

$= P$ (getting grade A) $+ P$ (getting grade B)

$+ P$ (getting grade C)

$= 0.35 + 0.25 + 0.35 = 0.95$

Hence, the probability that a student gets atleast grade C is 0.95.

8. Total number of cartons, $n(S) = 700$

(i) Number of cartons which has no defective bulb, $n(E_1) = 400$

$\therefore$ Probability that no defective bulb $= \dfrac{n(E_1)}{n(S)} = \dfrac{400}{700} = \dfrac{4}{7}$

Hence, the probability that no defective bulb is $\dfrac{4}{7}$.

(ii) Number of cartons which has defective bulbs from 2 to 6, $n(E_2)$

$= 48 + 41 + 18 + 8 + 3 = 118$

$\therefore$ Probability that the defective bulbs from 2 to 6

$= \dfrac{n(E_2)}{n(S)} = \dfrac{118}{700} = \dfrac{59}{350}$

Hence, the probability that the defective bulbs from 2 to 6 is $\dfrac{59}{350}$.

(iii) Number of cartons which has defective bulbs less than 4, $n(E_3) = 400 + 180 + 48 + 41 = 669$

$\therefore$ The probability that the defective bulbs less than 4

$= \dfrac{n(E_3)}{n(S)} = \dfrac{669}{700}$

Hence, the probability that the defective bulb less than 4 is $\dfrac{669}{700}$.

9. After observing in front of the school gate in time interval 6:30 to 7:30 am respective frequencies of different types of vehicles are

Types of vehicles	Frequency
Two-wheelers	550
Three-wheelers	250
Four-wheelers	80

$\therefore$ Total number of vehicle, $n(S) = 550 + 250 + 80 = 880$

Number of two-wheelers, $n(E) = 550$

$\therefore$ Probability of observing two-wheelers $= \dfrac{n(E)}{n(S)} = \dfrac{550}{880} = \dfrac{5}{8}$

10. Here, 200 telephone numbers are given on one page of a telephone directory.

$\therefore$ Total number of selected telephone numbers = 200

The frequency of digit 6 at unit place is 14. i.e. In 14 telephone numbers 6 is at unit place.

$\therefore$ Required probability

$= \dfrac{\text{Frequency of 6}}{\text{Total number of selected telephone numbers}} = \dfrac{14}{200} = 0.07$

11. Total number of engineers lives, $n(S) = 40$

(i) The number of engineers whose residence is less than 7 km from their place, $n(E) = 9$

$\therefore$ The probability, that an engineer lives less than 7 km from their place of work

$= \dfrac{n(E)}{n(S)} = \dfrac{9}{40}$

(ii) The number of engineers whose residence is more than or equal to 7 km from their place of work, $n(F) = 40 - 9 = 31$

$\therefore$ The probability, that an engineer lives more than or equal to 7 km from their place of work $= \dfrac{n(F)}{n(S)} = \dfrac{31}{40}$

(iii) The number of engineers whose residence within $\dfrac{1}{2}$ km from their place of work, i.e. $n(G) = 0$

$\therefore$ The probability, that an engineer lives within $\dfrac{1}{2}$ km from their place $= \dfrac{n(G)}{n(S)} = \dfrac{0}{40} = 0$

12. Total number of workers in a factory,

$n(S) = 38 + 27 + 86 + 46 + 3 = 200$

(i) Number of persons selected at the age of 40 yr or more,

$n(E_1) = 86 + 46 + 3 = 135$

$\therefore$ Probability that the person selected at the age of 40 yr or more,

$P(E_1) = \dfrac{n(E_1)}{n(S)} = \dfrac{135}{200} = 0.675$

Hence, the probability that the person selected at the age of 40 yr or more is 0.675.

(ii) Number of persons selected under the age of 40 yr

$n(E_2) = 38 + 27 = 65$

$\therefore$ Probability that the person selected under the age of 40 yr,

$P(E_2) = \dfrac{n(E_2)}{n(S)}$

$= \dfrac{65}{200} = 0.325$

Hence, the probability that the person selected under the age of 40 yr is 0.325.

(iii) Number of persons selected having age from 30 to 39 yr, $n(E_3) = 27$

$\therefore$ Probability that the person selected having age from 30 to 39 yr,

$P(E_3) = \dfrac{n(E_3)}{n(S)}$

$= \dfrac{27}{200} = 0.135$

Hence, the probability that the person selected having age from 30 to 39 yr is 0.135.

(iv) Number of persons selected having age under 60 but over 39 yr,

$n(E_4) = 86 + 46 = 132$

$\therefore$ Probability that the person selected having age under 60 but over 39 yr,

$$P(E_4) = \frac{n(E_4)}{n(S)} = \frac{132}{200} = 0.66$$

Hence, the probability that the person selected having age under 60 but over 39 yr is 0.66.

13. Here, results of 1000 cases are given.

So, total number of trials = 1000

   (i) The frequency of tyres that needs to be replaced before it covers 4000 km is 20.

   So, P (tyre to be replaced before it covers 4000 km)
   $$= \frac{20}{1000} = 0.02$$

   (ii) The frequency of tyres that will last more than 9000 km is $325 + 445 = 770$.

   So, P (tyre will last more than 9000 km)
   $$= \frac{770}{1000} = 0.77$$

   (iii) The frequency of tyres that requires replacement between 4000 km and 14000 km is $210 + 325 = 535$.

   So, P (tyre requiring replacement between 4000 km and 14000 km) $= \frac{535}{1000} = 0.535$

14. Given that, total number of bulbs = 80

Number of bulbs having life less than 900 h
$$= 10 + 15 + 23 = 48$$

$\therefore$ Required probability $= \dfrac{48}{80} = \dfrac{3}{5}$

15. Let p be the probability of success and q be the probability of failure.

Here, we have, $\qquad p - q = \dfrac{5}{19}$ $\qquad$ ...(i)

Also, we know $\qquad p + q = 1$ $\qquad$ ...(ii)

On solving Eqs. (i) and (ii), we get
$$2p = \frac{5}{19} + 1 \Rightarrow p = \frac{24}{2 \times 19} = \frac{24}{38} = \frac{12}{19}$$

From Eq. (ii), $\dfrac{12}{19} + q = 1 \Rightarrow q = 1 - \dfrac{12}{19} = \dfrac{7}{19}$

16. Given, a batswoman play 30 balls, therefore total number of trials = 30 and number of events of hitting the boundary = 6

Now, number of balls in which she is not hitting the boundary $= 30 - 6 = 24$

$\therefore$ The probability that she did not hit a boundary $= \dfrac{24}{30} = \dfrac{4}{5}$

17. (i) There are total 33 students, who live atmost 15 km away from school.

   P (student lives atmost 15 km away from school) $= \dfrac{33}{40}$

   So, the probability is $\dfrac{33}{40}$.

   (ii) P (student lives within 1 km from their school) $= \dfrac{0}{40} = 0$

18. Here, two coins are tossed simultaneously 300 times.

So, total number of trials = 300

   (i) Let E_1 be the event of getting 2 heads appeared 135 times.

   $\therefore$ Number of trials in which 2 heads occur = 135

   Hence, probability of getting 2 heads,
   $$P(E_1) = \frac{135}{300} = 0.45$$

   (ii) Let E_2 be the event of getting 1 head appeared 111 times.

   $\therefore$ Number of trials in which 1 head occur = 111

   Hence, probability of getting 1 head,
   $$P(E_2) = \frac{111}{300} = 0.37$$

   (iii) Let E_3 be the event of getting 0 head (no head) appeared 54 times.

   $\therefore$ Number of trials in which 0 head occur = 54

   Hence, probability of getting 0 head,
   $$P(E_3) = \frac{54}{300} = 0.18$$

19. Here, a die is thrown 250 times.

So, total number of trials = 250

In a random throw of a die, let E_1, E_2, E_3, E_4, E_5 and E_6 be the events of getting 1, 2, 3, 4, 5 and 6, respectively.

   (i) Here, frequency of outcome 1 is 65 i.e. 1 occurs on a die 65 times.

   $\therefore$ P (getting 1) $= P(E_1) = \dfrac{\text{Number of times 1 occurs}}{\text{Total number of trials}}$
   $$= \frac{65}{250} = 0.26$$

   (ii) Here, 2 occurs on a die 40 times.

   $\therefore$ P (getting 2) $= P(E_2) = \dfrac{\text{Number of times 2 occurs}}{\text{Total number of trials}}$
   $$= \frac{40}{250} = 0.16$$

   (iii) Here, 3 occurs on a die 42 times.

   $\therefore$ P (getting 3) $= P(E_3) = \dfrac{\text{Number of times 3 occurs}}{\text{Total number of trials}}$
   $$= \frac{42}{250} = 0.168$$

   (iv) Here, 4 occurs on a die 25 times.

   $\therefore$ P (getting 4) $= P(E_4) = \dfrac{\text{Number of times 4 occurs}}{\text{Total number of trials}}$
   $$= \frac{25}{250} = 0.10$$

   (v) Here, 5 occurs on a die 33 times.

   $\therefore$ P (getting 5) $= P(E_5) = \dfrac{\text{Number of times 5 occurs}}{\text{Total number of trials}}$
   $$= \frac{33}{250} = 0.132$$

   (vi) Here, 6 occurs on a die 45 times

   $\therefore P$ (getting 6) $= P(E_6) = \dfrac{\text{Number of times 6 occurs}}{\text{Total number of trials}}$
   $$= \frac{45}{250} = 0.18$$

20. Total number of times, when two dice are thrown simultaneously, $n(S) = 500$

(i) Number of times of getting a sum 3, $n(E) = 30$

$\therefore$ Probability of getting a sum $3 = \dfrac{n(E)}{n(S)} = \dfrac{30}{500}$

$= \dfrac{3}{50} = 0.06$

Hence, the probability of getting a sum 3 is 0.06.

(ii) Number of times of getting a sum more than 10,

$n(E_1) = 28 + 15 = 43$

$\therefore$ Probability of getting sum more than 10

$= \dfrac{n(E_1)}{n(S)} = \dfrac{43}{500} = 0.086$

Hence, the probability of getting a sum more than 10 is 0.086

(iii) Number of times of getting a sum less than or equal to 5,

$n(E_2) = 55 + 42 + 30 + 14 = 141$

$\therefore$ Probability of getting a sum less than or equal to 5

$= \dfrac{n(E_2)}{n(S)} = \dfrac{141}{500} = 0.282$

Hence, the probability of getting a sum less than or equal to 5 is 0.282.

(iv) The number of times of getting a sum between 8 and 12,

$n(E_3) = 53 + 46 + 28 = 127$

$\therefore$ Required probability $= \dfrac{n(E_3)}{n(S)}$

$= \dfrac{127}{500} = 0.254$

Hence, the probability of getting a sum between 8 and 12 is 0.254.

21. Total number of unit tests held $= 5$

(i) Number of unit tests in which the student gets a first class i.e. atleast 60% marks $= 4$

$\therefore$ Probability that the student gets a first class $= \dfrac{4}{5} = 0.8$

(ii) Number of unit tests in which the student gets marks between 70% and 80% $= 2$

$\therefore$ Probability that the student gets marks between 70% and 80% $= \dfrac{2}{5} = 0.4$

(iii) Number of unit tests in which the student gets distinction or marks equal and more than 75% $= 2$

$\therefore$ Probability that the student gets distinction $= \dfrac{2}{5} = 0.4$

(iv) Number of unit tests in which the student gets less than 65% marks $= 2$

$\therefore$ Probability that the student gets less than 65% marks $= \dfrac{2}{5} = 0.4$

22. Total number of families $= 1500$ [given]

Let E_1, E_2 and E_3 be the events choosing 2 girls, 1 girl and no girl, respectively.

(i) The number of families having 2 girls $= 475$

$\therefore$ The probability of chosen a family having 2 girls,

$P(E_1) = \dfrac{475}{1500} = \dfrac{19}{60}$

(ii) The number of families having 1 girl $= 814$

$\therefore$ The probability of chosen a family having 1 girl,

$P(E_2) = \dfrac{814}{1500} = \dfrac{407}{750}$

(iii) The number of families having no girl $= 211$

$\therefore$ The probability of chosen a family having no girl,

$P(E_3) = \dfrac{211}{1500}$

Now, sum of probabilities $= P(E_1) + P(E_2) + P(E_3)$

$= \dfrac{19}{60} + \dfrac{407}{750} + \dfrac{211}{1500}$

$= \dfrac{19 \times 25 + 407 \times 2 + 211}{1500}$

$= \dfrac{475 + 814 + 211}{1500}$

$= \dfrac{1500}{1500} = 1$

Hence, the sum of calculated probabilities is 1.

23. Total number of working days, $n(S) = 200$

(i) Number of days in which no defective part is, $n(E_1) = 50$

$\therefore$ Probability that no defective part

$= \dfrac{n(E_1)}{n(S)} = \dfrac{50}{200} = \dfrac{1}{4} = 0.25$

Hence, the probability that no defective part is 0.25.

(ii) Number of days in which atleast one defective part, is

$n(E_2) = 32 + 22 + 18 + 12 + 12 + 10 + 10 + 10$
$\qquad\qquad + 8 + 6 + 6 + 2 + 2$

$= 150$

$\therefore$ Probability that atleast one defective part

$= \dfrac{n(E_2)}{n(S)} = \dfrac{150}{200} = \dfrac{3}{4} = 0.75$

Hence, the probability that atleast one defective part is 0.75.

(iii) Number of days in which not more than 5 defective parts,

$n(E_3) = 50 + 32 + 22 + 18 + 12 + 12 = 146$

$\therefore$ Probability that not more than 5 defective parts

$= \dfrac{n(E_3)}{n(S)} = \dfrac{146}{200} = 0.73$

Hence, the probability that not more than 5 defective parts is 0.73.

(iv) Number of days in which more than 13 defective parts, $n(E_4) = 0$

$\therefore$ Probability that more than 13 defective parts

$= \dfrac{n(E_4)}{n(S)} = \dfrac{0}{200} = 0$

Hence, the probability that more than 13 defective parts is 0.

24. The total number of workers = 30　　　　　　　　[given]

(i) Number of workers whose wages is less than ₹ 150
$$= 3 + 4 = 7$$
∴ Probability that a worker gets wages less than ₹ 150
$$= \frac{7}{30}$$

(ii) Number of workers whose wages is atleast ₹ 210
$$= 4 + 3 = 7$$
∴ Probability that a worker gets wages of atleast ₹ 210
$$= \frac{7}{30}$$

(iii) Number of workers whose wages is more than or equal to ₹ 150 but less than ₹ 210 $= 5 + 6 + 5 = 16$

∴ Probability that a worker gets wages is more than or equal to ₹ 150 but less than ₹ 210 $= \dfrac{16}{30} = \dfrac{8}{15}$

(iv) Number of workers whose wages lies in the interval ₹ 190 - ₹ 250 $= 5 + 4 + 3 = 12$

∴ Probability that a worker gets wages lies in the interval ₹ 190 - ₹ 250 $= \dfrac{12}{30} = \dfrac{2}{5}$

25. Given, percentage of marks obtained by a student in monthly test.

Number of sample space = {70, 72, 65, 68, 85}

(i) Let E be the possible outcomes.
$$E = \{72, 85\}$$
$$P(E) = \frac{\text{Number of possible outcomes}}{\text{Total number of outcomes}}$$
$$\Rightarrow P(E) = \frac{2}{5} = 0.4$$

(ii) $P(E) = 0$

26. Here, total number of people = 200

(i) P (both good living and delhi pavilion)
$$= \frac{95 + 45}{200} = \frac{140}{200} = \frac{7}{10}$$

(ii) P (only defence pavilion) $= \dfrac{20}{200} = \dfrac{1}{10}$

(iii) P (only toy pavilion) $= \dfrac{40}{200} = \dfrac{1}{5}$

(iv) P (both toy and defence pavilion) $= \dfrac{40 + 20}{200} = \dfrac{3}{10}$

27. (i) Total number of bags = 5

Bags, where more than 40 seeds germinated
$$= \text{Bag 2, Bag 3 and Bag 5}$$

P (germination of more than 40 seeds in a bag) $= \dfrac{3}{5} = 0.6$

(ii) Number of bags in which 49 seeds germinated = 0

P (germination of 49 seeds in a bag) $= \dfrac{0}{5} = 0$

(iii) Bags, where more than 35 seeds germinated = Bags 1, 2, 3, 4 and 5.

Number of bags in which more than 35 seeds germinated = 5

P (germination of more than 35 seeds in a bag) $= \dfrac{5}{5} = 1$

28. Total number of tyres $= 120 + 150 + 80 + 200 + 250 = 800$

Frequency of tyre that needs to be replaced before it covers 700 km = 200

(i) So, P (tyre to be placed before it covers 700 km)
$$= \frac{200}{800} = 0.25$$

(ii) Total number of tyres = 800

Frequency of tyres that will last more than 1100 km
$$= 150 + 250 = 400$$

So, P(tyre will last more than 1100 km) $= \dfrac{400}{800} = \dfrac{1}{2}$

(iii) So, frequency of tyre that will last between 300 km to 1500 km $= 200 + 120 + 150 = 470$

So, $P(\varepsilon) = \dfrac{470}{800} = \dfrac{47}{80}$

(iv) P(tyre requiring replacing between) $= \dfrac{250}{800} = \dfrac{5}{16}$.

29. (i) Total number of drivers = 2000

Number of drivers who are (18-29) yr old and have exactly 3 accidents in one year = 61

P (driver is 18-29 yr old with exactly 3 accidents)
$$= \frac{\text{Number of drivers who are (18-29) yr old and have exactly 3 accidents in one year}}{\text{Total number of drivers}}$$
$$= \frac{61}{2000} = 0.0305$$

(ii) Total number of drivers = 2000

Number of drivers (30-50) yr of age and having one or more accidents in one yr.
$$= 125 + 60 + 22 + 18 = 225$$

P (30-50 yr of age and having one or more accidents)
$$= \frac{\text{Number of drivers who are (30-50) yr of age and having one or more accidents in one year}}{\text{Total number of drivers}}$$
$$= \frac{225}{2000} = 0.1125$$

(iii) Total number of drivers = 2000

The number of drivers having no accidents in one year
$$= 440 + 505 + 360 = 1305$$

P (driver having no accidents in one year)
$$= \frac{\text{Number of drivers who have no accidents in one year}}{\text{Total number of drivers}}$$
$$= \frac{1305}{2000} = 0.653$$

Chapter Test

Multiple Choice Questions

1. In 50 tosses of a coin, tail appears 32 times. If a coin is tossed at random, what is the probability of getting a head?

(a) $\dfrac{1}{32}$　　(b) $\dfrac{1}{18}$　　(c) $\dfrac{16}{25}$　　(d) $\dfrac{9}{25}$

2. Two coins are tossed 1000 times and the outcomes are recorded as under.

Number of heads	2	1	0
Frequency	266	540	194

A coin is thrown at random. What is the probability of getting at most one head?

(a) $\dfrac{403}{500}$　　　　(b) $\dfrac{27}{50}$

(c) $\dfrac{367}{500}$　　　　(d) $\dfrac{97}{500}$

Cased Based MCQs

3. One day Raju visited mall along with his friend. There, he saw a game of chance that consists of spinning an arrow (as shown in below figure) that comes to rest pointing at one of the numbers 1, 2, 3, 4, 5 6, 7 and 8 and these are equally likely outcomes.

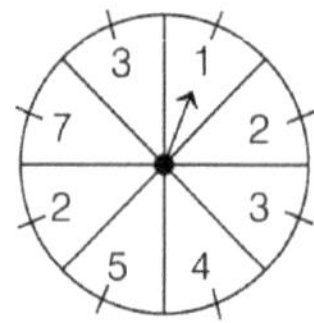

(i) Find the probability that the arrow will point at 2.

(a) $\dfrac{1}{4}$　　(b) $\dfrac{1}{8}$　　(c) $\dfrac{3}{8}$　　(d) $\dfrac{5}{8}$

(ii) Find the probability that the arrow will point at an even number.

(a) $\dfrac{1}{2}$　　(b) $\dfrac{1}{8}$　　(c) $\dfrac{3}{8}$　　(d) $\dfrac{1}{4}$

(iii) Find the probability that the arrow will point at a prime number.

(a) $\dfrac{1}{2}$　　(b) $\dfrac{1}{8}$　　(c) $\dfrac{3}{8}$　　(d) $\dfrac{5}{8}$

(iv) Find the probability that the arrow will point at a number divisible by 3.

(a) $\dfrac{1}{2}$　　(b) $\dfrac{1}{8}$　　(c) $\dfrac{3}{8}$　　(d) $\dfrac{1}{4}$

(v) Find the probability that the arrow will point at a number greater than 2.

(a) $\dfrac{1}{2}$　　(b) $\dfrac{1}{8}$　　(c) $\dfrac{3}{4}$　　(d) $\dfrac{1}{4}$

Short Answer Type Questions

4. 1500 families with 2 children each, were selected randomly and the following data were recorded.

Number of girls in a family	2	1	0
Number of families	102	675	723

Out of these families, one family is selected at random. What is the probability that the selected family has (i) 2 girls, (ii) 1 girl and (iii) no girl?

5. According to a meteorological report for 300 consecutive days in a year, its weather forecasts were correct 180 times.

Out of these days, one day is chosen at random.

What is the probability that the weather forecast was

(i) correct on that day?

(ii) not correct on that day?

Long Answer Type Questions

6. A die is thrown 250 times and the outcomes are noted as given below.

Outcome	1	2	3	4	5	6
Frequency	65	40	42	25	33	45

If a die is thrown at random, find the probability of getting.

(i) 1　　　　(ii) 2　　　　(iii) 3

(iv) 4　　　　(v) 5　　　　(vi) 6

7. The table given below shows the ages of 75 teachers in a school.

Age (in years)	18-29	30-39	40-49	50-59
Number of teachers	3	27	37	8

A teacher from this school is chosen at random.

What is the probability that the selected teacher is

(i) 40 or more than 40 yr old?

(ii) of an age lying between (30-39) yr (including both)?

(iii) 18 yr or more old?

(iv) Above 60 yr of age?

Answers

1. (d)　2. (c)　3. (i) (a) (ii) (c)　(iii) (a)　(iv) (d) (v) (a)

4. (i) 0.068 (ii) 0.45 (iii) 0.482　　5. (i) 0.6, (ii) 0.4

6. (i) 0.26, (ii) 0.16, (iii) 0.168, (iv) 0.1 (v) 0.132, (vi) 1

7. (i) 0.6, (ii) 0.36, (iii) 1, (iv) 0

For Detailed Solutions

Scan the code

Practice Paper 1*
(Solved)

Instructions

- Time : 2 Hr
- Max. Marks : 40

1. The question paper contains three sections A, B and C.
2. Section A has 5 questions with 3 internal choices.
3. Section B has 4 questions with 3 internal choices.
4. Section C has 1 Case Based MCQs comprises of 5 MCQs.
5. There is no negative marking.

** As exact Blue-print and Pattern for CBSE Term II exams is not released yet. So the pattern of this paper is designed by the author on the basis of trend of past CBSE Papers. Students are advised not to consider the pattern of this paper as official, it is just for practice purpose.*

Section A
(3 Marks Each)

This section consists of 5 questions of Short Answer Type.

1. Verify that whether -1 is zeroes of the polynomial $p(x) = 2x^3 - 9x^2 + x + 12$ and find the value of $p(0)$, $p(1)$ and $p(2)$.

2. The diagonals AC and BD of a parallelogram $ABCD$ intersect each other at the point O. If $\angle DAC = 32°$ and $\angle AOB = 70°$, then find $\angle DBC$.

Or

Two circles of radii 4 cm and 3 cm intersect at two points and the distance between their centres is 5 cm. Find the length of the common chord.

3. A survey of 600 students about their liking on coffee was conducted and recorded as under:

Opinion	Like	Dislike
Number of students	360	140

Out of these students one is chosen at random. What is the probability that the chosen student?

(i) Likes coffee?

(ii) Dislikes coffee.

Or

The ratio of the curved surface area to the total surface area of a right circular cylinder is 1 : 2. Find the volume of the cylinder, if its total surface area is 616 cm^2.

$$\left[\text{take, } \pi = \frac{22}{7} \right]$$

4. The distance (in km) of 40 engineers from their residence to their place of work were found as follows.

5	3	10	20	25	11	13	7	12	31
19	10	12	17	18	11	32	17	16	2
7	9	7	8	3	5	12	15	18	3
12	14	2	9	6	15	15	7	6	12

What is the empirical probability that an engineer lives

(i) less than 7 km from her place of work?

(ii) more than or equal to 7 km from her place of work?

(iii) within 1/2 km from her place of work?

Or

If $x^2 + \dfrac{1}{x^2} = 62$, then find the value of $x^3 + \dfrac{1}{x^3}$.

5. Two cones have their heights in the ratio 1 : 3 and the radii of their bases are in the ratio 3 : 1. Show that their volumes are in the ratio 3 : 1.

Section B   (5 Marks Each)

This section consists of 4 questions of Long Answer Type.

6. In the given figure, O is the centre of the circle $\angle BCO = 30°$. Find x and y.

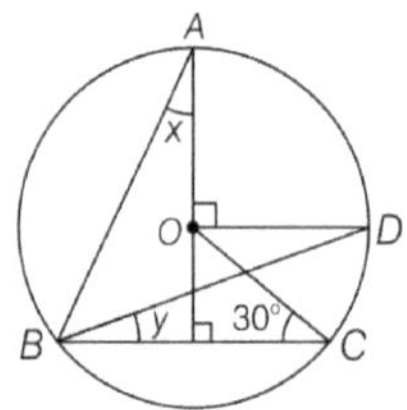

Or

ABC is a triangle. D is a point on AB such that $AD = \dfrac{1}{4} AB$ and E is a point on AC such that $AE = \dfrac{1}{4} AC$. Prove that $DE = \dfrac{1}{4} BC$.

7. Construct an angle of $22\dfrac{1}{2}^\circ$.

8. Water in a canal, 30 dm wide and 12 dm deep, is flowing with a velocity of 20 km per hour. How much area will it irrigate in 30 min, if 9 cm of standing water is desired?

Or Over the past 200 working days, the number of defective parts produced by a machine is given in the following table

Number of defective parts	0	1	2	3	4	5	6	7	8	9	10	11	12	13
Days	50	32	22	18	12	12	10	10	10	8	6	6	2	2

Determine the probability that tomorrow's output will have

(i) no defective part.

(ii) atleast one defective part.

(iii) not more than 5 defective parts.

(iv) more than 13 defective parts.

9. Simplify $(a+b)^3 - (a-b)^3 - 6b(a^2 - b^2)$.

Or On one page of a telephone directory, there are 150 phone numbers. The frequency distribution of their units digit is given below

Unit digit	0	1	2	3	4	5	6	7	8	9
Frequency	10	20	15	10	20	20	10	15	15	15

One of the numbers is chosen at random from the page. What is the probability that the units digit of the chosen number is

(i) less than 3?

(ii) greater than 8?

Section C
(1 Mark Each)

This section consists of 1 Case Based comprises of 5 MCQs.

10. Mathematics teacher of a D.A.V school took her 9th standard students to show Buland Darwaja. It was a part of their Educational trip. She narrated the facts of Buland darwaja to students. There are 2 pillars which are cylindrical in shape. Also 2 domes at the corners which are conical.

(i) Write the formula to find the total surface area of a cylindrical structure.

(a) $2\pi r\,(r+h)$ (b) $\pi r^2 h$

(c) $\pi r\,(r+h)$ (d) $2\pi r$

(ii) Find the curved surface area of each conical tomb if slant height and base diameter are 25 m and 14 m, respectively.

(a) $450\ m^2$ (b) $750\ m^2$

(c) $650\ m^2$ (d) $550\ m^2$

(iii) Find the cost of white-washing of curved surface area of each tomb at the rate of ₹ 210 per 100 m²?

(a) ₹ 1255   (b) ₹ 1155

(c) ₹ 1355   (d) ₹ 1455

(iv) Find the lateral surface area of two pillors if height of the pillor is 21 m and radius of the base is 2.1 m.

(a) $454.4\ m^2$ (b) $554.4\ m^2$

(c) $1054.4\ m^2$ (d) $954.4\ m^2$

(v) Write the formula to find the value of conical tomb.

(a) $\pi r m$ (b) $\pi r^2 h$

(c) $\dfrac{1}{3}\pi r^2 h$ (d) $2\pi r h$

Solutions

1. Let given polynomial be

$$p(x) = 2x^3 - 9x^2 + x + 12 \qquad \text{...(i)}$$

On putting $x = -1$ in Eq. (i) we get

$$p(-1) = 2(-1)^3 - 9(-1)^2 + (-1) + 12$$
$$= -2 - 9 - 1 + 12 = -12 + 12 = 0$$

$p(-1) = 0$, so $x = -1$ is zeroes of the given polynomial.

Now, $p(x) = 2x^3 - 9x^2 + x + 12$

$$p(0) = 2(0)^3 - 9(0)^2 + 0 + 12 = 12$$

$$p(1) = 2(1)^3 - 9(1)^2 + 1 + 12$$
$$= 2 - 9 + 1 + 12 = 6$$

$$p(2) = 2(2)^3 - 9(2)^2 + 2 + 12$$
$$= 2 \times 8 - 9 \times 4 + 14$$
$$= 16 - 36 + 14$$

$$p(2) = 30 - 36 = -6$$

$\therefore p(0) = 12, p(1) = 6$ and $p(2) = -6$

2. Given, $\angle AOB = 70°$ and $\angle DAC = 32°$

$$\Rightarrow \quad \angle ACB = 32° \qquad \text{[alternate angle]}$$

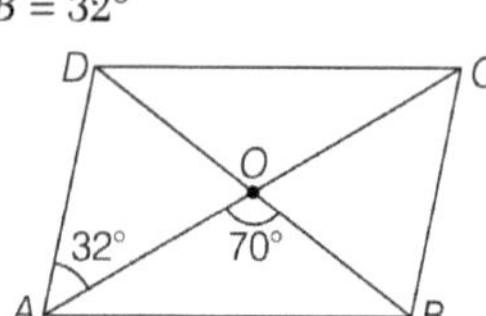

Now, $\angle BOC = 180° - \angle AOB \qquad$ [linear pair axiom]

$$\Rightarrow \quad \angle BOC = 180° - 70°$$
$$\Rightarrow \quad \angle BOC = 110°$$

Now, in $\triangle BOC$, $\angle BOC + \angle BCO + \angle OBC = 180°$

[$\because$ sum of all angles of a triangles is 180°]

$$\Rightarrow 110° + 32° + \angle OBC = 180° \qquad [\because \angle BCO = \angle BCA]$$
$$\Rightarrow \quad 142° + \angle OBC = 180°$$
$$\Rightarrow \quad \angle OBC = 180° - 142°$$
$$\Rightarrow \quad \angle OBC = 38°$$
$$\therefore \quad \angle DBC = \angle OBC = 38°$$

Or

Let O and O' be the centres of the circles of radii 4 cm and 3 cm, respectively.

Again, let AB be their common chord.

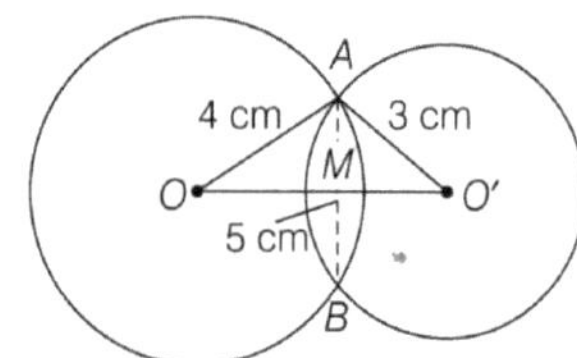

Given, $OA = 4$ cm, $O'A = 3$ cm and $OO' = 5$ cm

Now, $(AO')^2 + (OA)^2 = 3^2 + 4^2 = 9 + 16 = 25 = (OO')^2$

$\therefore \triangle OAO'$ is a right angled triangle, right angled at A.

Area of $\triangle OAO' = \dfrac{1}{2} \times O'A \times OA$

$$\left[\because \text{ area of triangle } = \frac{1}{2} \times \text{base} \times \text{altitude}\right]$$

$$= \frac{1}{2} \times 3 \times 4 = 6 \text{ sq units} \qquad \text{...(i)}$$

Also, area of $\triangle OAO' = \dfrac{1}{2} \times OO' \times AM$

$$= \frac{1}{2} \times 5 \times AM = \frac{5}{2} AM \qquad \text{...(ii)}$$

From Eqs. (i) and (ii), we get

$$\frac{5}{2} AM = 6 \Rightarrow AM = \frac{12}{5}$$

Since, when two circles intersect at two points, then their centres lie on the perpendicular bisector of the common chord.

$$\therefore \quad AB = 2 \times AM = 2 \times \frac{12}{5} = \frac{24}{5} = 4.8 \text{ cm}$$

3. Total number of students = 600

Total number of students that likes coffee = 360

Total number of students that dislikes coffee = 140

(i) P(student likes coffee)

$$= \frac{\text{number of students that likes coffee}}{\text{total number of students}}$$

$$= \frac{360}{600} = \frac{3}{5}$$

(ii) P(students dislike coffee)

$$= \frac{\text{number of students that dislikes coffee}}{\text{total number of students}}$$

$$= \frac{140}{600} = \frac{7}{30}$$

Or

Given, total surface area of a cylinder = 616 cm^2

Let radius of the cylinder = r and its height = h

$$\because \quad \frac{\text{Curved surface area of a cylinder}}{\text{Total surface area of a cylinder}} = \frac{1}{2}$$

$$\therefore \quad \frac{2\pi rh}{2\pi rh + 2\pi r^2} = \frac{1}{2}$$

$$\Rightarrow \quad \frac{(2\pi r)h}{(2\pi r)(h + r)} = \frac{1}{2}$$

$$\Rightarrow \quad \frac{h}{h + r} = \frac{1}{2}$$

$$\Rightarrow \quad 2h = h + r \Rightarrow h = r \qquad \text{... (i)}$$

Now, total surface area of a cylinder = 616 cm^2

$$\Rightarrow \quad 2\pi rh + 2\pi r^2 = 616$$
$$\Rightarrow \quad 2\pi r \times r + 2\pi r^2 = 616 \qquad \text{[from Eq. (i), } h = r]$$
$$\Rightarrow \quad 4\pi r^2 = 616$$
$$\Rightarrow \quad 4 \times \frac{22}{7} \times r^2 = 616$$
$$\Rightarrow \quad r^2 = \frac{616 \times 7}{88} = 49$$

$$\Rightarrow \qquad r = 7\,\text{cm}$$

$$\Rightarrow \qquad h = r = 7\,\text{cm}$$

$\therefore$ Volume of the cylinder $= \pi r^2 h$

$$= \frac{22}{7} \times (7)^2 \times 7 = 1078 \text{ cm}^3$$

4. Given, total number of engineers lives $= 40$

(i) The number of engineers, whose residence is less than 7 km from their place $= 9$

$\therefore$ The probability, that an engineer lives less than 7 km from their place of work $= \dfrac{9}{40}$

(ii) The number of engineers, whose residence is more than or equal to 7 km from their place of work

$$= 40 - 9 = 31$$

$\therefore$ The probability, that an engineer lives more than or equal to 7 km from their place of work $= \dfrac{31}{40}$

(iii) The number of engineers, whose residence within $\dfrac{1}{2}$ km from their place of work $= 0$

$\therefore$ The probability, that an engineer lives within $\dfrac{1}{2}$ km from their place $= \dfrac{0}{40} = 0$

Or

We have, $x^2 + \dfrac{1}{x^2} = 62$

$$\Rightarrow \quad x^2 + \frac{1}{x^2} + 2 = 62 + 2 \qquad \text{[adding 2 both sides]}$$

$$\Rightarrow \quad \left(x + \frac{1}{x}\right)^2 = 64 \qquad [\because a^2 + b^2 + 2ab = (a+b)^2]$$

$$\Rightarrow \quad x + \frac{1}{x} = \sqrt{64} = 8 \qquad \text{[taking square root]}$$

$$\Rightarrow \quad x + \frac{1}{x} = 8 \qquad\qquad \text{... (i)}$$

We know that,

$$\left(x + \frac{1}{x}\right)^3 = x^3 + \frac{1}{x^3} + 3 \cdot x \cdot \frac{1}{x}\left(x + \frac{1}{x}\right)$$

$$\Rightarrow \quad (8)^3 = x^3 + \frac{1}{x^3} + 3(8) \qquad \text{[from Eq. (i)]}$$

$$\Rightarrow \quad 512 = x^3 + \frac{1}{x^3} + 24$$

$$\therefore \quad x^3 + \frac{1}{x^3} = 512 - 24 = 488$$

5. Let the height of two cones be h, $3h$ and their radii be $3r$, r, respectively.

$\because$ Volume of cone $= \dfrac{1}{3}\pi R^2 H$

$\therefore \qquad V_1 = \dfrac{1}{3}\pi (3r)^2 h = 3\pi r^2 h$

and $\qquad V_2 = \dfrac{1}{3}\pi r^2 (3h) = \pi r^2 h$

$\therefore$ Ratio of volumes of the cones,

$$\frac{V_1}{V_2} = \frac{3\pi r^2 h}{\pi r^2 h}$$

$$= \frac{3}{1} = 3 : 1$$

6. Given, O is the centre of the circle and $\angle BCO = 30°$. Join OB and AC.

In $\triangle BOC$,

$$CO = BO \qquad\qquad \text{[both are the radius of circle]}$$

$\therefore \qquad \angle OBC = \angle OCB = 30°$

$$[\because \text{ angles opposite to equal sides are equal}]$$

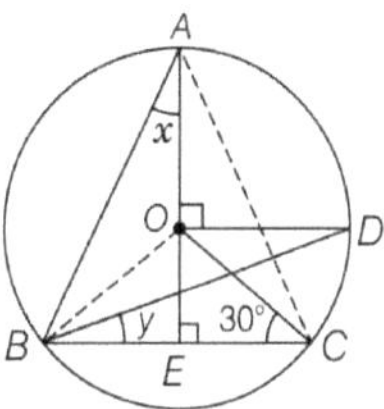

$\therefore \qquad \angle BOC = 180° - (\angle OBC + \angle OCB)$

$$\text{[by angle sum property of a triangle]}$$

$$= 180° - (30° + 30°) = 120°$$

We know that in a circle, the angle subtended by an arc at the centre is twice the angle subtended by it at the remaining part of the circle.

$\therefore \qquad \angle BOC = 2\,\angle BAC$

$$\Rightarrow \qquad \angle BAC = \frac{120°}{2} = 60°$$

Also, $\qquad \angle BAE = \angle CAE = 30°$

$$[AE \text{ is an angle bisector of angle } A]$$

$$\Rightarrow \qquad \angle BAE = x = 30°$$

In $\triangle ABE$,

$$\angle BAE + \angle EBA + \angle AEB = 180°$$

$$\text{[by angle sum property of a triangle]}$$

$$\Rightarrow \qquad 30° + \angle EBA + 90° = 180°$$

$\therefore \qquad \angle EBA = 180° - (90° + 30°)$

$$= 180° - 120° = 60°$$

Now, $\angle EBA = 60°$

$$\Rightarrow \qquad \angle ABD + y = 60°$$

$$\Rightarrow \qquad \frac{1}{2} \times \angle AOD + y = 60°$$

$$[\because \text{ in a circle, the angle subtended by an arc at the centre is twice the angle subtended by it at the remaining part of the circle}]$$

$$\Rightarrow \qquad \frac{90°}{2} + y = 60° \qquad [\because \angle AOD = 90°, \text{ given}]$$

$$\Rightarrow \qquad 45° + y = 60°$$

$$\Rightarrow \qquad y = 60° - 45°$$

$$\therefore \qquad y = 15°$$

Or

Given In $\triangle ABC$,

$$AD = \frac{1}{4} AB \text{ and } AE = \frac{1}{4} AC$$

To prove $DE = \frac{1}{4} BC$

Proof Let M and N be the mid-points of sides AB and AC, respectively.

By mid-point theorem,

$$MN \parallel BC \text{ and } MN = \frac{1}{2} BC \qquad \ldots(i)$$

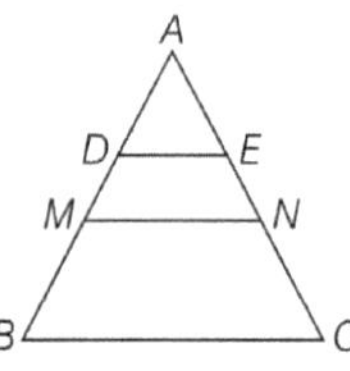

We have, $\qquad AM = \frac{1}{2} AB \qquad [\because M \text{ is mid-point of } AB]$

$\Rightarrow \qquad \frac{1}{2} AM = \frac{1}{4} AB$

$\Rightarrow \qquad \frac{1}{2} AM = AD \qquad [\because AD = \frac{1}{4} AB]$

So, D is the mid-point of AM.

Similarly, $\quad AN = \frac{1}{2} AC \qquad [\because N \text{ is the mid-point of } AC]$

$\Rightarrow \qquad \frac{1}{2} AN = \frac{1}{4} AC$

$\Rightarrow \qquad \frac{1}{2} AN = AE \qquad [\because AE = \frac{1}{4} AC]$

So, E is the mid-point of AN.

In $\triangle AMN$, D and E are the mid-points of AM and AN, respectively.

By mid-point theorem, $DE \parallel MN$ and $DE = \frac{1}{2} MN$

$\Rightarrow \qquad DE = \frac{1}{2}\left(\frac{1}{2} BC\right) \qquad [\text{from Eq. (i)}]$

$\Rightarrow \qquad DE = \frac{1}{4} BC \qquad \textbf{Hence proved.}$

7. Steps of Construction

(i) First, draw a ray OA with initial point O.

(ii) Taking O as centre and some radius, draw an arc of a circle which intersects OA, at a point, say B.

(iii) Taking B as centre and with the same radius as before, draw an arc intersecting the previously drawn arc, at a point, say C.

(iv) Taking C as centre and with the same radius as before, draw an arc intersecting the arc drawn in step (ii), at a point, say D.

(v) Draw the ray OE passing through C and the ray OF passing through D. Then, $\angle EOA = 60°$ and $\angle FOA = 120°$.

(vi) Next, taking C and D as centres and with radius more than $\frac{1}{2} CD$, draw arcs to intersect each other, at a point, say G.

(vii) Draw the ray OG. This ray OG is the bisector of $\angle FOE$.

i.e. $\angle GOA = \angle GOE + \angle EOA$

$\qquad = 30° + 60° = 90°$

(viii) Now, taking O as centre and any radius, draw an arc to intersect the rays OA and OG, say at H and I, respectively.

(ix) Next, taking H and I as centres and with the radius more than $\frac{1}{2} HI$, draw arcs to intersect each other, say at J.

(x) Draw the ray OJ. This ray OJ is the bisector of $\angle GOA$.

i.e. $\angle GOJ = \angle AOJ = \frac{1}{2} \angle GOA$

$\qquad = \frac{1}{2}(90°) = 45°$

(xi) Now, taking O as centre and any radius, draw an arc to intersect the rays OA and OJ, say at K and L, respectively.

(xii) Next, taking K and L as centres and with the radius more than $\frac{1}{2} KL$, draw arcs to intersect each other, say at M.

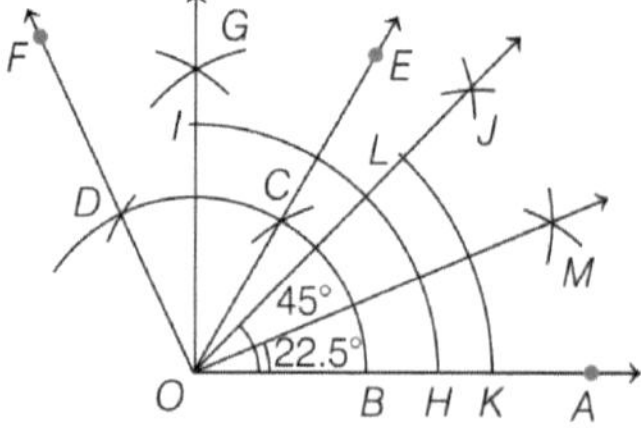

(xiii) Draw the ray OM. This ray OM is the bisector of $\angle AOJ$.

i.e. $\angle JOM = \angle AOM$

$\qquad = \frac{1}{2} \angle AOJ$

$\qquad = \frac{1}{2}(45°) = 22\frac{1}{2}°$

Hence, $\angle AOM$ is the required angle of $22\frac{1}{2}°$.

8. Water in the canal forms a cuboid of breadth $= 12\,\text{dm}$

$$= \frac{12}{10}\,\text{m} = 1.2\,\text{m} \qquad \left[\because 10\,\text{dm} = \frac{1}{10}\,\text{m}\right]$$

Height $= 30\,\text{dm}$

$$= \frac{30}{10}\,\text{m} = 3\,\text{m}$$

and length = distance covered by water in 30 min

$$= \text{Velocity of water} \times \text{time}$$

$$= 20000 \times \frac{30}{60} \, \text{m} = 10000 \, \text{m}$$

$\therefore$ Volume of water flown in 30 min

$$= lbh = (1.2 \times 3 \times 10000) \, \text{m}^3 = 36000 \, \text{m}^3$$

Suppose area irrigated be $A \, \text{m}^2$.

Then, $\quad A \times \dfrac{9}{100} = \text{Volume flown in 30 min}$

$$\Rightarrow \quad A \times \frac{9}{100} = 36000$$

$$\Rightarrow \quad A = 400000 \, \text{m}^2$$

Hence, the area irrigated is $400000 \, \text{m}^2$.

Or

Given, total number of working days $= 200$

(i) The number of days in which no defective part $= 50$

$\therefore$ The probability that no defective part

$$= \frac{50}{200} = \frac{1}{4} = 0.25$$

(ii) The number of days in which atleast one defective part

$$= 32 + 22 + 18 + 12 + 12 + 10 + 10 + 10 + 8 + 6$$
$$+ \, 6 + 2 + 2$$
$$= 150$$

$\therefore$ The probability that atleast one defective part

$$= \frac{150}{200} = \frac{3}{4} = 0.75$$

(iii) The number of days in which not more than 5 defective parts

$$= 50 + 32 + 22 + 18 + 12 + 12 = 146$$

$\therefore$ The probability that not more than 5 defective parts

$$= \frac{146}{200} = 0.73$$

(iv) The number of days in which more than 13 defective parts $= 0$

$\therefore$ The probability that more than 13 defective parts

$$= \frac{0}{200} = 0$$

9. We have, $(a + b)^3 - (a - b)^3 - 6b(a^2 - b^2)$

$$= (a + b)^3 - (a - b)^3 - 3 \times 2 \times b \times (a + b)(a - b)$$

$$[\because a^2 - b^2 = (a + b)(a - b)]$$

$$= (a + b)^3 - (a - b)^3 - 3(a + b)(a - b)\{(a + b) - (a - b)\}$$

$$[\because 2b = (a + b) - (a - b)]$$

$$= x^3 - y^3 - 3xy\,(x - y) \qquad [\text{put } x = a + b \text{ and } y = a - b]$$

$$= (x - y)^3 \qquad [\because (a - b)^3 = a^3 - b^3 - 3ab(a - b)]$$

$$= \{(a + b) - (a - b)\}^3 \qquad [\text{substitute } x = a + b \text{ and } y = a - b]$$

$$= (2b)^3 = 8\,b^3$$

Or

Given, total number of phone numbers $= 150$

$\therefore$ Total number of trials $= 150$

(i) Let E be the event of getting the number with unit digit less than 3.

$\therefore$ Number of trials in which the event E happened $= 10 + 20 + 15 = 45$

Now, $P(E) = \dfrac{\text{Number of trials in which E happened}}{\text{Total number of trials}}$

$$= \frac{45}{150} = \frac{3}{10}$$

(ii) Let F be the event of getting number with unit digit greater than 8.

$\therefore$ Number of trials in which F happened $= 15$

Now,

$$P(F) = \frac{\text{Number of trials in which F happened}}{\text{Total number of trials}}$$

$$= \frac{15}{150} = \frac{1}{10}$$

10. (i) (a) Total surface area of cylinder $= 2\pi r\,(r + h)$

(ii) (d) Given diameter of conical tomb $= 14\text{m}$ and slant height of conical tomb $= 25 \, \text{m}$

$\therefore$ Radius of conical tomb $(r) = \dfrac{14}{2} = 7 \, \text{m}$

$\therefore$ Curved surface area of each conical tomb

$$= \pi r l = \frac{22}{7} \times 7 \times 25 = 550 \, \text{m}^2$$

(iii) (b) Cost of white washing ₹ 210 per 100m²

$$\therefore \quad \text{Cost of } 550 \, \text{m}^2 = \frac{210}{100} \times 550$$

$$= ₹1155$$

(iv) (b) Lateral surface area of two pillars

$$= 2 \times 2\pi r h$$

$$= 4 \times \frac{22}{7} \times 2.1 \times 21$$

$$= 554.4 \, \text{m}^2$$

(v) (c) Volume of cone $= \dfrac{1}{3}\,\pi r^2 h$

Practice Paper 2*
(Solved)

Instructions

- Time : 2 Hr
- Max. Marks : 40

1. The question paper contains three sections A, B and C.
2. Section A has 5 questions with 3 internal choices.
3. Section B has 4 questions with 3 internal choices.
4. Section C has 1 Case Based MCQs comprises of 5 MCQs.
5. There is no negative marking.

As exact Blue-print and Pattern for CBSE Term II exams is not released yet. So the pattern of this paper is designed by the author on the basis of trend of past CBSE Papers. Students are advised not to consider the pattern of this paper as official, it is just for practice purpose.

Section A
(3 Marks Each)

This section consists of 5 questions of Short Answer Type.

1. If $x + \dfrac{1}{x} = 7$, then find the value of $x^3 + \dfrac{1}{x^3}$.

Or In the following figure, $ABCD$ is a rectangle such that $\angle CFE = 144°$ and $\angle ABE = 30°$ Find the measure of $\angle BEF$.

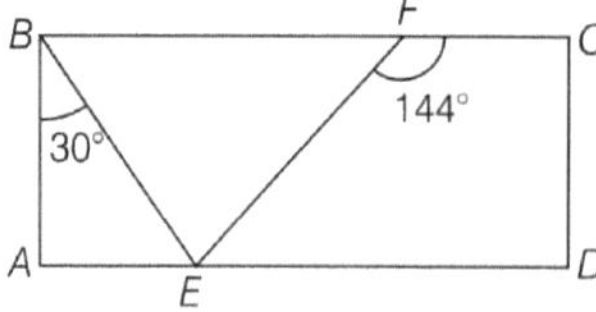

2. Two concentric circles with centre O have A, B, C, D as the points of intersection with the line l as shown in the figure. If $AD = 12$ cm and $BC = 8$ cm, then find the lengths of AB, CD, AC and BD, respectively.

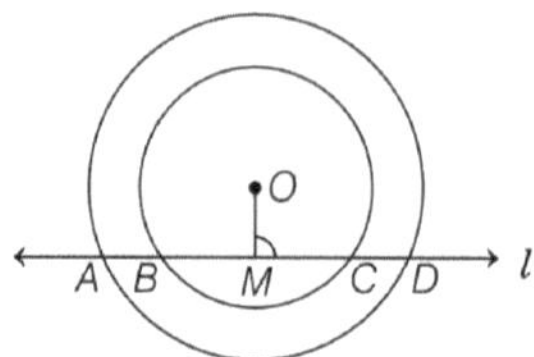

Or Draw a line segment $AB = 12$ cm. Divide it into $\dfrac{3}{4}$th part. Measure the length of $\dfrac{3}{4}$th part of AB.

3. It is required to make a closed cylindrical tank of height 1 m and base diameter 140 cm from a metal sheet. How many square metres of the sheet are required for the same? [take, $\pi = 22/7$]

4. The record of a weather station shows that out of the past 250 consecutive days, its weather forecast were correct 175 times.

(i) What is the probability that on a given day it was correct?

(ii) What is the probability that it was not correct on a given day?

5. In the given figure, if $\angle AOB = 90°$ and $\angle ABC = 30°$, then find the measure of $\angle CAO$.

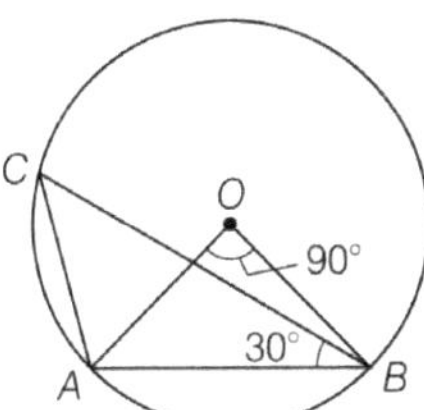

Or The percentage of marks obtained by a student in the monthly unit tests are given below

Unit test	I	II	III	IV	V
Percentage of marks obtained	58	64	76	62	85

Find the probability that the student gets

(i) a first class i.e. atleast 60% marks

(ii) marks between 70% and 80%

(iii) a distinction i.e. 75% or above

(iv) less than 65% marks.

Section B

(5 Marks Each)

This section consists of 4 questions of Long Answer Type.

6. In the given figure, $ABCD$ is a square, if $\angle PQR = 90°$ and $PB = QC = DR$, then prove that $QB = RC$, $PQ = QR$ and $\angle QPR = 45°$.

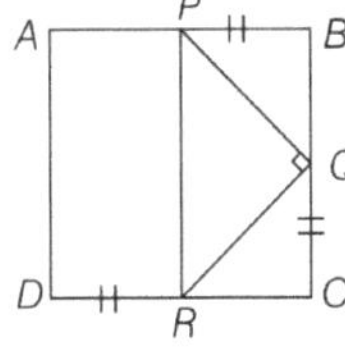

7. In the given figure, AB is a diameter of the circle, CD is a chord equal to the radius of the circle. AC and BD when extend/ed intersect at a point E. Prove that $\angle AEB = 60°$.

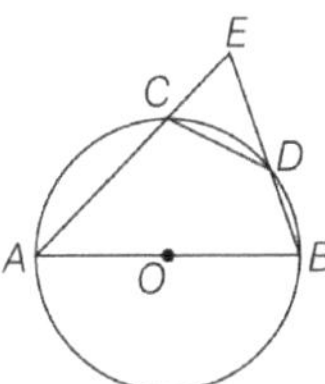

Or In the given figure, $RS = QT$ and $QS = RT$. Prove that $PQ = PR$.

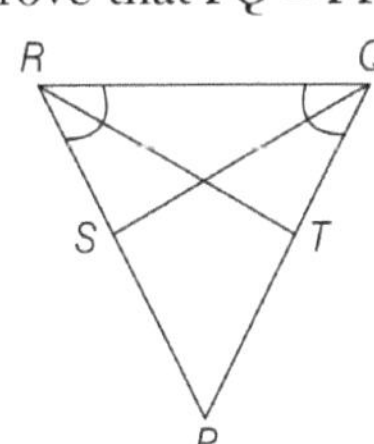

8. Cards marked with the numbers 2 to 101 are placed in a box and mixed thoroughly. One card is drawn from this box. Find the probability that the number on the card is

(i) an even number. (ii) a number less than 14. (iii) a number which is a perfect square.

Or Construct a $\triangle ABC$ in which $BC = 4.6$ cm, $\angle B = 45°$ and $AB + CA = 8.2$ cm.

9. Draw a bar graph to represent the data regarding life expectancy of Animals.

Name of Animals	Dog	Horse	Cow	Cat	Goat	Monkey
Life Expectancy	10	15	5	20	27	35

Or If $p(x) = x^3 - 4x^2 + x + 6$, then show that $p(3) = 0$ and hence factorise $p(x)$.

Section C
(1 Mark Each)

This section consists of 1 Case Based comprises of 5 MCQs.

10. In economy of any country, women are as equally important as men. As almost 40% population of any country is women, so they should also given chance to work and to help in improving the economy. The department of health and family welfare of Government of NCR of Delhi collected data related to ratio between male and female children in families. 2000 families with 4 children each were selected randomly and the following data were recorded.

Number of girls in a family	4	3	2	1	0
Number of families	700	350	250	400	300

(i) Compute the probability of a family having 4 girls.

(a) $\dfrac{9}{20}$ (b) $\dfrac{7}{20}$ (c) $\dfrac{11}{20}$ (d) $\dfrac{13}{20}$

(ii) Compute the probability of a family having 3 girls.

(a) $\dfrac{7}{40}$ (b) $\dfrac{9}{40}$ (c) $\dfrac{7}{20}$ (d) None of these

(iii) Compute the probability of a family having atleast 1 girl.

(a) $\dfrac{17}{20}$ (b) $\dfrac{19}{20}$ (c) $\dfrac{11}{20}$ (d) $\dfrac{13}{20}$

(iv) Compute the probability of a family having 2 girls.

(a) $\dfrac{1}{8}$ (b) $\dfrac{1}{6}$ (c) $\dfrac{1}{9}$ (d) $\dfrac{1}{10}$

(v) Compute the probability of a family having no girls

(a) $\dfrac{5}{14}$ (b) $\dfrac{3}{20}$ (c) $\dfrac{7}{20}$ (d) $\dfrac{11}{20}$

Answers

1. 322 or 84°   **2.** $AB = 2$ cm, $CD = 2$ cm, $AC = 10$ cm and $BD = 10$ cm or 9 cm   **3.** 7.48 m^2 **4.** (i) 0.7 (ii) 0.3

5. 60° or (i) 0.8 (ii) 0.2 (iii) 0.4 (iv) 0.6   **8.** (i) $\dfrac{1}{2}$ (ii) $\dfrac{3}{25}$ (iii) $\dfrac{9}{100}$ **10.** (i) (b) (ii) (a) (iii) (a) (iv) (a) (v) (b)

Practice Paper 3*

(Solved)

Instructions

- Time : 2 Hr
- Max. Marks : 40

1. The question paper contains three sections A, B and C.
2. Section A has 5 questions with 3 internal choices.
3. Section B has 4 questions with 3 internal choices.
4. Section C has 1 Case Based MCQs comprises of 5 MCQs.
5. There is no negative marking.

** As exact Blue-print and Pattern for CBSE Term II exams is not released yet. So the pattern of this paper is designed by the author on the basis of trend of past CBSE Papers. Students are advised not to consider the pattern of this paper as official, it is just for practice purpose.*

Section A

(3 Marks Each)

This section consists of 5 questions of Short Answer Type.

1. If $a + b = 10$ and $a^2 + b^2 = 58$, then find the value of $a^3 + b^3$.

Or Prove that the line joining the mid-points of the diagonals of a trapezium is parallel to the parallel sides of the trapezium.

2. AB and AC are two chords of a circle or radius r, such that $AB = 2AC$. If p and q are the distance of AB and AC from the centre, then prove that $4q^2 = p^2 + 3r^2$.

Or Construct a ΔPQR, in which $QR = 5.5$ cm. $\angle Q = 60°$ and $PR - PQ = 1.4$ cm.

3. The diameter of a sphere is decreased by 25%. By what per cent does its curved surface area decrease?

4. A company selected 4000 households at random and surveyed them to find out a relationship between income level and the number of television sets in a home.

The information so obtained is listed in the following table

Monthly income (in ₹)	Number of televisions/households			
	0	1	2	Above 2
< 10000	20	80	10	0
10000-14999	10	240	60	0
15000-19999	0	380	120	30
20000-24999	0	520	370	80
25000 and above	0	1100	760	220

Find the probability

(i) of a household earning ₹ 10000 - ₹ 14999 per year and having exactly one television.

(ii) of a household earning ₹ 25000 and more per year owing 2 televisions.

(iii) of a household not having any television.

Or Construct a rhombus, whose side is of length 3.4 cm and one of its angle is 45°.

5. Prove that the mid-point of the hypotenuse of a right angled triangle is equidistant from its vertices.

Section B   (5 Marks Each)

This section consists of 4 questions of Long Answer Type.

6. Construct the angle of 15°. Do you think that the angle of $7\dfrac{1}{2}^{\circ}$ can be constructed by the bisector of 15°?

Or $ABCD$ is a cyclic quadrilateral whose diagonals intersect at a point E. If $\angle DBC = 70°$ and $\angle BAC = 30°$, then find $\angle BCD$. Further, if $AB = BC$, find $\angle ECD$.

7. The internal and external diameters of a hollow hemispherical vessel are 24 cm and 25 cm, respectively. The cost to paint 1 cm^2 the surface is ₹ 0.05. Find the total cost to paint the vessel all over.

$$\left[\text{take, } \pi = \dfrac{22}{7}\right]$$

Or In the given figure, AB is a diameter of a circle with centre O and $DO \parallel CB$.

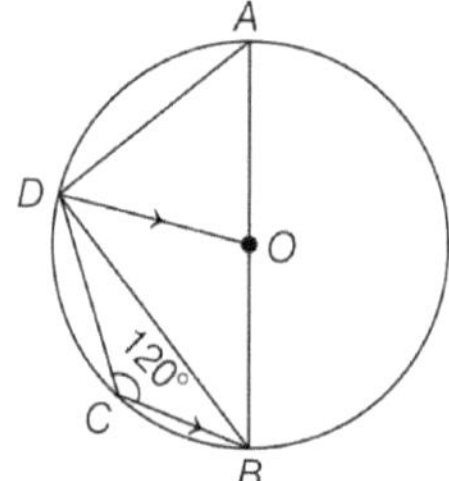

If $\angle BCD = 120°$ and $\angle DAB = 60°$, then calculate

(i) $\angle DBA$ (ii) $\angle CBD$

Also, show that $\triangle AOD$ is an equilateral triangle.

8. In 50 throws of a die, the outcomes were noted as under

Outcomes	1	2	3	4	5	6
Number of times	8	9	6	7	12	8

A die is thrown at random. What is the probability of getting

(i) even number?

(ii) odd number?

(iii) greater than 4?

Or Construct a $\triangle PQR$ in which $QR = 6$ cm, $\angle Q = 60°$ and $PR - PQ = 2$ cm.

9. Evaluate

(i) Evaluate $(106)^3$ by using suitable identity.

(ii) $\dfrac{8.73 \times 8.73 \times 8.73 + 4.27 \times 4.27 \times 4.27}{8.73 \times 8.73 - 8.73 \times 4.27 + 4.27 \times 4.27}.$

Section C   (1 Mark Each)

This section consists of 1 Case Based comprises of 5 MCQs.

10. The class teacher of IX class gave students coloured papers made by recycling of waste products in shape of quadrilateral. She asked them to make a parallelogram from it using paper folding.

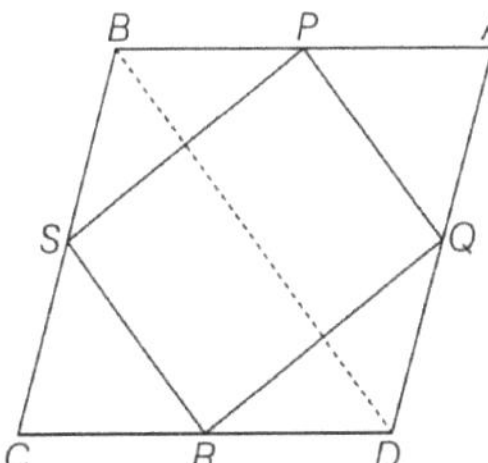

Then teacher ask them some questions. To answer these questions, choose the correct option.

(i) How can a parallelogram be formed by using paper folding?
   (a) Joining the sides of quadrilateral
   (b) Joining the mid-points of sides of quadrilateral
   (c) Joining the vertices of quadrilateral
   (d) None of these

(ii) Which of the following is correct condition?
   (a) $PQ = BD$ (b) $PQ = \dfrac{1}{2} BD$ (c) $3PQ = BD$ (d) $PQ = 2BD$

(iii) Which of the following is correct condition.
   (a) $2RS = BD$ (b) $RS = \dfrac{BD}{3}$ (c) $RS = BD$ (d) $RS = 2BD$

(iv) Which of the following is correct condition.
   (a) $PQ = \dfrac{SR}{2}$ (b) $PQ = SR$ (c) $PQ = \dfrac{SR}{3}$ (d) $4PQ = SR$

(v) Write the formula to find the perimeter of $\square PQRS$.
   (a) $PQ + QR + RS + PS$
   (b) $PQ - QR - RS + PS$
   (c) $\dfrac{PQ + QR + RS + PS}{2}$
   (d) $\dfrac{PQ + QR + RS + PS}{3}$

Answers

1. 370   *3.* 43.75 %   *4.* (i) 0.06 (ii) 0.19 (iii) $\dfrac{3}{400}$ *6.* or $\angle BCD - 80°$, $\angle ECD - 50°$

7. ₹ 96.28 or (i) $\angle DBA = 30°$, (ii) $\angle CBD = 30°$ *8.* (i) $\dfrac{12}{25}$ (ii) $\dfrac{13}{25}$ (iii) $\dfrac{2}{5}$ *9.* (i) 1191016 (ii) 13

10. (i) (b) (ii) (b) (iii) (a) (iv) (b) (v) (a)

Printed by Libri Plureos GmbH in Hamburg,
Germany